# From COVID-19 to Resilience: Quantitative Methods in Economics and Business

# From COVID-19 to Resilience: Quantitative Methods in Economics and Business

Editors

**Lina Novickytė**
**Jolanta Droždz**
**Radosław Pastusiak**
**Michał Soliwoda**

MDPI • Basel • Beijing • Wuhan • Barcelona • Belgrade • Manchester • Tokyo • Cluj • Tianjin

*Editors*

Lina Novickytė
Government Strategic
Analysis Center
Vilnius, Lithuania

Jolanta Droždz
Vilnius University
Vilnius, Lithuania

Radosław Pastusiak
University of Lodz
Lodz, Poland

Michał Soliwoda
University of Lodz
Lodz, Poland

*Editorial Office*
MDPI
St. Alban-Anlage 66
4052 Basel, Switzerland

This is a reprint of articles from the Special Issue published online in the open access journal *Mathematics* (ISSN 2227-7390) (available at: https://www.mdpi.com/si/mathematics/Quant_Methods_Econ_Bus).

For citation purposes, cite each article independently as indicated on the article page online and as indicated below:

Lastname, A.A.; Lastname, B.B. Article Title. *Journal Name* **Year**, *Volume Number*, Page Range.

**ISBN 978-3-0365-7764-7 (Hbk)**
**ISBN 978-3-0365-7765-4 (PDF)**
doi.org/10.3390/books978-3-0365-7765-4

© 2023 by the authors. Articles in this book are Open Access and distributed under the Creative Commons Attribution (CC BY) license. The book as a whole is distributed by MDPI under the terms and conditions of the Creative Commons Attribution-NonCommercial-NoDerivs (CC BY-NC-ND) license.

# Contents

**About the Editors** . . . . . . . . . . . . . . . . . . . . . . . . . . . . . . . . . . . . . . . . . . . . . . . . . . . . . . . . . . . . . . vii

**Preface** . . . . . . . . . . . . . . . . . . . . . . . . . . . . . . . . . . . . . . . . . . . . . . . . . . . . . . . . . . . . . . . . . . . . . . ix

**Lanndon Ocampo, Joerabell Lourdes Aro, Samantha Shane Evangelista, Fatima Maturan, Egberto Selerio, Jr., Nadine May Atibing and Kafferine Yamagishi**
On K-Means Clustering with IVIF Datasets for Post-COVID-19 Recovery Efforts
Reprinted from: *Mathematics* **2021**, *9*, 2639, doi:10.3390/math9202639 . . . . . . . . . . . . . . . . . 1

**Artur I. Petrov, Victor I. Kolesov and Daria A. Petrova**
Theory and Practice of Quantitative Assessment of System Harmonicity: Case of Road Safety in Russia before and during the COVID-19 Epidemic
Reprinted from: *Mathematics* **2021**, *9*, 2812, doi:10.3390/math9212812 . . . . . . . . . . . . . . . . . 31

**Ming-Chin Hung, Yung-Kang Ching and Shih-Kuei Lin**
Impact of COVID-19 on the Robustness of the Probability of Default Estimation Model
Reprinted from: *Mathematics* **2021**, *9*, 3087, doi:10.3390/math9233087 . . . . . . . . . . . . . . . . . 65

**Juan Antonio Galán-Gutiérrez and Rodrigo Martín-García**
Fundamentals vs. Financialization during Extreme Events: From Backwardation to Contango, a Copper Market Analysis during the COVID-19 Pandemic
Reprinted from: *Mathematics* **2022**, *10*, 559, doi:10.3390/math10040559 . . . . . . . . . . . . . . . . 79

**Alaa M. S. Azazz and Ibrahim A. Elshaer**
Amid COVID-19 Pandemic, Entrepreneurial Resilience and Creative Performance with the Mediating Role of Institutional Orientation: A Quantitative Investigation Using Structural Equation Modeling
Reprinted from: *Mathematics* **2022**, *10*, 2127, doi:10.3390/math10122127 . . . . . . . . . . . . . . . 103

**Raúl Katz and Juan Jung**
The Role of Broadband Infrastructure in Building Economic Resiliency in the United States during the COVID-19 Pandemic
Reprinted from: *Mathematics* **2022**, *10*, 2988, doi:10.3390/math10162988 . . . . . . . . . . . . . . . 121

**Dominika Gajdosikova, Katarina Valaskova, Tomas Kliestik and Veronika Machova**
COVID-19 Pandemic and Its Impact on Challenges in the Construction Sector: A Case Study of Slovak Enterprises
Reprinted from: *Mathematics* **2022**, *10*, 3130, doi:10.3390/math10173130 . . . . . . . . . . . . . . . 135

**Ibrahim A. Elshaer, Ahmad M. AboAlkhair, Sameh Fayyad and Alaa M. S. Azazz**
Post-COVID-19 Family Micro-Business Resources and Agritourism Performance: A Two-Mediated Moderated Quantitative-Based Model with a PLS-SEM Data Analysis Method
Reprinted from: *Mathematics* **2023**, *11*, 359, doi:10.3390/math11020359 . . . . . . . . . . . . . . . . 155

**Semei Coronado, Jose N. Martinez, Victor Gualajara, Rafael Romero-Meza and Omar Rojas**
Time-Varying Granger Causality of COVID-19 News on Emerging Financial Markets: The Latin American Case
Reprinted from: *Mathematics* **2023**, *11*, 394, doi:10.3390/math11020394 . . . . . . . . . . . . . . . . 171

**Jireh Yi-Le Chan, Seuk Wai Phoong, Seuk Yen Phoong, Wai Khuen Cheng and Yen-Lin Chen**
The Bitcoin Halving Cycle Volatility Dynamics and Safe Haven-Hedge Properties: A MSGARCH Approach
Reprinted from: *Mathematics* **2023**, *11*, 698, doi:10.3390/math11030698 . . . . . . . . . . . . . . . . 189

**Claudiu Tiberiu Albulescu and Eugenia Grecu**
Government Interventions and Sovereign Bond Market Volatility during COVID-19: A Quantile Analysis
Reprinted from: *Mathematics* **2023**, *11*, 1171, doi:10.3390/math11051171 . . . . . . . . . . . . . . . **209**

# About the Editors

**Lina Novickytė**

Dr. Lina Novickytė is the Head of the Strategic Insights Group from the Government Strategic Analysis Centre (Lithuania). She is the author of approximate fifty publications and co-author of three scientific monographs on behavior finance, agricultural finance, and risk management (h index=12), and she has more than 15 years of research experience. Dr. L. Novickytė is an expert in international and national projects on finance and risk management; she has been the leader and principal researcher of scientific and applied projects. Dr. L. Novickytė has actively participated in international conferences, being involved as a reviewer of scientific journal editorials. Her main interests include multiple-criteria decision-making (MCDM) analysis, efficiency, banks, behavioral economics and finance, agricultural economics, risk management, and M&A.

**Jolanta Droždz**

Dr. Jolanta Droždz is an Associate Professor at Vilnius University, Faculty of Economics and Business Administration (Lithuania). She is a coordinator of international and national research projects with significant experience in working with the European Commission and international research organizations. She has more than 18 years of applied science and research experience, has prepared more than 30 research reports, authored 22 scientific publications, and is a co-author of 2 scientific monographs. The results of the conducted research are intended for the European Commission, international research organizations, the Chancellery of the Government of the Republic of Lithuania, the Ministry of Agriculture of the Republic of Lithuania, etc. Jolanta Droždz actively contributes to the presentation of scientific information in understandable lexicon, having published dozens of articles in science popularization journals, promoting interaction between the fields of science and policy making. Her main interests include risk management, agricultural finance, agricultural policy, international economics, international trade, and foreign direct investments.

**Radosław Pastusiak**

Prof. Dr. Radosław Pastusiak is a Professor from the University of Lodz, Faculty of Economics and Sociology. Earning his Master's in Economics and a MBA from the University of Lodz and the Polish-American Management Center respectively, he later achieved his doctoral degree in 2002 with a focus on financing in the energy sector. From 2012 to 2021, he directed the Corporate Finance Department at the university. His main interests include capital markets, corporate finance, agricultural finance, and sustainability.

**Michał Soliwoda**

Dr. Michał Soliwoda is from the University of Lodz, Faculty of Economics and Sociology. Holding advanced doctoral credentials from the Warsaw University of Life Sciences in the fields of economic sciences, with a specific focus on economics and finance, Dr. Soliwoda has contributed to public policy as an expert since 2013. In 2020, he established an affiliation with the Corporate Finance Department at the University of Lodz, where he serves as an Associate Professor. His main interests include risk management household finance, SME finance, agricultural finance, and agricultural policy.

# Preface

The COVID-19 pandemic represents a particularly important challenge for empirical research in economics and finance. The category of resilience enters numerous, usually overly complex interactions with many important socio-economic and public categories, important for various spheres of the economy, politics, and life of citizens. The main aim of the Special Issue is to explore quantitative methods of measuring resilience in the context of the COVID-19 pandemic. The measurement and assessment of resilience at different levels require advanced quantitative and qualitative methods that are based on dynamic approaches and interaction with other socio-economic categories, which, consequently, makes it exceedingly difficult to develop public policies that are oriented towards strengthening resilience in general.

The response of the scientific community has been significant, with many papers being submitted for consideration, and, finally, 11 papers were accepted for publication after going through a careful peer-review process based on quality and novelty criteria.

The paper prepared by Albulescu and Grecu (2023) tests the interaction between governments' COVID-19 interventions, COVID-19-induced uncertainty, and the volatility of sovereign bonds.

Chan et al. (2023), in their paper, introduce a unique perspective towards Bitcoin safe-haven and hedge properties through the Bitcoin halving cycle using the MSGARCH approach.

Coronado et al. (2023) assess whether U.S. financial markets react differently to COVID-19 news than emerging markets and if such markets are impacted differently by country-specific and global news. To detect the spillover effects from news on market volatility, the authors applied a time-varying DCC-GARCH model.

Elshaer et al. (2023) analyzed family micro-business resources and agritourism performance post-COVID-19 using a two-mediated moderated quantitative-based model with a PLS-SEM data analysis method.

Gajdosikova et al. (2022), in their paper, pay attention to how the COVID-19 pandemic changed the construction sector, which is considered a crucial sector of the Slovak economy.

The paper authored by Katz and Jung (2022) studies the role of broadband in mitigating the economic losses resulting from COVID-19 in the United States. The authors apply an empirical framework underlined by a Cobb–Douglas production function and estimate within a structural multi-equation model through the three-stage least squares approach.

Azazz and Elshaer (2022) investigate the resilience of entrepreneurs as well as the relationship between resilience and creative performance using the structural equation modeling data analysis technique.

Galán-Gutiérrez and Martín-García (2022) intended to evaluate copper market analysis during the COVID-19 pandemic. They try to explain the evolution of warehouses and copper price structure and its utility for hedging in the context of an extreme event.

Hung et al. (2021) explored the robustness of a PD model with a GDP determinant (the test model) in comparison with that of a PD model with a credit default swap index (CDX) determinant (the alternative model).

Petrov et al. (2021) explained road safety in Russia before and during the COVID-19 pandemic using systemic harmonicity models.

The paper authored by Ocampo et al. (2021) proposed K-Means clustering with IVIF datasets for post-COVID-19 recovery efforts.

As the Guest Editors of the Special Issue From COVID-19 to Resilience: Quantitative Methods in Economics and Business, we are grateful to all authors who contributed with their articles. We would also like to express our gratitude to all reviewers for their valuable comments toward the improvement of the quality of submitted papers and to the administrative staff of the MDPI journal for their support in completing this book. Special thanks are due to the Managing Editor of the special issue Dr. Syna Mu for his excellent collaboration and valuable assistance. The goal of this

Special Issue was to attract quality and novelty of scientific papers in the field of using different quantitative methods in economics and business, which could be useful tools to analyze resilience. It is hoped that these selected research papers will be found to be impactful by the international scientific community and that these papers will facilitate further research on quantitative techniques for solving complex problems in various disciplines and application fields.

- Albulescu, C.T.; Grecu, E. Government Interventions and Sovereign Bond Market Volatility during COVID-19: A Quantile Analysis. Mathematics 2023, 11, 1171. https://doi.org/10.3390/math11051171
- Chan, J.Y.-L.; Phoong, S.W.; Phoong, S.Y.; Cheng, W.K.; Chen, Y.-L. The Bitcoin Halving Cycle Volatility Dynamics and Safe Haven-Hedge Properties: A MSGARCH Approach. Mathematics 2023, 11, 698. https://doi.org/10.3390/math11030698
- Coronado, S.; Martinez, J.N.; Gualajara, V.; Romero-Meza, R.; Rojas, O. Time-Varying Granger Causality of COVID-19 News on Emerging Financial Markets: The Latin American Case. Mathematics 2023, 11, 394. https://doi.org/10.3390/math11020394
- Elshaer, I.A.; AboAlkhair, A.M.; Fayyad, S.; Azazz, A.M.S. Post-COVID-19 Family Micro-Business Resources and Agritourism Performance: A Two-Mediated Moderated Quantitative-Based Model with a PLS-SEM Data Analysis Method. Mathematics 2023, 11, 359. https://doi.org/10.3390/math11020359
- Gajdosikova, D.; Valaskova, K.; Kliestik, T.; Machova, V. COVID-19 Pandemic and Its Impact on Challenges in the Construction Sector: A Case Study of Slovak Enterprises. Mathematics 2022, 10, 3130. https://doi.org/10.3390/math10173130
- Katz, R.; Jung, J. The Role of Broadband Infrastructure in Building Economic Resiliency in the United States during the COVID-19 Pandemic. Mathematics 2022, 10, 2988. https://doi.org/10.3390/math10162988
- Azazz, A.M.S.; Elshaer, I.A. Amid COVID-19 Pandemic, Entrepreneurial Resilience and Creative Performance with the Mediating Role of Institutional Orientation: A Quantitative Investigation Using Structural Equation Modeling. Mathematics 2022, 10, 2127. https://doi.org/10.3390/math10122127
- Galán-Gutiérrez, J.A.; Martín-García, R. Fundamentals vs. Financialization during Extreme Events: From Backwardation to Contango, a Copper Market Analysis during the COVID-19 Pandemic. Mathematics 2022, 10, 559. https://doi.org/10.3390/math10040559
- Hung, M.-C.; Ching, Y.-K.; Lin, S.-K. Impact of COVID-19 on the Robustness of the Probability of Default Estimation Model. Mathematics 2021, 9, 3087. https://doi.org/10.3390/math9233087
- Petrov, A.I.; Kolesov, V.I.; Petrova, D.A. Theory and Practice of Quantitative Assessment of System Harmonicity: Case of Road Safety in Russia before and during the COVID-19 Epidemic. Mathematics 2021, 9, 2812. https://doi.org/10.3390/math9212812
- Ocampo, L.; Aro, J.L.; Evangelista, S.S.; Maturan, F.; Selerio, E., Jr.; Atibing, N.M.; Yamagishi, K. On K-Means Clustering with IVIF Datasets for Post-COVID-19 Recovery Efforts. Mathematics 2021, 9, 2639. https://doi.org/10.3390/math9202639

Lina Novickytė, Jolanta Droždz, Radosław Pastusiak, and Michał Soliwoda

*Editors*

*Article*

# On *K*-Means Clustering with IVIF Datasets for Post-COVID-19 Recovery Efforts

**Lanndon Ocampo** [1,2,*], **Joerabell Lourdes Aro** [2], **Samantha Shane Evangelista** [2], **Fatima Maturan** [2], **Egberto Selerio, Jr.** [2], **Nadine May Atibing** [2] **and Kafferine Yamagishi** [2,3]

[1] Department of Industrial Engineering, Cebu Technological University, Cebu City 6000, Philippines
[2] Center for Applied Mathematics and Operations Research, Cebu Technological University, Cebu City 6000, Philippines; joerabellaro@gmail.com (J.L.A.); sammievangelista@gmail.com (S.S.E.); fatimamaturan1013@gmail.com (F.M.); egbertoselerio@gmail.com (E.S.J.); nadinemayatibing@gmail.com (N.M.A.); kafferineyamagishi@gmail.com (K.Y.)
[3] Department of Tourism Management, Cebu Technological University, Cebu City 6000, Philippines
* Correspondence: lanndonocampo@gmail.com

**Citation:** Ocampo, L.; Aro, J.L.; Evangelista, S.S.; Maturan, F.; Selerio, E., Jr.; Atibing, N.M.; Yamagishi, K. On *K*-Means Clustering with IVIF Datasets for Post-COVID-19 Recovery Efforts. *Mathematics* **2021**, *9*, 2639. https://doi.org/10.3390/math9202639

Academic Editors: Lina Novickytė, Jolanta Drozdz, Radosław Pastusiak and Michał Soliwoda

Received: 12 September 2021
Accepted: 12 October 2021
Published: 19 October 2021

**Publisher's Note:** MDPI stays neutral with regard to jurisdictional claims in published maps and institutional affiliations.

**Copyright:** © 2021 by the authors. Licensee MDPI, Basel, Switzerland. This article is an open access article distributed under the terms and conditions of the Creative Commons Attribution (CC BY) license (https://creativecommons.org/licenses/by/4.0/).

**Abstract:** The recovery efforts of the tourism and hospitality sector are compromised by the emergence of COVID-19 variants that can escape vaccines. Thus, maintaining non-pharmaceutical measures amidst massive vaccine rollouts is still relevant. The previous works which categorize tourist sites and restaurants according to the perceived degree of tourists' and customers' exposure to COVID-19 are deemed relevant for sectoral recovery. Due to the subjectivity of predetermining categories, along with the failure of capturing vagueness and uncertainty in the evaluation process, this work explores the use *k*-means clustering with dataset values expressed as interval-valued intuitionistic fuzzy sets. In addition, the proposed method allows for the incorporation of criteria (or attribute) weights into the dataset, often not considered in traditional *k*-means clustering but relevant in clustering problems with attributes having varying priorities. Two previously reported case studies were analyzed to demonstrate the proposed approach, and comparative and sensitivity analyses were performed. Results show that the priorities of the criteria in evaluating tourist sites remain the same. However, in evaluating restaurants, customers put emphasis on the physical characteristics of the restaurants. The proposed approach assigns 12, 15, and eight sites to the "low exposure", "moderate exposure", and "high exposure" cluster, respectively, each with distinct characteristics. On the other hand, 16 restaurants are assigned "low exposure", 16 to "moderate exposure", and eight to "high exposure" clusters, also with distinct characteristics. The characteristics described in the clusters offer meaningful insights for sectoral recovery efforts. Findings also show that the proposed approach is robust to small parameter changes. Although idiosyncrasies exist in the results of both case studies, considering the characteristics of the resulting clusters, tourists or customers could evaluate any tourist site or restaurant according to their perceived exposure to COVID-19.

**Keywords:** COVID-19; tourism industry; hospitality sector; interval-valued intuitionistic fuzzy set; k-means clustering

## 1. Introduction

The current pandemic has adversely impacted the tourism and hospitality industry through travel restrictions and physical distancing measures. Following these prolonged measures, tourists' behavior after reopening is linked to their perceived degree of exposure to COVID-19 [1,2]. The perceived degree of exposure may vary depending on the characteristics associated with the tourist sites and the hospitality establishments under consideration. For instance, the proximity of the destination, the duration of stay, and the volume of tourist arrivals may prompt the difference in the degree of exposure to COVID-19. Gaining insights on the degree of exposure is crucial for the decision-makers in implementing measures that would mitigate the fear of travel and reverberate the entire tourism value chain. This agenda has been explored in the recent work of Yamagishi and Ocampo [2], with subsequent and more comprehensive reports of Ocampo and Yamagishi [3] and Ocampo et al. [4]. They adopted an approach based on multi-attribute decision-making (MADM) methods in sorting tourist sites (restaurants) for perceived COVID-19 exposure of tourists (customers) under multiple relevant criteria. Their approaches involve the introduction of various attributes that would evaluate numerous alternatives (e.g., tourist sites, restaurants) under a computational platform that would capture the subjectivity and uncertainty of the evaluation environment. Their work allows the evaluation of the susceptibility of tourists to COVID-19 infection when visiting tourist sites, which is a relevant recovery effort of the industry.

While previous works [2–4] reported an interesting agenda for tourism and hospitality recovery, their approach may suffer certain drawbacks. First, the multiple criteria sorting methods employed in both studies in sorting tourist sites into classes are highly susceptible to subjective bias. In sorting methods, the characteristics of classes are predetermined by the analyst or by the decision-makers. The limited knowledge and inclinations of the analyst likely impose a bias on defining the classes and, in turn, on the overall sorting process. This drawback can be overcome by using clustering instead of sorting. In clustering, the characteristics of the clusters are determined by the shared characteristics of the alternatives that the clustering algorithm assigns to the cluster. With it, the need to predetermine the characteristics of clusters is eliminated along with the bias that it introduces. Secondly, their evaluation platform failed to account for a more encompassing agenda in addressing vagueness and uncertainty in the evaluation process. Such a limited approach in capturing judgment uncertainty brought about by factors such as the incomplete knowledge and experience of decision-makers with the problem domain may yield counterintuitive results. Reports in the literature suggest that capturing vagueness and uncertainty in decision-making represents a more robust and representative approach in addressing evaluation problems [4], particularly with those agendas having crucial impacts (e.g., public health). This work advances these gaps by offering a methodology in clustering a pre-determined number of alternatives or destinations (e.g., tourist sites, restaurants) based on the customers' perception of their degree of exposure to COVID-19.

In this work, the same problem domain reported by our previous works [3,4] is addressed through clustering analysis, where homogeneous decision clusters are determined by the similarity of the alternatives (e.g., tourist sites, restaurants). Clustering describes a process of grouping a set of objects into classes of similar characteristics such that the objects within a given group should be similar to each other, whereas the objects within different groups should be dissimilar to each other. It has been extensively used in many areas such as image processing and segmentation [5], data mining [6], pattern recognition [7], among others. Clustering algorithms can be broadly divided into two groups: hierarchical and partitional. This work utilizes a partitioning clustering algorithm that simultaneously finds all the clusters as partitions of the data and does not impose a hierarchical structure. A partitional algorithm can use either an $n \times d$ pattern matrix, where $n$ objects are embedded in a $d$-dimensional feature space, or an $n \times n$ similarity matrix. The most popular partitional clustering algorithm in various domains is the $k$-means clustering, first introduced by Mac Queen in 1967. It has been widely used in several applications, such as environmental science [8], education [9], medicine [10], transportation [11], tourism [12,13], among others. In most applications in the literature, little regard is placed on the relative importance of the attributes of the observations that are being clustered. Only very few consider such an essential aspect of the clustering process [14,15]. In most applications, the assumption of equal attribute importance is implicitly invoked. However, this assumption might be unsuitable in some cases. For instance, each criterion may present a different priority to the decision-maker for clustering alternatives (i.e., considered as observations) based on multiple criteria [15]. This issue is addressed in this study by pre-processing data inputs for the $k$-means clustering to incorporate weights representing the importance of the attributes (i.e., criteria).

Moreover, when *k*-means clustering is associated with a dataset obtained from human judgments, evaluation scores expressed in crisp values would yield limited information on the uncertainty of the decision-making process. Thus, in this work, linguistic variables representative of those scores are introduced with corresponding interval-valued intuitionistic fuzzy (IVIF) sets. In many practical decision-making problems, the decision-makers often provide their preferences over a list of alternatives. This preference is usually imprecise or uncertain, along with the hesitation about the preference due to several factors such as lack of sufficient information or decision-makers having limited information processing capacities [16]. The rise of the use of fuzzy sets in data management has been popular in addressing this concern. Zadeh [17] first proposed the notion of a fuzzy set to model qualitative information with non-sharp boundaries, and Atanassov [18] generalized this idea to intuitionistic fuzzy set (IFS) by introducing both membership and non-membership degrees, extending the previous proposal of Zadeh [17] on membership functions to represent a fuzzy set. The use of IFS in modeling uncertainty has been widespread in the recent decade [19]. However, the membership and non-membership degrees in IFS are expressed as crisp values with limited capability in completely representing uncertainty and hesitation. Thus, Atanassov and Gargov [20] introduced interval membership and non-membership degrees, coining the term interval-valued intuitionistic fuzzy set (IVIFS). Recent works on the use of IVIFS values have been emerging in various applications, such as energy systems [21], medical diagnosis [22], image processing [23], transportation [24], tourism [25], hospitality [26], among others. Note that this list is not intended to be comprehensive. The integration of IVIFS in the datasets for *k*-means clustering augments the representation of judgment uncertainty involved in evaluation problems that attempt to identify resultant clusters of decision alternatives. In summary, this work contributes by (1) introducing a platform for *k*-means clustering based on datasets with IVIFS values, and (2) applying such a platform to advance our previous works [3,4] in tourism and hospitality recovery efforts.

This paper is outlined as follows: Section 2 provides a brief literature review of the recovery efforts of the tourism and hospitality sector. Section 3 illustrates the preliminaries of IVIFS and *k*-means clustering. Section 4 presents the application of the proposed *k*-means clustering with IVIFS datasets in two case studies in the Philippines. The sensitivity of the results, along with the comparative analysis on the performance of the proposed approach with the VIKORSORT and IF-TOPSIS-Sort, is presented in Section 5. It proceeds with a discussion of findings in Section 6. It ends with a conclusion and discussion of future works in Section 7.

**2. Literature Review**

A highly transmittable disease identified as coronavirus disease 2019 (COVID-19) with symptoms such as fever, dry cough, fatigue, shortness of breath, chills, muscles pain, headache, gastric discomforts, and weight loss was declared as a global pandemic on the 11 of March 2020 by the World Health Organization (WHO) [27,28]. Since its emergence in Wuhan, China, in November 2019, a total of 195 million confirmed cases of COVID-19, including 4 million deaths as of July 2021, has been recorded (WHO) [29]. To mitigate the spread of the virus and "flatten the curve", non-pharmaceutical measures such as travel and mobility restrictions, social distancing protocols, and community lockdowns have been imposed globally [30]. The Organization for Economic Co-operation and Development (OCED) pointed out that the tourism sector was among the first industries highly affected by the coronavirus outbreak [31]. Before the pandemic, the collective direct, indirect, and induced contributions of the tourism industry accounted for 10.6% of all jobs and 10.4% of global GDP [32]. The tourism industry thrives through physical visits and face-to-face interactions, and its growth relies heavily on demand for its goods and services. Due to travel bans, event cancellations, quarantine requirements, and fear of spread, the industry faces commercial, operational, and financial crises [33]. Records in 2020 indicate that the unemployment rate has increased by approximately 18.5%, while the global GDP contribution of the industry decreased to 5.5% due to ongoing restrictions on mobility [32].

A case in point, the Philippine government recognizes the tourism sector as the most vulnerable amidst the COVID-19 pandemic. For the full-year report of 2020, the direct GDP contribution of the tourism industry is only Php 973.31 billion (19.53 billion USD), lower by 61.2% compared to Php 2.51 trillion (50.35 billion USD) of 2019 [34]. The decline of the GDP was caused by the restrictions imposed by the government to ensure the safety of the people, such as lowering the operational capacity of the establishment to enable social distancing measures. In fact, a survey conducted by the Asia Development Bank [35] for the Philippines reported that 89.9% of the businesses in the hospitality sector are not more than 50% operational, while 22.2% of them are now permanently closed. Consequently, the hospitality sector has a $-42.7\%$ GDP growth in 2020 and is among the main contributors to the decline of the country's GDP [36]. Furthermore, restricted operations of the sector resulted in a 17.98% decrease in the labor force [37]. Thus, both tourism and labor and employment departments led the Financial Assistance and Cash-for-Work Program, providing financial support for displaced workers in the tourism industry, including the hospitality sector.

Amidst the enormous blow, industry decision-makers endeavor to promote initiatives that serve as coping mechanisms until some stability is obtained. These initiatives include robust negotiations with suppliers for sustenance, extensive cost reduction practices, or a minimum mandatory period for accommodation bookings when visiting tourist destinations and hospitality businesses [38]. For customer safety, restaurants and food establishments implement proactive measures, such as contactless menu boards, payment systems, changed sitting arrangements, health checks of diners, and regular sanitation of chairs and tables [39]. At record speed, the development and deployment of COVID-19 vaccines open a critical window to fight the COVID-19 pandemic and promote the safe resumption of international travel alongside other risk mitigation tools such as COVID-19 testing [40]. As of July 2021, approximately 4 billion doses of vaccines have been administered worldwide [41]. According to Gursoy et al. [42], COVID-19 vaccines have significantly raised the hopes for recovery as they can effectively mitigate the disease spread, which would lead to lifting global travel bans and improving the demand for tourism and hospitality products. Even though vaccination can speed up socio-economic recovery, several factors hinder countries from attaining herd immunity, including the willingness of the population to get vaccinated, lack of resources (e.g., budget), and improper allocation of doses [43,44].

However, alongside the introduction of vaccines and the consequent relaxation of preventive measures (e.g., restricted outings, avoidance of gatherings, self-isolation, and lockdowns), a quick escalation of COVID-19 cases across Europe arises. As a response, governments reimpose measures that would limit social activities to counter succeeding waves of COVID-19 [45]. The second wave of COVID-19 cases made way for the viral mutation and emergence of new variants (e.g., Alpha variant, Delta variant), more contagious and fatal than their parent virus [46]. The existence of new COVID-19 variants has been threatening countries in achieving herd immunity and inducing a reduced sense of safety for tourists to travel [45]. Thus, despite heightened vaccine rollouts, the tourism and hospitality sector needs a set of recovery efforts that would still maintain a certain degree of non-pharmaceutical measures. Our recently reported works [2–4] explored this agenda by evaluating the degree of exposure of tourists or customers in the facilities managed by the sector (i.e., tourist sites, restaurants). The computational platforms demonstrated in the previous works offer crucial insights to the sectoral recovery efforts in informing the design of measures of various stakeholders in managing the operations of the facilities. However, some methodological issues (e.g., the drawbacks of sorting items to pre-determined groups, the uncertainty of judgments) of these platforms are valid, which may require a different analytical perspective.

## 3. Preliminaries

### 3.1. Fuzzy Set Theory

Zadeh developed the fuzzy set theory in 1965, initially motivated by applying numerous valued logics as means of illustrating the behavior of complex electrical systems, which later turned into the idea of a fuzzy set [17]. In real-life scenarios, it is understood that conversations do not always lead to true or to false statements. Many statements exist between true and false, and these are called "statements of gradual truth" [47]. Fuzzy set theory is an established mathematical framework that measures uncertainties associated with vague and perception-based situations, opposing randomness [17]. It was derived from Boolean logic, where the absolute truth values 0 and 1 are described as being entirely false and entirely true, respectively. On the other hand, in the case of the fuzzy set theory, the degree of truth values assumes a closed interval $[0,1]$ defined by a membership function [17]. The notion of the framework of a fuzzy set provides a natural way of handling problems in which the lack of precisely defined criteria of class membership is the basis of indistinctness rather than the existence of random variables [17]. For an element that belongs to the fuzzy set $A$ in $X$, several possibilities such as "that element belongs to $A$", "partially belongs to $A$", and "does not belong to $A$" are applicable.

**Definition 1:** Let $X$ be the universe of discourse. The set of pairs $A = \{x, \mu_A(x) | x \in X\}$ is called a fuzzy set, or standard fuzzy set, where $\mu_A(x)$ is the membership function of $x$ in $A$. In a standard fuzzy set $A$, each element $x$ is mapped to the closed interval $[0,1]$ by $\mu_A : X \to [0,1]$, which includes all real numbers between 0 and 1, including 0 and 1.

The membership function of $A$ can also be expressed as $A(x) \in [0,1]$. A fuzzy set can also be written as:

$$A = \{\mu_A(x)/x : x \in X\} \quad (1)$$

or:

$$A = \bigcup_x \mu_A(x)/x \quad (2)$$

Assuming that the elements are continuous, then the set can be expressed as:

$$A = \int \mu_A(x)/x \quad (3)$$

In the context of fuzzy set, the crisp set can be considered as a special case where the crisp interval $A = [a,b] \subseteq \mathbb{R}, a < b$, has a membership function $\mu_A(x)$ defined by:

$$\mu_A(x) = \begin{cases} 0 & x < a \\ 1 & a \leq x \leq b \\ 0 & x > b \end{cases} \quad (4)$$

### 3.2. Intuitionistic Fuzzy Set Theory

The intuitionistic fuzzy set theory, introduced by Atanassov [18], generalizes the fuzzy set theory of Zadeh [17] for computing information with vagueness and impression. It extends the fuzzy set theory by introducing a non-membership function in addition to the membership function and a resulting hesitancy function [18]. The non-membership function expresses opposition, while the hesitancy function represents neutrality in eliciting information. These additional components improve the efficacy of fuzzy computing, particularly in applications that require making decisions under uncertainty. The fundamentals of the IFS theory can be found in Atanassov [48] and several succeeding foundational works thereafter. For brevity, the following provides some useful and relevant concepts.

**Definition 2 ([18]).** Suppose $X$ is a finite, non-empty set. Then an intuitionistic fuzzy set $A$ in $X$ is defined as:

$$A = \{x, \mu_A(x), \nu_A(x) : x \in X\}, \quad (5)$$

where $\mu_A(x) : X \to [0,1]$ and $\nu_A(x) : X \to [0,1]$ such that $0 \le \mu_A(x) + \nu_A(x) \le 1, \forall x \in X$. Here, two mappings of $x \in X$ to $A$ are introduced: (1) the membership function $\mu_A(x)$, and (2) the non-membership function $\nu_A(x)$. From these functions, the hesitancy function $\pi_A(x)$, i.e., the degree of the lack of knowledge on $x$ in $A$, is generated and is defined as $\pi_A(x) = 1 - \mu_A(x) - \nu_A(x)$.

**Definition 3 ([20]).** Let $D[0,1]$ be the set of all closed subintervals of $[0,1]$. Let $X \ne \varnothing$ be a given set. An interval-valued intuitionistic fuzzy (IVIF) set $A$ in $X$ is given by $A = \{x, \mu_A^I(x), \gamma_A^I(x) : x \in X\}$, where $\mu_A^I(x) : X \longrightarrow D[0,1], \gamma_A^I(x) \longrightarrow D[0,1]$, with the condition that

$$0 < \sup_x \mu_A^I(x) + \sup_x \gamma_A^I(x) < 1 \tag{6}$$

The intervals $\mu_A^I(x)$ and $\gamma_A^I(x)$, respectively, denote the degree of membership and non-membership of $x$ to the set $A$.

For each $x \in X$, $\mu_A^I(x)$ and $\gamma_A^I(x)$ are closed intervals whose lower- and upper-end points are, respectively, denoted by $\mu_{AL}^I(x), \mu_{AU}^I(x)$ and $\gamma_{AL}^I(x), \gamma_{AU}^I(x)$. With these, $A$ can be written as $= \{x, [\mu_{AL}^I(x), \mu_{AU}^I(x)], [\gamma_{AL}^I(x), \gamma_{AU}^I(x)] : x \in X\}$, where $0 \le \mu_{AL}^I(x)$, $0 \le \gamma_{AL}^I(x)$, and $0 < \mu_{AU}^I(x) + \gamma_{AU}^I(x) \le 1$.

For each $x \in X$, the hesitancy degree $\pi_A(x)$ of $x \in X$ in $A$ is defined as follows:

$$\pi_A^I(x) = 1 - \mu_A^I(x) - \gamma_A^I(x) = \left[1 - \mu_{AU}^I(x) - \gamma_{AU}^I(x), 1 - \mu_{AL}^I(x) - \gamma_{AL}^I(x)\right] \tag{7}$$

We will denote IVIFS $(X)$ as the set of all IVIF sets in $X$. For convenience, we will write the IVIFS value $A = ([a,b],[c,d])$.

**Definition 4 ([49,50]).** Let $A = ([a,b],[c,d])$, $A_1 = ([a_1,b_1],[c_1,d_1])$, and $A_2 = ([a_2,b_2],[c_2,d_2])$ be IVIFS values, and $\lambda > 0$. The following shows some of their basic operational laws:

$$1 - A = A^c = ([c,d],[a,b]) \tag{8}$$

$$A_1 \cup A_2 = ([\max(a_1,a_2), \max(b_1,b_2)], [\min(c_1,c_2), \min(d_1,d_2)]) \tag{9}$$

$$A_1 \cap A_2 = ([\min(a_1,a_2), \min(b_1,b_2)], [\max(c_1,c_2), \max(d_1,d_2)]) \tag{10}$$

$$A_1 + A_2 = ([a_1 + a_2 - a_1 a_2, b_1 + b_2 - b_1 b_2], [c_1 c_2, d_1 d_2]) \tag{11}$$

$$A_1 \cdot A_2 = ([a_1 a_2, b_1 b_2], [c_1 + c_2 - c_1 c_2, d_1 + d_2 - d_1 d_2]) \tag{12}$$

$$\lambda A = \left(\left[1 - (1-a)^\lambda, 1 - (1-b)^\lambda\right], \left[c^\lambda, d^\lambda\right]\right) \tag{13}$$

$$A^\lambda = \left(\left[a^\lambda, b^\lambda\right], \left[1 - (1-c)^\lambda, 1 - (1-d)^\lambda\right]\right) \tag{14}$$

The following provides the two major approaches of aggregating IVIFS values: (1) the weighted arithmetic average operator and (2) the weighted geometric average operator.

**Definition 5 ([49]).** Let $A_j(1,\ldots,n) \in IVIFS(X)$. The weighted arithmetic average operator $(F_w)$ is defined by:

$$F_w = (A_1,\ldots,A_n) = \sum_{j=1}^{n} w_j A_j = \left[1 - \prod_{j \in \{1,\ldots,n\}} \left(1 - \mu_{A_j L}^I(x)\right)^{w_j}, 1 - \prod_{j \in \{1,\ldots,n\}} \left(1 - \mu_{A_j U}^I(x)\right)^{w_j}\right], \left[\left(\prod_{j \in \{1,\ldots,n\}} \left(\gamma_{A_j L}^I(x)\right)^{w_j}\right), \left(\prod_{j \in \{1,\ldots,n\}} \left(\gamma_{A_j U}^I(x)\right)^{w_j}\right)\right] \tag{15}$$

where $w_j$ is the weight of $A_j(1,\ldots,n)$, $w_j \in [0,1]$, $\sum_{j=1}^{n} w_j = 1$.

**Definition 6 ([49]).** Let $A_j(1,\ldots,n) \in IVIFS(X)$. The weighted geometric average operator ($G_w$) is defined by

$$G_w = (A_1,\ldots,A_n) = \sum_{j=1}^{n} w_j A_j = \left( \left[ \left( \prod_{j\in\{1,\ldots,n\}} \left(\mu^I_{A_j L}(x)\right)^{w_j} \right), \left( \prod_{j\in\{1,\ldots,n\}} \left(\mu^I_{A_j U}(x)\right)^{w_j} \right) \right], \left[ 1 - \prod_{j\in\{1,\ldots,n\}} \left(1 - \gamma^I_{A_j L}(x)\right)^{w_j}, 1 - \prod_{j\in\{1,\ldots,n\}} \left(1 - \gamma^I_{A_j U}(x)\right)^{w_j} \right] \right) \quad (16)$$

where $w_j$ is the weight of $A_j(1,\ldots,n)$, $w_j \in [0,1]$, $\sum_{j=1}^{n} w_j = 1$

The following discusses various approaches in comparing IVIFS values.

**Definition 7 ([49]).** Let $A = ([a,b],[c,d])$ be an IVIFS value, where $0 \le a \le b \le 1, 0 \le c \le d \le 1$, and $b + d \le 1$. A score function $S(A)$ is defined as:

$$S(A) = \frac{(a-b) + (c-d)}{2} \quad (17)$$

where $S(A) \in [0,1]$

**Definition 8 ([49]).** [Let $A = ([a,b],[c,d])$ be an IVIFS value, where $0 \le a \le b \le 1, 0 \le c \le d \le 1$, and $b + d \le 1$. An accuracy function $H(A)$ based on an unknown degree is defined as:

$$H(A) = \frac{(a+b) + (c+d)}{2} \quad (18)$$

where $H(A) \in [0,1]$.

Based on Definitions 7 and 8, Xu and Jian [39] proposed an approach to compare two IVIFS values. Theorem 1 offers such an approach.

**Theorem 1 ([51]).** Let $A_1 = ([a_1,b_1],[c_1,d_1])$ and $A_2 = ([a_2,b_2],[c_2,d_2])$ be two IVIFS values. Then:
(i)  If $S(A_1) < S(A_2)$, then $A_1 < A_2$
(ii) If $S(A_1) = S(A_2)$, then:
- If $H(A_1) = H(A_2)$, then $A_1 = A_2$
- If $H(A_1) < H(A_2)$, then $A_1 < A_2$

Ye [52] offered a new formulation of the accuracy function (i.e., the novel accuracy function) that allows comparison among IVIFS values.

**Definition 9 ([52]).** Let $A = ([a,b],[c,d])$ be an IVIFS value, where $0 \le a \le b \le 1, 0 \le c \le d \le 1$, and $b + d \le 1$. A novel accuracy function of in IVIFS values, based on an unknown degree, is proposed as:

$$M(A) = \frac{a - (1-a-c) + b - (1-b-d)}{2} = a + b - 1 + \frac{c+d}{2} \quad (19)$$

where $M(A) \in [-1,+1]$.

Shown in various examples, the novel accuracy function demonstrates a promising approach that improves the efficacy of the formulation proposed by Xu and Jian [51]. However, Nayagam et al. [53] argued that the previous two formulations might fail to compare IVIFS values in some instances. Thus, they devised an alternative formulation of an accuracy function.

**Definition 10 ( [53]).** *Let $A = ([a,b], [c,d])$ be an IVIFS value, where $0 \leq a \leq b \leq 1, 0 \leq c \leq d \leq 1$, and $b + d \leq 1$. A novel accuracy function $L(A)$ of in IVIFS values, based on an unknown degree, can be formulated as:*

$$L(A) = \frac{a + b - d(1-b) - c(1-a)}{2} \qquad (20)$$

*where $L(A) \in [-1, +1]$.*

Given Definition 10, the following result provides a basis for comparing two IVIFS values.

**Theorem 2 ( [53]).** *For any two comparable IVIFS values $A$ and $B$, if $A \leq B$, then $L(A) \leq L(B)$.*

### 3.3. K-Means Clustering

Clustering divides a set of data into clusters. Several clustering methods were employed for a variety of applications in the literature. Abualigah et al. [54] proposed an improved krill herd algorithm for text clustering. Janani and Vijayarani [55] employed the spectral clustering algorithm with particle swarm optimization for text document clustering. Ramirez et al. [56] employed the k-means clustering algorithm to determine clusters of education graduate students based on motivation. Selerio et al. [57] employed the fuzzy C-means clustering to improve sustainable urban water management. Although clustering algorithms are found to be useful in various domains, their application in tourism and hospitality recovery is not well explored. Among multiple algorithms, the k-means clustering algorithm is arguably the most popular due to its simplicity and strong theoretical foundations. It has been used in various applications, such as analyzing customer behavior [58], in situ additive manufacturing process monitoring [59], seismic attribute selection [60], and intelligent broadcasting [61], to name a few. Here, a novel application of k-means clustering is demonstrated for tourism and hospitality recovery amidst the COVID-19 pandemic.

The k-means clustering divides a set of data into k number of distinct clusters. The process is partitioned into phases. It determines the k centroid in the first phase and then moves each point to the cluster with the closest centroid to the data point in the second phase. The Euclidean distance is widely used for determining the distance to the nearest centroid. It recalculates the new centroid of each cluster once the grouping is complete. Based on that centroid, a new Euclidean distance between each center and each data point is calculated, and the cluster's points with the shortest Euclidean distance are assigned. The member objects and centroid of each cluster in the partition define it. The centroid of each cluster is where the sum of the distances between all the items in the cluster is the smallest. The k-means algorithm is an iterative technique that minimizes the sum of distances between each item and its cluster centroid over all clusters. The Lloyd-Forgy algorithm [62,63] is used in this work.

The general formulation of the algorithm is as follows: Given a set of observations $(x_1, x_2, \ldots, x_n)$ where each observation is a $d$-dimensional real vector, k-means clustering aims to partition the $n$ observations into $k \leq n$ sets $S = \{S_1, S_2, \ldots, S_k\}$ to minimize the within-cluster sum of squares (i.e., variance). The objective function is defined as follows:

$$\arg\min_S \sum_{i=1}^{k} \sum_{x \in S_i} \|x - \mu_i\|^2 = \arg\min_S \sum_{i=1}^{k} |S_i| \text{ Var } S_i \qquad (21)$$

where $\mu_i$ is the mean of the points in $S$. This is equivalent to minimizing the pairwise squared deviations of points in the same cluster, as illustrated:

$$\arg\min_S \sum_{i=1}^{k} \frac{1}{2|S_i|} \sum_{x,y \in S_i} \|x - y\|^2 \qquad (22)$$

and the equivalence can be deducted from the identity presented as follows:

$$\sum_{x \in S_i} {x - \mu_i}^2 = \sum_{x \neq y \in S_i} (x - \mu_i)^T (\mu_i - y) \tag{23}$$

## 4. Proposed Procedure: The Application of K-Means Clustering Based on IVIF Datasets

*4.1. Case Study 1: Clustering Tourist Sites for Perceived COVID-19 Exposure*

The Philippine government recognizes the tourism sector as the most vulnerable amidst the COVID-19 pandemic. Hundreds of thousands of people have been unemployed due to the Philippines' extended and widespread lockdown. With careful relaxation of containment measures [64], the government pushes for economic recovery while keeping public health a priority. The Department of Tourism (DOT), the government's tourism arm, has been emphasizing the need for tourist trust and confidence for a healthy recovery, highlighting the necessity of safety measures and stakeholder participation in ensuring that public health standards are met [65]. In this regard, some standard protocols across tourist destinations were released [66]. Furthermore, the DOT introduced a personalized package trip as a key to encouraging more Filipinos for domestic travel and a way of faster tourism recovery. They also welcome the approval of uniform travel protocols for all local government units (LGUs), although some require a COVID-19 test before travel [66].

As tourism activities slowly resume, health and safety are deemed primary among travelers, and vaccination is considered essential to the industry's full recovery [67]. Vaccination is deemed a cost-effective measure to control the spread of pandemics and minimize economic losses [68]. Progress on the vaccination rollout in the country is forecasted to contribute a 4.5% economic growth in 2021, according to the Asian Development Bank [69]. Mass vaccination in the Philippines began in March 2021, and in July 2021, the Philippines already can administer 500,000 daily vaccine doses. With the continuing effort of the government to implement the inoculation of vaccines to the population, the economy is expected to reopen with more relaxed movement restrictions. However, authorities are almost in consensus about some required forms of social distancing and other non-pharmaceutical measures, despite the presence of vaccines. For instance, several states in the U.S. mandate an indoor mask. On the other hand, some states, such as Hawaii, Nevada, and Washington D.C., allow the exemption to fully vaccinated individuals only after at least two weeks of their last shot. Nevertheless, with the current threat brought about by the Delta variant and other emerging variants, the U.S. Centers for Disease Control and Prevention recommends that vaccinated people wear masks in indoor areas with high rates of COVID-19 transmission [70]. Thus, while implementing recovery efforts in the tourism sector, putting up measures and safeguards for the tourists and enterprises remains crucial amidst the emergence of COVID-19 variants that can escape vaccines.

With this, the agenda of evaluating tourists' perceived degree of exposure to COVID-19 in tourist sites is deemed relevant for tourism recovery. To address the limitations of multiple criteria sorting methods adopted in previous works, the proposed k-means clustering based on datasets with IVIFS values is adopted. Following the previous problem of sorting 35 tourist sites under six evaluation criteria, the required computational steps are as follows:

**Step 1**: Identify the necessary criteria.

Yamagishi and Ocampo [2] identified six criteria representing the degree of exposure of tourists to COVID-19 in various tourist sites. These include proximity (C1), available modes of transportation (C2), duration of stay (C3), tourist activities (C4), area of the site's premises (C5), and volume of tourist arrivals (C6). The process of identifying these criteria was discussed thoroughly [3] and is not repeated here for brevity. However, activities such as literature review, focus group discussions, expert interviews, and other group consensus-generating techniques may be necessary to identify these criteria.

**Step 2**: Determine the list of evaluation alternatives.

The alternatives are represented by 35 tourist sites under a local geographical region [3]. These tourist sites are participating in tourism recovery efforts via domestic tourism and were pre-selected for the study. In general, the selection of tourist sites is problem-specific and is within the scope of the interests of decision-makers. Table 1 shows the list of 35 tourist sites with their corresponding codes for easier recall. The comprehensive characteristics of these sites are previously illustrated [3].

Table 1. List of tourist sites [3].

| Type | Code | Tourist Site | Type | Code | Tourist Site |
| --- | --- | --- | --- | --- | --- |
| | S1 | Sumilon island | | S18 | Bojo river |
| | S2 | Panagsama beach | Ecotourism | S19 | Sanctuaries in Olango |
| | S3 | Sardine run | | S20 | Omagieca mangrove garden |
| Sun, sea, sand | S4 | Basdaku | Farm tourism | S21 | AO farm gardens |
| | S5 | Virgin island | | S22 | Eskapo Verde ecotourism |
| | S6 | Malapascua island | | S23 | Oslob whale watching |
| | S7 | Orongan beach resort | Water-based tourism | S24 | Kawasan falls |
| | S8 | Lambug beach | | S25 | Pescador island |
| | S9 | Tingko beach | | S26 | Canyoneering |
| | S10 | Camotes beach | | S27 | Cebu Ocean Park |
| | S11 | Fort San Pedro | | S28 | Danasan eco adventure park |
| | S12 | Casa Gorordo | Adventure tourism | S29 | Cebu safari |
| | S13 | Yap-Sandiego museum | | S30 | Anjo World |
| Heritage and culture | S14 | Museo sa Sugbo | | S31 | Sirao flower garden |
| | S15 | Parian museum | | S32 | Tops lookout |
| | S16 | Sugbo Chinese heritage museum | Park tourism | S33 | D'Family park |
| | S17 | Mactan shrine | | S34 | Baluarte park |
| | | | | S35 | Lake Danao |

**Step 3**: Determine the priority weights of the criteria.

The dataset reported in our previous work [3] involves respondents evaluating the importance of the six criteria within the context of COVID-19 exposure using a 9-point scale. Two hundred twenty-one (221) respondents participated in an online survey. To capture the vagueness and uncertainty within the dataset, the 9-point scale is provided with an equivalent linguistic evaluation scale with corresponding IVIFS values, as shown in Table 2. The presence of IVIFS values allows the integration of two aspects of uncertainty prevalent in judgment mapping, i.e., the membership and non-membership degrees of the evaluation ratings.

Table 2. Linguistic evaluation scale for the priority weights of the criteria.

| Rating | Linguistic Variable | Equivalent IVIFS Value |
| --- | --- | --- |
| 1 | Extremely irrelevant | ([0,0.1],[0.8,0.9]) |
| 2 | Very irrelevant | ([0.2,0.2],[0.7,0.7]) |
| 3 | Irrelevant | ([0.3,0.4],[0.5,0.6]) |
| 4 | Slightly irrelevant | ([0.4,0.5],[0.5,0.5]) |
| 5 | Fairly relevant | ([0.5,0.5],[0.4,0.5]) |
| 6 | Slightly relevant | ([0.6,0.7],[0.2,0.3]) |
| 7 | Relevant | ([0.7,0.8],[0.2,0.2]) |
| 8 | Very relevant | ([0.8,0.8],[0.1,0.1]) |
| 9 | Extremely relevant | ([0.9,1],[0,0]) |

Let $A_j^k = \left( \left[ \mu_{A_j^k L}^I, \mu_{A_j^k U}^I \right], \left[ \gamma_{A_j^k L}^I, \gamma_{A_j^k U}^I \right] \right)$ be the IVIFS value representing the perception of the $k$th decision-maker on the importance of the $j$th criterion. Using the weighted arithmetic average operator found in Definition 5, the IVIF weight $F_{A_j}$ of the criterion $j$ is computed as:

$$F_{A_j} = \left(\left[\mu^I_{A_jL}, \mu^I_{A_jU}\right], \left[\gamma^I_{A_jL}, \gamma^I_{A_jU}\right]\right) = \sum_{k=1}^{K} w_k A_j^k = \left(\left[1 - \prod_{k\in\{1,...,K\}}\left(1-\mu^I_{A_j^kL}\right)^{w_k}, 1 - \prod_{k\in\{1,...,K\}}\left(1-\mu^I_{A_j^kU}\right)^{w_k}\right], \left[\left(\prod_{k\in\{1,...,K\}}\left(\gamma^I_{A_j^kL}\right)^{w_k}\right), \left(\prod_{k\in\{1,...,K\}}\left(\gamma^I_{A_j^kU}\right)^{w_k}\right)\right]\right) \quad (24)$$

where $K$ is the total number of decision-makers, and $w_k = \frac{1}{K}$ with the assumption that all $K$ decision-makers have equal significance to the problem domain. Note that the required operations in Equation (24) are described in Definition 4. Following the required computations, the IVIF weights are shown in Table 3. By way of the novel accuracy function $L(A)$ of Definition 10, Theorem 2 provides a way of ranking these criteria. Results show that proximity is on top of the list, followed by the volume of tourist arrivals, available modes of transportation, area of site premises, tourist activities, and duration of stay.

Table 3. The IVIF weights of the evaluation criteria of tourist sites.

| Codes | Criteria | IVIF Weights | Novel Accuracy Function $L(A)$ | Rank |
|---|---|---|---|---|
| C1 | Proximity | ([0.9,1],[0,0]) | 0.950 | 1 |
| C2 | Available modes of transportation | ([0.78,1],[0,0]) | 0.891 | 3 |
| C3 | Duration of stay | ([0.75,1],[0,0]) | 0.875 | 6 |
| C4 | Tourist activities | ([0.76,1],[0,0]) | 0.879 | 5 |
| C5 | Area of site premises | ([0.76,1],[0,0]) | 0.880 | 4 |
| C6 | Volume of tourist arrivals | ([0.82,1],[0,0]) | 0.912 | 2 |

**Step 4**: Evaluate the relevance of the alternatives for all criteria.

The same set of respondents evaluated the relevance of the 35 tourist sites under the six criteria using the same 9-point scale. With the equivalent linguistic variables presented in Table 2, the resulting datasets contain IVIFS data, where each entry $f_{ij}^k = \left(\left[\mu^I_{f_{ij}^kL}, \mu^I_{f_{ij}^kU}\right], \left[\gamma^I_{f_{ij}^kL}, \gamma^I_{f_{ij}^kU}\right]\right)$ represents the IVIFS score of each tourist site $i(1,...,m)$ with respect to a criterion $j(1,...,n)$ as perceived by the decision-maker $k(1,...,K)$. Table 4 presents a sample dataset of a respondent in IVIFS values. The aggregate IVIFS score denoted by $f_{ij}$ is obtained as follows:

$$f_{ij} = \left(\left[\mu^I_{f_{ij}L}, \mu^I_{f_{ij}U}\right], \left[\gamma^I_{f_{ij}L}, \gamma^I_{f_{ij}U}\right]\right) = \left(\left[1 - \prod_{k\in\{1,...,K\}}\left(1-\mu^I_{f_{ij}^kL}\right)^{w_k}, 1 - \prod_{k\in\{1,...,K\}}\left(1-\mu^I_{f_{ij}^kU}\right)^{w_k}\right], \left[\left(\prod_{k\in\{1,...,K\}}\left(\gamma^I_{f_{ij}^kL}\right)^{w_k}\right), \left(\prod_{k\in\{1,...,K\}}\left(\gamma^I_{f_{ij}^kU}\right)^{w_k}\right)\right]\right) \quad (25)$$

where $w_k = \frac{1}{K}$. The aggregate dataset with IVIFS values is shown in Table 5.

**Step 5**: Obtain the weighted evaluation score of the alternatives under all criteria.

The weighted evaluation score $f_{ij}^w$ is obtained by multiplying the IVIF weight of a criterion $j$ obtained through Equation (24) and the aggregate IVIF score of an alternative $i$ under criterion $j$ generated by Equation (25) using the operation defined in Equation (12). The computational process is shown in Equation (26):

$$f_{ij}^w = F_{A_j} \cdot f_{ij} = \left(\left[\mu^I_{f_{ij}^wL}, \mu^I_{f_{ij}^wU}\right], \left[\gamma^I_{f_{ij}^wL}, \gamma^I_{f_{ij}^wU}\right]\right) = \left(\left[\mu^I_{A_jL}\mu^I_{f_{ij}L}, \mu^I_{A_jU}\mu^I_{f_{ij}U}\right], \left[\gamma^I_{A_jL} + \gamma^I_{f_{ij}L} - \gamma^I_{A_jL}\gamma^I_{f_{ij}L}, \gamma^I_{A_jU} + \gamma^I_{f_{ij}U} - \gamma^I_{A_jU}\gamma^I_{f_{ij}U}\right]\right) \quad (26)$$

Table 6 presents the resulting weighted dataset with IVIFS values.

**Step 6**: Generate the equivalent crisp value of $f_{ij}^w$.

As shown in Definition (10), the corresponding crisp score of $f_{ij}^w$ can be obtained using the novel accuracy function proposed by Nayagam et al. [41]. Let $L\left(f_{ij}^w\right)$ be the crisp score of the weighted relevance of tourist site $i$ on criterion $j$. Then:

$$L\left(f_{ij}^w\right) = \frac{\mu_{f_{ij}^w L}^I + \mu_{f_{ij}^w U}^I - \gamma_{f_{ij}^w U}^I\left(1 - \mu_{f_{ij}^w U}^I\right) - \gamma_{f_{ij}^w L}^I\left(1 - \mu_{f_{ij}^w L}^I\right)}{2} \quad (27)$$

Table 7 illustrates the resulting crisp dataset for the evaluation of tourist sites.

**Table 4.** Sample IVIF dataset representing a respondent evaluating the tourist sites.

| Tourist Sites | C1 | C2 | C3 | C4 | C5 | C6 |
|---|---|---|---|---|---|---|
| S1 | ([0.4,0.5],[0.5,0.5]) | ([0.5,0.5],[0.4,0.5]) | ([0.5,0.5],[0.4,0.5]) | ([0.5,0.5],[0.4,0.5]) | ([0.4,0.5],[0.5,0.5]) | ([0.5,0.5],[0.4,0.5]) |
| S2 | ([0.4,0.5],[0.5,0.5]) | ([0.5,0.5],[0.4,0.5]) | ([0.5,0.5],[0.4,0.5]) | ([0.5,0.5],[0.4,0.5]) | ([0.5,0.5],[0.4,0.5]) | ([0.5,0.5],[0.4,0.5]) |
| S3 | ([0.7,0.8],[0.2,0.2]) | ([0.8,0.8],[0.1,0.1]) | ([0.9,1],[0,0]) | ([0.9,1],[0,0]) | ([0.8,0.8],[0.1,0.1]) | ([0.9,1],[0,0]) |
| S4 | ([0.5,0.5],[0.5,0.5]) | ([0.5,0.5],[0.4,0.5]) | ([0.5,0.5],[0.4,0.5]) | ([0.5,0.5],[0.4,0.5]) | ([0.5,0.5],[0.5,0.5]) | ([0.5,0.5],[0.4,0.5]) |
| S5 | ([0.5,0.5],[0.4,0.5]) | ([0.5,0.5],[0.4,0.5]) | ([0.5,0.5],[0.4,0.5]) | ([0.5,0.5],[0.4,0.5]) | ([0.5,0.5],[0.4,0.5]) | ([0.5,0.5],[0.4,0.5]) |
| S6 | ([0.5,0.5],[0.4,0.5]) | ([0.5,0.5],[0.4,0.5]) | ([0.5,0.5],[0.4,0.5]) | ([0.5,0.5],[0.4,0.5]) | ([0.5,0.5],[0.4,0.5]) | ([0.5,0.5],[0.4,0.5]) |
| S7 | ([0.6,0.7],[0.2,0.3]) | ([0.6,0.7],[0.2,0.3]) | ([0.6,0.7],[0.2,0.3]) | ([0.6,0.7],[0.2,0.3]) | ([0.6,0.7],[0.2,0.3]) | ([0.6,0.7],[0.2,0.3]) |
| S8 | ([0.6,0.7],[0.2,0.3]) | ([0.6,0.7],[0.2,0.3]) | ([0.6,0.7],[0.2,0.3]) | ([0.6,0.7],[0.2,0.3]) | ([0.6,0.7],[0.2,0.3]) | ([0.6,0.7],[0.2,0.3]) |
| S9 | ([0.7,0.8],[0.2,0.2]) | ([0.7,0.8],[0.2,0.2]) | ([0.7,0.8],[0.2,0.2]) | ([0.7,0.8],[0.2,0.2]) | ([0.7,0.8],[0.2,0.2]) | ([0.7,0.8],[0.2,0.2]) |
| S10 | ([0.6,0.7],[0.2,0.3]) | ([0.6,0.7],[0.2,0.3]) | ([0.6,0.7],[0.2,0.3]) | ([0.6,0.7],[0.2,0.3]) | ([0.6,0.7],[0.2,0.3]) | ([0.6,0.7],[0.2,0.3]) |
| S11 | ([0.7,0.8],[0.2,0.2]) | ([0.7,0.8],[0.2,0.2]) | ([0.7,0.8],[0.2,0.2]) | ([0.7,0.8],[0.2,0.2]) | ([0.7,0.8],[0.2,0.2]) | ([0.7,0.8],[0.2,0.2]) |
| S12 | ([0.7,0.8],[0.2,0.2]) | ([0.7,0.8],[0.2,0.2]) | ([0.7,0.8],[0.2,0.2]) | ([0.7,0.8],[0.2,0.2]) | ([0.7,0.8],[0.2,0.2]) | ([0.7,0.8],[0.2,0.2]) |
| S13 | ([0.7,0.8],[0.2,0.2]) | ([0.7,0.8],[0.2,0.2]) | ([0.7,0.8],[0.2,0.2]) | ([0.7,0.8],[0.2,0.2]) | ([0.7,0.8],[0.2,0.2]) | ([0.7,0.8],[0.2,0.2]) |
| S14 | ([0.7,0.8],[0.2,0.2]) | ([0.7,0.8],[0.2,0.2]) | ([0.7,0.8],[0.2,0.2]) | ([0.7,0.8],[0.2,0.2]) | ([0.7,0.8],[0.2,0.2]) | ([0.7,0.8],[0.2,0.2]) |
| S15 | ([0.7,0.8],[0.2,0.2]) | ([0.7,0.8],[0.2,0.2]) | ([0.7,0.8],[0.2,0.2]) | ([0.7,0.8],[0.2,0.2]) | ([0.7,0.8],[0.2,0.2]) | ([0.7,0.8],[0.2,0.2]) |
| S16 | ([0.7,0.8],[0.2,0.2]) | ([0.7,0.8],[0.2,0.2]) | ([0.7,0.8],[0.2,0.2]) | ([0.7,0.8],[0.2,0.2]) | ([0.7,0.8],[0.2,0.2]) | ([0.7,0.8],[0.2,0.2]) |
| S17 | ([0.7,0.8],[0.2,0.2]) | ([0.7,0.8],[0.2,0.2]) | ([0.7,0.8],[0.2,0.2]) | ([0.7,0.8],[0.2,0.2]) | ([0.7,0.8],[0.2,0.2]) | ([0.7,0.8],[0.2,0.2]) |
| S18 | ([0.5,0.5],[0.4,0.5]) | ([0.5,0.5],[0.4,0.5]) | ([0.5,0.5],[0.4,0.5]) | ([0.5,0.5],[0.4,0.5]) | ([0.5,0.5],[0.4,0.5]) | ([0.5,0.5],[0.4,0.5]) |
| S19 | ([0.5,0.5],[0.4,0.5]) | ([0.5,0.5],[0.4,0.5]) | ([0.5,0.5],[0.4,0.5]) | ([0.5,0.5],[0.4,0.5]) | ([0.5,0.5],[0.4,0.5]) | ([0.5,0.5],[0.4,0.5]) |
| S20 | ([0.5,0.5],[0.4,0.5]) | ([0.5,0.5],[0.4,0.5]) | ([0.5,0.5],[0.4,0.5]) | ([0.5,0.5],[0.4,0.5]) | ([0.5,0.5],[0.4,0.5]) | ([0.5,0.5],[0.4,0.5]) |
| S21 | ([0.7,0.8],[0.2,0.2]) | ([0.7,0.8],[0.2,0.2]) | ([0.7,0.8],[0.2,0.2]) | ([0.7,0.8],[0.2,0.2]) | ([0.7,0.8],[0.2,0.2]) | ([0.6,0.7],[0.2,0.3]) |
| S22 | ([0.6,0.7],[0.2,0.3]) | ([0.6,0.7],[0.2,0.3]) | ([0.6,0.7],[0.2,0.3]) | ([0.6,0.7],[0.2,0.3]) | ([0.6,0.7],[0.2,0.3]) | ([0.7,0.8],[0.2,0.2]) |
| S23 | ([0.7,0.8],[0.2,0.2]) | ([0.7,0.8],[0.2,0.2]) | ([0.7,0.8],[0.2,0.2]) | ([0.7,0.8],[0.2,0.2]) | ([0.7,0.8],[0.2,0.2]) | ([0.6,0.7],[0.2,0.3]) |
| S24 | ([0.6,0.7],[0.2,0.3]) | ([0.6,0.7],[0.2,0.3]) | ([0.6,0.7],[0.2,0.3]) | ([0.6,0.7],[0.2,0.3]) | ([0.6,0.7],[0.2,0.3]) | ([0.5,0.5],[0.4,0.5]) |
| S25 | ([0.5,0.5],[0.4,0.5]) | ([0.5,0.5],[0.4,0.5]) | ([0.5,0.5],[0.4,0.5]) | ([0.5,0.5],[0.4,0.5]) | ([0.5,0.5],[0.4,0.5]) | ([0.6,0.7],[0.2,0.3]) |
| S26 | ([0.6,0.7],[0.2,0.3]) | ([0.6,0.7],[0.2,0.3]) | ([0.6,0.7],[0.2,0.3]) | ([0.6,0.7],[0.2,0.3]) | ([0.6,0.7],[0.2,0.3]) | ([0.7,0.8],[0.2,0.2]) |
| S27 | ([0.7,0.8],[0.2,0.2]) | ([0.7,0.8],[0.2,0.2]) | ([0.7,0.8],[0.2,0.2]) | ([0.7,0.8],[0.2,0.2]) | ([0.7,0.8],[0.2,0.2]) | ([0.6,0.7],[0.2,0.3]) |
| S28 | ([0.6,0.7],[0.2,0.3]) | ([0.6,0.7],[0.2,0.3]) | ([0.6,0.7],[0.2,0.3]) | ([0.6,0.7],[0.2,0.3]) | ([0.6,0.7],[0.2,0.3]) | ([0.5,0.5],[0.4,0.5]) |
| S29 | ([0.5,0.5],[0.4,0.5]) | ([0.5,0.5],[0.4,0.5]) | ([0.5,0.5],[0.4,0.5]) | ([0.5,0.5],[0.4,0.5]) | ([0.5,0.5],[0.4,0.5]) | ([0.7,0.8],[0.2,0.2]) |
| S30 | ([0.7,0.8],[0.2,0.2]) | ([0.7,0.8],[0.2,0.2]) | ([0.7,0.8],[0.2,0.2]) | ([0.7,0.8],[0.2,0.2]) | ([0.7,0.8],[0.2,0.2]) | ([0.6,0.7],[0.2,0.3]) |
| S31 | ([0.6,0.7],[0.2,0.3]) | ([0.6,0.7],[0.2,0.3]) | ([0.6,0.7],[0.2,0.3]) | ([0.6,0.7],[0.2,0.3]) | ([0.6,0.7],[0.2,0.3]) | ([0.6,0.7],[0.2,0.3]) |
| S32 | ([0.6,0.7],[0.2,0.3]) | ([0.6,0.7],[0.2,0.3]) | ([0.6,0.7],[0.2,0.3]) | ([0.6,0.7],[0.2,0.3]) | ([0.6,0.7],[0.2,0.3]) | ([0.7,0.8],[0.2,0.2]) |
| S33 | ([0.7,0.8],[0.2,0.2]) | ([0.7,0.8],[0.2,0.2]) | ([0.7,0.8],[0.2,0.2]) | ([0.6,0.7],[0.2,0.3]) | ([0.7,0.8],[0.2,0.2]) | ([0.5,0.5],[0.4,0.5]) |
| S34 | ([0.5,0.5],[0.4,0.5]) | ([0.5,0.5],[0.4,0.5]) | ([0.5,0.5],[0.4,0.5]) | ([0.5,0.5],[0.4,0.5]) | ([0.5,0.5],[0.4,0.5]) | ([0.5,0.5],[0.4,0.5]) |
| S35 | ([0.5,0.5],[0.4,0.5]) | ([0.5,0.5],[0.4,0.5]) | ([0.5,0.5],[0.4,0.5]) | ([0.5,0.5],[0.4,0.5]) | ([0.5,0.5],[0.4,0.5]) | ([0.5,0.5],[0.4,0.5]) |

**Table 5.** Aggregate IVIF dataset for the evaluation of tourist sites.

| Tourist Sites | C1 | C2 | C3 | C4 | C5 | C6 |
|---|---|---|---|---|---|---|
| S1 | ([0.63,1],[0,0]) | ([0.73,1],[0,0]) | ([0.66,1],[0,0]) | ([0.69,1],[0,0]) | ([0.67,1],[0,0]) | ([0.77,1],[0,0]) |
| S2 | ([0.68,1],[0,0]) | ([0.73,1],[0,0]) | ([0.7,1],[0,0]) | ([0.72,1],[0,0]) | ([0.71,1],[0,0]) | ([0.78,1],[0,0]) |
| S3 | ([0.65,1],[0,0]) | ([0.71,1],[0,0]) | ([0.67,1],[0,0]) | ([0.68,1],[0,0]) | ([0.68,1],[0,0]) | ([0.75,1],[0,0]) |
| S4 | ([0.68,1],[0,0]) | ([0.74,1],[0,0]) | ([0.7,1],[0,0]) | ([0.72,1],[0,0]) | ([0.71,1],[0,0]) | ([0.78,1],[0,0]) |
| S5 | ([0.64,1],[0,0]) | ([0.71,1],[0,0]) | ([0.66,1],[0,0]) | ([0.69,1],[0,0]) | ([0.69,1],[0,0]) | ([0.75,1],[0,0]) |

Table 5. *Cont.*

| Tourist Sites | C1 | C2 | C3 | C4 | C5 | C6 |
|---|---|---|---|---|---|---|
| S6 | ([0.67,1],[0,0]) | ([0.72,1],[0,0]) | ([0.68,1],[0,0]) | ([0.7,1],[0,0]) | ([0.7,1],[0,0]) | ([0.76,1],[0,0]) |
| S7 | ([0.63,1],[0,0]) | ([0.69,1],[0,0]) | ([0.66,1],[0,0]) | ([0.67,1],[0,0]) | ([0.67,1],[0,0]) | ([0.74,1],[0,0]) |
| S8 | ([0.68,1],[0,0]) | ([0.72,1],[0,0]) | ([0.68,1],[0,0]) | ([0.7,1],[0,0]) | ([0.7,1],[0,0]) | ([0.77,1],[0,0]) |
| S9 | ([0.66,1],[0,0]) | ([0.72,1],[0,0]) | ([0.67,1],[0,0]) | ([0.7,1],[0,0]) | ([0.71,1],[0,0]) | ([0.77,1],[0,0]) |
| S10 | ([0.67,1],[0,0]) | ([0.72,1],[0,0]) | ([0.67,1],[0,0]) | ([0.7,1],[0,0]) | ([0.69,1],[0,0]) | ([0.77,1],[0,0]) |
| S11 | ([0.74,1],[0,0]) | ([0.74,1],[0,0]) | ([0.71,1],[0,0]) | ([0.72,1],[0,0]) | ([0.76,1],[0,0]) | ([0.8,1],[0,0]) |
| S12 | ([0.72,1],[0,0]) | ([0.74,1],[0,0]) | ([0.7,1],[0,0]) | ([0.72,1],[0,0]) | ([0.75,1],[0,0]) | ([0.79,1],[0,0]) |
| S13 | ([0.7,1],[0,0]) | ([0.72,1],[0,0]) | ([0.69,1],[0,0]) | ([0.71,1],[0,0]) | ([0.74,1],[0,0]) | ([0.78,1],[0,0]) |
| S14 | ([0.71,1],[0,0]) | ([0.73,1],[0,0]) | ([0.7,1],[0,0]) | ([0.72,1],[0,0]) | ([0.75,1],[0,0]) | ([0.78,1],[0,0]) |
| S15 | ([0.73,1],[0,0]) | ([0.73,1],[0,0]) | ([0.7,1],[0,0]) | ([0.73,1],[0,0]) | ([0.75,1],[0,0]) | ([0.78,1],[0,0]) |
| S16 | ([0.71,1],[0,0]) | ([0.72,1],[0,0]) | ([0.69,1],[0,0]) | ([0.71,1],[0,0]) | ([0.73,1],[0,0]) | ([0.77,1],[0,0]) |
| S17 | ([0.71,1],[0,0]) | ([0.73,1],[0,0]) | ([0.68,1],[0,0]) | ([0.7,1],[0,0]) | ([0.72,1],[0,0]) | ([0.77,1],[0,0]) |
| S18 | ([0.66,1],[0,0]) | ([0.7,1],[0,0]) | ([0.65,1],[0,0]) | ([0.69,1],[0,0]) | ([0.67,1],[0,0]) | ([0.74,1],[0,0]) |
| S19 | ([0.67,1],[0,0]) | ([0.72,1],[0,0]) | ([0.67,1],[0,0]) | ([0.7,1],[0,0]) | ([0.69,1],[0,0]) | ([0.76,1],[0,0]) |
| S20 | ([0.65,1],[0,0]) | ([0.7,1],[0,0]) | ([0.65,1],[0,0]) | ([0.67,1],[0,0]) | ([0.67,1],[0,0]) | ([0.74,1],[0,0]) |
| S21 | ([0.71,1],[0,0]) | ([0.67,1],[0,0]) | ([0.69,1],[0,0]) | ([0.7,1],[0,0]) | ([0.75,1],[0,0]) | ([0.65,1],[0,0]) |
| S22 | ([0.7,1],[0,0]) | ([0.65,1],[0,0]) | ([0.68,1],[0,0]) | ([0.67,1],[0,0]) | ([0.74,1],[0,0]) | ([0.7,1],[0,0]) |
| S23 | ([0.73,1],[0,0]) | ([0.7,1],[0,0]) | ([0.74,1],[0,0]) | ([0.73,1],[0,0]) | ([0.8,1],[0,0]) | ([0.7,1],[0,0]) |
| S24 | ([0.74,1],[0,0]) | ([0.71,1],[0,0]) | ([0.74,1],[0,0]) | ([0.73,1],[0,0]) | ([0.8,1],[0,0]) | ([0.67,1],[0,0]) |
| S25 | ([0.71,1],[0,0]) | ([0.68,1],[0,0]) | ([0.71,1],[0,0]) | ([0.69,1],[0,0]) | ([0.77,1],[0,0]) | ([0.69,1],[0,0]) |
| S26 | ([0.73,1],[0,0]) | ([0.71,1],[0,0]) | ([0.74,1],[0,0]) | ([0.72,1],[0,0]) | ([0.78,1],[0,0]) | ([0.74,1],[0,0]) |
| S27 | ([0.76,1],[0,0]) | ([0.75,1],[0,0]) | ([0.76,1],[0,0]) | ([0.78,1],[0,0]) | ([0.81,1],[0,0]) | ([0.68,1],[0,0]) |
| S28 | ([0.71,1],[0,0]) | ([0.67,1],[0,0]) | ([0.71,1],[0,0]) | ([0.69,1],[0,0]) | ([0.75,1],[0,0]) | ([0.67,1],[0,0]) |
| S29 | ([0.72,1],[0,0]) | ([0.68,1],[0,0]) | ([0.7,1],[0,0]) | ([0.7,1],[0,0]) | ([0.76,1],[0,0]) | ([0.73,1],[0,0]) |
| S30 | ([0.74,1],[0,0]) | ([0.74,1],[0,0]) | ([0.77,1],[0,0]) | ([0.77,1],[0,0]) | ([0.81,1],[0,0]) | ([0.69,1],[0,0]) |
| S31 | ([0.7,1],[0,0]) | ([0.67,1],[0,0]) | ([0.69,1],[0,0]) | ([0.71,1],[0,0]) | ([0.77,1],[0,0]) | ([0.69,1],[0,0]) |
| S32 | ([0.71,1],[0,0]) | ([0.69,1],[0,0]) | ([0.69,1],[0,0]) | ([0.71,1],[0,0]) | ([0.77,1],[0,0]) | ([0.69,1],[0,0]) |
| S33 | ([0.71,1],[0,0]) | ([0.68,1],[0,0]) | ([0.7,1],[0,0]) | ([0.7,1],[0,0]) | ([0.74,1],[0,0]) | ([0.65,1],[0,0]) |
| S34 | ([0.65,1],[0,0]) | ([0.68,1],[0,0]) | ([0.64,1],[0,0]) | ([0.66,1],[0,0]) | ([0.66,1],[0,0]) | ([0.73,1],[0,0]) |
| S35 | ([0.65,1],[0,0]) | ([0.7,1],[0,0]) | ([0.66,1],[0,0]) | ([0.67,1],[0,0]) | ([0.66,1],[0,0]) | ([0.74,1],[0,0]) |

Table 6. The weighted IVIF dataset for the evaluation of tourist sites.

| Tourist Sites | C1 | C2 | C3 | C4 | C5 | C6 |
|---|---|---|---|---|---|---|
| S1 | ([0.57,1],[0,0]) | ([0.57,1],[0,0]) | ([0.5,1],[0,0]) | ([0.53,1],[0,0]) | ([0.51,1],[0,0]) | ([0.63,1],[0,0]) |
| S2 | ([0.61,1],[0,0]) | ([0.57,1],[0,0]) | ([0.52,1],[0,0]) | ([0.55,1],[0,0]) | ([0.54,1],[0,0]) | ([0.64,1],[0,0]) |
| S3 | ([0.58,1],[0,0]) | ([0.56,1],[0,0]) | ([0.5,1],[0,0]) | ([0.52,1],[0,0]) | ([0.52,1],[0,0]) | ([0.62,1],[0,0]) |
| S4 | ([0.61,1],[0,0]) | ([0.58,1],[0,0]) | ([0.53,1],[0,0]) | ([0.55,1],[0,0]) | ([0.54,1],[0,0]) | ([0.64,1],[0,0]) |
| S5 | ([0.58,1],[0,0]) | ([0.55,1],[0,0]) | ([0.5,1],[0,0]) | ([0.53,1],[0,0]) | ([0.52,1],[0,0]) | ([0.62,1],[0,0]) |
| S6 | ([0.61,1],[0,0]) | ([0.56,1],[0,0]) | ([0.51,1],[0,0]) | ([0.53,1],[0,0]) | ([0.53,1],[0,0]) | ([0.63,1],[0,0]) |
| S7 | ([0.57,1],[0,0]) | ([0.54,1],[0,0]) | ([0.49,1],[0,0]) | ([0.51,1],[0,0]) | ([0.51,1],[0,0]) | ([0.61,1],[0,0]) |
| S8 | ([0.61,1],[0,0]) | ([0.57,1],[0,0]) | ([0.51,1],[0,0]) | ([0.53,1],[0,0]) | ([0.53,1],[0,0]) | ([0.63,1],[0,0]) |
| S9 | ([0.6,1],[0,0]) | ([0.56,1],[0,0]) | ([0.51,1],[0,0]) | ([0.53,1],[0,0]) | ([0.54,1],[0,0]) | ([0.63,1],[0,0]) |
| S10 | ([0.61,1],[0,0]) | ([0.56,1],[0,0]) | ([0.5,1],[0,0]) | ([0.53,1],[0,0]) | ([0.52,1],[0,0]) | ([0.63,1],[0,0]) |
| S11 | ([0.66,1],[0,0]) | ([0.58,1],[0,0]) | ([0.53,1],[0,0]) | ([0.55,1],[0,0]) | ([0.58,1],[0,0]) | ([0.66,1],[0,0]) |
| S12 | ([0.65,1],[0,0]) | ([0.58,1],[0,0]) | ([0.53,1],[0,0]) | ([0.55,1],[0,0]) | ([0.57,1],[0,0]) | ([0.65,1],[0,0]) |
| S13 | ([0.63,1],[0,0]) | ([0.56,1],[0,0]) | ([0.52,1],[0,0]) | ([0.54,1],[0,0]) | ([0.56,1],[0,0]) | ([0.64,1],[0,0]) |
| S14 | ([0.64,1],[0,0]) | ([0.57,1],[0,0]) | ([0.53,1],[0,0]) | ([0.55,1],[0,0]) | ([0.57,1],[0,0]) | ([0.64,1],[0,0]) |
| S15 | ([0.66,1],[0,0]) | ([0.57,1],[0,0]) | ([0.53,1],[0,0]) | ([0.55,1],[0,0]) | ([0.57,1],[0,0]) | ([0.64,1],[0,0]) |
| S16 | ([0.64,1],[0,0]) | ([0.56,1],[0,0]) | ([0.52,1],[0,0]) | ([0.54,1],[0,0]) | ([0.55,1],[0,0]) | ([0.63,1],[0,0]) |
| S17 | ([0.64,1],[0,0]) | ([0.57,1],[0,0]) | ([0.51,1],[0,0]) | ([0.53,1],[0,0]) | ([0.55,1],[0,0]) | ([0.64,1],[0,0]) |
| S18 | ([0.59,1],[0,0]) | ([0.55,1],[0,0]) | ([0.49,1],[0,0]) | ([0.52,1],[0,0]) | ([0.51,1],[0,0]) | ([0.61,1],[0,0]) |
| S19 | ([0.6,1],[0,0]) | ([0.56,1],[0,0]) | ([0.51,1],[0,0]) | ([0.53,1],[0,0]) | ([0.52,1],[0,0]) | ([0.62,1],[0,0]) |
| S20 | ([0.58,1],[0,0]) | ([0.55,1],[0,0]) | ([0.49,1],[0,0]) | ([0.51,1],[0,0]) | ([0.51,1],[0,0]) | ([0.61,1],[0,0]) |

Table 6. *Cont.*

| Tourist Sites | C1 | C2 | C3 | C4 | C5 | C6 |
|---|---|---|---|---|---|---|
| S21 | ([0.64,1],[0,0]) | ([0.52,1],[0,0]) | ([0.52,1],[0,0]) | ([0.53,1],[0,0]) | ([0.57,1],[0,0]) | ([0.54,1],[0,0]) |
| S22 | ([0.63,1],[0,0]) | ([0.51,1],[0,0]) | ([0.51,1],[0,0]) | ([0.51,1],[0,0]) | ([0.56,1],[0,0]) | ([0.58,1],[0,0]) |
| S23 | ([0.66,1],[0,0]) | ([0.55,1],[0,0]) | ([0.56,1],[0,0]) | ([0.55,1],[0,0]) | ([0.61,1],[0,0]) | ([0.58,1],[0,0]) |
| S24 | ([0.66,1],[0,0]) | ([0.56,1],[0,0]) | ([0.55,1],[0,0]) | ([0.55,1],[0,0]) | ([0.61,1],[0,0]) | ([0.56,1],[0,0]) |
| S25 | ([0.64,1],[0,0]) | ([0.53,1],[0,0]) | ([0.53,1],[0,0]) | ([0.53,1],[0,0]) | ([0.59,1],[0,0]) | ([0.57,1],[0,0]) |
| S26 | ([0.66,1],[0,0]) | ([0.55,1],[0,0]) | ([0.56,1],[0,0]) | ([0.54,1],[0,0]) | ([0.59,1],[0,0]) | ([0.61,1],[0,0]) |
| S27 | ([0.68,1],[0,0]) | ([0.59,1],[0,0]) | ([0.57,1],[0,0]) | ([0.59,1],[0,0]) | ([0.62,1],[0,0]) | ([0.56,1],[0,0]) |
| S28 | ([0.64,1],[0,0]) | ([0.53,1],[0,0]) | ([0.53,1],[0,0]) | ([0.52,1],[0,0]) | ([0.57,1],[0,0]) | ([0.55,1],[0,0]) |
| S29 | ([0.64,1],[0,0]) | ([0.53,1],[0,0]) | ([0.53,1],[0,0]) | ([0.53,1],[0,0]) | ([0.58,1],[0,0]) | ([0.6,1],[0,0]) |
| S30 | ([0.67,1],[0,0]) | ([0.58,1],[0,0]) | ([0.58,1],[0,0]) | ([0.58,1],[0,0]) | ([0.61,1],[0,0]) | ([0.57,1],[0,0]) |
| S31 | ([0.63,1],[0,0]) | ([0.53,1],[0,0]) | ([0.52,1],[0,0]) | ([0.54,1],[0,0]) | ([0.59,1],[0,0]) | ([0.57,1],[0,0]) |
| S32 | ([0.64,1],[0,0]) | ([0.54,1],[0,0]) | ([0.51,1],[0,0]) | ([0.54,1],[0,0]) | ([0.58,1],[0,0]) | ([0.57,1],[0,0]) |
| S33 | ([0.64,1],[0,0]) | ([0.53,1],[0,0]) | ([0.52,1],[0,0]) | ([0.53,1],[0,0]) | ([0.56,1],[0,0]) | ([0.53,1],[0,0]) |
| S34 | ([0.58,1],[0,0]) | ([0.53,1],[0,0]) | ([0.48,1],[0,0]) | ([0.5,1],[0,0]) | ([0.5,1],[0,0]) | ([0.6,1],[0,0]) |
| S35 | ([0.59,1],[0,0]) | ([0.54,1],[0,0]) | ([0.49,1],[0,0]) | ([0.51,1],[0,0]) | ([0.5,1],[0,0]) | ([0.61,1],[0,0]) |

Table 7. The equivalent crisp dataset for the evaluation of tourist sites.

| Tourist Sites | C1 | C2 | C3 | C4 | C5 | C6 |
|---|---|---|---|---|---|---|
| S1 | 0.78323 | 0.78492 | 0.74933 | 0.76333 | 0.75612 | 0.81525 |
| S2 | 0.80713 | 0.78431 | 0.76150 | 0.77316 | 0.76840 | 0.82021 |
| S3 | 0.79093 | 0.77899 | 0.75061 | 0.75938 | 0.75996 | 0.80885 |
| S4 | 0.80545 | 0.78977 | 0.76442 | 0.77340 | 0.76996 | 0.82098 |
| S5 | 0.78830 | 0.77595 | 0.74900 | 0.76261 | 0.76114 | 0.80988 |
| S6 | 0.80264 | 0.78132 | 0.75637 | 0.76497 | 0.76472 | 0.81299 |
| S7 | 0.78320 | 0.77128 | 0.74641 | 0.75577 | 0.75377 | 0.80389 |
| S8 | 0.80601 | 0.78339 | 0.75655 | 0.76601 | 0.76406 | 0.81671 |
| S9 | 0.79785 | 0.78110 | 0.75267 | 0.76486 | 0.76867 | 0.81712 |
| S10 | 0.80315 | 0.78109 | 0.75235 | 0.76542 | 0.76043 | 0.81606 |
| S11 | 0.83107 | 0.79146 | 0.76452 | 0.77348 | 0.78758 | 0.83039 |
| S12 | 0.82326 | 0.78809 | 0.76338 | 0.77440 | 0.78349 | 0.82513 |
| S13 | 0.81550 | 0.78215 | 0.75780 | 0.77034 | 0.78125 | 0.81919 |
| S14 | 0.82142 | 0.78600 | 0.76384 | 0.77319 | 0.78347 | 0.82014 |
| S15 | 0.82897 | 0.78705 | 0.76419 | 0.77517 | 0.78501 | 0.82091 |
| S16 | 0.81853 | 0.78197 | 0.75818 | 0.76888 | 0.77580 | 0.81657 |
| S17 | 0.81827 | 0.78435 | 0.75329 | 0.76520 | 0.77274 | 0.81898 |
| S18 | 0.79556 | 0.77468 | 0.74541 | 0.76045 | 0.75354 | 0.80476 |
| S19 | 0.80030 | 0.78088 | 0.75282 | 0.76620 | 0.76229 | 0.81158 |
| S20 | 0.79118 | 0.77262 | 0.74358 | 0.75327 | 0.75486 | 0.80261 |
| S21 | 0.81867 | 0.76183 | 0.76006 | 0.76641 | 0.78332 | 0.76904 |
| S22 | 0.81489 | 0.75569 | 0.75490 | 0.75303 | 0.77981 | 0.78954 |
| S23 | 0.82957 | 0.77583 | 0.77793 | 0.77620 | 0.80465 | 0.79000 |
| S24 | 0.83176 | 0.77919 | 0.77591 | 0.77668 | 0.80263 | 0.77760 |
| S25 | 0.82023 | 0.76669 | 0.76566 | 0.76310 | 0.79335 | 0.78538 |
| S26 | 0.82782 | 0.77636 | 0.77867 | 0.77239 | 0.79678 | 0.80661 |
| S27 | 0.83988 | 0.79451 | 0.78582 | 0.79535 | 0.80863 | 0.78058 |
| S28 | 0.81842 | 0.76274 | 0.76696 | 0.76085 | 0.78307 | 0.77720 |
| S29 | 0.82199 | 0.76510 | 0.76313 | 0.76452 | 0.79026 | 0.80083 |
| S30 | 0.83274 | 0.78772 | 0.79064 | 0.79179 | 0.80711 | 0.78267 |
| S31 | 0.81716 | 0.76361 | 0.75818 | 0.76894 | 0.79302 | 0.78527 |
| S32 | 0.81887 | 0.76965 | 0.75728 | 0.76980 | 0.79152 | 0.78389 |
| S33 | 0.81937 | 0.76594 | 0.76148 | 0.76545 | 0.78200 | 0.76676 |
| S34 | 0.79157 | 0.76621 | 0.74010 | 0.75053 | 0.75179 | 0.79921 |
| S35 | 0.79458 | 0.77215 | 0.74666 | 0.75576 | 0.75008 | 0.80319 |

**Step 7**: Perform *k*-means clustering.

With the equivalent crisp dataset from Step 6, *k*-means clustering is performed on the tourist sites. Using RapidMiner®version 9.9, the Clustering (*k*-means) operator was used to process the crisp dataset presented in Table 7 with the parameter *k* set to 3, and the maximum runs set to 200, NumericalMeasures set as the measure type, Euclidean distance set as the numerical measure, and the maximum optimization steps set to 100. The $k = 3$ is set purposively so that the clusters may be comparable to the classes defined previously [3].

Three distinguishable clusters were obtained from the analysis. As observed on the heat map presented in Figure 1, the "low exposure" cluster is characterized by a 68.12% smaller area of premises, 60.34% closer in proximity, and 52.68% shorter stay duration than the other two clusters. Despite smaller premises where physical distancing measures may be compromised, these sites are accessible with shorter travel time, implying shorter exposure time for tourists during travel, coupled with tourists having a shorter duration of stay. Thus, exposure to COVID-19 is regarded as minimal, as proximity is considered the most crucial exposure criterion (i.e., see Table 3), and this cluster of sites portrays such a characteristic. Due to these characteristics, this cluster can be associated with tourists having a low risk of exposure to COVID-19, comparable to the "low exposure" class in our previous work [3].

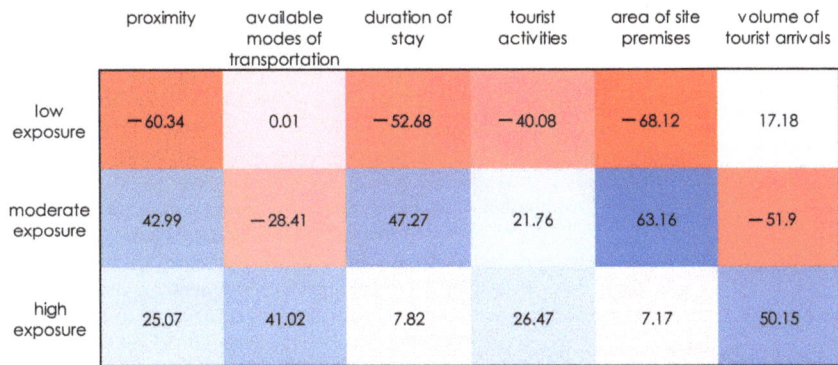

**Figure 1.** Differentiators (%) of the three clusters of tourist sites based on average.

Based on average values, the "moderate exposure" cluster is characterized by 63.16% larger in the area of premises, 51.90% smaller in the volume of tourist arrival, and 47.27% longer in the duration of stay compared to the other clusters. Table 3 suggests that tourists assign more premium to the volume of tourist arrivals when exposure to COVID-19 is considered. Although the duration of stay is longer than the average, the volume of tourist arrivals is minimum. Lastly, the "high exposure" cluster is characterized by 51.15% larger in the volume of tourist arrival, 26.47% higher in the number of tourist activities, and 41.02% more available modes of transportation than the other two clusters. A similar argument to how the "high exposure" cluster is framed, higher tourist arrivals would compromise the physical distancing measures at the sites; thus, exposure to COVID-19 is considered high. The "high exposure" cluster is comparable to the "high exposure" class in our previous work [3]. The list of tourist sites with their corresponding clusters is presented in Table 8.

**Table 8.** Assignment of tourist sites to clusters using the proposed approach.

| Low Exposure Cluster | Moderate Exposure Cluster | High Exposure Cluster |
|---|---|---|
| S1, S3, S5, S6, S7, S8, S9, S10, S18, S19, S20, S34, S35 | S21, S22, S23, S24, S25, S26, S27, S28, S29, S30, S31, S32, S33 | S2, S4, S11, S12, S13, S14, S15, S16, S17 |

## 4.2. Case Study 2: Clustering Restaurants for Perceived COVID-19 Exposure

The accommodation and food sector or the hospitality sector employs millions of people and contributes significantly to the global economy [39]. However, mobility restrictions imposed by the Philippine government during the countrywide lockdown have had adverse effects on the sector's business operations. Furthermore, minimum health protocols (i.e., social distancing, the single flow of entry and exit, mask compliance) that the government imposed to ensure the safety of both the workers and customers also affected the operational capacity of most businesses, particularly in the hospitality industry. In particular, measures for improved dine-in systems are required for establishments, such as proper ventilation, one-meter distance arrangement for each table, visible floor markers, provision of food menus per table, appropriate table dividers for face-to-face seating, disinfection of high-risk areas, defined take-away or pick-up area, prohibition of meal buffet, provision of a self-service station, and constant temperature monitoring. Despite the strict compliance of health and safety measures implemented by the industry, and the continuous effort of the government to administer the vaccines to the general population, customers found themselves under stigma regarding their possible exposure to COVID-19. The stigma prevails even to those vaccinated customers, given recent reports about the emergence of COVID-19 variants that may escape vaccines. Thus, a systematic evaluation of the levels of perceived exposure to different food services is an important initiative. Furthermore, the insights gained from the evaluation may serve as guidelines to the industry in encouraging customers to dine in.

In this regard, an online survey was conducted in our previous work [4] to evaluate customers' exposure to COVID-19 in various restaurants. Table 9 shows the list of 40 restaurants with their corresponding codes. A set of six criteria, 40 restaurants in the vicinity of Cebu (i.e., central Philippines), were evaluated. These criteria include proximity (C1), available mode of transportation (C2), available hygiene facilities and equipment (C3), physical environment (C4), duration of stay (C5), and consumer traffic (C6). The online survey questionnaires were sent to over 400 respondents, and 250 of them participated. The questionnaire contains two parts. First, respondents are required to evaluate the importance of the criteria set in the context of customers' exposure to COVID-19 using the same 9-point scale with corresponding linguistic variables and IVIFS values in Table 2. Secondly, they were prompted to evaluate the pre-defined set of 40 restaurants with a 6-point evaluation scale in Table 10, along with the corresponding linguistic variables and IVIFS values.

Table 9. List of restaurants under evaluation [4].

| Code | Restaurants | Code | Restaurants |
| --- | --- | --- | --- |
| R1 | Vikings Luxury Buffet, SM City Cebu | R21 | Entoy's Bakasihan, Cordova |
| R2 | Buffet 101, City Time Square Mandaue City | R22 | Matias BBQ, Mandaue City |
| R3 | Cabalen Restaurant, SM City Cebu | R23 | Pungko pungko sa Fuente, Cebu City |
| R4 | Tinderbox Wine and Deli Shop, Banilad Cebu City | R24 | Chinese Ngohiong, Downtown Cebu City |
| R5 | Acacia Steakhouse, Capitol Cebu City | R25 | Larangan sa Pasil - the original, Pasil Cebu City |
| R6 | Top of Cebu, Busay, Cebu City | R26 | Nonki Japanese Restaurant, SM City Cebu |
| R7 | Rico's Lechon, Mandaue City | R27 | La Vie Parisienne, Gorordo Cebu City |
| R8 | Hukad, SM City Cebu | R28 | Casa Verde Main Cebu City |
| R9 | Lantaw Floating Restaurant, Cordova Cebu | R29 | Lemon Grass, Ayala Center Cebu |
| R10 | Choobi-choobi, Mabolo Cebu City | R30 | Samguypsalamat Unli-Korean Meat, Cabahug St, Cebu City |
| R11 | Starbucks, Ayala Cebu | R31 | Maya Mexican, Cebu City |
| R12 | Bo's Coffee, BTC Banilad Cebu City | R32 | Jollibee, Highway Mandaue City |
| R13 | Macau Imperial Tea, SM City Cebu | R33 | McDonald's, Jones Avenue Cebu City |
| R14 | KM 21, Cantipla Cebu City | R34 | Chowking, Sto. Nino Cebu City |
| R15 | Chatime, SM City Cebu | R35 | Mang Inasal, Parkmall Mandaue City |
| R16 | Sugbo Mercado, IT Park Cebu City | R36 | Orange Brutus, Fuente Cebu City |
| R17 | Larsian Barbecue Food Park | R37 | Cafe Bai, Bai Hotel Mandaue City |
| R18 | Tambayan Food Park, Consolacion | R38 | Cafe Marco, Marco Polo Cebu City |
| R19 | SM Food Court, SM City Cebu | R39 | Feria, Radisson Blue Cebu City |
| R20 | Sutukil Seafood Market, Mactan | R40 | Pusô Bistro & Bar, Quest Hotel Cebu City |

Table 10. Linguistic evaluation scale for rating the restaurants.

| Rating | Linguistic Variable | Equivalent IVIFS Value |
|---|---|---|
| 1 | very irrelevant | ([0.05,0.25],[0.65,0.75]) |
| 2 | irrelevant | ([0.30,0.45],[0.40,0.55]) |
| 3 | slightly irrelevant | ([0.45,0.55],[0.30,0.45]) |
| 4 | slightly relevant | ([0.55,0.75],[0.10,0.25]) |
| 5 | relevant | ([0.75,0.85],[0.05,0.10]) |
| 6 | very relevant | ([0.85,0.95],[0,0.05]) |

Following the steps carried out in Case study 1 (Section 3.1.), this section presents the results. Table 11 shows the IVIF weights of the six evaluation criteria while applying a similar computational process in Equation (24). The priority ranking yields $C3 \succ C4 \succ C6 \succ C2 \succ C5 \succ C1$. The aggregate IVIF scores of respondents in their evaluation of the relevance of restaurants under the six criteria are presented in Table 12. Using similar computations in Equation (26), the weighted IVIF scores are shown in Table 13. Finally, using Equation (27), the equivalent dataset for the $k$-means clustering is reported in Table 14.

Table 11. The IVIF weights of the evaluation criteria of restaurants.

| Codes | Criteria | IVIF Weights | Novel Accuracy Function $L(A)$ | Rank |
|---|---|---|---|---|
| C1 | proximity | ([0.66,1],[0,0]) | 0.831 | 6 |
| C2 | available mode of transportation | ([0.70,1],[0,0]) | 0.850 | 4 |
| C3 | available hygiene facilities and equipment | ([0.75,1],[0,0]) | 0.874 | 1 |
| C4 | physical environment | ([0.74,1],[0,0]) | 0.868 | 2 |
| C5 | duration of stay | ([0.69,1],[0,0]) | 0.843 | 5 |
| C6 | consumer traffic | ([0.70,1],[0,0]) | 0.851 | 3 |

Table 12. Aggregate IVIF dataset for the evaluation of restaurants.

| Restaurants | C1 | C2 | C3 | C4 | C5 | C6 |
|---|---|---|---|---|---|---|
| R1 | ([0.59,0.74],[0,0.24]) | ([0.61,0.76],[0,0.22]) | ([0.62,0.77],[0,0.21]) | ([0.63,0.78],[0,0.2]) | ([0.61,0.76],[0,0.21]) | ([0.63,0.78],[0,0.2]) |
| R2 | ([0.59,0.74],[0,0.24]) | ([0.61,0.76],[0,0.22]) | ([0.6,0.76],[0,0.22]) | ([0.63,0.78],[0,0.2]) | ([0.6,0.75],[0,0.22]) | ([0.62,0.77],[0,0.21]) |
| R3 | ([0.59,0.74],[0,0.24]) | ([0.6,0.75],[0,0.23]) | ([0.61,0.76],[0,0.23]) | ([0.62,0.77],[0,0.21]) | ([0.61,0.76],[0,0.22]) | ([0.63,0.78],[0,0.2]) |
| R4 | ([0.58,0.73],[0,0.25]) | ([0.59,0.75],[0,0.24]) | ([0.6,0.75],[0,0.23]) | ([0.61,0.76],[0,0.22]) | ([0.59,0.75],[0,0.23]) | ([0.61,0.76],[0,0.22]) |
| R5 | ([0.57,0.73],[0,0.25]) | ([0.59,0.74],[0,0.24]) | ([0.6,0.76],[0,0.22]) | ([0.62,0.76],[0,0.21]) | ([0.59,0.74],[0,0.23]) | ([0.61,0.76],[0,0.22]) |
| R6 | ([0.57,0.73],[0,0.26]) | ([0.6,0.75],[0,0.23]) | ([0.6,0.75],[0,0.23]) | ([0.58,0.74],[0,0.24]) | ([0.58,0.73],[0,0.25]) | ([0.58,0.74],[0,0.24]) |
| R7 | ([0.6,0.75],[0,0.23]) | ([0.59,0.74],[0,0.24]) | ([0.61,0.77],[0,0.22]) | ([0.61,0.76],[0,0.22]) | ([0.59,0.75],[0,0.23]) | ([0.61,0.76],[0,0.22]) |
| R8 | ([0.6,0.75],[0,0.23]) | ([0.61,0.76],[0,0.22]) | ([0.61,0.76],[0,0.22]) | ([0.62,0.77],[0,0.21]) | ([0.6,0.75],[0,0.23]) | ([0.62,0.77],[0,0.2]) |
| R9 | ([0.59,0.75],[0,0.24]) | ([0.6,0.76],[0,0.23]) | ([0.61,0.77],[0,0.22]) | ([0.6,0.75],[0,0.23]) | ([0.59,0.75],[0,0.23]) | ([0.61,0.76],[0,0.22]) |
| R10 | ([0.59,0.74],[0,0.24]) | ([0.59,0.74],[0,0.24]) | ([0.62,0.77],[0,0.21]) | ([0.62,0.77],[0,0.21]) | ([0.59,0.74],[0,0.24]) | ([0.61,0.76],[0,0.22]) |
| R11 | ([0.6,0.75],[0,0.23]) | ([0.61,0.76],[0,0.22]) | ([0.62,0.77],[0,0.21]) | ([0.62,0.77],[0,0.21]) | ([0.6,0.75],[0,0.23]) | ([0.64,0.79],[0,0.19]) |
| R12 | ([0.6,0.75],[0,0.23]) | ([0.6,0.76],[0,0.23]) | ([0.61,0.77],[0,0.22]) | ([0.63,0.77],[0,0.2]) | ([0.61,0.76],[0,0.22]) | ([0.62,0.77],[0,0.21]) |
| R13 | ([0.6,0.75],[0,0.23]) | ([0.61,0.76],[0,0.22]) | ([0.62,0.77],[0,0.21]) | ([0.63,0.78],[0,0.2]) | ([0.59,0.74],[0,0.23]) | ([0.63,0.78],[0,0.2]) |
| R14 | ([0.56,0.72],[0,0.26]) | ([0.58,0.74],[0,0.25]) | ([0.6,0.75],[0,0.23]) | ([0.58,0.73],[0,0.25]) | ([0.58,0.73],[0,0.25]) | ([0.58,0.74],[0,0.24]) |
| R15 | ([0.59,0.74],[0,0.24]) | ([0.6,0.75],[0,0.23]) | ([0.62,0.77],[0,0.21]) | ([0.63,0.78],[0,0.2]) | ([0.6,0.76],[0,0.23]) | ([0.63,0.78],[0,0.2]) |
| R16 | ([0.65,0.79],[0,0.19]) | ([0.64,0.79],[0,0.19]) | ([0.67,0.81],[0,0.17]) | ([0.68,0.82],[0,0.16]) | ([0.65,0.8],[0,0.18]) | ([0.68,0.82],[0,0.16]) |
| R17 | ([0.65,0.8],[0,0.19]) | ([0.64,0.79],[0,0.19]) | ([0.67,0.82],[0,0.17]) | ([0.68,0.83],[0,0.16]) | ([0.66,0.81],[0,0.18]) | ([0.67,0.82],[0,0.17]) |
| R18 | ([0.65,0.8],[0,0.18]) | ([0.64,0.79],[0,0.19]) | ([0.66,0.81],[0,0.17]) | ([0.67,0.82],[0,0.17]) | ([0.65,0.8],[0,0.18]) | ([0.67,0.81],[0,0.17]) |
| R19 | ([0.62,0.77],[0,0.21]) | ([0.63,0.78],[0,0.2]) | ([0.65,0.8],[0,0.18]) | ([0.66,0.81],[0,0.17]) | ([0.64,0.79],[0,0.19]) | ([0.66,0.81],[0,0.18]) |
| R20 | ([0.62,0.77],[0,0.21]) | ([0.63,0.78],[0,0.21]) | ([0.65,0.8],[0,0.19]) | ([0.65,0.8],[0,0.18]) | ([0.62,0.77],[0,0.21]) | ([0.64,0.78],[0,0.19]) |
| R21 | ([0.61,0.76],[0,0.22]) | ([0.61,0.76],[0,0.22]) | ([0.63,0.78],[0,0.2]) | ([0.63,0.78],[0,0.2]) | ([0.6,0.75],[0,0.23]) | ([0.63,0.78],[0,0.2]) |
| R22 | ([0.6,0.75],[0,0.23]) | ([0.61,0.76],[0,0.22]) | ([0.62,0.78],[0,0.21]) | ([0.63,0.78],[0,0.2]) | ([0.62,0.77],[0,0.21]) | ([0.63,0.78],[0,0.2]) |
| R23 | ([0.66,0.81],[0,0.18]) | ([0.64,0.79],[0,0.19]) | ([0.7,0.84],[0,0.15]) | ([0.7,0.84],[0,0.15]) | ([0.68,0.83],[0,0.16]) | ([0.69,0.84],[0,0.15]) |
| R24 | ([0.63,0.78],[0,0.2]) | ([0.63,0.78],[0,0.2]) | ([0.67,0.82],[0,0.17]) | ([0.67,0.81],[0,0.17]) | ([0.65,0.8],[0,0.19]) | ([0.66,0.81],[0,0.18]) |
| R25 | ([0.65,0.8],[0,0.18]) | ([0.65,0.8],[0,0.19]) | ([0.69,0.83],[0,0.16]) | ([0.7,0.85],[0,0.14]) | ([0.67,0.82],[0,0.17]) | ([0.68,0.83],[0,0.16]) |
| R26 | ([0.59,0.74],[0,0.24]) | ([0.6,0.75],[0,0.23]) | ([0.59,0.75],[0,0.24]) | ([0.6,0.75],[0,0.23]) | ([0.59,0.74],[0,0.24]) | ([0.6,0.74],[0,0.23]) |
| R27 | ([0.58,0.73],[0,0.24]) | ([0.58,0.73],[0,0.25]) | ([0.59,0.75],[0,0.24]) | ([0.6,0.75],[0,0.23]) | ([0.58,0.73],[0,0.25]) | ([0.59,0.74],[0,0.24]) |
| R28 | ([0.58,0.74],[0,0.24]) | ([0.59,0.74],[0,0.24]) | ([0.6,0.76],[0,0.22]) | ([0.62,0.77],[0,0.21]) | ([0.59,0.75],[0,0.23]) | ([0.6,0.75],[0,0.23]) |
| R29 | ([0.58,0.73],[0,0.25]) | ([0.57,0.73],[0,0.26]) | ([0.6,0.75],[0,0.23]) | ([0.6,0.75],[0,0.23]) | ([0.57,0.73],[0,0.25]) | ([0.58,0.74],[0,0.24]) |
| R30 | ([0.61,0.76],[0,0.22]) | ([0.6,0.75],[0,0.23]) | ([0.62,0.78],[0,0.21]) | ([0.63,0.78],[0,0.2]) | ([0.62,0.78],[0,0.21]) | ([0.63,0.78],[0,0.2]) |

Table 12. Cont.

| Restaurants | C1 | C2 | C3 | C4 | C5 | C6 |
|---|---|---|---|---|---|---|
| R31 | ([0.58,0.73],[0,0.25]) | ([0.58,0.73],[0,0.25]) | ([0.6,0.75],[0,0.23]) | ([0.59,0.74],[0,0.24]) | ([0.57,0.73],[0,0.25]) | ([0.58,0.73],[0,0.25]) |
| R32 | ([0.62,0.77],[0,0.21]) | ([0.61,0.76],[0,0.22]) | ([0.62,0.78],[0,0.21]) | ([0.63,0.79],[0,0.2]) | ([0.62,0.77],[0,0.21]) | ([0.64,0.79],[0,0.19]) |
| R33 | ([0.63,0.78],[0,0.2]) | ([0.62,0.77],[0,0.21]) | ([0.62,0.78],[0,0.21]) | ([0.65,0.8],[0,0.18]) | ([0.63,0.78],[0,0.2]) | ([0.65,0.79],[0,0.19]) |
| R34 | ([0.63,0.78],[0,0.2]) | ([0.63,0.78],[0,0.21]) | ([0.64,0.8],[0,0.19]) | ([0.66,0.81],[0,0.17]) | ([0.65,0.8],[0,0.18]) | ([0.66,0.81],[0,0.18]) |
| R35 | ([0.62,0.77],[0,0.21]) | ([0.62,0.77],[0,0.21]) | ([0.64,0.79],[0,0.2]) | ([0.65,0.79],[0,0.19]) | ([0.64,0.78],[0,0.2]) | ([0.64,0.79],[0,0.19]) |
| R36 | ([0.61,0.76],[0,0.22]) | ([0.61,0.75],[0,0.22]) | ([0.63,0.77],[0,0.2]) | ([0.64,0.78],[0,0.2]) | ([0.61,0.76],[0,0.22]) | ([0.62,0.77],[0,0.21]) |
| R37 | ([0.6,0.75],[0,0.23]) | ([0.6,0.75],[0,0.23]) | ([0.59,0.75],[0,0.24]) | ([0.6,0.75],[0,0.23]) | ([0.59,0.74],[0,0.24]) | ([0.6,0.75],[0,0.23]) |
| R38 | ([0.58,0.74],[0,0.25]) | ([0.59,0.74],[0,0.25]) | ([0.59,0.75],[0,0.24]) | ([0.59,0.75],[0,0.24]) | ([0.58,0.73],[0,0.25]) | ([0.57,0.73],[0,0.25]) |
| R39 | ([0.58,0.73],[0,0.25]) | ([0.58,0.74],[0,0.25]) | ([0.58,0.75],[0,0.24]) | ([0.58,0.73],[0,0.25]) | ([0.57,0.72],[0,0.26]) | ([0.56,0.72],[0,0.26]) |
| R40 | ([0.58,0.74],[0,0.25]) | ([0.58,0.74],[0,0.25]) | ([0.58,0.74],[0,0.24]) | ([0.59,0.74],[0,0.24]) | ([0.58,0.73],[0,0.25]) | ([0.57,0.73],[0,0.25]) |

Table 13. The weighted IVIF dataset for the evaluation of restaurants.

| Restaurants | C1 | C2 | C3 | C4 | C5 | C6 |
|---|---|---|---|---|---|---|
| R1 | ([0.39,0.74],[0,0.24]) | ([0.42,0.76],[0,0.22]) | ([0.46,0.77],[0,0.21]) | ([0.47,0.78],[0,0.2]) | ([0.42,0.76],[0,0.21]) | ([0.44,0.78],[0,0.2]) |
| R2 | ([0.39,0.74],[0,0.24]) | ([0.42,0.76],[0,0.22]) | ([0.45,0.76],[0,0.22]) | ([0.46,0.78],[0,0.2]) | ([0.41,0.75],[0,0.22]) | ([0.43,0.77],[0,0.21]) |
| R3 | ([0.39,0.74],[0,0.24]) | ([0.42,0.75],[0,0.23]) | ([0.46,0.76],[0,0.22]) | ([0.46,0.77],[0,0.21]) | ([0.42,0.76],[0,0.22]) | ([0.44,0.78],[0,0.2]) |
| R4 | ([0.38,0.73],[0,0.25]) | ([0.41,0.75],[0,0.24]) | ([0.45,0.75],[0,0.23]) | ([0.45,0.76],[0,0.22]) | ([0.41,0.75],[0,0.23]) | ([0.43,0.76],[0,0.22]) |
| R5 | ([0.38,0.73],[0,0.25]) | ([0.41,0.74],[0,0.24]) | ([0.45,0.76],[0,0.22]) | ([0.45,0.76],[0,0.21]) | ([0.4,0.74],[0,0.23]) | ([0.43,0.76],[0,0.22]) |
| R6 | ([0.38,0.73],[0,0.26]) | ([0.42,0.75],[0,0.23]) | ([0.45,0.75],[0,0.23]) | ([0.43,0.74],[0,0.24]) | ([0.4,0.73],[0,0.25]) | ([0.41,0.74],[0,0.24]) |
| R7 | ([0.39,0.75],[0,0.23]) | ([0.41,0.74],[0,0.24]) | ([0.46,0.77],[0,0.22]) | ([0.45,0.76],[0,0.22]) | ([0.41,0.75],[0,0.23]) | ([0.43,0.76],[0,0.22]) |
| R8 | ([0.39,0.75],[0,0.23]) | ([0.43,0.76],[0,0.22]) | ([0.46,0.76],[0,0.22]) | ([0.46,0.77],[0,0.21]) | ([0.41,0.75],[0,0.23]) | ([0.44,0.77],[0,0.2]) |
| R9 | ([0.39,0.75],[0,0.24]) | ([0.42,0.76],[0,0.23]) | ([0.46,0.77],[0,0.22]) | ([0.44,0.75],[0,0.23]) | ([0.41,0.75],[0,0.23]) | ([0.43,0.76],[0,0.22]) |
| R10 | ([0.39,0.74],[0,0.24]) | ([0.41,0.74],[0,0.24]) | ([0.46,0.77],[0,0.21]) | ([0.45,0.77],[0,0.21]) | ([0.41,0.74],[0,0.24]) | ([0.43,0.76],[0,0.22]) |
| R11 | ([0.4,0.75],[0,0.23]) | ([0.43,0.76],[0,0.22]) | ([0.46,0.77],[0,0.21]) | ([0.45,0.77],[0,0.21]) | ([0.41,0.75],[0,0.23]) | ([0.45,0.79],[0,0.19]) |
| R12 | ([0.4,0.75],[0,0.23]) | ([0.42,0.76],[0,0.23]) | ([0.46,0.77],[0,0.22]) | ([0.46,0.77],[0,0.2]) | ([0.42,0.76],[0,0.22]) | ([0.44,0.77],[0,0.21]) |
| R13 | ([0.39,0.75],[0,0.23]) | ([0.43,0.76],[0,0.22]) | ([0.46,0.77],[0,0.21]) | ([0.46,0.78],[0,0.2]) | ([0.41,0.74],[0,0.23]) | ([0.44,0.78],[0,0.2]) |
| R14 | ([0.37,0.72],[0,0.26]) | ([0.4,0.74],[0,0.25]) | ([0.45,0.75],[0,0.23]) | ([0.43,0.73],[0,0.25]) | ([0.4,0.73],[0,0.23]) | ([0.41,0.74],[0,0.24]) |
| R15 | ([0.39,0.75],[0,0.24]) | ([0.42,0.75],[0,0.23]) | ([0.46,0.77],[0,0.21]) | ([0.46,0.78],[0,0.2]) | ([0.41,0.76],[0,0.23]) | ([0.44,0.78],[0,0.2]) |
| R16 | ([0.43,0.79],[0,0.19]) | ([0.45,0.79],[0,0.19]) | ([0.5,0.81],[0,0.17]) | ([0.5,0.82],[0,0.16]) | ([0.45,0.8],[0,0.18]) | ([0.48,0.82],[0,0.16]) |
| R17 | ([0.43,0.8],[0,0.19]) | ([0.45,0.79],[0,0.19]) | ([0.5,0.82],[0,0.17]) | ([0.5,0.83],[0,0.16]) | ([0.45,0.81],[0,0.18]) | ([0.47,0.82],[0,0.17]) |
| R18 | ([0.43,0.8],[0,0.18]) | ([0.45,0.79],[0,0.19]) | ([0.5,0.81],[0,0.17]) | ([0.5,0.82],[0,0.17]) | ([0.45,0.8],[0,0.18]) | ([0.47,0.81],[0,0.17]) |
| R19 | ([0.41,0.77],[0,0.21]) | ([0.44,0.78],[0,0.2]) | ([0.49,0.8],[0,0.18]) | ([0.49,0.81],[0,0.17]) | ([0.44,0.79],[0,0.19]) | ([0.46,0.81],[0,0.18]) |
| R20 | ([0.41,0.77],[0,0.21]) | ([0.44,0.78],[0,0.21]) | ([0.48,0.8],[0,0.19]) | ([0.48,0.8],[0,0.18]) | ([0.43,0.77],[0,0.21]) | ([0.45,0.78],[0,0.19]) |
| R21 | ([0.4,0.76],[0,0.22]) | ([0.42,0.76],[0,0.22]) | ([0.47,0.78],[0,0.2]) | ([0.46,0.78],[0,0.2]) | ([0.41,0.75],[0,0.23]) | ([0.44,0.78],[0,0.2]) |
| R22 | ([0.4,0.75],[0,0.23]) | ([0.42,0.76],[0,0.22]) | ([0.47,0.78],[0,0.21]) | ([0.46,0.78],[0,0.2]) | ([0.42,0.77],[0,0.21]) | ([0.45,0.78],[0,0.2]) |
| R23 | ([0.43,0.81],[0,0.18]) | ([0.45,0.79],[0,0.19]) | ([0.52,0.84],[0,0.15]) | ([0.51,0.84],[0,0.15]) | ([0.47,0.83],[0,0.16]) | ([0.49,0.84],[0,0.15]) |
| R24 | ([0.41,0.78],[0,0.2]) | ([0.44,0.78],[0,0.2]) | ([0.5,0.82],[0,0.17]) | ([0.49,0.81],[0,0.17]) | ([0.44,0.8],[0,0.19]) | ([0.46,0.81],[0,0.18]) |
| R25 | ([0.43,0.8],[0,0.18]) | ([0.45,0.8],[0,0.19]) | ([0.52,0.83],[0,0.16]) | ([0.52,0.85],[0,0.14]) | ([0.46,0.82],[0,0.17]) | ([0.48,0.83],[0,0.16]) |
| R26 | ([0.39,0.74],[0,0.24]) | ([0.42,0.75],[0,0.23]) | ([0.44,0.75],[0,0.24]) | ([0.44,0.75],[0,0.23]) | ([0.4,0.74],[0,0.24]) | ([0.42,0.74],[0,0.23]) |
| R27 | ([0.39,0.73],[0,0.24]) | ([0.4,0.73],[0,0.25]) | ([0.44,0.75],[0,0.24]) | ([0.44,0.75],[0,0.23]) | ([0.4,0.73],[0,0.25]) | ([0.41,0.74],[0,0.24]) |
| R28 | ([0.39,0.74],[0,0.24]) | ([0.41,0.74],[0,0.24]) | ([0.45,0.76],[0,0.22]) | ([0.46,0.77],[0,0.21]) | ([0.41,0.75],[0,0.23]) | ([0.42,0.75],[0,0.23]) |
| R29 | ([0.38,0.73],[0,0.25]) | ([0.4,0.73],[0,0.26]) | ([0.45,0.75],[0,0.23]) | ([0.44,0.75],[0,0.23]) | ([0.39,0.73],[0,0.25]) | ([0.41,0.74],[0,0.24]) |
| R30 | ([0.4,0.76],[0,0.22]) | ([0.42,0.75],[0,0.23]) | ([0.46,0.78],[0,0.21]) | ([0.47,0.78],[0,0.2]) | ([0.43,0.78],[0,0.21]) | ([0.44,0.78],[0,0.2]) |
| R31 | ([0.39,0.73],[0,0.25]) | ([0.41,0.73],[0,0.25]) | ([0.45,0.75],[0,0.23]) | ([0.43,0.74],[0,0.24]) | ([0.39,0.73],[0,0.25]) | ([0.4,0.73],[0,0.25]) |
| R32 | ([0.41,0.77],[0,0.21]) | ([0.43,0.76],[0,0.22]) | ([0.47,0.78],[0,0.21]) | ([0.47,0.79],[0,0.2]) | ([0.43,0.77],[0,0.21]) | ([0.45,0.79],[0,0.19]) |
| R33 | ([0.41,0.78],[0,0.2]) | ([0.43,0.77],[0,0.21]) | ([0.47,0.78],[0,0.21]) | ([0.48,0.8],[0,0.18]) | ([0.43,0.78],[0,0.2]) | ([0.45,0.79],[0,0.19]) |
| R34 | ([0.42,0.78],[0,0.2]) | ([0.44,0.78],[0,0.21]) | ([0.48,0.8],[0,0.19]) | ([0.49,0.81],[0,0.17]) | ([0.45,0.8],[0,0.18]) | ([0.46,0.81],[0,0.18]) |
| R35 | ([0.41,0.77],[0,0.21]) | ([0.44,0.77],[0,0.21]) | ([0.48,0.79],[0,0.2]) | ([0.48,0.79],[0,0.19]) | ([0.44,0.78],[0,0.2]) | ([0.45,0.79],[0,0.19]) |
| R36 | ([0.4,0.76],[0,0.22]) | ([0.42,0.75],[0,0.22]) | ([0.47,0.77],[0,0.2]) | ([0.47,0.78],[0,0.2]) | ([0.42,0.76],[0,0.22]) | ([0.43,0.77],[0,0.21]) |
| R37 | ([0.4,0.75],[0,0.23]) | ([0.42,0.75],[0,0.23]) | ([0.44,0.75],[0,0.24]) | ([0.44,0.75],[0,0.23]) | ([0.41,0.74],[0,0.24]) | ([0.42,0.75],[0,0.23]) |
| R38 | ([0.38,0.74],[0,0.25]) | ([0.41,0.74],[0,0.25]) | ([0.44,0.75],[0,0.24]) | ([0.44,0.75],[0,0.24]) | ([0.39,0.73],[0,0.25]) | ([0.4,0.73],[0,0.25]) |
| R39 | ([0.38,0.73],[0,0.25]) | ([0.41,0.74],[0,0.25]) | ([0.44,0.75],[0,0.24]) | ([0.43,0.73],[0,0.25]) | ([0.39,0.72],[0,0.26]) | ([0.4,0.72],[0,0.26]) |
| R40 | ([0.38,0.74],[0,0.25]) | ([0.41,0.74],[0,0.25]) | ([0.44,0.74],[0,0.24]) | ([0.43,0.75],[0,0.24]) | ([0.4,0.73],[0,0.25]) | ([0.4,0.73],[0,0.25]) |

Table 14. The equivalent crisp dataset for the evaluation of restaurants.

| Restaurants | C1 | C2 | C3 | C4 | C5 | C6 |
|---|---|---|---|---|---|---|
| R1 | 0.53421 | 0.56409 | 0.59061 | 0.60444 | 0.56786 | 0.59290 |
| R2 | 0.53362 | 0.56410 | 0.57716 | 0.60098 | 0.55618 | 0.57810 |
| R3 | 0.53511 | 0.55534 | 0.58291 | 0.59113 | 0.56382 | 0.58536 |
| R4 | 0.52143 | 0.55008 | 0.57281 | 0.57704 | 0.54630 | 0.56536 |
| R5 | 0.51954 | 0.54784 | 0.57863 | 0.58246 | 0.54324 | 0.56927 |

Table 14. Cont.

| Restaurants | C1 | C2 | C3 | C4 | C5 | C6 |
|---|---|---|---|---|---|---|
| R6 | 0.51741 | 0.55765 | 0.57158 | 0.55017 | 0.53290 | 0.54025 |
| R7 | 0.54220 | 0.54890 | 0.58595 | 0.57845 | 0.54813 | 0.56753 |
| R8 | 0.54293 | 0.56549 | 0.58131 | 0.59176 | 0.54815 | 0.58268 |
| R9 | 0.53767 | 0.56389 | 0.58580 | 0.56693 | 0.54751 | 0.57026 |
| R10 | 0.53074 | 0.54837 | 0.59502 | 0.58507 | 0.54342 | 0.56732 |
| R11 | 0.54462 | 0.56724 | 0.59247 | 0.58825 | 0.55248 | 0.59765 |
| R12 | 0.54243 | 0.56125 | 0.58965 | 0.59448 | 0.56076 | 0.58112 |
| R13 | 0.54388 | 0.57041 | 0.59431 | 0.59821 | 0.54466 | 0.58675 |
| R14 | 0.50988 | 0.53809 | 0.56912 | 0.54742 | 0.53281 | 0.54043 |
| R15 | 0.54009 | 0.55795 | 0.59302 | 0.59668 | 0.55615 | 0.58586 |
| R16 | 0.59227 | 0.59576 | 0.64019 | 0.64741 | 0.60692 | 0.63773 |
| R17 | 0.59734 | 0.60137 | 0.64806 | 0.64962 | 0.61513 | 0.62845 |
| R18 | 0.59422 | 0.59936 | 0.63902 | 0.64258 | 0.60643 | 0.62362 |
| R19 | 0.56741 | 0.58410 | 0.62578 | 0.63197 | 0.59208 | 0.61719 |
| R20 | 0.56554 | 0.58363 | 0.62140 | 0.62281 | 0.57485 | 0.59438 |
| R21 | 0.55603 | 0.56765 | 0.60576 | 0.60195 | 0.55570 | 0.58618 |
| R22 | 0.54836 | 0.56350 | 0.59751 | 0.60073 | 0.57205 | 0.59179 |
| R23 | 0.60461 | 0.60160 | 0.67186 | 0.66636 | 0.63395 | 0.64827 |
| R24 | 0.57513 | 0.58726 | 0.64198 | 0.63540 | 0.60119 | 0.62022 |
| R25 | 0.60066 | 0.60786 | 0.66176 | 0.67201 | 0.62789 | 0.64021 |
| R26 | 0.53234 | 0.55240 | 0.56663 | 0.56672 | 0.53671 | 0.55193 |
| R27 | 0.52815 | 0.52963 | 0.56719 | 0.56717 | 0.53115 | 0.54879 |
| R28 | 0.53037 | 0.54644 | 0.58061 | 0.58911 | 0.54585 | 0.55911 |
| R29 | 0.52551 | 0.52872 | 0.57163 | 0.56874 | 0.52429 | 0.54145 |
| R30 | 0.55412 | 0.55894 | 0.59852 | 0.60132 | 0.57948 | 0.59142 |
| R31 | 0.52583 | 0.53378 | 0.56989 | 0.55628 | 0.52448 | 0.53097 |
| R32 | 0.56553 | 0.56814 | 0.59961 | 0.60552 | 0.57475 | 0.60100 |
| R33 | 0.57310 | 0.57768 | 0.59783 | 0.62193 | 0.58485 | 0.60464 |
| R34 | 0.57720 | 0.58520 | 0.61934 | 0.63428 | 0.60579 | 0.61668 |
| R35 | 0.57075 | 0.58152 | 0.61109 | 0.61624 | 0.58815 | 0.60309 |
| R36 | 0.55791 | 0.56115 | 0.59852 | 0.60560 | 0.56505 | 0.57784 |
| R37 | 0.54299 | 0.55936 | 0.56791 | 0.57141 | 0.54289 | 0.55592 |
| R38 | 0.52747 | 0.54540 | 0.56211 | 0.56284 | 0.52848 | 0.53357 |
| R39 | 0.52307 | 0.53953 | 0.56042 | 0.54760 | 0.51972 | 0.51974 |
| R40 | 0.52759 | 0.53839 | 0.55839 | 0.55786 | 0.53135 | 0.53015 |

Figure 2 summarizes the differentiators of the clusters obtained from k-means clustering. Based on average values, restaurants belonging to the "low exposure" cluster are characterized by 61.78% lower duration of stay, 51.91% lower consumer traffic, and 54.58% closer proximity.

On the other hand, the "high exposure" cluster is associated with 76.61% higher consumer traffic, 112.10% longer duration of stay, and 111.32% farther proximity. Restaurants located at a distance are associated with customers having more prolonged exposure at transportation facilities, while the other characteristics (i.e., higher consumer traffic and longer duration of stay) would compromise physical distancing measures at the restaurants, especially those that are air-conditioned.

Lastly, those restaurants belonging to the "moderate exposure" cluster are associated with 3.92% farther proximity, 10.41% larger physical environment, 5.73% longer duration of stay, 13.60% higher consumer traffic, and 0.94% lesser available hygiene facilities and equipment. The assignment of restaurants to clusters based on k-means clustering is presented in Table 15.

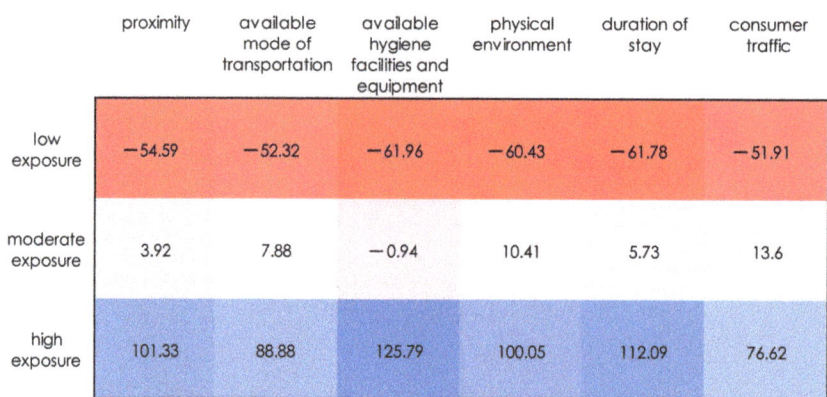

**Figure 2.** Differentiators (%) of the three clusters of restaurants based on average.

**Table 15.** Assignment of restaurants to clusters using the proposed approach.

| Low Exposure Cluster | Moderate Exposure Cluster | High Exposure Cluster |
| --- | --- | --- |
| R4, R5, R6, R7, R9, R10, R14, R26, R27, R28, R29, R31, R37, R38, R39, R40 | R1, R2, R3, R8, R11, R12, R13, R15, R20, R21, R22, R30, R32, R33, R35, R36 | R16, R17, R18, R19, R23, R24, R25, R34 |

## 5. Comparative and Sensitivity Analysis

This section reports both comparative and sensitivity analyses of the proposed approach. We compare the findings of the $k$-means clustering with IVIF datasets with those detailed previously [3,4] using multiple criteria sorting methods. In addition, we report some insights on the results of the proposed approach when compared to the $k$-means clustering with crisp datasets, i.e., observations are not expressed in IVIFS values. Finally, to avoid arriving at whimsical evaluation, we performed a sensitivity analysis of the proposed approach by investigating the changes of the clusters brought about by minor changes of the model parameters, i.e., the choice of IVIFS value representing a linguistic variable in the evaluation process.

*5.1. Comparative Analysis*

Case Study 1: Tourist Sites

In Figure 3, we compare the results of the proposed approach in Case study 1 with that of the VIKORSORT [3] and offer some insights. Using the proposed approach, the assignments yield 12, 15, and eight sites to "low exposure", "moderate exposure", and "high exposure" cluster, respectively. Note that these assignments vary significantly with the results of the VIKORSORT, with no site assigned to the "low exposure" cluster, 27 sites to "moderate exposure", and eight sites to the "high exposure" cluster. Ten sites (i.e., S4, S5, S6, S7, S9, S10, S14, S28, S29, S31) from the "moderate exposure" cluster [3] were considered in the "low exposure" cluster with the proposed approach, while two sites (S26, S27) initially assigned by the VIKORSORT to the "high exposure" cluster are downgraded to "low exposure" cluster. These two sites belong to water-based tourism, and tourist arrivals are currently controlled via capacity restrictions of the government. All but three sites (i.e., S11, S12, S30) assigned to the "moderate exposure" cluster (proposed approach) are also assigned to the same cluster (VIKORSORT). While the area of these three sites is limited, tourist arrivals and duration of stay are minimum due to the limited activities available in these sites and the imposed limits on capacity by the government. Six sites (i.e., S16, S17, S18, S19, 25, 34) assigned to the "moderate exposure" cluster (VIKORSORT) are transferred to the "high exposure" cluster (proposed method). On the other hand, four sites (i.e., S11, S12, S15, S30) in the "high exposure" cluster (VIKORSORT) are downgraded to the "moderate exposure" cluster (proposed approach). When comparing the proposed approach with *k*-means clustering with the crisp dataset, minor differences can be observed. For instance, two sites (i.e., S7, S10) are assigned to the "low exposure" (proposed method) instead of "moderate exposure" (VIKORSORT). This assignment seems necessary as these two sites are beaches with low tourist arrivals; thus, physical distancing measures can be easily implemented. Lake Danao (S35) is assigned to the "high exposure" cluster (crisp *k*-means clustering), while this site has a low volume of tourist arrivals. Thus, the proposed method is plausible in assigning S35 to the "moderate exposure" cluster.

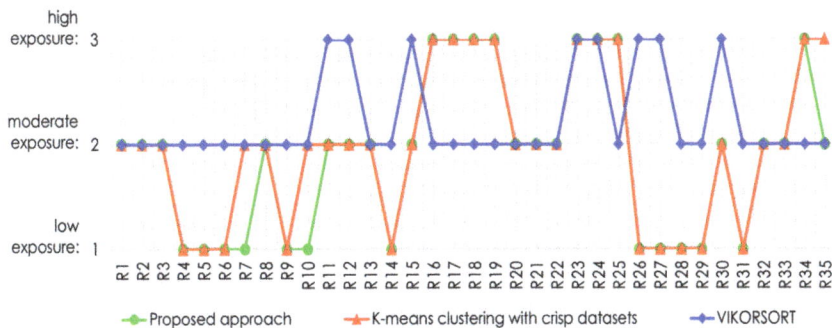

**Figure 3.** Assignments of tourist sites to clusters with VIKORSORT, *k*-means clustering with crisp datasets, and the proposed approach.

A more detailed analysis suggests that the sun, sea, sand sites have mostly downgraded from "moderate exposure" (VIKORSORT) to "low exposure" (proposed approach), except for Panagsama beach (S2) and Basdaku (S4). The two beach sites are considered top popular beach sites in the locality, in comparison with other beach sites (i.e., S7, S8, S9, S10), with their high volume of tourist arrivals and the jump-off point to various tourist activities (e.g., island tours, snorkeling, scuba diving). Thus, S2 and S4 are justifiably assigned at the "moderate exposure" cluster. Other sun, sea, sand sites are remote small island sites (e.g., S1, S5, S6) with proximity and area criteria affecting tourist choice. Hence, the proposed methods provide a reasonable assignment of these sites. Secondly, the heritage and culture sites have greatly differing assignments, from "moderate exposure" (VIKORSORT) to "high exposure" (proposed method), making all sites in this type assigned to the "high exposure" cluster. The proximity of these sites is overwhelmed with their enclosed environment, which increases the exposure of tourists to COVID-19. Third, ecotourism sites have mostly downgraded from "moderate exposure" (VIKORSORT) to "low exposure" (proposed approach). Ecotourism sites have been practicing social and environmental carrying capacity with their relatively low tourist arrivals, implying "low exposure" to COVID-19. Fourth, water-based sites have mostly been downgraded from high (VIKORSORT) to "moderate exposure" (proposed method). Water-based sites mainly limit the duration of stay of the tourists, most activities are undertaken in-group and by batches (i.e., family, friends), imposing carrying capacity, and the area is wide and open if not well ventilated. Water-based sites have already implemented proper monitoring and management before the pandemic due to stakeholders' pressure to manage increasing tourist arrivals. Despite that, current government restrictions discouraged this type of tourist's travel (e.g., travel age restriction, site closure). Lastly, park sites yield the same assignments (i.e., "moderate exposure"), except for Baluarte Park (S34) and Lake Danao (S35) that are situated in rural areas with limited tourist activities. Both approaches (i.e., VIKORSORT, proposed method) agree on farm tourism sites belonging to the "moderate exposure" cluster.

To illustrate further the performance of the proposed method with the VIKORSORT and $k$-means clustering with crisp datasets, we subscribe to the similarity ratio metric ($S_r$) introduced by Ghorabaee et al. [71]. Equation (28) illustrates such a metric:

$$S_r = \frac{\sum_{i=1}^{m} w_i(x_i, y_i)}{m}, \quad x_i, y_i \in \{\text{"low exposure", "moderate exposure", "high exposure"}\} \quad (28)$$

where, $w_i(x_i, y_i) = \begin{cases} 1 & \text{if } x_i = y_i, \\ 0 & \text{if } x_i \neq y_i, \end{cases}$ . $m$ denotes the number of alternatives (i.e., tourist sites), $x_i$ is the cluster of the $i$th alternative using the first method, and $y_i$ is the cluster of the $i$th alternative using the second method. As a consequence, full agreement of all assignments for any two methods implies yields $S_r = 1$. Table 16 provides the values of $S_r$. Table 16 reveals noticeable differences in the assignments between using the VIKORSORT [3] and the proposed approach, as implied by its low $S_r = 0.371$. This is comparable with the $S_r$ value between the VIKORSORT and the crisp $k$-means clustering. However, the crisp $k$-means clustering and the proposed approach yield high similarity of assignments, having $S_r = 0.914$. Nevertheless, the minor differences may become more profound at scale application. These findings imply that the $k$-means clustering algorithms offer an entirely different view with plausible results.

**Table 16.** Comparing the assignments of tourist sites to clusters with VIKORSORT, $k$-means clustering with crisp datasets, and the proposed approach based on $S_r$.

|  | Vikorsort | K-Means Clustering with Crisp Datasets | Proposed Approach |
|---|---|---|---|
| VIKORSORT | 1 | 0.400 | 0.371 |
| $k$-means clustering with crisp datasets | - | 1 | 0.914 |
| Proposed approach | - | - | 1 |

Case Study 2: Restaurants

The analysis employed for Case study 1 was carried out for Case study 2. In Figure 4, we compare the efficacy of the proposed approach in Case study 2 with that of the IF-TOPSIS-Sort carried out by Ocampo et al. [4] and offer some insights. Using the proposed approach, the assignments yield 14, 17, and 9 sites to "low exposure", "moderate exposure", and "high exposure" cluster, respectively. Note that these assignments do not vary a lot with the results of both the IF-TOPSIS-Sort and the $k$-means clustering with crisp datasets, which is apparent in Table 17 based on $S_r$ metric. However, some slight differences among the approaches are observable. For instance, unlike the IF-TOPSIS-Sort and the proposed approach, which assigns Hukad (R8) and Choobi-choobi (R10) to the "moderate exposure" cluster, the $k$-means clustering with crisp datasets downgrades the assignment of these restaurants to the "low exposure" cluster.

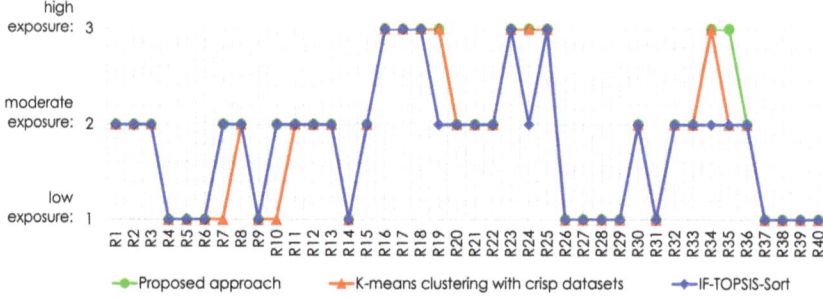

**Figure 4.** Assignments of tourist sites to clusters with IF-TOPSIS-Sort, $k$-means clustering with crisp datasets, and the proposed approach.

**Table 17.** Comparing the assignments of tourist sites to clusters with IF-TOPSIS-Sort, $k$-means clustering with crisp datasets, and the proposed approach based on $S_r$.

|  | IF-TOPSIS-Sort | K-Means Clustering with Crisp Datasets | Proposed Approach |
| --- | --- | --- | --- |
| IF-TOPSIS-Sort | 1 | 0.875 | 0.9 |
| $k$-means clustering with crisp datasets | - | 1 | 0.925 |
| Proposed approach | - | - | 1 |

On the other hand, while the proposed approach and $k$-means clustering with crisp datasets assign Matias BBQ (R22) and Chinese Ngohiong (R24) to the "high exposure" cluster, the IF-TOPSIS-Sort downgrades the assignment of these restaurants to the "moderate exposure" cluster. The IF-TOPSIS-Sort also downgrades the assignment of McDonald's (R33) to the "moderate exposure" cluster while the other two approaches classify it in the "high exposure" cluster. The last difference observed is when the proposed approach appreciates the assignment of Orange Brutus (R36) to the "high exposure" cluster. At the same time, the other approaches classify it in the "moderate exposure" cluster. These inconsistencies in cluster assignment are considered relatively minimal, which is evident in the results wherein most of the assignments in one cluster are consistent with the other approaches. On the basis of these results, the proposed approach may, thus, be likened to both the IF-TOPSIS-Sort and $k$-means clustering with crisp datasets.

*5.2. Sensitivity Analysis*

A sensitivity analysis is carried out to evaluate the robustness of the proposed approach with minor changes in the model parameters (i.e., equivalent IVIFS values of the linguistic variables). Robustness is defined here as the tendency of the clustering results to resist change despite changes in key parameter values. The evaluation of robustness is critical as IVIFS values may be arbitrarily assigned to linguistic terms, which can alter inputs and, in turn, alter the results of the proposed clustering procedure. In performing the sensitivity analysis, the following conditions are set: Let $X = \{x_1, x_2, \ldots, x_n\}$ be the set of linguistic ratings in the scale where $x_1 \prec x_2 \prec \ldots \prec x_n$. Note that the rating scale referred to here is the scale used to represent the linguistic variables used by the decision-makers (respondents) to elicit judgments. Also, let $M = \{m_1, m_2, \ldots, m_n\}$ be such that $m_1 = 0.5\psi_o$ and $m_i = m_{i-1} + d$, $\forall i \in \{2, \ldots, n\}$, where $d = (1 - \psi_o)(n-1)^{-1}$. Here, $M$ is the set of the centers of the interval membership degrees of the elements in $X$ assuming $\mu_{AL}^I(x_1) = 0$ and $\mu_{AL}^I(x_n) = 0.95$, while $d$ is the uniform distance of the centers from one another. The parameter $d$ ensures the uniform spacing of memberships of the ratings in the scale. Also, $\psi_o \in [0,1]$ is the parameter defining the "interval length" of the membership of $x$, hence $\psi_o = \mu_{AU}^I(x) - \mu_{AL}^I(x)$, $\forall x \in X$. It is also assumed that $\gamma_{AL}^I(x) = 0.5\gamma_{AU}^I(x)$ and $\gamma_{AU}^I(x) = 1 - \mu_{AU}^I(x)$, $\forall x \in X$. Finally, the following are introduced:

$$\mu_{AL}^I(x_i) = m_i - (0.5\psi_o), \forall i \in \{1, 2, \ldots, n\} \tag{29}$$

$$\mu_{AU}^I(x_i) = m_i + (0.5\psi_o), \forall i \in \{1, 2, \ldots, n\} \tag{30}$$

These conditions are set to establish a standard method for varying the IVIFS values through the parameter $\psi_o$. In this analysis, $\psi_o = \{0.15, 0.20, 0.25, 0.30, 0.35\}$ is used in both case studies to test how the results vary with different overlapping IVIFS values. Note that, in both cases, the original IVIFS values are not overlapping (see Tables 2 and 8). The resulting IVIFS values corresponding to the five $\psi_o$ values are presented in Table 18 (for the assignment of tourist sites) and Table 19 (for the assignment of restaurants).

Table 18. Resulting IVIFS values for the case of assigning tourist sites.

| Rating | $\psi_o = 0.15$ | $\psi_o = 0.20$ | $\psi_o = 0.25$ | $\psi_o = 0.30$ | $\psi_o = 0.35$ |
|---|---|---|---|---|---|
| 1 | [(0,0.15),(0.43,0.85)] | [(0,0.2),(0.4,0.8)] | [(0,0.25),(0.38,0.75)] | [(0,0.3),(0.35,0.7)] | [(0,0.35),(0.33,0.65)] |
| 2 | [(0.1,0.25),(0.38,0.75)] | [(0.09,0.29),(0.35,0.71)] | [(0.09,0.34),(0.33,0.66)] | [(0.08,0.38),(0.31,0.62)] | [(0.08,0.43),(0.29,0.58)] |
| 3 | [(0.2,0.35),(0.33,0.65)] | [(0.19,0.39),(0.31,0.61)] | [(0.18,0.43),(0.29,0.58)] | [(0.16,0.46),(0.27,0.54)] | [(0.15,0.5),(0.25,0.5)] |
| 4 | [(0.3,0.45),(0.28,0.55)] | [(0.28,0.48),(0.26,0.52)] | [(0.26,0.51),(0.24,0.49)] | [(0.24,0.54),(0.23,0.46)] | [(0.23,0.58),(0.21,0.43)] |
| 5 | [(0.4,0.55),(0.23,0.45)] | [(0.38,0.58),(0.21,0.43)] | [(0.35,0.6),(0.2,0.4)] | [(0.33,0.63),(0.19,0.38)] | [(0.3,0.65),(0.18,0.35)] |
| 6 | [(0.5,0.65),(0.18,0.35)] | [(0.47,0.67),(0.17,0.33)] | [(0.44,0.69),(0.16,0.31)] | [(0.41,0.71),(0.15,0.29)] | [(0.38,0.73),(0.14,0.28)] |
| 7 | [(0.6,0.75),(0.13,0.25)] | [(0.56,0.76),(0.12,0.24)] | [(0.53,0.78),(0.11,0.23)] | [(0.49,0.79),(0.11,0.21)] | [(0.45,0.8),(0.1,0.2)] |
| 8 | [(0.7,0.85),(0.08,0.15)] | [(0.66,0.86),(0.07,0.14)] | [(0.61,0.86),(0.07,0.14)] | [(0.57,0.87),(0.07,0.13)] | [(0.53,0.88),(0.06,0.13)] |
| 9 | [(0.8,0.95),(0.03,0.05)] | [(0.75,0.95),(0.03,0.05)] | [(0.7,0.95),(0.03,0.05)] | [(0.65,0.95),(0.03,0.05)] | [(0.6,0.95),(0.03,0.05)] |

Table 19. Resulting IVIFS values for the case of assigning restaurants.

| Rating | $\psi_o = 0.15$ | $\psi_o = 0.20$ | $\psi_o = 0.25$ | $\psi_o = 0.30$ | $\psi_o = 0.35$ |
|---|---|---|---|---|---|
| 1 | [(0,0.15),(0.43,0.85)] | [(0,0.2),(0.4,0.8)] | [(0,0.25),(0.38,0.75)] | [(0,0.3),(0.35,0.7)] | [(0,0.35),(0.33,0.65)] |
| 2 | [(0.16,0.31),(0.35,0.69)] | [(0.15,0.35),(0.33,0.65)] | [(0.14,0.39),(0.31,0.61)] | [(0.13,0.43),(0.29,0.57)] | [(0.12,0.47),(0.27,0.53)] |
| 3 | [(0.32,0.47),(0.27,0.53)] | [(0.3,0.5),(0.25,0.5)] | [(0.28,0.53),(0.24,0.47)] | [(0.26,0.56),(0.22,0.44)] | [(0.24,0.59),(0.21,0.41)] |
| 4 | [(0.48,0.63),(0.19,0.37)] | [(0.45,0.65),(0.18,0.35)] | [(0.42,0.67),(0.17,0.33)] | [(0.39,0.69),(0.16,0.31)] | [(0.36,0.71),(0.15,0.29)] |
| 5 | [(0.64,0.79),(0.11,0.21)] | [(0.6,0.8),(0.1,0.2)] | [(0.56,0.81),(0.1,0.19)] | [(0.52,0.82),(0.09,0.18)] | [(0.48,0.83),(0.09,0.17)] |
| 6 | [(0.8,0.95),(0.03,0.05)] | [(0.75,0.95),(0.03,0.05)] | [(0.7,0.95),(0.03,0.05)] | [(0.65,0.95),(0.03,0.05)] | [(0.6,0.95),(0.03,0.05)] |

Three cluster performance metrics are used to evaluate the clustering performance of the proposed procedure for each value of $\psi_o$. First is the average within centroid distance ($\xi_{cent}$). This metric pertains to the average distance of the observations (i.e., tourist sites, restaurants) to the cluster centroid. It measures the variability of the observations within each cluster. The next metric is the average within-cluster distance ($\xi_{clust}$). This metric measures the cluster density performance, calculated using the average distance between points in a cluster, and multiplies this by the number of points minus one. Lastly, the Davies-Bouldin index ($\xi_{DBI}$) is used to evaluate the goodness of split by the clustering procedure. The $\xi_{DBI}$ is calculated as the average similarity of each cluster with a cluster most similar to it. For all the metrics mentioned here, lower values suggest the better the clusters are separated and the better is the result of the clustering. The performance of the clustering procedure for the five values of the parameter $\psi_o$ is presented in Table 20 (Case study 1) and Table 21 (Case study 2).

For both cases, the elements in each cluster for all values of $\psi_o$ are the same as the initial results of the case studies. This finding suggests that the proposed approach is robust to minor changes in the model parameters. Also, note that as the value of $\psi_o$ increases, the overlap of the interval membership functions of the ratings also increases for all cluster performance metrics considered in this work. Tables 20 and 21 show a consistent improvement in the clustering performance of the proposed method as $\psi_o$ increases.

Table 20. Sensitivity analysis of the proposed method for the assignment of tourist sites.

| $\psi_o$ | Overall $\xi_{cent}$ | Low Exposure: $\xi_{cent}$ | Moderate Exposure: $\xi_{cent}$ | High Exposure: $\xi_{cent}$ | Overall $\xi_{clust}$ | Low Exposure: $\xi_{clust}$ | Moderate Exposure: $\xi_{clust}$ | High Exposure: $\xi_{clust}$ | $\xi_{DBI}$ |
|---|---|---|---|---|---|---|---|---|---|
| 0.15 | 0.004 | 0.002 | 0.002 | 0.006 | 0.862 | 0.734 | 0.438 | 1.283 | 0.767 |
| 0.20 | 0.003 | 0.002 | 0.001 | 0.006 | 0.806 | 0.684 | 0.408 | 1.203 | 0.765 |
| 0.25 | 0.003 | 0.002 | 0.001 | 0.005 | 0.750 | 0.634 | 0.379 | 1.123 | 0.763 |
| 0.30 | 0.002 | 0.001 | 0.001 | 0.004 | 0.694 | 0.584 | 0.351 | 1.042 | 0.761 |
| 0.35 | 0.002 | 0.001 | 0.001 | 0.004 | 0.639 | 0.535 | 0.322 | 0.961 | 0.760 |

Table 21. Sensitivity analysis of the proposed method for the assignment of restaurants.

| $\psi_0$ | Overall $\zeta_{cent}$ | Low Exposure: $\zeta_{cent}$ | Moderate Exposure: $\zeta_{cent}$ | High Exposure: $\zeta_{cent}$ | Overall $\zeta_{clust}$ | Low Exposure: $\zeta_{clust}$ | Moderate Exposure: $\zeta_{clust}$ | High Exposure: $\zeta_{clust}$ | $\zeta_{DBI}$ |
|---|---|---|---|---|---|---|---|---|---|
| 0.15 | 0.002 | 0.001 | 0.003 | 0.002 | 0.721 | 0.770 | 0.476 | 0.795 | 0.637 |
| 0.20 | 0.001 | 0.001 | 0.002 | 0.001 | 0.660 | 0.705 | 0.436 | 0.726 | 0.637 |
| 0.25 | 0.001 | 0.001 | 0.002 | 0.001 | 0.601 | 0.643 | 0.398 | 0.660 | 0.637 |
| 0.30 | 0.001 | 0.001 | 0.001 | 0.001 | 0.545 | 0.583 | 0.361 | 0.598 | 0.637 |
| 0.35 | 0.001 | 0.001 | 0.001 | 0.001 | 0.491 | 0.526 | 0.326 | 0.538 | 0.637 |

## 6. Discussion

The proposed approach offers insightful contributions to both practical and methodological aspects of $k$-means clustering. As demonstrated in this work, the agenda of categorizing the degree of exposure of tourists or customers to COVID-19, previously explored in our works [2–4], is crucial to the recovery of the tourism and hospitality sector despite the availability of vaccines. With the identified evaluation criteria for tourist site evaluation, the proposed approach yields the same priority ranking [3], which suggests that proximity with the top priority, followed by the volume of tourist arrivals, available modes of transportation, area of site premises, tourist activities, and duration of stay at the bottom of the list. Accordingly, authorities can set these insights as guidelines in developing measures that would promote sectoral recovery while curbing disease spread. Our previous works offered some plausible directions rooted in this ranking of criteria. On the other hand, evaluating the set of restaurants results in a different ranking of criteria associated with the exposure of customers to COVID-19. While proximity ranks on top for tourist sites, the same criterion has the least priority compared to other criteria. Instead, the availability of hygiene facilities and equipment emerges with the highest priority, followed by the physical environment, consumer traffic, available mode of transportation, and duration of stay. This implies that customers give a premium to the availability of hygiene facilities and equipment and the physical environment when dining in restaurants amidst the pandemic. This finding is almost straightforward, as COVID-19 spread is highly linked to the physical characteristics of the restaurants. Aside from these two attributes, customers are mindful of consumer traffic when dining in, indicating the importance of physical distancing measures. These top three attributes imply that customers put more emphasis on the characteristics of the restaurants themselves, not on the manner of getting into the location.

To initiate a comparison with the previous categorization, the proposed approach assumes three clusters for the $k$-means clustering of tourist sites. Distinct characteristics for each cluster are revealed. The "low exposure" cluster includes tourist sites with small premises, closer to home, with activities that allow tourists not to stay longer. The "moderate exposure" cluster, on the other hand, characterizes tourist sites with large premises where tourists can stay longer but with minimal tourist arrivals. Finally, the "high exposure" cluster involves sites with a huge volume of tourist arrivals that would engage in a higher number of tourist activities. Tourist arrivals in this cluster are encouraged by more available modes of transportation. These characterizations of clusters advance our previously reported findings [3], where multiple criteria sorting methods set these categories merely *a priori* by the analysts who might have limited knowledge of the domain problem. On the other hand, the proposed $k$-means clustering with IVIF datasets provides a practical approach by analyzing patterns within the dataset and reveals the shared characteristics of those tourist sites within the same cluster. Extracting these characteristics offers practical insights to tourists and tourism enterprises, as well as the government for policy- and decision-making. The proposed approach assigns 12 sites to the "low exposure" cluster, 15 sites to the "moderate exposure" cluster, and eight sites to the "high exposure cluster. While these assignments are idiosyncratic, meaningful insights that would associate the type of the tourist site and the cluster can be revealed to the case stakeholders and the general tourism sector.

Using the similar methodological framework adopted in the assignment of tourist sites, the evaluation of restaurants according to the perceived degree of exposure of customers to COVID-19 is demonstrated as a second case study. With $k = 3$ set similarly, the "low exposure" cluster is characterized by restaurants that are just nearby, with low consumer traffic, and customers' stay is shorter (e.g., food orders are served fast). The "moderate exposure" cluster contains restaurants that have an average rating on all evaluation criteria. That is, their evaluation scores lie on the average of all restaurants assessed in every criterion. Lastly, the "high exposure" cluster is associated with restaurants located at a distance, with high consumer traffic and longer service times (i.e., customers staying longer). Again, these characteristics that could not be gained from multiple criteria sorting methods are the major advantage of a clustering approach. In addition, the hospitality sector and the government would benefit from these characteristics as they would serve as guidelines for the post-pandemic recovery of the sector. On the other hand, customers can associate these characteristics of restaurants to other similar restaurants that are outside the evaluation reported in this work. This practical value is crucial to the recovery of the hospitality sector amidst the pandemic, with the emergence of variants that can escape vaccines. The proposed approach yields 16 restaurants assigned to the "low exposure" cluster, 16 labeled having "moderate exposure", and eight in the "high exposure" cluster. Exploring the characteristics of these restaurants to assess other restaurants in other local regions is an added value.

Comparing with the multiple criteria sorting method (i.e., VIKORSORT) suggests that the results of the $k$-means clustering with IVIF datasets are more plausible as validated by the actual experiences of tourists in those sites under consideration. The proposed method yields better results; thus, it is preferable to use. This argument is motivated by the capability of the $k$-means clustering to extract patterns on the performance of each site on every criterion, as opposed to the predetermined identification of categories or clusters by the analysts who may have limited knowledge on the scope of the evaluation problem. Compared to the $k$-means clustering with crisp datasets, the proposed approach yields similar assignments 90% of the time for both cases. The minor difference in their assignments is associated with the integration of the IVIFS theory of $k$-means clustering, which better captures the vagueness and uncertainty of judgment elicitation of respondents. While the difference seems minor, its impact may become more profound when applied to a large-scale problem. Finally, by running a systematic sensitivity analysis, the proposed approach is robust to minor changes in the model parameters represented by the equivalent IVIFS values of the linguistic variables used in the evaluation process. On the other hand, comparing the proposed approach to that of the IF-TOPSIS-Sort by Ocampo et al. [4] yields minor differences, which is interesting because IF-TOPSIS-Sort does not abide by the principle of pattern extraction, which is the capability harnessed by the proposed approach. Nevertheless, these findings could indicate similarity between the proposed approach that incorporates IVIFs into the $k$-means clustering algorithm and the IF-TOPSIS-Sort, which may link pattern recognition approaches (i.e., $k$-means clustering) to MADM techniques (e.g., the TOPSIS method). Such an investigation is, however, beyond the scope of this work.

## 7. Conclusions and Future Works

The emergence of COVID-19 variants that can escape available vaccines further delays the full recovery of the tourism and hospitality sector. The fear of exposure to COVID-19 even among vaccinated individuals hinders tourists and customers in availing of the products and services offered by the sector. Thus, our prior works, which reported computational platforms of evaluating tourist sites (restaurants) according to the perceived exposure of tourists (customers) to COVID-19, remain a relevant approach to safe sectoral recovery and curb disease spread. However, the VIKORSORT, IF-TOPSIS-Sort, and other multiple-criteria sorting methods suffer from two major drawbacks. First, tourist sites and restaurants are assigned to predetermined categories defined by the analyst who may have limited knowledge of the problem domain. Secondly, the elicitation of judgments of the respondents (or decision-makers) fails to consider the vagueness and uncertainty brought about by the decision-makers lack of knowledge and experience or their limited information processing capabilities. Thus, this work advances these gaps by performing $k$-means clustering with IVIF datasets. The $k$-means clustering offers a more practical evaluation by extracting clusters based on the shared characteristics of the tourist sites; thus, eliminating the subjectivity of introducing pre-determined categories as in multi-criteria sorting methods (i.e., VIKORSORT, IF-TOPSIS-Sort). The integration of the IVIFS theory augments the limitation of $k$-means clustering in handling datasets with vague and imprecise observations, especially in application domains where observations represent human judgments. In addition, the proposed approach incorporates the weights of the attributes (or criteria), which are not addressed in traditional $k$-means clustering. This mechanism, an enhancement of $k$-means clustering, is particularly useful in evaluation problems where attributes have varying priorities.

To demonstrate the proposed approach, the same problem domain, reported elsewhere, of evaluating 35 tourist sites under six criteria elucidating the degree of exposure of tourists to COVID-19 is carried out in this work. Similarly, a second case study, also reported elsewhere, evaluates restaurants according to customers' exposure to COVID-19. Results suggest that the priority ranking of criteria for evaluating tourist sites shares similarity with the previous findings: proximity emerges on top, followed by the volume of tourist arrivals, available modes of transportation, area of site premises, tourist activities, and duration of stay. This ranking seems in contrast with the priority ranking of criteria for evaluating restaurants, which indicates that customers emphasize the physical characteristics of the restaurants, such as the availability of hygiene facilities and equipment, physical environment, and consumer traffic. By fixing $k = 3$ for both case studies, the proposed approach yields distinct characteristics of the three clusters, which can be associated with "low exposure", "moderate exposure", and "high exposure" of tourists to COVID-19. In the first case study, 12 sites, 15 sites, and eight sites are assigned to the "low exposure" cluster, "moderate exposure" cluster, and "high exposure" cluster, respectively. Although idiosyncrasies exist, the value of associating the type of the tourist site and its resulting cluster is crucial for establishing measures that could contribute to the sectoral recovery. Similarly, the proposed method provides distinct characteristics of the three clusters (i.e., "low exposure", "moderate exposure", and "high exposure") where restaurants in the second case study are assigned to. Results reveal that 16 restaurants are assigned to "low exposure", 16 to "moderate exposure", and eight to "high exposure" clusters, respectively. Considering the characteristics of the clusters, customers may evaluate any restaurant according to their perceived exposure to COVID-19.

Finally, compared to the VIKORSORT and IF-TOPSIS-Sort, the proposed approach offers more verifiable and practical results, owing to the capability of the $k$-means clustering to extract patterns of the characteristics of the alternatives in establishing distinct clusters. These characteristics can provide better guidelines to tourists, customers, and authorities in the safe recovery of the tourism and hospitality sector. The proposed approach is also robust to small changes in the model parameters (i.e., equivalent IVIFS values in judgment elicitation). As opposed to $k$-means clustering with crisp datasets, integrating the IVIFS theory and the inclusion of criteria weights offers a promising approach for clustering problems with attributes having varying weights and with datasets represented by human judgments containing inherent vagueness and uncertainty. Future works could explore other possible applications of the proposed approach outside the tourism and hospitality sector. The use of the proposed approach for big datasets with non-sharp data is an interesting future direction. Other fuzzy set extensions such as type-2 fuzzy sets, intuitionistic fuzzy sets, neutrosophic sets, Pythagorean fuzzy sets, among others, could be used instead of IVIF sets.

**Author Contributions:** Conceptualization, L.O.; methodology, L.O., J.L.A., S.S.E., F.M. and E.S.J.; software, J.L.A., S.S.E., F.M. and E.S.J.; validation, L.O., J.L.A., S.S.E., F.M. and E.S.J.; formal analysis, L.O., J.L.A., S.S.E., F.M. and E.S.J.; investigation, L.O., J.L.A., S.S.E., F.M., E.S.J. and K.Y.; resources, L.O.; data curation, L.O., J.L.A., S.S.E., F.M., E.S.J. and K.Y.; writing—original draft preparation, L.O., J.L.A., S.S.E., F.M., E.S.J., N.M.A. and K.Y.; writing—review and editing, L.O., J.L.A., S.S.E., F.M., E.S.J. and N.M.A.; visualization, L.O., J.L.A., S.S.E., F.M. and E.S.J.; supervision, L.O.; project administration, L.O.; funding acquisition, L.O. All authors have read and agreed to the published version of the manuscript.

**Funding:** This research is funded by the 2019 CHED Institutional Development and Innovation Grant entitled "Creation of Interdisciplinary Graduate Program Courses for Applied Mathematics and Operations Research as Tools for Innovation".

**Institutional Review Board Statement:** Not applicable.

**Informed Consent Statement:** Not applicable.

**Data Availability Statement:** Not applicable.

**Acknowledgments:** We acknowledge the financial support provided by the Commission on Higher Education of the Republic of the Philippines through the 2019 CHED Institutional Development and Innovation Grant.

**Conflicts of Interest:** The authors declare no conflict of interest.

## References

1. Dryhurst, S.; Schneider, C.R.; Kerr, J.; Freeman, A.L.J.; Recchia, G.; van der Bles, A.M.; Spiegelhalter, D.; van der Linden, S. Risk perceptions of COVID-19 around the world. *J. Risk Res.* **2020**, *23*, 994–1006. [CrossRef]
2. Yamagishi, K.; Ocampo, L. Utilizing TOPSIS-Sort for sorting tourist sites for perceived COVID-19 exposure. *Curr. Issues Tour.* **2021**, 1–11. [CrossRef]
3. Ocampo, L.; Yamagishi, K. Multiple criteria sorting of tourist sites for perceived COVID-19 exposure: The use of VIKORSORT. *Kybernetes* **2021**. [CrossRef]
4. Ocampo, L.; Tanaid, R.A.; Tiu, A.M.; Selerio, E., Jr.; Yamagishi, K. Classifying the degree of exposure of customers to COVID-19 in the restaurant industry: A novel intuitionistic fuzzy set extension of the TOPSIS-Sort. *Appl. Soft Comput.* **2021**, *113*, 107906. [CrossRef]
5. Cong, L.; Ding, S.; Wang, L.; Zhang, A.; Jia, W. Image segmentation algorithm based on superpixel clustering. *IET Image Process.* **2018**, *12*, 2030–2035. [CrossRef]
6. Hossain, Z.; Akhtar, N.; Ahmad, R.; Rahman, M. A dynamic K-means clustering for data mining. *Indones. J. Electr. Eng. Comput. Sci.* **2019**, *13*, 521–526. [CrossRef]
7. Wen, L.; Zhou, K.; Yang, S. A shape-based clustering method for pattern recognition of residential electricity consumption. *J. Clean. Prod.* **2019**, *212*, 475–488. [CrossRef]
8. Shi, W.; Zeng, W. Application of k-means clustering to environmental risk zoning of the chemical industrial area. *Front. Environ. Sci. Eng.* **2014**, *8*, 117–127. [CrossRef]
9. Kuswandi, D.; Surahman, E.; Thaariq, Z.Z.A.; Muthmainnah, M. K-Means Clustering of Student Perceptions on Project-Based Learning Model Application. In Proceedings of the 2018 4th International Conference on Education and Technology (ICET), Malang, Indonesia, 26–28 October 2018; IEEE: Manhattan, NY, USA, 2018; pp. 9–12.
10. Khanmohammadi, S.; Adibeig, N.; Shanehbandy, S. An improved overlapping k-means clustering method for medical applications. *Expert Syst. Appl.* **2017**, *67*, 12–18. [CrossRef]
11. Pustokhina, I.V.; Pustokhin, D.A.; Rodrigues, J.J.P.C.; Gupta, D.; Khanna, A.; Shankar, K.; Seo, C.; Joshi, G.P. Automatic Vehicle License Plate Recognition Using Optimal K-Means with Convolutional Neural Network for Intelligent Transportation Systems. *IEEE Access* **2020**, *8*, 92907–92917. [CrossRef]
12. Rani, S.; Kholidah, K.N.; Huda, S.N. A Development of Travel Itinerary Planning Application using Traveling Salesman Problem and K-Means Clustering Approach. In Proceedings of the 2018 7th International Conference on Software and Computer Applications, Kuantan, Malaysia, 8–10 February 2018; ACM: New York, NY, USA, 2018; pp. 327–331.
13. Monica, S.; Natalia, F.; Sudirman, S. Clustering Tourism Object in Bali Province Using K-Means and X-Means Clustering Algorithm. In *2018 IEEE 20th International Conference on High Performance Computing and Communications; IEEE 16th International Conference on Smart City; IEEE 4th International Conference on Data Science and Systems (HPCC/SmartCity/DSS)*; IEEE: Manhattan, NY, USA, 2018; pp. 1462–1467.
14. Yang, H.; Luo, J.-D.; Fan, Y.; Zhu, L. Using weighted k-means to identify Chinese leading venture capital firms incorporating with centrality measures. *Inf. Process. Manag.* **2020**, *57*, 102083. [CrossRef]
15. Mahmoudi, A.; Deng, X.; Javed, S.A.; Yuan, J. Large-scale multiple criteria decision-making with missing values: Project selection through TOPSIS-OPA. *J. Ambient. Intell. Humaniz. Comput.* **2021**, *12*, 9341–9362. [CrossRef]

16. Park, J.H.; Park, I.Y.; Kwun, Y.C.; Tan, X. Extension of the TOPSIS method for decision making problems under interval-valued intuitionistic fuzzy environment. *Appl. Math. Model.* **2011**, *35*, 2544–2556. [CrossRef]
17. Zadeh, L.A. Fuzzy sets. *Inf. Control.* **1965**, *3*, 338–353. [CrossRef]
18. Atanassov, K.T. Intuitionistic fuzzy sets. *Fuzzy Sets Syst.* **1986**, *20*, 87–96. [CrossRef]
19. Ngan, R.T.; Son, L.H.; Ali, M.; Tamir, D.E.; Rishe, N.D.; Kandel, A. Representing complex intuitionistic fuzzy set by quaternion numbers and applications to decision making. *Appl. Soft Comput.* **2020**, *87*, 105961. [CrossRef]
20. Atanassov, K.; Gargov, G. Interval valued intuitionistic fuzzy sets. *Fuzzy Sets Syst.* **1989**, *31*, 343–349. [CrossRef]
21. Hu, K.; Tan, Q.; Zhang, T.; Wang, S. Assessing technology portfolios of clean energy-driven desalination-irrigation systems with interval-valued intuitionistic fuzzy sets. *Renew. Sustain. Energy Rev.* **2020**, *132*, 109950. [CrossRef]
22. Luo, M.; Liang, J. A Novel Similarity Measure for Interval-Valued Intuitionistic Fuzzy Sets and Its Applications. *Symmetry* **2018**, *10*, 441. [CrossRef]
23. Ananthi, V.; Balasubramaniam, P. A new image denoising method using interval-valued intuitionistic fuzzy sets for the removal of impulse noise. *Signal. Process.* **2016**, *121*, 81–93. [CrossRef]
24. Oztaysi, B.; Onar, S.C.; Kahraman, C.; Yavuz, M. Multi-criteria alternative-fuel technology selection using interval-valued intuitionistic fuzzy sets. *Transp. Res. Part D Transp. Environ.* **2017**, *53*, 128–148. [CrossRef]
25. Wu, L.; Wei, G.; Gao, H.; Wei, Y. Some Interval-Valued Intuitionistic Fuzzy Dombi Hamy Mean Operators and Their Application for Evaluating the Elderly Tourism Service Quality in Tourism Destination. *Mathematics* **2018**, *6*, 294. [CrossRef]
26. Cheng, S.-H. Autocratic multiattribute group decision making for hotel location selection based on interval-valued intuitionistic fuzzy sets. *Inf. Sci.* **2018**, *427*, 77–87. [CrossRef]
27. Kaur, S.P.; Gupta, V. COVID-19 Vaccine: A comprehensive status report. *Virus Res.* **2020**, *288*, 198114. [CrossRef]
28. Abu Bakar, N.; Rosbi, S. Effect of Coronavirus disease (COVID-19) to tourism industry. *Int. J. Adv. Eng. Res. Sci.* **2020**, *7*, 189–193. [CrossRef]
29. John Hopkins Coronavirus Resource Center. COVID-19 Dashboard by the Center for Systems Science and Engineering (CSSE) at Johns Hopkins University (JHU). Available online: https://coronavirus.jhu.edu/map.html (accessed on 31 July 2021).
30. Davahli, M.R.; Karwowski, W.; Sonmez, S.; Apostolopoulos, Y. The Hospitality Industry in the Face of the COVID-19 Pandemic: Current Topics and Research Methods. *Int. J. Environ. Res. Public Health* **2020**, *17*, 7366. [CrossRef]
31. Organization for Economic Co-Operation and Development. Tourism Policy Responses to Coronavirus (COVID-19). 2020. Available online: https://www.oecd.org/coronavirus/policy-responses/tourism-policy-responses-to-the-coronavirus-covid-19-6466aa20/ (accessed on 2 August 2021).
32. World Travel & Tourism Council (WTTC). Economic Impact Reports. *World Travel & Tourism Council.* 2021. Available online: https://wttc.org/Research/Economic-Impact (accessed on 30 July 2021).
33. Zhang, H.; Cho, T.; Wang, H. The Impact of a Terminal High Altitude Area Defense Incident on Tourism Risk Perception and Attitude Change of Chinese Tourists Traveling to South Korea. *Sustainability* **2020**, *12*, 7. [CrossRef]
34. Philippine Statistics Authority. Share of Tourism to GDP is 5.4 Percent in 2020. 2021. Available online: https://psa.gov.ph/tourism/satellite-accounts/id/164617 (accessed on 27 July 2021).
35. Asian Development Bank. The COVID-19 Impact on Philippine Business. June 2020. Available online: https://www.adb.org/sites/default/files/publication/622161/covid-19-impact-philippine-business-enterprise-survey.pdf (accessed on 25 July 2021).
36. Philippine Statistics Authority. Philippine GDP Posts -8.3 Percent in the Fourth Quarter 2020; -9.5 Percent for Full-Year 2020. Available online: https://psa.gov.ph/content/philippine-gdp-posts-83-percent-fourth-quarter-2020-95-percent-full-year-2020 (accessed on 28 January 2021).
37. Philippine Statistics Authority. Employed Persons by Sector, Subsector, and Hours Worked, Philippines. 2021. Available online: https://psa.gov.ph/system/files/Table%202-Employed%20Persons%20by%20Sector%2C%20Sub-sector%20and%20Hours%20Worked%2C%20Philippines%2C%20February%202021%2C%20March%202021%2C%20April%202021%20and%20May%202021_0.xlsx (accessed on 26 July 2021).
38. Kaushal, V.; Srivastava, S. Hospitality and tourism industry amid COVID-19 pandemic: Perspectives on challenges and learnings from India. *Int. J. Hosp. Manag.* **2021**, *92*, 102707. [CrossRef] [PubMed]
39. Dube, K.; Nhamo, G.; Chikodzi, D. COVID-19 cripples global restaurant and hospitality industry. *Curr. Issues Tour.* **2021**, *24*, 1487–1490. [CrossRef]
40. United Nations World Tourism Organization (UNWTO). UNWTO Launches a Call for Action for Tourism's COVID-19 Mitigation and Recovery. 2020. Available online: https://www.unwto.org/news/unwto-launches-a-call-for-action-for-tourisms-covid-19-mitigation-and-recovery (accessed on 30 July 2021).
41. World Health Organization. WHO Coronavirus (COVID-19) Dashboard. Available online: https://covid19.who.int/ (accessed on 28 July 2021).
42. Gursoy, D.; Can, A.S.; Williams, N.; Ekinci, Y. Evolving impacts of COVID-19 vaccination intentions on travel intentions. *Serv. Ind. J.* **2021**, *41*, 719–733. [CrossRef]
43. Buhat, C.A.H.; Duero, J.C.C.; Felix, F.O.; Rabajante, J.F.; Mamplata, J.B. Optimal Allocation of COVID-19 Test Kits Among Accredited Testing Centers in the Philippines. *J. Heal. Inform. Res.* **2021**, *5*, 54–69. [CrossRef]
44. Gursoy, D.; Chi, C.G.; Chi, O.H. Effects of COVID 19 pandemic on restaurant and hotel customers' sentiments towards dining out, traveling to a destination and staying at hotels. *J. Hosp.* **2021**, *3*, 1–17.

45. Hafeez, S.; Din, M.; Zia, F.; Ali, M.; Shinwari, Z.K. Emerging concerns regarding COVID-19; second wave and new variant. *J. Med. Virol.* **2021**, *93*, 4108. [CrossRef] [PubMed]
46. Padhi, A.K.; Tripathi, T. Can SARS-CoV-2 accumulate mutations in the S-protein to increase pathogenicity? *ACS Pharmacol. Transl. Sci.* **2020**, *3*, 1023–1026. [CrossRef] [PubMed]
47. Šostaks, A. Mathematics in the context of fuzzy sets: Basic ideas, concepts, and some remarks on the history and recent trends of development. *Math. Model. Anal.* **2011**, *16*, 173–198. [CrossRef]
48. Atanassov, K.T. Interval valued intuitionistic fuzzy sets. In *Intuitionistic Fuzzy Sets*; Physical: Heidelberg, Germany, 1999; pp. 139–177.
49. Xu, Z. Methods for aggregating interval-valued intuitionistic fuzzy information and their application to decision making. *Control. Decis.* **2007**, *22*, 215–219.
50. Xu, Z. A method based on distance measure for interval-valued intuitionistic fuzzy group decision making. *Inf. Sci.* **2010**, *180*, 181–190. [CrossRef]
51. Xu, Z.; Chen, J. Approach to group decision making based on interval-valued intuitionistic judgment matrices. *Syst. Eng. Theory Pract.* **2007**, *27*, 126–133. [CrossRef]
52. Ye, J. Multicriteria fuzzy decision-making method based on a novel accuracy function under interval-valued intuitionistic fuzzy environment. *Expert Syst. Appl.* **2009**, *36*, 6899–6902. [CrossRef]
53. Nayagam, V.L.G.; Muralikrishnan, S.; Sivaraman, G. Multi-criteria decision-making method based on interval-valued intuitionistic fuzzy sets. *Expert Syst. Appl.* **2011**, *38*, 1464–1467. [CrossRef]
54. Abualigah, L.M.; Khader, A.T.; Hanandeh, E.S. Hybrid clustering analysis using improved krill herd algorithm. *Appl. Intell.* **2018**, *48*, 4047–4071. [CrossRef]
55. Janani, R.; Vijayarani, S. Text document clustering using Spectral Clustering algorithm with Particle Swarm Optimization. *Expert Syst. Appl.* **2019**, *134*, 192–200. [CrossRef]
56. Ramirez, A.; Himang, C.; Selerio, E.; Manalastas, R.; Himang, M.; Giango, W.; Tenerife, P.; Ocampo, L. Exploring the Hedonic and Eudaimonic Motivations of Teachers for Pursuing Graduate Studies. *Asia-Pac. Educ. Res.* **2020**. [CrossRef]
57. Selerio, E.F.; Arcadio, R.D.; Medio, G.J.; Natad, J.R.P.; Pedregosa, G.A. On the complex causal relationship of barriers to sustainable urban water management: A fuzzy multi-criteria analysis. *Urban. Water J.* **2021**, *18*, 12–24. [CrossRef]
58. Anitha, P.; Patil, M.M. RFM model for customer purchase behavior using K-Means algorithm. *J. King Saud Univ. Comput. Inf. Sci.* **2019**, in press. [CrossRef]
59. Taheri, H.; Koester, L.W.; Bigelow, T.A.; Faierson, E.J.; Bond, L.J. In Situ Additive Manufacturing Process Monitoring with an Acoustic Technique: Clustering Performance Evaluation Using K-Means Algorithm. *J. Manuf. Sci. Eng.* **2019**, *141*, 1–27. [CrossRef]
60. Galvis, I.S.; Villa, Y.; Duarte, C.; Sierra, D.; Agudelo, W. Seismic attribute selection and clustering to detect and classify surface waves in multicomponent seismic data by using k-means algorithm. *Lead. Edge* **2017**, *36*, 239–248. [CrossRef]
61. Ramalingam, M.; Thangarajan, R. Mutated k-means algorithm for dynamic clustering to perform effective and intelligent broadcasting in medical surveillance using selective reliable broadcast protocol in VANET. *Comput. Commun.* **2020**, *150*, 563–568. [CrossRef]
62. Lloyd, S. Least squares quantization in PCM. *IEEE Trans. Inf. Theory* **1982**, *28*, 129–137. [CrossRef]
63. Forgy, E. Cluster analysis of multivariate data: Efficiency versus interpretability of classifications. *Biometrics* **1965**, *21*, 768–769.
64. Ocampo, L.; Yamagishi, K. Modeling the lockdown relaxation protocols of the Philippine government in response to the COVID-19 pandemic: An intuitionistic fuzzy DEMATEL analysis. *Socio-Econ. Plan. Sci.* **2020**, *72*, 100911. [CrossRef] [PubMed]
65. Department of Tourism DOT Pushes Stringent Guidelines for Stakeholders across the Nation. 2020. Available online: http://tourism.gov.ph/news_features/GuidelinesForStakeholders.aspx (accessed on 20 July 2021).
66. Department of Tourism DOT Statement on Uniform Travel Protocols. 2021. Available online: http://www.tourism.gov.ph/news_features/UniformTravelProtocols.aspx (accessed on 20 July 2021).
67. Rocamora, J.A.; Vaccination Key to Tourism Recovery. Philippine News Agency. 2021. Available online: https://www.pna.gov.ph/articles/1144200 (accessed on 31 July 2021).
68. Prosser, L.A.; Lavelle, T.A.; Fiore, A.E.; Bridges, C.B.; Reed, C.; Jain, S.; Dunham, K.M.; Meltzer, M.I. Cost-Effectiveness of 2009 Pandemic Influenza A(H1N1) Vaccination in the United States. *PLoS ONE* **2011**, *6*, e22308. [CrossRef] [PubMed]
69. Asian Development Bank. (28 April 2021). Philippine Economy Seen Recovering in 2021, with Stronger Growth in 2022—ADB. Available online: https://www.adb.org/news/philippine-economy-seen-recovering-2021-stronger-growth-2022-adb (accessed on 29 July 2021).
70. Markowitz, A. State-by-State Guide to Face Mask Requirements. AARP. Available online: https://www.aarp.org/health/healthy-living/info-2020/states-mask-mandates-coronavirus.html (accessed on 10 February 2021).
71. Ghorabaee, M.K.; Zavadskas, E.K.; Olfat, L.; Turskis, Z. Multi-Criteria Inventory Classification Using a New Method of Evaluation Based on Distance from Average Solution (EDAS). *Informatica* **2015**, *26*, 435–451. [CrossRef]

*Article*

# Theory and Practice of Quantitative Assessment of System Harmonicity: Case of Road Safety in Russia before and during the COVID-19 Epidemic

Artur I. Petrov [1,*], Victor I. Kolesov [1] and Daria A. Petrova [2]

1 Department of Road Transport Operation, The Institute of Transport, Industrial University of Tyumen, 625027 Tyumen, Russia; vikolesov@yandex.ru
2 The Institute of Natural Sciences and Mathematics, Ural Federal University named after the first President of Russia B.N. Yeltsin, 620002 Ekaterinburg, Russia; daartpetrova@mail.ru
* Correspondence: ArtIgPetrov@yandex.ru; Tel.: +7-(912)-079-19-91

**Citation:** Petrov, A.I.; Kolesov, V.I.; Petrova, D.A. Theory and Practice of Quantitative Assessment of System Harmonicity: Case of Road Safety in Russia before and during the COVID-19 Epidemic. *Mathematics* **2021**, *9*, 2812. https://doi.org/10.3390/math9212812

Academic Editors: Lina Novickytė, Jolanta Drozdz, Radosław Pastusiak and Michał Soliwoda

Received: 21 September 2021
Accepted: 24 October 2021
Published: 5 November 2021

**Publisher's Note:** MDPI stays neutral with regard to jurisdictional claims in published maps and institutional affiliations.

**Copyright:** © 2021 by the authors. Licensee MDPI, Basel, Switzerland. This article is an open access article distributed under the terms and conditions of the Creative Commons Attribution (CC BY) license (https://creativecommons.org/licenses/by/4.0/).

**Abstract:** People have had an interest in harmony issues for thousands of years; however, there is still no elaborated system of views on these questions. Ancient Greeks understood harmony as an agreement of opposites. A surge of interest in the study of the harmonic aspects of being occurred in the twentieth century due to the development of systems science, particularly regarding synergetic system effects. At the same time, there are still relatively few applications of synergetics because of the absence of an accurate methodology for the identification of system harmonicity. The aim of this research is to develop the methodology for the quantitative assessment of system harmonicity by considering a practical example: the quantitative assessment of the harmonicity of the road safety provision system (RSS) and its dynamics during the last 15 years (2006–2020). In addition, the impact of the COVID restrictions on population mobility in Russia in 2020, on the change in the harmonicity of the road safety provision system, is considered. During the research it was established that the quality factor $g$ of the Russian road safety provision system changed from $g_{2006}$ = 1.9565 to $g_{2020}$ = 2.4646, which promoted the decline of the relative entropy of the Russian road safety provision system from $H_{n\,RSS\,2006}$ = 0.8623 to $H_{n\,RSS\,2020}$ = 0.7553. The deep reason for that change was the modification of relation between "weights" or the significance of the contribution of different elements of the cause-and-effect chain in the formation of the factual level of the road accident rate in Russia in the last 15 years. The main conclusion of this research is that the harmonicity of the Russian road safety provision system, assessed by the normalized functional general utility $GU_n$, has been increased, and it has already exceeded the level of harmonious reference systems $GU_n$ = 0.618. In fact, the normalized functional general utility $GU_n$ of the Russian road safety provision system increased from $GU_{n\,RSS\,2006}$ = 0.615 to $GU_{n\,RSS\,2020}$ = 0.652 (by 6.0%), from 2006 to 2020. Simultaneously, the share of the normalized used resource $X_n$ declined, allowing a conclusion to be drawn about a significant improvement in the balance "efficiency-quality" of the Russian road safety provision system. The COVID lockdown played a positive role in this process. Harmonicity of the Russian road safety provision system, assessed by the normalized general utility $GU_{n\,RSS}$, increased by 0.46% from 2019 to 2020.

**Keywords:** system structural harmonicity; synergetics; orderliness; entropy; generalized golden ratio (GGR); quantitative assessment; road safety; COVID-19 epidemic; Russia

## 1. Introduction

The year 2020 will go down in history as a very unusual year. The Great Reset is a relevant slogan, the authors of which in the context of the events of 2020 and subsequent years are K. Schwab and T. Malleret [1]. Widespread lockdowns forced the transfer of activity from off-line to on-line. The forced decline in activity has changed people's lifestyles everywhere. Naturally, this caused a decrease in the transport mobility of people.

To a greater extent, this concerned citizens in the largest cities of the world whose transport traffic, according to the Tom Tom Traffic Index [2], decreased by 20–80% during the active lockdown phase (April–May 2020) [3]. Rural residents were also forced to reduce transport activity, although to a lesser extent than urban residents [4]. This could not but affect various aspects of the functioning of the transport sector of the economy. Primarily, this concerns road safety.

Data analysis of the Road Safety Annual Report 2020 [5] indicates two important facts. In countries with a hard lockdown in the spring of 2020, the number of deaths in road accidents significantly decreased; when comparing "April 2020 to April 2019", road traffic mortality reduced by 30–80%. Conversely, in those few countries where lockdown was not introduced, the death rate in road accidents increased; in Sweden and the Netherlands, the countries that are long-standing world leaders in road safety, the number of people killed in road accidents in April 2020 increased by 6% compared to April 2019. Of course, all this could not go unnoticed by the regional authorities, or by the global level of government.

One of the most important decisions of the 74th session (18.08.2020) of the United Nations (UN) General Assembly was resolution A/RES/74/299, "Improving global road safety" [6]. This document highlights the importance of the work already conducted in this area over the past decade. It also formulates the need to achieve a new goal by 2030, which is to reduce the number of deaths on roads by 50%. It should be assumed that this ambitious goal was formulated at the time when the first results of the assessment of the COVID lockdown's impact on road traffic accidents had already been received, and the connection between the restriction in transport mobility and the number of fatalities in road accidents was comprehended. Perhaps these statistics largely served as the basis for cautious optimism in promoting the concept of Mobility-as-a-Service (MaaS), which is the ideological basis for abandoning personal transport in favor of a transportation service provider. Expectation of the upcoming mass rejection of the individual car is perhaps the main reason for optimism about potential trends in road safety. In some countries, targets have been announced for a multiple reduction in the number of people killed in road accidents over the next decade [7,8]. An example of such goal-setting is the Russian Federation [9], where the task is to reach a level of human risk of four deaths in road accidents per hundred thousand people by 2024, and a level of zero mortality in road accidents by 2030 [10]. For reference, in 2020, the level of human risk in Russia was equal to 10.80 people killed in road accidents per hundred thousand people [11]. Meanwhile, no assessment of the real possibility of achieving this goal was carried out.

How possible is the success of the practical implementation of this target setting? How did the COVID restrictions affect the effectiveness, usefulness and harmony of state road safety systems? These are the most important issues and are discussed by the authors from the standpoint of the theory of system harmony, when comparing the situation in the field of assessing the organization of the state system for ensuring road safety in the Russian Federation during characteristic periods (between 2006 and 2020, and comparing the situation of 2019, a conditionally normal year, to 2020, the lockdown year).

## 2. Related Works

### 2.1. Synergetics, Orderliness and System Harmonicity

The subject of synergetics can be defined as the study of the process of system self-organization. Social synergetics studies the patterns of self-organization of society, i.e., the relationship between social order and social chaos (their mutual transition into one another and their synthesis). R. Benedict [12] is the author of the "synergy" concept and initially the authors specializing in the interaction between the individual and society were engaged in the problems of synergy [13]. Today, synergetics is mainly a tool of cognition in the social sciences [14–17].

However, it is generally recognized that the main ideas of synergetics were laid down in the works of scientists of the natural science profile: I. Prigogine, I. Stengers, and G. Nicolis [18–21].

Nevertheless, H. Haken can be considered the founder of synergetics [22–24]. He defined synergetics as the science of self-organization, the theory of "the joint action of many subsystems, that in result arises a structure and corresponding functioning at the macroscopic level" [23].

This is mentioned in analytical works [25,26].

Today, synergetics is recognized as a scientific direction all over the world. In Russia, the ideas of synergetics were actively promoted and developed by scientists of the scientific group of S. P. Kurdyumov [27,28].

Synergetics made a revolution by creating a new image of the world that continuously evolves according to nonlinear laws.

The basic concepts of synergetics are "order" and "chaos". The concept of "order" is usually used when describing a system of stable, repetitive in space and time relationships between elements of any nature. Conversely, the concept of "chaos" is usually used to describe a set of elements between which there are no stable repeating relationships. Dissipative systems, which include any socio-technical systems, can exist only in conditions of a constant exchange of matter, energy and information with the external environment [18]. The existence of a dissipative system is based on a constant synthesis of order and chaos. It has two aspects. Firstly, its system order exists only due to the chaos injected into the environment. Secondly, the system acquires the ability to adequately respond to chaotic influences of the external environment and thereby maintain its stability due to its system order. This remark primarily concerns structural stability preservation. It is possible if the system has a high level of orderliness.

Orderliness is the property of a system to preserve the structural composition, i.e., to restrict the freedom of change of both the system's element set and the connections between the elements. Usually, in a society, orderliness is a consequence of the practical implementation of functioning of a set of attitudes, laws and prohibitions that structure the system and organize its functioning within a clear system of rules. System orderliness is connected with its harmony.

The functioning of complex systems, which include all forms of transportation systems, is based on two global laws: the first law of dialectics and the law of the generalized golden ratio (GGR).

The first law of dialectics is the law of unity and the struggle of the opposites. Its essence can be expressed in the following form:

*Positive + negative = universe*

which, after normalization, is reduced to the form (1):

$$a + b = 1, \tag{1}$$

where

$a$—dominant;
$b$—subdominant.

In the structural identification of the concept of system sustainability, we will use the first law of dialectics in form (1), taking an increase in utility as a positive and a loss of sustainability as a negative:

*Positive (P) + negative (N) = universe (U).*

The law of the generalized golden ratio (S-ratio) was identified by E. M. Soroko [29] and it has the following analytical form (2):

$$\left(\frac{1}{a}\right)^s = \frac{a}{b} = \frac{a}{1-a} \tag{2}$$

where *s*—so-called multiplicity indicator.

In complex systems management, the law of the generalized golden ratio was the predecessor of modern F-technologies. In general, both laws are tools for building system functionality and structure close to the standard. The purpose of reference transport systems functionality is to form the general utility *(GU)* when consuming the provided resource. Thus, it is necessary to identify the general utility model. To do this, it is necessary to identify it structurally and parametrically.

*2.2. Road Safety Is a System Property. Road Safety as a Result of Functioning of a Specialized System for Preventing Conflict Road Traffic Situations*

A variety of authors have considered road safety from a system perspective. In the period of 1950–1970 many authors brought the consideration of road safety to the system level [30–35]. In many ways, this was promoted by the general theoretical work of L. Von Bertalanffy [36]. Road safety specialists relied on this work and considered the problems of road traffic accidents not as a set of special cases, but as a demonstration of a system peculiarity.

The result of this work was the concept of "Vision Zero", as Sweden's Traffic Safety Policy, declared in 1997 [37]. Two and a half decades of implementation of this concept, at first in the Scandinavian countries, and then, albeit partially, in many others, have shown the high efficiency of using the system approach in road safety provision.

P. Larsson et al. [38] believe that "the so-called zero-tolerance position, or Vision Zero approach, to road safety is built around two axioms; the system must be adapted to the psychological and physical conditions and limitations of the human being and the responsibility for road safety must be shared between the road-users and the designers and professional operators of the system". This is an important thesis that requires road traffic organizers to have a professional understanding of the cause-and-effect relationships of the process of forming of road traffic accidents and active actions to minimize the negative consequences in the chain of events.

A. Szymanek [39] has a similar opinion: "The road safety management methodology should be based on a system approach. This means that the road transport must be formalized as a complex system (CS), and then safety can be interpreted as an emergent feature of such a system. Road accidents should be interpreted as "organizational accidents".

B. P. Hughes et al. systematize various approaches of road safety provision in [40]. The analysis of 2620 literary sources conducted by the authors allowed them to summarize the experience in the road safety sphere in various countries in the form of 121 different types of models. This diversity of models for road safety provision is explained by a wide range of different targets and restrictions. This is an illustrative example of a wide variety of approaches, among which there may be the most unexpected ones.

*2.3. General Trends of Road Safety Changes*

At various times, scientists from all over the world were interested in the issues of road safety provision [41–51]. The analysis of the content of most of these studies allows us to conclude about the positive global changes in trends in road safety. The statistics of such organizations as the World Health Organization [52], IRTAD Group and permanent working group on road safety of the International Transport Forum [53] confirm this fact.

R. Elvik and R. Goel [54] state that "recent studies find a stronger tendency towards safety-in-numbers than older studies". This remark applies to the majority of the economically and socially developed countries of the world [55], but not to all of them. The economically and socially underdeveloped countries of Africa and Southeast Asia are characterized not only by a relatively high level of road traffic accidents, but also by trends in its increase. This spatial heterogeneity of road safety trends on a global scale is explained by the fact that different paradigms of road safety provision are currently relevant in different countries [56]. This means that some developing countries now have a level of road safety provision at approximately the same level as it was 30–70 years ago, from 1950 to 1990 in currently leading countries in the field of road safety.

While we consider the general trends in road safety, we should understand that the attention of states to the issues of reducing road traffic accidents and deaths in road accidents is largely related to the socio-economic aspects of life, particularly to one of the most important—the damage caused by the decrease in the quality of citizens' human potential. Thus, it is shown in [57] that the total costs of road crashes in 31 European countries are equivalent to 0.4–4.1% of Gross Domestic Product. Cost per fatality varies in different European countries in the range from €0.7 million to €3.0 million.

According to L. J. Blincoe et al. [58], the economic cost of US motor vehicle crashes that occurred in 2010 totaled $242 billion. This is equivalent to 1.6% of the US Gross Domestic Product.

These facts indicate that the problem of road traffic accident rate is highly significant both from the social and economic sides for most countries of the world. This is the reason for a serious increase in attention to the issue of road safety that has been paid in recent years in almost all countries of the world. As a result, in the vast majority of countries of the world, the general trends in changes in road safety are quite encouraging.

*2.4. Factors Influencing Road Safety*

2.4.1. The Road User Factor

Long-term experience [59–87] allowed us to establish that the contribution of the human factor to the road traffic accident rate is at least 90%. That is why autonomous car driving technologies have been rapidly developing in recent years [59–62], and the possibility of removing a person from the process of driving a vehicle has been actively studied [63]. However, in recent decades, there has been a huge improvement in the road transport infrastructure in various countries [64–66]. Many organizational and technical solutions are devoted to the minimization of the possibility of direct contact between a pedestrian and a driver [67,68]. Another direction of road safety improvement involves administrative actions, such as reducing the speed of vehicles in cities [69] and monitoring drivers' behavior [70,71]. In this regard, it is important to analyze the main approaches to assessing the driving style of drivers.

In 2004, O. Taubman-Ben-Ari et al. [72] published an article that proposed to classify the style of driving according to danger to others. The authors proposed to select eight typical driving styles. In the same article, the results of statistical research were presented, which aimed to identify a factor relationship between belonging to a particular driving style and the characteristic features of Israeli drivers who were representatives of different styles.

As indicated in the article by O. Taubman-Ben-Ari et al., the ideas of classifying drivers by driving styles are based on earlier works [73,74].

A little later, the method by O. Taubman-Ben-Ari et al. was modernized by Spanish [75] and Romanian authors [76].

In 2019, similar studies were conducted by Bulgarian researchers Z. Totkova and R. Racheva, who modernized the method and presented their version of factor analyses of the multidimensional driving style inventory (MDSI-BG) in [77].

The above studies were highly useful for understanding the psycho-physiological differences between different drivers and their different contributions to the formation of the actual road safety level.

A lot of works are also devoted to the issues of the impact of road users' sex and age on the road traffic accident rate [78–80]. Almost all of these studies indicate a greater tendency to unjustified risk, which is a risk factor for accidents, in young inexperienced male drivers with a low level of education and internal culture [81–83]. Conversely, women are more attentive and careful on the road than men [84]. It is also established that more educated professionals with a reliable workplace perform significantly less hazardous driving techniques than uneducated unemployed people [85]. There is also evidence of an inverse positive relationship between road traffic accidents and the general employment of people [86,87].

2.4.2. The Factor of Road Transport Infrastructure and Traffic Control Systems

Many works are devoted to the issues of the connection between road transport accidents and the quality of road transport infrastructure [88,89]. Numerous studies have been devoted to this topic in the context of the Third Paradigm of road safety [56]. Today, most developed countries make the highest requirements to the quality of the roadway, as well as to the engineering equipment of highways and the road network of cities. Nevertheless, even today, research on the further improvement of engineering systems for road safety provision is being conducted. One of the most important areas of such research is the identification of potentially dangerous locations for road users in the city. On the basis of these locations, new engineering solutions contributing to greater security will be developed and implemented [90–98].

The analysis of these works shows that creation of a high-quality road network is an expensive and resource-intensive task. Its solution has many limitations. In this regard, in the current situation, one of the most efficient ways to increase traffic safety is to identify dangerous locations, notify drivers about their existence and increase control of driving behavior on these sections of the road network.

2.4.3. The Factors of the Technical Level and Quality of the Vehicle

Researchers have been paying attention to car safety issues for more than 100 years. In this direction, especially effective research was carried out in the period from 1960 to 2010. During this time, cars have become much safer and much less demanding on the driver's qualifications. The level of active, passive and post-accident safety of individual cars has significantly increased. Duplication of safety systems, decrease in the probability of an accident and decline of the injury risks in an accident are the results of many years of work of designers, production technologists and researchers in the field of road safety. According to [99,100], the poor technical condition of vehicles and related technical failures were the cause of only 1–1.5% of accidents in EU countries (but 5–7% of accidents were caused by a combination of the technical failure of the car and incompetent actions of the driver in this critical situation).

2.4.4. The Factors of the External Environment That Negatively Affect Traffic Conditions

Many studies have been devoted to the influence of negative manifestations of the external environment on road safety [101–103]. In general, summarizing the results of these studies, it can be concluded that in adverse weather and weather-related road conditions, the accident rate increases significantly. That is why in countries with a high level of socio-economic development, active road signs and information boards are used on federal highways and in cities to regulate traffic flow modes taking into account environmental conditions [104–106]. This significantly reduces the risk of accidents. Unfortunately, such advanced technologies are used in a small number of countries. In most countries, the driver chooses the speed mode independently, without external informational support [107].

*2.5. COVID Lockdown and Its Influence on Road Safety*

In 2020 and 2021, a lot of works were published on the study of the impact of the COVID lockdown on changing people's transport behavior and, as a result, on changing the characteristics of road traffic accidents in various countries of the world [108–113]. Studies by [108,109] are devoted to changes in the patterns of using public and individual transport in the conditions of COVID-19. It was established that in 2020, people were afraid of the risks of infection and significantly reduced the frequency of using transport services. The same conclusion was made with regard to the use of individual cars and the mobility of citizens in general.

A study by Indian authors [110] shows that during the spring lockdown period (from 24.03.2020 to 31.06.2020), in comparison with the same period of 2019, India recorded a decrease in the number of road accidents by 68% and in the number of the dead and injured in road accidents by 62% and 72%, respectively.

According to the report "Impact of COVID-19 on Road Crashes in Australia" [111]: "fatalities among drivers (–5%), passengers (–11%), pedestrians (–20%) and motorcycle riders (–12%) decreased during the COVID lockdown, but pedal cyclist fatalities across Australia increased by 29%".

In [112], the Greek authors, on the basis of studies conducted in Greece and Saudi Arabia in March–April 2020, showed that "reduced traffic volumes due to lockdown, led to a slight increase in speeds by 6–11%, but more importantly to more frequent harsh acceleration and harsh braking events (up to 12% increase) as well mobile phone use (up to 42% increase) during March and April 2020, which were the months where COVID-19 spread was at its peak. On the bright side, accidents in Greece were reduced by 41% during the first month of COVID-19-induced measures and driving in the early morning hours (00:00–05:00), which are considered dangerous, dropped by up to 81%".

Summarizing the results of the above studies, it can be concluded that road safety during the lockdown restrictions in various countries of the world was largely determined by the peculiarities of the manifestation of transport activity. Based on these observations, L. Budd and S. Ison made conclusions about the need to develop new concepts and strategies of transport policy [113]. The main idea of these authors is that it is necessary to increase awareness of the choice of the method of mobility from the perspective of health safety in the future.

## 3. Theoretical Solution to the Problem of Assessing Systemic Harmonicity

### 3.1. Identification of the Concept of "Reference Systems"

Reference systems are open, interacting with the external environment, multicomponent systems with a number of specific features such as:

- they work in the mode of generalized golden ration (GGR) [29];
- their normalized utility function is described by the Equation (3):

$$GU_n = 1 - (1-x)^g \quad (3)$$

where

$GU$— the normalized general utility;
$x$—the share of consumed resource;
$g = 1 + s$—$Q$-factor-system quality indicator;
$s$—the multiplicity parameter, independent of $x$.

- they have real (independent of argument $x$) values of the quality factor $g$.

### 3.2. Functionality of Reference System

The essence of the functionality of reference systems of urban mobility management is to deliver the general utility of $GU$ in the consumption of the provided resource. The macro-model of the normalized general utility $GU_n$ is represented as (3). A significant advantage of this macro-model type is that it has fractal properties. Suppose that the argument $x$ is an analogous function of the new parameter $T_n$, i.e.,

$$x = 1 - (1 - T_n)^s \quad (4)$$

then normalized general utility $GU_n$ can be represented as:

$$GU_n(T_n) = 1 - (1-x)^g = 1 - \{1 - [1 - (1-T_n)^s]\}^g = 1 - [(1-T_n)^s]^g = 1 - (1-T_n)^q \quad (5)$$

Obviously, the new result (3) is again a fractal that has normalized time $T_n = t/T$ as an argument (here $T$ is a lifecycle time). The creation of the new model (3) allows us to proceed to the analysis of its dynamic characteristics.

### 3.3. Analysis of the Dynamic Characteristics of Reference Systems' Functionality

For the development of an algorithmic provision for road safety management systems it is necessary to have models of the basic dynamic characteristics of the information process. Article [114] is devoted to the topic of the development of such provision.

The functional scheme of the process (Figure 1) identifies dynamic models of the following process characteristics:

- speed of the change of process utility *SGU* (*speed of general utility*):

$$SGU(T_n) = dGU(T_n)/dT_n \qquad (6)$$

- process utility *GU* (*general utility*):

$$GU(T_n) = \int_0^{T_n} SGU_p(T_n) \cdot dT_n \qquad (7)$$

- vital power (performance) of process *VP* (*vital power*):

$$VP(T_n) = GU(T_n) \cdot SGU_p(T_n) \qquad (8)$$

- reserve of process vital power *S* (*stamina*):

$$S(T_n) = \int_0^{T_n} VP(T_n) \cdot dT_n \qquad (9)$$

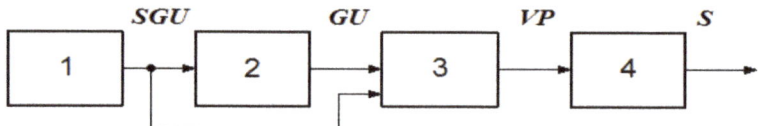

**Figure 1.** Functional scheme of the road safety management process (system).

Let us introduce the normalization of the above mentioned dynamic characteristics (Table 1).

**Table 1.** Dynamic models of system characteristics.

| Model | Determination Algorithm | |
|---|---|---|
| Normalized speed of the change of process utility $SGU_n$ | $SGU_n(T_n) = SGU_p(T_n)/SGU_{p\,max.} = (1 - T_n)^{q-1}$, where $SGU_{p\,max.} = q$. | (10) |
| Normalized process general utility $GU_n$ | $GU_n(T_n) = 1 - (1 - T_n)^q$ | (11) |
| Normalized vital power (performance) of process $VP_n$ | $VP_n(T_n) = \dfrac{VP(T_n)}{VP_{max}} = \dfrac{q \cdot Z^{q-1} \cdot (1 - Z^q)}{\left(\frac{q-1}{2q-1}\right)^{\frac{q-1}{q}} \cdot \frac{q^2}{2q-1}}$ | (12) |
| Normalized reserve of process vital power $S_n$ | $S_n(T_n) = \dfrac{S(T_n)}{S_{max}} = [GU(T_n)]^2$ | (13) |

Let us explain the models (10–13).

From the perspective of the quality of system changes management process it is preferable to have not only a high level of technology perfection (determined by the level of general utility $GU(T_n)$), but also a high growth rate $SGU_p(T_n) = dGU(T_n)/dT_n$.

In this regard, we can take as a criterion of effectiveness (vital power) of the system management process the next value (14):

$$VP(T_n) = GU(T_n) \cdot SGU_p(T_n) = q \cdot Z^{q-1} \cdot (1 - Z^q) \tag{14}$$

where $Z = (1 - T_n)$.

From the engineering point of view the question about the extremum of vital power $VP(T_n)$ is interesting. Its maximum is reached under the condition (15):

$$dVP(T_n)/dT_n = 0 \tag{15}$$

The solution of the Equation (15) is (16):

$$Z_{opt} = \left(\frac{q-1}{2q-1}\right)^{\frac{1}{q}} \tag{16}$$

The maximum possible value of the process vital power $VP$ is reached under the condition (17):

$$VP_{max} = \left(\frac{q-1}{2q-1}\right)^{\frac{q-1}{q}} \cdot \frac{q^2}{2q-1} \tag{17}$$

The normalized value of the process vital power $VP_n$ is determined by the algorithm (18):

$$VP_n(T_n) = \frac{VP(T_n)}{VP_{max}} = \frac{q \cdot Z^{q-1} \cdot (1 - Z^q)}{\left(\frac{q-1}{2q-1}\right)^{\frac{q-1}{q}} \cdot \frac{q^2}{2q-1}} \tag{18}$$

In Table 1 model (18) is denoted as (12).

Argument $T_{n\ opt}$, corresponding to the maximum of effectiveness of the controlled process, is determined by (19):

$$T_{n\ opt} = 1 - Z_{opt} = 1 - \left(\frac{q-1}{2q-1}\right)^{\frac{1}{q}} \tag{19}$$

The reserve of vital power of population mobility management process can be interpreted as cumulative sum of vital powers on the interval $T_n$ (20):

$$S(T_n) = \int_0^{T_n} VP(T_n) \cdot dT_n = \int_0^{T_n} GU \cdot dGU/dT_n \cdot dT = \int_0^{GU(T_n)} GU \cdot dGU = \frac{GU^2(T_n)}{2} \tag{20}$$

The level of reserve of vital powers at the end of the lifecycle is (21):

$$S_{max} = \int_0^1 VP(T_v) \cdot dt_v = \int_0^1 GU \cdot dGU/dT_n \cdot dT = \int_0^1 GU \cdot dGU = \frac{1}{2} \tag{21}$$

Introduction of the normalization generates model (22):

$$S_n(T_n) = \frac{S(T_n)}{S_{max}} = [GU(T_n)]^2 \tag{22}$$

In Table 1 model (22) is denoted as (13).

### 3.4. The Research of the Structural Features of Utility Function of System Management

When analyzing the structure of general utility $GU$ in multicomponent systems we should take into account two main points:

- the general utility *GU* of a complex system is an additive composition of individual functions of utility of system components;
- the general utility *GU* of urban mobility management is a consequence of interaction between chaotic state and orderliness of processes in this sphere.

When assessing the general utility *GU* of a complex system we need to identify the contribution of each component to the total success. A Pareto chart (*PC*) is a traditional tool for this type of analysis. It represents a cumulative function of the contribution of individual components into a total balance. As a rule, *PC* is approximated by a function (23):

$$PC = 1 - (1-x)^g \qquad (23)$$

where

$x$—normalized rank; $x = r_i/r_{max}$;
$r_i$ and $r_{max}$—correspondingly current and maximal ranks;
$g = 1 + s$—*Q-factor*-system quality indicator;
$g$ and $s$—indicators.

Since *PC* is the increasing sum of "weights" of system components, it allows us to analytically deduce "weight" coefficients as (24):

$$\omega_i = PC_i - PC_{i-1} = \left(1 - \frac{i-1}{n}\right)^g - \left(1 - \frac{i}{n}\right)^g \qquad (24)$$

Essentially, the normalized Pareto chart also represents the function of general utility *GU*, where $x$ is a share of the consumed resource. A comparison of models (3) and (23) indicates their functional equivalence *PC(x)* = *GU(x)*.

Found "weight" coefficients $\omega_i$ are used to solve two significant problems:

- the estimation of relative structural entropy $H_n$ [29,115,116], characterizing the level of orderliness (and structural perfection) of a process or system (25):

$$H_n = \left[-\sum_{i=1}^{n}\omega_i \cdot \ln(\omega_i)\right]/\ln(n) \qquad (25)$$

- representation of utility function *GU(x)* in additive form (26):

$$GU(x) = \sum_{i=1}^{n} GU_i(x) = \sum_{i=1}^{n} \omega_i \cdot \left[1 - (1-x)^g\right] \qquad (26)$$

where

$GU_i(x)$—an individual utility function (the share of contribution of *i*-component to the final system result).

Let us examine the second approach in detail.

Its specifics are generated by the wide usage in modern computer-aided manufacturing systems of F-technologies (F—Fibonacci). F-technologies exploit Fibonacci algorithms to build highly efficient and harmonic technical, socio-economic and organizational systems. One of the leading experts in this sphere is E. M. Soroko [29,115,116]. He found that in the majority of situations the principle of generalized golden ratio (GGR) works when the proportion between parts of the unit interval $f_r$ and $f_s$ (meeting the condition of normalization $f_r + f_s = 1$) is right (27):

$$(1/f_r)^s = (f_r/f_s) = f_r/(1 - f_r) \qquad (27)$$

From (27) it follows, that (28):

$$f_r^g + f_r - 1 = 0 \qquad (28)$$

where

$f_r$—dominant;
$1 - f_r = f_s$—subdominant;
$g = 1 + s$—*Q-factor*-system quality indicator
$g$ and $s$—indicators.

The generalized golden ratio regime (GGR regime) directly relates to the functionality of reference management systems, presented as a macromodel of normalized general utility $GU_n$ (3). Its graphic representation as Pareto chart $PC(x)$ (taking into account equivalency $PC(x) = GU(x)$) is shown in Figure 2.

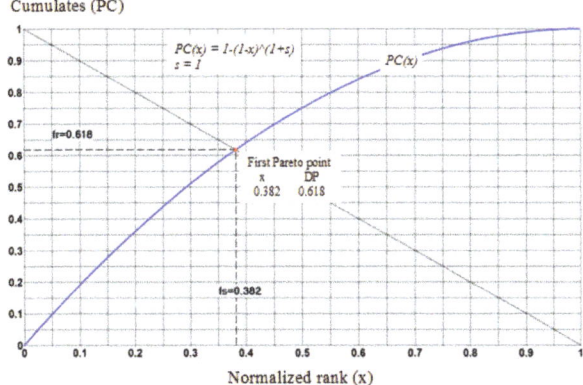

**Figure 2.** Macromodel of normalized general utility $GU_n$ in the form of Pareto chart.

The GGR regime is presented in the figure as a diagonal $y = (1 - x)$, where every point meets the condition $y + x = 1$. The point of intersection of the diagonal and Pareto chart (with coordinates $f_s$ and $f_r$) is called the first Pareto point. We want to highlight its properties. Firstly, it complies with the GGR principle. Secondly, it is related to indicator $g$ (system quality factor) by the correlation (29):

$$g = 1 + s = \frac{\ln(1 - f_r)}{\ln(1 - f_s)} \quad (29)$$

Thirdly, it is predetermined by proportion «order/chaos» in the management system. The meaning of the dominant $f_r$ and $f_s$ the subdominant is fundamentally important. The approach, evaluating levels of orderliness and chaos in an informational metric, where the maximal relative entropy of combination is taken as a unit, is foundational. The use of such approach allowed the creation of the theory of systems harmony [29]. However, at the same time, there is some non-transparency of the harmony concept in terms of engineering of efficient systems of urban mobility management. Let us consider the methodology of the optimal synthesis of harmonic systems in the examined domain sphere.

If we assume that the target management function is the retention of a process at the first Pareto point, then we need to prove that it provides an optimum in terms of predetermined parameter; in our case by default it is harmony. However, the harmonicity concept is not clearly formalized yet, and the question of an acceptable metric remains open. It is obvious that the total process utility in the first Pareto point is higher, the larger value of parameter $g$. However, the choice of the optimal value of the indicator $g$ is not simple. With a decline in the value of indicator $g$, system losses should increase due to the poor quality of the system. With the growth of the indicator $g$ the system efficiency should increase and, as a consequence, the additional expenses on the implementation of a system's functioning would grow. This problem belongs to the optimization category, where we need to establish which conditions provide minimal total expenses $Z$ and what is the value of the reached extremum $Z_{min}$.

The solution to this problem is given in the work [117]. A short explanation is given below.

In the paper it is supposed that the total expenses $Z$ are caused by the simultaneous effect of two mechanisms:

- on the one hand, a low value of the indicator g indicates a low system efficiency and, as a consequence, it is related to unwanted losses $Z_1$;
- on the other hand, a growth of the value g is impossible withoud additional expenses $Z_2$.

Equation (28), written in the form $1 - f = f^g$ ($f$ - is a dominant of GGR regime), reaches a compromise. The left part characterizes the negative of decline of the f dominant, while the right part characterizes the positive, provided by its growth.

The negative $(1-f)$ leads to proportianal losses $Z_1 = C_1 \cdot (1-f)$ (where $C_1$ — cost), when the positive $f^g$ demands proportional expenses $Z_2 = C_2 \cdot f^g$.

Therefore total expenses are (28):

$$Z = Z_1 + Z_2 = C_1 \cdot (1-f) + C_2 \cdot f^g \qquad (30)$$

It is important that the price $C_1$ can have a broad meaning. Price $C_1$ can be understood as money, energy, information, time and other resource types. The essence of article [117] consists in the fact that the harmonic regime is the regime of provision of the minimal total resource expenses in the first Pareto point.

It is established in [117] that the level of total expenses $Z$ is (31):

$$Z = Z_{max} \cdot (1 - f + m \cdot f^g) \qquad (31)$$

where $m = \frac{1}{g \cdot f_r^{g-1}}$.

The normalized value of expenses equals to $Z_n$ (32):

$$Z_n = Z/Z_{max} = (1 - f + m \cdot f^g) \qquad (32)$$

The minimum of expenses is reached under the condition $dZ_n/df_r = 0$. Value of extremum $Z_{n\ min}$ equals to (33):

$$Z_{n\ min} = 1 - f_r \cdot (1 - 1/g) \qquad (33)$$

and the level of minimal total expenses equals to (34):

$$Z_{min} = Z_{max} \cdot [1 - f_r \cdot (1 - 1/g)] \qquad (34)$$

*3.5. Establishment of the Relation between Functionality and Structure*

Associating the system functionality with the function of general utility $GU$, it was detected that the key characteristic of $GU$ is the indicator $g$, which determines the level of success (the positive) in the consumption of the available resource and the structure of "weight" coefficients (relation (23)). However, the "weight" structure in turn predetermines the level of relative entropy $H_n$ (25). Therefore, the relation between $g$ and $H_n$ is quite expected (Figure 3).

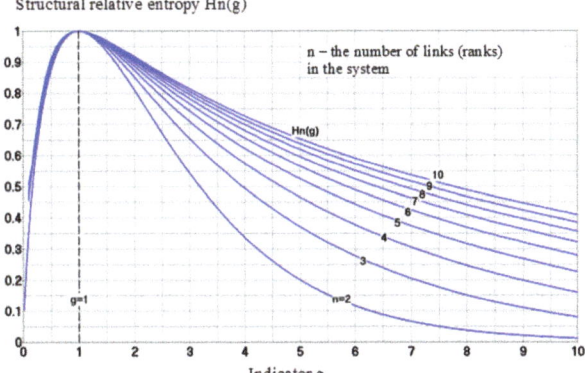

**Figure 3.** Model $H_n = f(g)$.

### 3.6. Identification of Model of Evaluation of Reference Systems' Efficiency

The successful solution of management problems is based on competent goal-setting, the quantitative measure of which is an efficiency. Formally, efficiency is a relation of performance to the resource expenses on results' achievement.

Let us consider the interpretation of the concept of "performance".

Traditionally, success is associated with the dominant $f_r$; the higher the dominant, the more positive the result. Since $f_r$ is a measure of the total utility, as a consequence, it can be a characteristic of the performance of the examined process. Model $GU = f(g)$ is a useful tool for success evaluation. It indicates that the quantitative characteristic of management performance can be presented both as general utility $GU$ and as a system (process) characteristic g, defined as a quality factor or *Q-factor*.

Therefore, there are two possible options for performance evaluation. Meanwhile, it is important to correctly evaluate resources expenses on the result achievement.

Analysis of efficiency of reference systems. If we define efficiency as a relation of performance to resource expenses, then we can consider two alternative options:

$$\text{criterion 1 } EF_1 = f_r/Z \to \max, \tag{35}$$

$$\text{criterion 2 } EF_2 = g/Z \to \max. \tag{36}$$

The analysis showed that the second option, i.e., analysis of the system efficiency with regard to the criterion 2 (36), is more preferable than the first, because it provides higher elasticity $EF$ relative to the total utility $GU$. The relation $EF_{2m}/EF_{1m} = g/f_r$ in the mode of the golden ratio (when $g = 2$; $f_r = 0.618$) is equal to 3.23.

The plot of dependency of efficiency $EF_2$ on dominant $f_r$ for reference systems (with different levels of quality factor *Q-factor* estimated g) is shown in Figure 4.

In the analysis of the model of process (system) efficiency, presented in Figure 4, it may seem as if the growth of the efficiency of reference systems is not limited at all. In fact, with the growth in the quality factor *Q-factor* estimated $g$, the system cost is increasing and according to the paper [118], this cost is proportional to $g$. Due to the high elasticity of the process efficiency relative to *Q-factor* estimated $g$, the system sustainability stock is decreasing and the possibility of bifurcation is increasing. The issue of the boundary of the efficient systems' sustainability is quite important but it requires individual consideration.

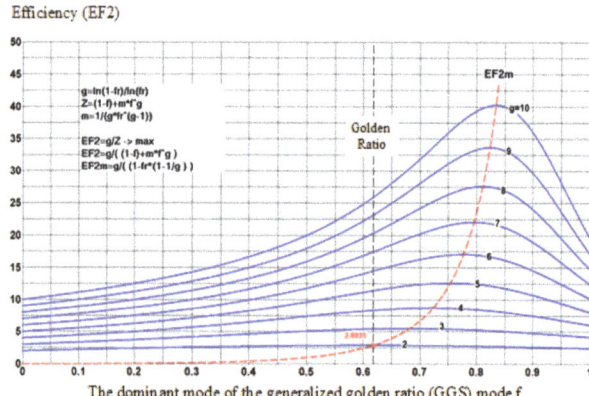

**Figure 4.** Model of process (system) efficiency $EF_2 = f(f_r)$.

### 3.7. Conceptual Model of Reference System Analysis

Key properties of any rational systems are integrity and goal-orientation. System goals can differ but their main humanistic destination is a creation of some positive (utility). Management of complex systems is directed towards the growth of the positive. However, there are always forces that prevent the growth. Counteraction of multidirectional vectors forms dialectical results of complex systems' functioning. The antagonistic force of the utility is a system's sustainability.

With the growth of the consumed resource, the utility should increase, but at the same time the remaining resource is declining and this fact determines system sustainability and its ability to stably function. Therefore, the utility growth is not unlimited. In this situation the suggestion about some optimal (harmonious) system working mode occurs. The traditional approach supposes hidden (latent) work of some global mechanism, called the golden ratio or golden mean.

Lately the principle of the general golden ratio (GGR), established by Belarusian scientist E. M. Soroko [29] started to be used for analysis. Researchers of the V.A. Trapeznikov Institute of Management Problems of the Russian Academy of Science [119,120] created new scientific field: *F-technologies* (F—Fibonacci), successfully solving complex application problems of efficient management in the systems of various purposes.

The conceptual model (Figure 5) that we use also relies on the GGR principle and the first dialectic law. This model defines two new entities: normalized total utility and normalized sustainability.

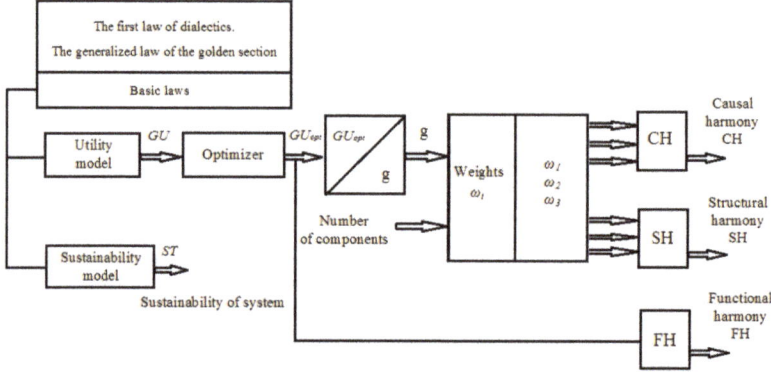

**Figure 5.** Conceptual model of complex system harmonycity formation.

The research into these characteristics allows us to solve two important problems: the problem of the optimization of the system utility $GU$ and the problem about the logical consequences generated by this optimization (casual, structural and functional system harmonies).

### 3.8. Definition of the System Utility Function

The system utility is characterized by the level of system functionality. Analytically it is set by the model of total utility $GU$.

In the structural identification of this model, we will assume that the first dialectic law works:

$$Positive + negative = universum.$$

We interpret the positive as a saved resource and the negative as an under-received utility. After normalization we have

$$a + b = 1$$

where

$a$—dominant, $a = 1 - x_c$;
$x_c$—the share of resource consumed on goal achievement;
$b$—subdominant; $b = 1 - GU$;
$GU$—the share of received utility relatively to maximal possible.

The GGR principle works as follows:

$$\left(\frac{1}{a}\right)^s = \frac{a}{b}$$

which gives (37):

$$\left(\frac{1}{1-x_c}\right)^s = \frac{1-x_c}{1-GU_n} \tag{37}$$

i.e.,

$$GU_n(x_c) = 1 - (1-x_c)^g \tag{38}$$

where

$g$—*Q-factor*-system quality indicator.

The plots of total utility functions for different values of the quality control $g$ are presented on Figure 6.

In Figure 6 the point C, corresponding to the classical golden ratio (under the condition $g = 2$), is highlighted. All sustainable solutions, conformed to GGR, are placed on the diagonal $Y_2 = 1 - x_c$.

The analysis of extremely possible utility $PU$ (37) showed that $GU$ meets the necessary requirements, i.e., it declines with the growth of consumed resource $x_c$ (39):

$$PU = dGU/dx_c = g \cdot (1-x_c)^{g-1} \tag{39}$$

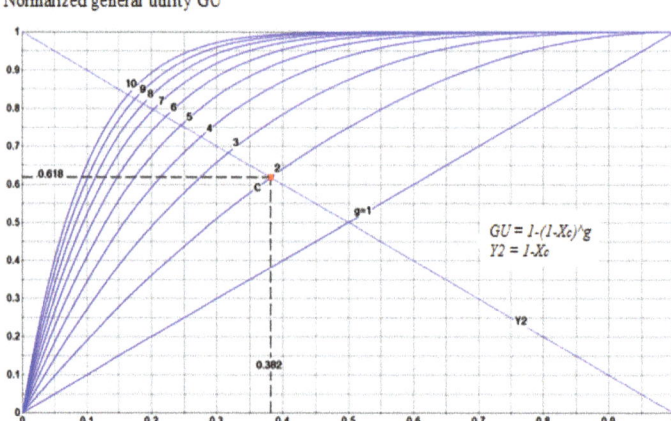

**Figure 6.** Plots of total utility functions $GU(x_c)$.

### 3.9. Optimization of the Total Utility (Criteria of Optimality, System Harmonization)

Taking into account the essence of the first dialectic law, we should expect a confrontation between the system positive and the system negative. The sustainable balance between them forms the system balance. Many authoritative scientists [121–123] suppose that system balance is identical to the concept of system harmony. In that point (denoted as $x_{opt}$) two conditions should simultaneously meet:

- with regard to the first dialectic law, $a + b = 1$, where $a = 1 - x_c$; $b = 1 - GU$), the next condition should be satisfied

$$a + b = (1 - x_c) + (1 - GU) = 1, \text{ i.e., } GU = 1 - x_c.$$

- with regard to GGR, $GU = 1 - (1 - x_c)^g$. Therefore, in the optimum point (where $x_c = x_{opt}$) we have

$$1 - x_{opt} = 1 - (1 - x_{opt})^g$$

which implies that the quality factor equals to (40):

$$g = \frac{\ln(x_{opt})}{\ln(1 - x_{opt})} \qquad (40)$$

In the regime of classical golden ration, when $g = 2$, $x_{opt} = 0.382$, substitution (40) into (37) gives an important result (41):

$$GU_{opt} = 1 - (1 - x_{opt})^{\frac{\ln(x_{opt})}{\ln(1 - x_{opt})}} = 1 - x_{opt} \qquad (41)$$

Therefore,

$$GU_{opt} = 1 - x_{opt} \qquad (42)$$

It means that:
- optimal solutions are always placed on the diagonal (42);
- system quality factor in the optimum point equals to $g = \frac{\ln(x_{opt})}{\ln(1 - x_{opt})}$;
- work state in optimum should be considered as harmonious system state;

- "weights" $\omega_i$ of system components, as shown in work [124], are predetermined by the system quality factor g (43):

$$\omega_i = \left(1 - \frac{i-1}{n}\right)^g - \left(1 - \frac{i}{n}\right)^g \quad (43)$$

where

$n$—the number of components of the system under study;
$i$—the rank of the component.

In the "golden ratio" regime (when g = 2) formula (41) takes the form (44):

$$\omega_i = \frac{2}{n} - \frac{(2 \cdot i - 1)}{n^2} \quad (44)$$

*3.10. Evaluation of the Complex Systems' Sustainability*

In recent times, in strategic management publications [125] the concept of sustainability is broadly used. Different authors variously interpret this concept [126]. The majority define it only from the economic or ecological point of view, but in fact this concept has a wider meaning. There is no unified point of the view on this issue yet. At the same time the sustainability concept is significant in system analysis. It predetermines the successfulness of functioning of an analyzed complex system.

Sustainability can be evaluated by different metrics. We will use the metric of the generalized golden ratio (GGR). As was shown earlier in Section 2.1:

*Positive + negative = universum.*

The positive *(P)* assumes the growth of system utility, while the negative *(N)* is defined by the loss of system sustainability.

In the growth of the system utility the first summand—the Positive *(P)*—is dominant and after the normalization it will take the form of $GU_{opt}$. $GU_{opt}$ is total utility in the operating point. The second summand—the Negative *(N)*—is a subdominant and it defines the share of the lost sustainability *(1 - $ST_{opt}$)*; here $ST_{opt}$ is a normalized sustainability in the operating point.

We will use GGR in the form $\left(\frac{1}{GU_{opt}}\right)^s = \frac{GU_{opt}}{1-ST_{opt}}$, and as a result we will have (45):

$$ST_{opt} = 1 - GU_{opt}^g \quad (45)$$

where

*g—Q-factor-system quality indicator; g = s + 1.*

Analysis of the formula (45) allows us to make a significant conclusion: The growth of the utility is not unlimited: it is restrained by the loss of the sustainability. Sustainability (as an ability to execute prescribed functionality) is defined by the remaining resource and with its decline it also declines.

*3.11. Establishment of the Relation between System Sustainability and Its Utility*

The relation between the sustainability and the utility in the operating point (i.e., $x_c = x_{c\ opt}$) is characterized by the relation (45). In points $x_c$ the structure of this relation is inherited and the sustainability model can be represented in the form (46):

$$ST(x_c) = 1 - [GU(x_c)]^g = 1 - \left[1 - (1 - x_c)^g\right]^g \quad (46)$$

Plots of the functions *ST($x_c$)* and *GU($x_c$)* are presented in Figure 7.

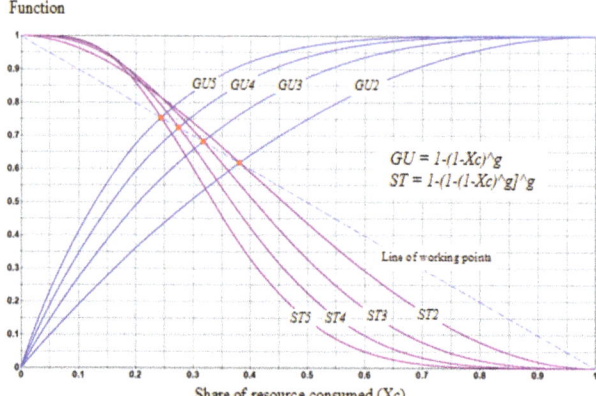

**Figure 7.** Plots of functions $GU(x_c)$ and $ST(x_c)$.

Operating points, corresponding to values of the quality factor $g$ = 2, 3, 4 and 5 are highlighted. The pair $GU_2$ and $GT_2$ belongs to the golden ratio regime ($g$ = 2). In the operating point the condition

$$GU_2(x_c) = ST_c(x_c) = 0.618 \text{ is met.}$$

### 3.12. Analysis of the Possibilities of System Sustainability Application

There is a series of spheres in which arises a need to evaluate the sustainability level. From the positions of the PEST analysis [125] there are several types of sustainability:

- social;
- ecological;
- economic;
- technological (energetical);
- political.

In cases of sustainable urban mobility development, we should use vector (generalized) sustainability evaluation (47):

$$ST = \sum_{i=1}^{n} \omega_i \cdot ST_i \quad (47)$$

where

$ST_i$—sustainability in the $i$-sphere;

$\omega_i$—the "weight" coefficients, meeting the normalization condition $\sum_{i=1}^{n} \omega_i = 1$.

### 3.13. Harmonization of Complex Systems

Usually, harmony is considered from three points of view [29]. Firstly, it is considered from the positions of the character and mechanism of harmonious impact of one system part on another (casual harmony). Secondly, it is considered as proportionality of the parts in the whole (structural harmony). Thirdly, it is considered as the mutual consistency and synchronicity of system components functioning (functional harmony). The authors agree with E. M. Soroko's point of view [29,115–117], consisting of the observation that system harmony is observed in the regime of the classical golden ratio, when the system quality factor equals $g$ = 2.

## 4. Identification of the Q-factor g of the Road Safety Provision System

*4.1. The System Orderliness and Its Relation to the System Quality Factor*

In Section 2.1 it was shown that the base of the system orderliness is the structural sustainability. Maintenance of the system structural sustainability in the conditions of the negative impact of chaos is a consequence of the high level of the system orderliness. The system orderliness is identified by the features of the "weight" distribution Pareto charts or the system/process elements' significance in the formation of the system functioning result. It is quantitatively evaluated by the level of the curvature of the Lorenz curve of the Pareto chart.

The normalized Pareto chart is presented as a function of the normalized generalized utility $GU_n$, where x is the share of the used resource (Equation (1)). As it was shown above in Section 3.4, the Pareto chart is an increscent sum of "weights" $\omega_i$ of the components of the considered system. As it was shown in Equation (22), the "weight" coefficients $\omega_i$ are defined by the equation:

$$\omega_i = DP_i - DP_{i-1} = \left(1 - \frac{i-1}{n}\right)^g - \left(1 - \frac{i}{n}\right)^g$$

In addition, earlier in Section 2.1, in Equation (23) it was presented that the found "weight" coefficients $\omega_i$ relative structural entropy $H_n$, characterizing the level of orderliness (or structural perfection) of the process or the system:

$$H_n = \left[-\sum_{i=1}^{n} \omega_i \cdot \ln(\omega_i)\right] / \ln(n)$$

The utility function *GU(x)* in the additive form can be presented as the sum of particular utility functions (or the sum of the shares of the contribution of *i*-components in the system result) (48):

$$GU(x) = \sum_{i=1}^{n} GU_i(x) = \sum_{i=1}^{n} \omega_i \cdot \left[1 - (1-x)^g\right] \qquad (48)$$

In this equation, x is a share of the used resource and g identifies the system quality factor. The determination of the relative structural entropy $H_n$ is important from the positions of the identification of the level of the system orderliness and the system quality factor g.

*4.2. Method of Definition of Relative Entropy of Road Safety Provision System*

Formula (41) connects "weights" $\omega_i$ of researched system components and the quality factor g. Consequently, this raises the question of the system itself, its components, their "weights" and the relative importance of each component to the formation of the system functioning result.

To consider the road safety provision system we need to define the size of the system (federal, regional, district, urban or microdistrict) and the cause-and-effect relationship of road accident rate formation.

4.2.1. The Cause-and-Effect Model of Road Accident Rate Formation

The cause-and-effect model for a road safety provision system is shown in Figure 8.

The goal of the analysis of the cause-and-effect model (Figure 8) is to establish the relationship between coefficients of the informational transfer of elements of the road accident rate formation process.

For the research into the examined process structure, we will use cybernetic modeling. The concept of cybernetic modeling is defined by V.I. Krutov et al. [127] in the following way: "cybernetic models are based on the receiving of relations between input and output function for some black box or grey box, representing examined an phenomenon, without disclosure of its inner structure".

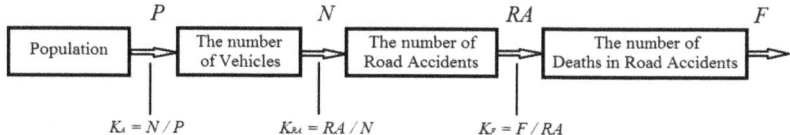

**Figure 8.** The cause-and-effect model of road accident rate formation.

We should pay attention not to the inner mechanism of each component of the examined process chain but only to coefficients $K_i$ of the informational transfer between elements of the cause-and-effect model. $K_i$ plays a special role in the analysis of the process model. It comprises the key characteristics of the elements of the complex system, the model of which is entirely defined by the behavior of its elements. The coefficient of the transfer of the $i$-element of the cause-and-effect model is a relation between its output ($A_{out}$) and input ($A_{in}$):

$$K_i = A_{out}/A_{in}$$

With regard to the structure of the road accident rate mechanism (Figure 8) we distinguish 3 subprocesses:

- the formation of the vehicle fleet, determining the average annual intensity of road traffic (with the transfer coefficient $K_A = N/P$);
- the formation of the road accidents (with the transfer coefficient $K_{RA} = RA/N$);
- the formation of the deaths rate in road accidents, the number of the deceased in road accidents (with the transfer coefficient $K_F = F/RA$);

4.2.2. Determination of the Priorities of the Process Elements (ABC Analysis)

The ABC analysis, based on the Pareto chart, is a tool of determination of the priorities of the examined process elements. The aim of the analysis is to identify main priorities. The essence of the ABC analysis consists of the search for the first and the second Pareto points (determining the position of the boundaries between A, B and C areas).

To hold this analysis, it is necessary to preliminarily make a decision on 3 issues: decide what to define as the positive; choose necessary metric; prepare data.

For the first problem, it is obvious that the lower the transfer coefficient $K$ of the element, the more positive the result. Generally, for the whole cause-and-effect process chain we can say that the lower the value of the through transfer coefficient $K_i$, the more positive the system result.

In the next step we need to learn how to measure the positive, i.e., introduce the necessary metric. It is reasonable to use an indicator of the process $Q$ positive as a measure (49):

$$Q_i = \ln(1/K_i) \tag{49}$$

Received results allow us to find "weak" elements in the chain of the cause-and-effect relations in the road accident rate formation process and set priorities in the road safety management sphere.

4.2.3. Evaluation of the "Weight" Coefficients $\omega_i$

Knowing the values of the positive of process elements $Q_i$, we determine the total process positive $Q$ (50):

$$Q = Q_A + Q_{RA} + Q_F = \ln(1/K_A) + \ln(1/K_{RA}) + \ln(1/K_F) \tag{50}$$

The "weight" coefficients $w_i$ show the share of each summand $Q_i$ in the total sum of the process positive $Q$ (51):

$$w_i = \frac{\ln(1/K_i)}{\sum_{i=1}^{3} \ln(1/K_i)} \quad (51)$$

4.2.4. Evaluation of the Entropy as A Characteristic of the Orderliness of the Road Safety Provision System

The structure of the "weight" coefficients $w_i$ of the road safety provision process defines the level of the orderliness. The numerical characteristic of the orderliness level is an entropy $H$ (52):

$$H = -\sum_{i=1}^{n} w_i \cdot \ln w_i \quad (52)$$

where

$n$—the number of system elements (in our case $n = 3$);

$w_i$—the "weight" coefficients, meeting the normalization condition $\sum_{i=1}^{n} w_i = 1$.

Relative entropy $H_n$ is more visual and convenient from the positions of the application characteristic of the evaluation of the road safety provision system's orderliness (53):

$$H_n = H / \ln(n) \quad (53)$$

where

$n$—the number of system elements (in our case $n = 3$);

From now on we will use this characteristic to evaluate the orderliness of the road safety provision systems.

*4.3. The Method of the Determination of the Quality Factor of the Road Safety Provision System*

As was shown in Sections 2.4 and 4.1, value $g$ is an exponent of the exponential equation, identifying the curvature of the change in the Pareto chart cumulate. Equation (27), presented in Section 3.4, illustrates the meaning of the system quality factor $g$:

$$g = 1 + s = \frac{\ln(1 - f_r)}{\ln(1 - f_s)}$$

By knowing the coordinates $f_r$ and $f_s$ of the curve, which identify the utility function $GU(x)$, we can determine the value of the quality factor of the system.

## 5. Example of the Theoretical Solution of the Problem of the Evaluation of the System Harmonicity in Relation to the Road Safety Provision System

As an example, we will provide results of the harmonic analysis of the complex systems in the road safety sphere, one of the key spheres of the urban mobility implementation. In this analysis the results of the authors' research relied on the database of the State Inspectorate for Road Traffic Safety [11].

The three "weight" coefficients of the rank Pareto chart are the subject of the analysis: "weight", characterizing the level of automobilization ($w_A$); "weight", characterizing the level of road accidents ($w_{RA}$) and "weight", characterizing the death rate ($w_F$). The sum of "weights" meets the normalization condition $\sum_{i=1}^{3} w_i = 1$

*5.1. Structural Harmony*

In reference systems, the "weight" coefficients are always determined (see relation (43), Figure 9).

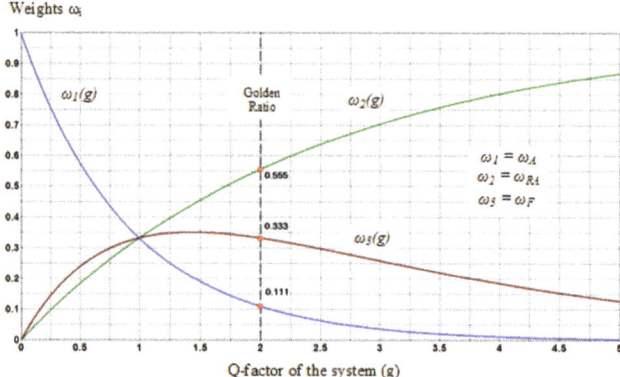

**Figure 9.** Structural harmony of the "weights" coefficients $\omega_i$.

In the golden ratio regime, when $g = 2$, components' "weights" (Figure 9) correspond to the proportions (44) and when $n = 3$ they are correspondingly equal: $\omega_A = 0.111$; $\omega_{RA} = 0.555$; $\omega_F = 0.333$.

### 5.2. Casual Harmony

In the analysis it was taken into account that the level of automobilization $A$ is the root cause, while the number of road accidents and the number of deceased in road accidents are consequences of the automobilization $A$. Therefore, it is reasonable to present the casual harmony in the form of the dependency of the "weights" $\omega_{RA}$ and $\omega_F$ on the "weight" $\omega_A$ (Figure 10).

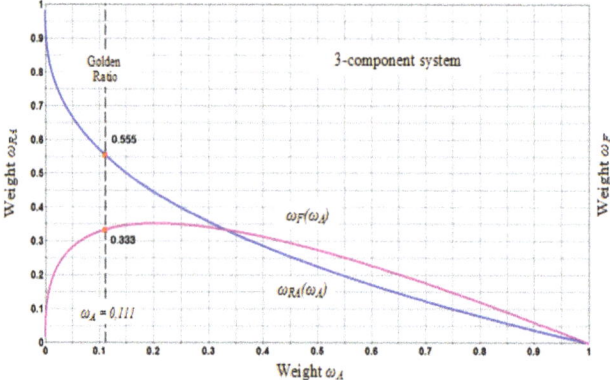

**Figure 10.** Casual harmony of the "weights" coefficients $\omega_i$.

The relation of the "weights" is of practical interest. It is presented in Figure 11.

### 5.3. Functional Harmony

According to Socrates [29], we connect functional harmony with the utility principle. The optimal level of the normalized utility is observed in the golden ratio conditions (Figure 12) and it is equal to 0.618.

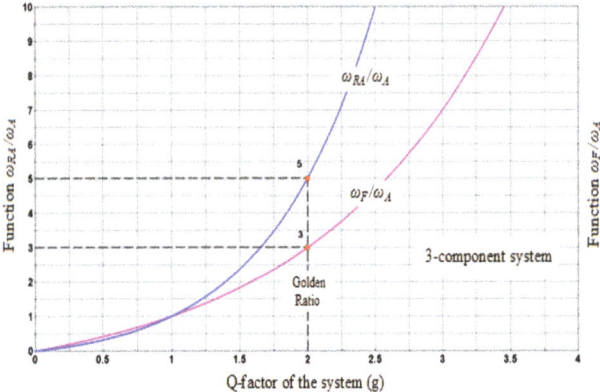

**Figure 11.** The relation of the "weights" coefficients $\omega_i$ for the road safety provision system case.

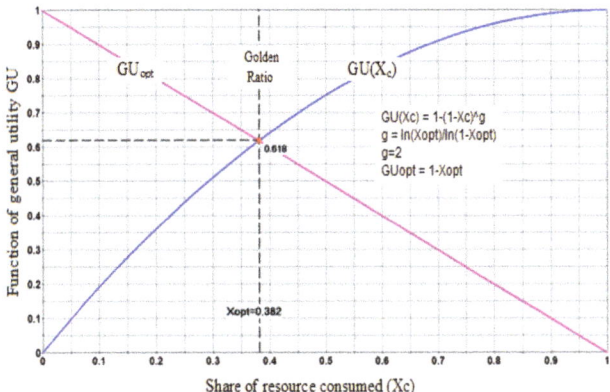

**Figure 12.** Functional harmony.

## 6. Quantitative Assessment of Changes in the Road Safety System Harmonicity in the Russian Federation

*6.1. Assessment of the General Trend in Changes in the Road Safety System Harmonicity in Russia from 2006 to 2020*

The data source was the official statistics of the State Inspectorate for Road Traffic Safety of the Russian Federation [11]. Over the past 15 years (2006–2020), the indicators of road safety in Russia have been constantly improving. A number of factors have contributed to this, such as a general increase in the transport culture of the country's population, a significant increase in the quality of the country's transport fleet and significant qualitative growth of the country's road transport infrastructure. It is also important that since 2006, a lot of attention has been paid to the issues of road safety provision by the Russian government [9,10].

The result of the improvement in the overall situation in the transport sphere was a decrease in the annual number of accidents and deaths in road accidents in Russia over the past 15 years (Table 2).

**Table 2.** Changes in the main road safety indicators in the Russian Federation from 2006 to 2020.

| Road Safety Indicators | Numerical Values of Indicators By Year | | | | | | | |
|---|---|---|---|---|---|---|---|---|
| | 2006 | 2008 | 2010 | 2012 | 2014 | 2016 | 2018 | 2020 |
| Number of accidents, units | 228,309 | 217,557 | 199,083 | 203,597 | 199,720 | 173,694 | 168,099 | 137,662 |
| The number of people killed in accidents, deceased people | 32,724 | 29,936 | 26,567 | 27,991 | 26,963 | 20,308 | 18,214 | 15,788 |

The natural result of a long-term decrease in road traffic accident rate in Russia was a significant decrease in the relative entropy $H_n$ of the road safety system and an increase in its Q-factor $g$ (Table 3).

**Table 3.** Changes in relative entropy $H_{n\,RSS}$ and Q-factor $g$ values of the road safety system in Russia.

| Characteristic | Numerical Values of Indicators By Year | | | | | | | |
|---|---|---|---|---|---|---|---|---|
| | 2006 | 2008 | 2010 | 2012 | 2014 | 2016 | 2018 | 2020 |
| Relative entropy of the road safety system $H_{n\,RSS}$ | 0.862 | 0.847 | 0.831 | 0.817 | 0.797 | 0.780 | 0.775 | 0.755 |
| Q-factor of the road safety system $g$ | 1.956 | 2.027 | 2.098 | 2.166 | 2.262 | 2.346 | 2.374 | 2.465 |

The dynamics of the change in Q-factor $g$ of the road safety system of the Russian Federation from 2006 to 2020 is very impressive.

At the same time, the ratio of "weight" coefficients $\omega_i$ changes over time. Based on these dynamics, it is possible to estimate changes in all three types of system harmony: structural, causal and functional.

Let us consider the actual data characterizing the "weight" coefficients $\omega_i$, and draw conclusions about the dynamics of the road safety system harmony in Russia over the past 15 years (2006–2020).

Table 4 presents data on the change in the numerical values of the "weight" coefficients $\omega_i$ from 2006 to 2020.

**Table 4.** Changes in the numerical values of the "weight" coefficients $\omega_i$ from 2006 to 2020.

| Characteristic | Numerical Values of Indicators By Year | | | | | | | |
|---|---|---|---|---|---|---|---|---|
| | 2006 | 2008 | 2010 | 2012 | 2014 | 2016 | 2018 | 2020 |
| $\omega_A$ | 0.170 | 0.155 | 0.143 | 0.134 | 0.120 | 0.104 | 0.098 | 0.093 |
| $\omega_{RA}$ | 0.598 | 0.610 | 0.622 | 0.633 | 0.647 | 0.654 | 0.655 | 0.670 |
| $\omega_F$ | 0.232 | 0.235 | 0.235 | 0.232 | 0.233 | 0.242 | 0.247 | 0.237 |

Figure 13 shows the graphs of the dynamics of the "weight" coefficients of the road safety system in Russia from 2006 to 2020.

Figure 14 shows a comparison of the theoretical and actual dynamics of changes in the "weight" coefficients $\omega_i$ of the road safety system in Russia over a 15-year period.

The analysis of the dynamics of the values of the weight coefficients $\omega_i$ allows us to conclude that the value of "weight" $\omega_A$ has decreased almost by half over the past 15 years, the value of "weight" $\omega_{RA}$ has increased by 12%, and the value of "weight" $\omega_F$ has increased by 6% from 2016 to 2018. However, in 2020, the "weight" $\omega_F$ significantly dropped again. This happened due to a significant increase in the severity of road accidents in 2020. The reason is the increase in the speed of vehicle movement in Russia in 2020 in the conditions of a relative rarefaction of the traffic flow associated with pandemic restrictions on the population mobility.

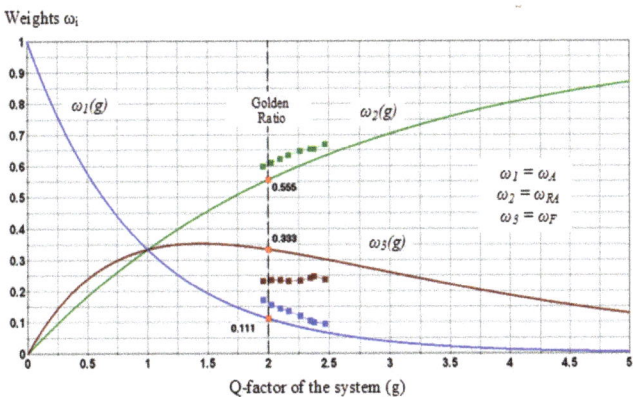

**Figure 13.** The actual dynamics of the "weights" coefficients of the road safety system in Russia.

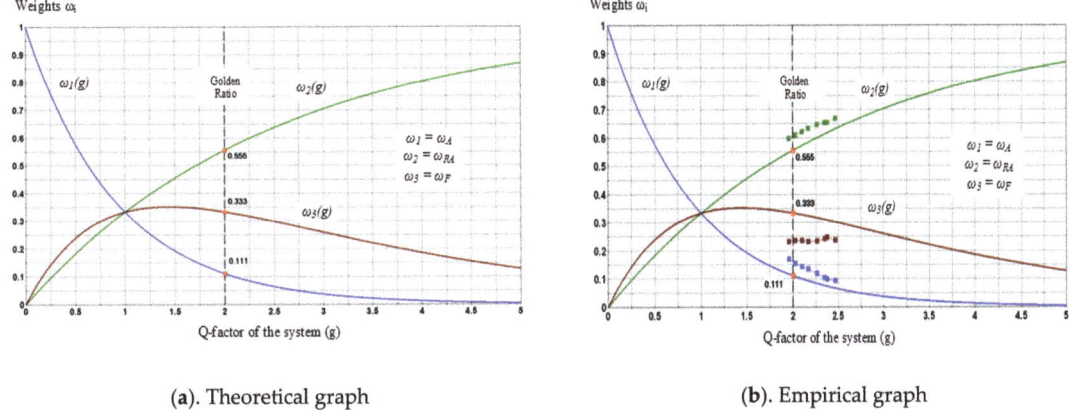

(a). Theoretical graph  (b). Empirical graph

**Figure 14.** Comparison of the theoretical and actual dynamics of changes in the "weights" coefficients of the road safety system in Russia over a 15-year period (2006–2020).

This is also evidenced by the statistics of penalties for violating the requirements of traffic rules and the share of those that fall on violation of the requirements of the speed limits (Table 5).

**Table 5.** General statistics of penalties for violators of traffic rules in Russia (2016–2020).

| Indicator | Numerical Values of Indicators By Year | | | | |
|---|---|---|---|---|---|
| | 2016 | 2017 | 2018 | 2019 | 2020 |
| The number of penalties, mln. units | 87.1 | 108.7 | 131.3 | 142.1 | 167.0 |
| Of these, for violation of the speed limit, mln. units | 54.0 | 74.4 | 92.2 | 101.8 | 124.0 |
| The share of speed limit violations in the total number of violations, % | 62.0 | 68.4 | 70.2 | 71.6 | 74.2 |

The data analysis in Table 5 shows that over the past 5 years in Russia, not only the number of penalties for violating traffic rules, but also the share of speed violations has increased. This indirectly indicates an increase in the quality of Russian roads and an improvement in the system of monitoring the speed limits of traffic flows. It is known that at the end of 2020, about 19,000 automated complexes for photo-video recording of traffic violations by drivers were used in Russia.

Figure 15 shows a comparison of the theoretical and actual dynamics of causal harmony of the road safety provision system in Russia over a 15-year period.

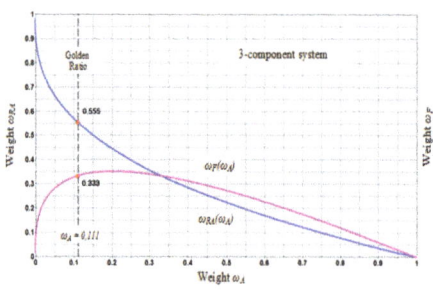
(a). Theoretical graph

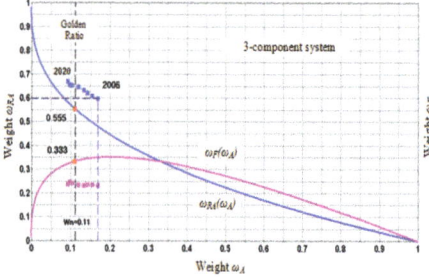
(b). Empirical graph

**Figure 15.** Comparison of the theoretical and actual dynamics of causal harmony of the road safety system in Russia over a 15-year period (2006–2020).

The functionality of the road safety system is estimated by the ratio of the actual level of normalized functional utility $GU_n$ and the share of consumed resource $X_c$, and is actually identified by the coordinate of the first Pareto point on the graph $GU_n = f(X_c)$. Table 6 shows the data on changes in the numerical values of the actual level of the normalized functional utility $GU_{n\ RSS}$ of the Russian road safety provision system.

**Table 6.** Changes in the numerical values of the normalized general utility $GU_{n\ RSS}$ of the Russian RSS from 2006 to 2020.

| Characteristic | Numerical Values of Indicators By Year | | | | | | | |
|---|---|---|---|---|---|---|---|---|
| | 2006 | 2008 | 2010 | 2012 | 2014 | 2016 | 2018 | 2020 |
| Normalized general utility $GU_{n\ RSS}$ | 0.615 | 0.620 | 0.626 | 0.631 | 0.639 | 0.644 | 0.646 | 0.652 |

Figure 16 shows the dynamics of the actual numerical values of the normalized general utility $GU_{n\ RSS}$ of the Russian road safety provision system from 2006 to 2020.

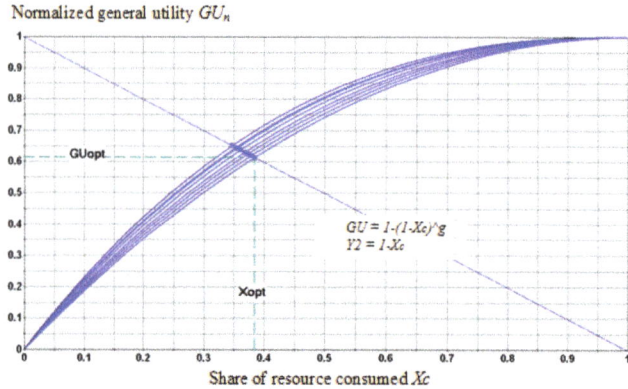

**Figure 16.** The actual dynamics of the values of the normalized general utility $GU_n$.

Comparing the data in Figure 16 with the known optimal value of the normalized utility $GU_{opt} = 0.618$, it is easy to conclude about the current state of the Russian road safety provision system harmonicity.

*6.2. Comparison of the Road Safety System Harmonicity in Russia during the COVID Restriction Period (2020) and during the Pre-COVID Period (2019)*

COVID-restrictions on mobility of all types (pedestrian, transport and general) have very seriously affected the change in all characteristics that define the process of road traffic accident formation in Russia.

Table 7 presents data describing the process of road accident rate formation in Russia in 2019 and 2020.

**Table 7.** Numerical values of the characteristics of the causal path of road traffic accident formation in Russia before (2019) and during (2020) the COVID-19 pandemic.

| Year | Population of Russian Federation (on 1 January the Following Year), People | The Average Annual Number of the Fleet of Vehicles of the Russian Federation, Units | Annual Number of Road Accidents in the Russian Federation, Case/Year | The Annual Number of Deaths in Road Accidents in the Russian Federation, Deceased/Year |
|---|---|---|---|---|
| 2019 | 146,748,590 | 61,739,156 | 164,358 | 16,981 |
| 2020 | 146,171,015 | 62,721,765 | 137,662 | 15,788 |
| *Absolute change, unit* | | | | |
| $\Delta_{2020/2019}$ | −577,575 | +982,609 | −26,696 | −1193 |
| *Relative change, %* | | | | |
| $\Delta_{2020/2019}$, % | −0.39 | +1.59 | −16.25 | −7.02 |

Tables 8 and 9 present the intermediate (according to the methodology of Section 4.2 of the article) and final results of calculating the relative entropy of the Russian road safety system $H_{n\ RSS\ RF}$ in 2019 and 2020.

**Table 8.** Intermediate and final results of calculating the relative entropy $H_{n\ RS\ SRF}$ of the Russian road safety system in 2019.

| Numerical Values of the Elements of the Three-Link Mechanism of Informational Transformation of the Road Safety System in the Russian Federation, 2019 | | | |
|---|---|---|---|
| $Y_1$ – Country population | $Y_2$ – Size of vehicle fleet | $Y_3$ – Annual number of road accidents | $Y_4$ – Annual number of deaths in road accidents |
| 146,748,590 | 61,739,56 | 164,358 | 16,981 |
| $K_i$ numerical values | | | |
| $K_A$ | $K_{RA}$ | | $K_F$ |
| 61,739,156/146,748,590 = 0.4207 | 164,358/61,739,156 = 0.0026 | | 16,981/164,358 = 0.1033 |
| Numerical values of the positive $Q_i = \ln(1/K_i)$ | | | |
| 0.8658 | 5.9286 | | 2.2700 |
| Numerical values of relative "weight" of the positive $\omega_i(Q_i)$ | | | |
| 0.096 | 0.654 | | 0.250 |
| Numerical values ($\ln \omega_i$) | | | |
| −2.3485 | −0.4246 | | −1.3846 |
| Numerical values ($\omega_i \cdot \ln \omega_i$) | | | |
| −0.2243 | −0.2777 | | −0.3467 |
| Numerical value of absolute entropy $H_{RSS\ RF} = 0.8487$ | | | |
| Numerical value of relative entropy $H_{n\ RSS\ RF} = 0.7726$ | | | |

**Table 9.** Intermediate and final results of calculating the relative entropy $H_{n\ RSS\ RF}$ of the Russian road safety system in 2020.

| Numerical Values of the Elements of the Three-Link Mechanism of Informational Transformation of the Road Safety System in the Russian Federation, 2020 | | | |
|---|---|---|---|
| $Y_1$ – Country population | $Y_2$ – Number of vehicle fleet | $Y_3$ – Annual number of road accidents | $Y_4$ – Annual number of deaths in road accidents |
| 146,171,015 | 62,721,765 | 137,662 | 15,788 |
| $K_i$ numerical values | | | |
| $K_A$ | | $K_{RA}$ | $K_F$ |
| 62,721,765/146,171,015 = 0.4291 | | 137,662/62,721,765 = 0.0022 | 15,788/137,662 = 0.1147 |
| Numerical values of the positive $Q_i = \ln(1/K_i)$ | | | |
| 0.8461 | | 6.1217 | 2.1656 |
| Numerical values of relative "weight" of the positive $\omega_i(Q_i)$ | | | |
| 0.093 | | 0.670 | 0.237 |
| Numerical values ($\ln \omega_i$) | | | |
| −2.34791 | | −0.4001 | −1.4393 |
| Numerical values ($\omega_i \cdot \ln \omega_i$) | | | |
| −0.2204 | | −0.2682 | −0.3413 |
| Numerical value of absolute entropy $H_{RSS\ RF}$ = 0.8298 | | | |
| Numerical value of relative entropy $H_{n\ RSS\ RF}$ = 0.7553 | | | |

On the basis of the numerical values of $H_{n\ RSS\ RF-2019}$ = 0.7726 and $H_{n\ RSS\ RF-2020}$ = 0.7553 we determined the appropriate Q-factor levels of the road safety system for the versions of 2019 and 2020.

Q-factor of the road safety system in the Russian Federation in 2019 $g_{RSS\ RF-2019}$ = 2.3754, and its analogue for 2020 $g_{RSS\ RF-2020}$ = 2.4646.

The calculations show that the changes in the Russian road safety system that occurred during COVID restrictions (2020) ensured a decrease in its relative entropy $H_n$ by 2.24%, from $H_{n\ RSS\ 2019}$ = 0.7726 to $H_{n\ RSS\ 2020}$ = 0.7553. The orderliness of the road safety system in Russia has improved.

The Q-factor of the Russian road safety system $g_{RSS}$ increased by 3.75% during COVID restrictions (2020).

Normalized general utility $GU_{n\ RSS}$ increased by 0.46% from 2019 to 2020 ($GU_{n\ RSS\ 2019}$ = 0.649 and $GU_{n\ RSS\ 2019}$ = 0.652).

## 7. Conclusions

During the research it was established that the Q-factor g of the Russian road safety provision system changed from $g_{2006}$ = 1.9565 to $g_{2020}$ = 2.4646. This promotes the decline of the relative entropy of the Russian road safety provision system from $H_{n\ RSS\ 2006}$ = 0.8623 to $H_{n\ RSS\ 2020}$ = 0.7553. The deep reason for that change was the modification of the relation between "weights" or the significance of the contribution of different elements of the cause-and-effect chain in the formation of the factual level of the road accident rate in Russia in the last 15 years.

The main conclusion is that the harmonicity of the Russian road safety provision system, assessed by the normalized functional general utility $GU_n$, has been increased and it already exceeded the level of harmonious reference systems $GU_n$ = 0.618.

Actually, the normalized functional general utility $GU_{n\ RSS}$ of the Russian road safety provision system increased from $GU_{n\ RSS\ 2006}$ = 0.615 to $GU_{n\ RSS\ 2020}$ = 0.652 (by 6.0%) from 2006 to 2020. Simultaneously, the share of the normalized used resource $X_n$ declined. That allowed us to make a conclusion about a significant improvement in the balance "efficiency-quality" of the Russian road safety provision system. The COVID lockdown played a positive role in this process. The harmonicity of the Russian road safety provision system, assessed by the normalized general utility $GU_{n\,RSS}$, increased by 0.46% from 2019 to 2020.

It is important to note that the methodology of the quantitative assessment of the system harmonicity can be applied to a variety of spheres of human activity. The road safety system is just one example. Exactly the same calculations can be carried out to assess the harmonicity of the functioning of a variety of socio-technical and socio-cultural systems.

**Author Contributions:** Conceptualization, A.I.P. and V.I.K.; methodology, V.I.K.; software, A.I.P., V.I.K. and D.A.P.; validation, A.I.P. and V.I.K.; formal analysis, A.I.P. and D.A.P.; investigation, A.I.P.; resources, A.I.P.; data curation, A.I.P. and D.A.P.; writing—original draft preparation, A.I.P. and V.I.K.; writing—review and editing, A.I.P. and D.A.P.; visualization, A.I.P., V.I.K. and D.A.P.; supervision, A.I.P.; project administration, A.I.P.; funding acquisition, A.I.P. All authors have read and agreed to the published version of the manuscript.

**Funding:** This research was funded by the Russian Ministry of Education and Science, grant number 0825-2020-0014, 2020–2022. «New patterns and solutions for the functioning of urban transport systems in the paradigm "Transition from owning a personal car to mobility as a service"».

**Institutional Review Board Statement:** Not applicable.

**Informed Consent Statement:** Not applicable.

**Data Availability Statement:** Not applicable.

**Acknowledgments:** 1. The authors would like to thank the Russian Ministry of Education and Science on the project: «New patterns and solutions for the functioning of urban transport systems in the paradigm "Transition from owning a personal car to mobility as a service"» (No. 0825-2020-0014, 2020–2022). 2. The authors would like to thank the anonymous reviewers for their very useful suggestions.

**Conflicts of Interest:** The authors declare no conflict of interest.

# References

1. Schwab, K.; Malleret, T. *COVID-19. The Great Reset*; World Economic Forum: Cologny, Geneva, 2020; 212p.
2. TomTom Traffic Index. Available online: https://www.tomtom.com/en_gb/traffic-index/ (accessed on 9 August 2021).
3. Sharifi, A.; Khavarian-Garmsir, A.R. The COVID-19 pandemic: Impacts on cities and major lessons for urban planning, design and management. *Sci. Total Environ.* **2020**, *749*, 142391. [CrossRef]
4. Rutz, C.; Loretto, M.C.; Bates, A.E.; Davidson, S.C.; Duarte, C.M. COVID-19 lockdown allows researchers to quantify the effects of human activity on wildlife. *Nat. Ecol. Evol.* **2020**, *4*, 1156–1159. [CrossRef]
5. Road Safety Annual Report. 2020. Available online: www.itf-oecd.org/road-safety-annual-report-2020 (accessed on 10 August 2021).
6. Resolution A/RES/74/299. Improving Global Road Safety. Available online: un.org\T1\guilsinglrightpga/74---uploads---Resolution-Road-Safety.pdf (accessed on 10 August 2021).
7. Voas, R.B.; Fell, J.C.; McKnight, A.S.; Sweedler, B.M. Controlling Impaired Driving Through Vehicle Programs: An Overview. *Traffic Inj. Prev.* **2004**, *5*, 292–298. [CrossRef]
8. Amador, L.; Willis, C.J. Demonstrating a Correlation between the Maturity of Road Safety Practices and Road Safety Incidents. *Traffic Inj. Prev.* **2014**, *15*, 591–597. [CrossRef]
9. Mayorov, V.I.; Sevryugin, V.E. International experience of developing complex target programs of road users' safety. *Criminol. J. Baikal Natl. Univ. Econ. Law* **2015**, *9*, 766–776. (In Russian) [CrossRef]
10. Decree of the Government of the Russian Federation of 8.01.2018, No 1-r, On Approval of the Road Safety Strategy in the Russian Federation for 2018–2024. Available online: https://docs.cntd.ru/document/556323639 (accessed on 11 August 2021).
11. The Official Website of the State Traffic Inspectorate of the Russian Federation. Indicators of the State of Road Safety. Available online: http://stat.gibdd.ru/ (accessed on 11 August 2021).
12. Benedict, R. Synergy: Some Notes of Ruth Benedict. *Am. Anthropologist. New Ser.* **1970**, *72*, 320–333.
13. Maslow, A.H. Synergy in the Society and in the Individual. *J. Individ. Psychol.* **1964**, *20*, 153.
14. Evans, P. Government action, social capital and development: Reviewing the evidence on synergy. *World Dev.* **1996**, *24*, 1119–1132. [CrossRef]
15. Evans, P.; Berkeley, C.A. (Eds.) *State-Society Synergy: Government and Social Capital in Development*; Institute for International Studies: Berkeley, CA, USA, 1996.
16. Hauert, C.; Michor, F.; Nowak, M.A.; Doebeli, M. Synergy and discounting of cooperation in social dilemmas. *J. Theor. Biol.* **2006**, *239*, 195–202. [CrossRef] [PubMed]

17. Jaffe, K. Quantifying social synergy in insect and human societies. *Behav. Ecol. Sociobiol.* **2010**, *64*, 1721–1724. [CrossRef]
18. Prigogine, I.; Stengers, I. *Order out of Chaos: Man's New Dialogue with Nature*; A Bantam Book: Toronto, ON, Canada; New York, NY, USA; London, UK; Sydney, Australia, 1984; 349p.
19. Prigogine, I. The philosophy of instability. *Futures* **1989**, *21*, 396–400. [CrossRef]
20. Nicolis, G.; Prigogine, I. *Self-Organization in Nonequilibrium Systems*; John Wiley & Sons: New York, NY, USA, 1977; 491p.
21. Othmer, H.G. Self-Organization in Nonequilibrium Systems (G. Nicolis and I. Prigogine). *SIAM Rev.* **1982**, *24*, 483–485. [CrossRef]
22. Haken, H. *The Science of Structure: Synergetics*; Prentice Hall: New York, NY, USA, 1984.
23. Haken, H. *Synergetics: An Introduction*; Springer Ser. Synergetics: Berlin/Heidelberg, Germany, 1983.
24. Haken, H. *Advanced Synergetics*; Springer Ser. Synergetics: Berlin/Heidelberg, Germany, 1987.
25. Liening, A. Synergetics—Fundamental Attributes of the Theory of Self-Organization and Its Meaning for Economics. *Mod. Econ.* **2014**, *5*, 841–847. [CrossRef]
26. Yakimtsov, V.V. History and development of Haken's synergetics. *Sci. Bull. UNFU* **2018**, *28*, 119–125. [CrossRef]
27. Kurdyumov, S.P.; Malinetskii, G.G. *Synergetics-Theory of Self-Organization. Ideas, Methods, Perspectives*; Nauka: Moscow, Russia, 1983; 280p. (In Russian)
28. Kurdyumov, S.P.; Malinetskii, G.G. *Prologue. Synergetics and System Synthesis. Looking to the Third Millennium*; Nauka: Moscow, Russia, 2002; 420p. (In Russian)
29. Soroko, E.M. *Golden Sections, Processes of Self-Organization and Evolution of Systems: An Introduction to the General Theory of Harmony of Systems*, 4rd ed.; Book House "Librocom": Moscow, Russia, 2012; 264p. (In Russian)
30. Gordon, J.E. The epidemiology of accidents. *Am. J. Public Health* **1949**, *39*, 504–515. [CrossRef]
31. Gibson, J.J. *The Contribution of Experimental Psychology to the Formulation of the Problem of Safety—A Brief for Basic Research. Behavioural Approaches to Accident Research*; Assoc. for the Aid of Crippled Children: New York, NY, USA, 1961; pp. 77–89.
32. Haddon, W. The changing approach to the epidemiology, prevention, and amelioration of trauma: The transition to approaches etiologically rather than descriptively based. *Am. J. Public Health* **1968**, *58*, 1431–1438. [CrossRef]
33. Haddon, W. A logical framework for categorizing highway safety phenomena and activity. *J. Trauma* **1972**, *12*, 193–207. [CrossRef] [PubMed]
34. Haddon, W. Energy damage and 10 countermeasure strategies. *J. Trauma Inj. Infect. Crit. Care* **1973**, *13*, 321–331. [CrossRef] [PubMed]
35. Haddon, W. Options for the prevention of motor vehicle crash injury. *Isr. J. Med. Sci.* **1980**, *16*, 45–65.
36. Von Bertalanffy, L. *General System Theory: Foundations, Development, Applications*; Penguin: London, UK, 1968.
37. Johansson, R. Vision Zero—Implementing a policy for traffic safety. *Saf. Sci.* **2009**, *47*, 826–831. [CrossRef]
38. Larsson, P.; Dekker, S.W.; Tingvall, C. The need for a systems theory approach to road safety. *Saf. Sci.* **2010**, *48*, 1167–1174. [CrossRef]
39. Szymanek, A. System Approach in Road Safety Studies. *Commun. Sci. Lett. Univ. Zilina* **2020**, *22*, 201–210. [CrossRef]
40. Hughes, B.P.; Newstead, S.; Anund, A.; Shu, C.C.; Falkmer, T. A review of models relevant to road safety. *Accid. Anal. Prev.* **2015**, *74*, 250–270. [CrossRef]
41. Smeed, R.J. Some statistical aspects of road safety research. *J. R. Stat. Soc.* **1949**, *12*, 1–34. [CrossRef]
42. Haight, F.A. Traffic safety in developing countries. *J. Saf. Res.* **1980**, *12*, 50–58. [CrossRef]
43. Jacobs, G.D.; Cutting, C.A. Further research on accident rates in developing countries. *Accid Anal. Prev.* **1986**, *18*, 119–127. [CrossRef]
44. Nicholson, A.J.; Jadaan, K.S. A review of recent developments and current issues in road safety. *J. Traffic Med.* **1989**, *17*, 13–22.
45. Zwi, A.B.; Forjouh, S.; Murugusamphillay, S. Injuries in developing countries: Policy response needed now. *Trans. R. Soc. Trop. Med. Hyg.* **1996**, *90*, 593–595. [PubMed]
46. Murray, C.J.L.; Lopez, A.D. Mortality by cause for eight regions of the World: Global burden of disease Study. *Lancet* **1997**, *349*, 1269–1276. [CrossRef]
47. Bener, A.; Abu-Zidan, F.M.; Bensiali, A.K.; Al-Mulla, A.A.; Jadaan, K.S. Strategy to improve road safety in developing countries. *Saudi Med. J.* **2003**, *24*, 603–608. [PubMed]
48. Belin, M.-Å.; Tillgren, P.; Vedung, E. Vision Zero—A road safety policy innovation. *Int. J. Inj. Control Saf. Promot.* **2012**, *19*, 171–179. [CrossRef]
49. Haagsma, J.A.; Graetz, N.; Bolliger, I.; Naghavi, M.; Higashi, H.; Mullany, E.C.; Abera, S.F.; Abraham, J.P.; Adofo, K.; Alsharif, U.; et al. The global burden of injury: Incidence, mortality, disability-adjusted life years and time trends from the Global Burden of Disease study 2013. *Inj. Prev.* **2016**, *22*, 3–18. [PubMed]
50. Goniewicz, K.; Goniewicz, M.; Pawłowski, W.; Fiedor, P. Road accident rates: Strategies and programmes for improving road traffic safety. *Eur. J. Trauma Emerg. Surg.* **2016**, *42*, 433–438. [CrossRef]
51. Beck, B.; Cameron, P.A.; Fitzgerald, M.C.; Judson, R.T.; Teague, W.; Lyons, R.A.; Gabbe, B.J. Road safety: Serious injuries remain a major unsolved problem. *Med. J. Aust.* **2017**, *207*, 244–249. [CrossRef] [PubMed]
52. WHO. Available online: https://www.who.int/ (accessed on 13 August 2021).
53. Website of the International Traffic Safety Data and Analysis Group (IRTAD). Available online: https://www.itf-oecd.org/IRTAD (accessed on 14 August 2021).
54. Elvik, R.; Goel, R. Safety-in-numbers: An updated meta-analysis of estimates. *Accid. Anal. Prev.* **2019**, *129*, 136–147. [CrossRef]

55. WHO. Global Status Report on Road Safety, Geneva. 2015. Available online: http://www.who.int/violence_injury_prevention/road_traffic/en/ (accessed on 15 August 2021).
56. Blinkin, M.Y.; Reshetova, E.M. *Road Safety: The History of the Issue, International Experience, Basic Institutions*; Publishing House of the Higher School of Economics: Moscow, Russia, 2013; 240p. (In Russian)
57. Wijnen, W.; Weijermars, W.; Schoeters, A.; van den Berghe, W.; Bauer, R.; Carnis, L.; Elvik, R.; Martensen, H. An analysis of official road crash cost estimates in European countries. *Saf. Sci.* **2019**, *113*, 318–327. [CrossRef]
58. Blincoe, L.J.; Miller, T.R.; Zaloshnja, E.; Lawrence, B.A. *The Economic and Societal Impact of Motor Vehicle Crashes, 2010*; (Revised) (Report No. DOT HS 812 013); National Highway Traffic Safety Administration: Washington, DC, USA, 2015.
59. Kato, S.; Takeuchi, E.; Ishiguro, Y.; Ninomiya, Y.; Takeda, K.; Hamada, T. An Open Approach to Autonomous Vehicles. *IEEE Micro* **2015**, *35*, 60–68. [CrossRef]
60. Fagnant, D.J.; Kockelman, K. Preparing a nation for autonomous vehicles: Opportunities, barriers and policy recommendations. *Transp. Res. Part A Policy Pract.* **2015**, *77*, 167–181. [CrossRef]
61. Bonnefon, J.-F.; Shariff, A.; Rahwan, I.Y. The social dilemma of autonomous vehicles. *Science* **2016**, *352*, 1573–1576. [CrossRef]
62. Faisal, A.; Kamruzzaman, M.; Yigitcanlar, T.; Currie, G. Understanding autonomous vehicles: A systematic literature review on capability, impact, planning and policy. *J. Transp. Land Use* **2019**, *12*, 45–72. [CrossRef]
63. Hulse, L.M.; Xie, H.; Galea, E.R. Perceptions of autonomous vehicles: Relationships with road users, risk, gender and age. *Saf. Sci.* **2018**, *102*, 1–13. [CrossRef]
64. Khadaroo, J.; & Seetanah, B. The Role of Transport Infrastructure in International Tourism Development: A Gravity Model Approach. *Tour. Manag.* **2008**, *29*, 831–840. [CrossRef]
65. Kolik, A.; Radziwill, A.; Turdyeva, N. Improving Transport Infrastructure in Russia. In *OECD Economics Department Working Papers*; No. 1193; OECD Publishing: Paris, France, 2015. [CrossRef]
66. Qin, Y. China's Transport Infrastructure Investment: Past, Present, and Future. *Asian Econ. Policy Rev.* **2016**, *11*, 199–217. [CrossRef]
67. Hamed, M.M. Analysis of pedestrians' behavior at pedestrian crossings. *Saf. Sci.* **2001**, *38*, 63–82. [CrossRef]
68. Sucha, M.; Dostal, D.; Risser, R. Pedestrian-driver communication and decision strategies at marked crossings. *Accid. Anal. Prev.* **2017**, *102*, 41–50. [CrossRef]
69. Van den Elshout, S.; Molenaar, R.; Wester, B. Adaptive traffic management in cities—Comparing decision-making methods. *Sci. Total Environ.* **2014**, *488–489*, 382–388. [CrossRef]
70. Wouters, P.I.J.; Bos, J.M.J. Traffic accident reduction by monitoring driver behaviour with in-car data recorders. *Accid. Anal. Prev.* **2000**, *32*, 643–650. [CrossRef]
71. Warner, H.W.; Åberg, L. Drivers' decision to speed: A study inspired by the theory of planned behavior. *Transp. Res. Part F Traffic Psychol. Behav.* **2006**, *9*, 427–433. [CrossRef]
72. Taubman-Ben-Ari, O.; Mikulincer, M.; Gillath, O. The multidimensional driving style inventory—Scale construct and validation. *Accid. Anal. Prev.* **2004**, *36*, 323–332. [CrossRef]
73. Burger, J.M.; Cooper, H.M. The desirability of control. *Motiv. Emot.* **1979**, *3*, 381–393. [CrossRef]
74. Zuckerman, M.; Kuhlman, D.M.; Joireman, M.; Kraft, H. Five robust questionnaire scale factors of personality without culture. *Personal. Individ. Differ.* **1993**, *12*, 929–941. [CrossRef]
75. Poó, F.; Taubman-Ben-Ari, O.; Ledesma, R.; Díaz-Lázaro, C. Reliability and validity of a Spanish-language version of the multidimensional driving style inventory. *Transp. Res. Part F Traffic Psychol. Behav.* **2013**, *17*, 75–87. [CrossRef]
76. Holman, A.; Havârneanu, C. The Romanian version of the multidimensional driving style inventory: Psychometric properties and cultural specificities. *Transp. Res. Part F Traffic Psychol. Behav.* **2015**, *35*, 45–59. [CrossRef]
77. Totkova, Z.; Racheva, R. The Bulgarian Version of the Multidimensional Driving Style Inventory: Psychometric Properties. *Behav. Sci.* **2019**, *9*, 145. [CrossRef]
78. Evans, L. Risks older drivers face themselves and threats they pose to other road users. *Int. J. Epidemiol.* **2000**, *29*, 315–322. [CrossRef]
79. Bernhoft, I.M.; & Carstensen, G. Preferences and behaviour of pedestrians and cyclists by age and gender. *Transp. Res. Part F Traffic Psychol. Behav.* **2008**, *11*, 83–95. [CrossRef]
80. Gonawala, R.J.; Badami, N.B.; Electicwala, F.; Kumar, R. Impact of Elderly Road Users Characteristics at Intersection. *Procedia Soc. Behav. Sci.* **2013**, *104*, 1088–1094. [CrossRef]
81. Zaidel, D.M. A modeling perspective on the culture of driving. *Accid. Anal. Prev.* **1992**, *24*, 585–597. [CrossRef]
82. Guldenmund, F.W. The nature of safety culture: A review of theory and research. *Saf. Sci.* **2000**, *34*, 215–257.
83. Zhang, W.; Huang, Y.; Roetting, M.; Wang, Y.; Wei, H. Driver's views and behaviours about safety in China: What do they not know about driving? *Accid. Anal. Prev.* **2006**, *38*, 22–27. [PubMed]
84. Özkan, T.; Lajunen, T. Person and Environment. In *Handbook of Traffic Psychology*; Porter, B.E., Waltham, M.A., Eds.; Academic Press: London, UK, 2011; pp. 179–192. [CrossRef]
85. Gaygisiz, E. Cultural values and governance quality as correlates of road traffic fatalities: A nation level analysis. *Accid. Anal. Prev.* **2010**, *42*, 1894–1901.
86. Horne, J.A.; Reyner, L.A. Sleep related vehicle accidents. *BMJ* **1995**, *310*, 565–567. [PubMed]
87. Strohl, K.P. Sleep apnea, sleepiness, and driving risk. *Am. J. Respir. Crit. Care Med.* **1994**, *150*, 1463.

88. Bell, M.G.H. Policy issues for the future intelligent road transport infrastructure. *IEE Proc. Intell. Transp. Syst.* **2006**, *153*, 147. [CrossRef]
89. Losurdo, F.; Dileo, I.; Siergiejczyk, M.; Krzykowska, K.; Krzykowski, M. Innovation in the ICT Infrastructure as a Key Factor in Enhancing Road Safety: A Multi-sectoral Approach. In Proceedings of the 2017 25th International Conference on Systems Engineering (ICSEng), Las Vegas, NV, USA, 22–24 August 2017; pp. 157–162. [CrossRef]
90. Hegyi, P.; Borsos, A.; Koren, C. Searching possible accident black spot locations with accident analysis and gis software based on GPS coordinates. *Pollack Period* **2017**, *12*, 129–140. [CrossRef]
91. Dereli, M.A.; Erdogan, S. A new model for determining the traffic accident black spots using GIS-aided spatial statistical methods. *Transp. Res. Part A Policy Pract.* **2017**, *103*, 106–117.
92. Al-Jameel, H.A.; AbdAbas, A.Y. Identifying black spot locations at karbala city by using GIS system. *Int. J. Civ. Eng.* **2018**, *9*, 933–938.
93. Shen, L.; Lu, J.; Long, M.; Chen, T. Identification of accident blackspots on rural roads using grid clustering and principal component clustering. *Math. Probl. Eng.* **2019**, *2019*, 2151284. [CrossRef]
94. Bisht, L.S.; Tiwari, G. Assessing the Black Spots Focused Policies for Indian National Highways. *Transp. Res. Procedia* **2019**, *48*, 2537–2549. [CrossRef]
95. Vindhya Shree, M.P.; Shashikiran, C.R.; Nandish Shanabog, C.S. Prioritization of Accident Black Spots using GIS. *Int. J. Eng. Res.* **2020**, *9*, 653–666. [CrossRef]
96. Yuan, T.; Zeng, X.; Shi, T. Identifying Urban road black spots with a novel method based on the firefly clustering algorithm and a geographic information system. *Sustainability* **2020**, *12*, 2091. [CrossRef]
97. Chen, Y.; Wang, K.; Zhang, Y.; Shi, Q. Identification of black spots on highways using fault tree analysis and vehicle safety boundaries. *J. Transp. Saf. Secur.* **2021**, *13*, 46–68. [CrossRef]
98. Almoshaogeh, M.; Abdulrehman, R.; Haider, H.; Alharbi, F.; Jamal, A.; Alarifi, S.; Shafiquzzaman, M. Traffic Accident Risk Assessment Framework for Qassim, Saudi Arabia: Evaluating the Impact of Speed Cameras. *Appl. Sci.* **2021**, *11*, 6682. [CrossRef]
99. European Accident Research and Safety Report. 2017. Available online: https://ec.europa.eu/transport/road_safety/sites/roadsafety/files/pdf/statistics/dacota/asr2017.pdf (accessed on 18 August 2021).
100. European Accident Research and Safety Report. 2018. Available online: https://ec.europa.eu/transport/road_safety/sites/roadsafety/files/pdf/statistics/dacota/asr2018.pdf (accessed on 18 August 2021).
101. Thiffault, P.; Bergeron, J. Monotony of road environment and driver fatigue: A simulator study. *Accid. Anal. Prev.* **2003**, *35*, 381–391. [CrossRef]
102. Saneinejad, S.; Roorda, M.J.; Kennedy, C. Modelling the impact of weather conditions on active transportation travel behaviour. *Transp. Res. Part D Transp. Environ.* **2012**, *17*, 129–137. [CrossRef]
103. Chu, W.; Wu, C.; Atombo, C.; Zhang, H.; Özkan, T. Traffic climate, driver behaviour, and accidents involvement in China. *Accid. Anal. Prev.* **2019**, *122*, 119–126. [CrossRef]
104. Horowitz, R.; Varaiya, P. Control design of an automated highway system. *Proc. IEEE* **2000**, *88*, 913–925. [CrossRef]
105. Giannopoulos, G. The application of information and communication technologies in transport. *Eur. J. Oper. Res.* **2004**, *152*, 302–320. [CrossRef]
106. Hamdi, S.; Faiedh, H.; Souani, C.; Besbes, K. Road signs classification by ANN for real-time implementation. In Proceedings of the 2017 International Conference on Control, Automation and Diagnosis (ICCAD), Hammamet, Tunisia, 19–21 January 2017; pp. 328–332. [CrossRef]
107. Michon, J.A. A Critical View of Driver Behavior Models: What Do We Know, What Should We Do? In *Human Behavior and Traffic Safety*; Evans, L., Schwing, R.C., Eds.; Springer: Boston, MA, USA, 1985.
108. Dingil, A.E.; Esztergár-Kiss, D. The Influence of the Covid-19 Pandemic on Mobility Patterns: The First Wave's Results. *Transp. Lett.* **2021**, *13*, 434–446. [CrossRef]
109. Cho, S.-H.; Park, H.-C. Exploring the Behaviour Change of Crowding Impedance on Public Transit due to COVID-19 Pandemic: Before and After Comparison. *Transp. Lett.* **2021**, *13*, 367–374. [CrossRef]
110. Velmurugan, S.; Mukti, A.; Padma, S. Impacts of COVID-19 on the Transport Sector and Measures as Well as Recommendations of Policies and Future Research: Report on India. 27 September 2020. [CrossRef]
111. Catchpole, J.; Naznin, F. Impact of COVID-19 on Road Crashes in Australia. Available online: https://www.arrb.com.au/latest-research/report-reveals-facts-about-covid-19-lockdown-road-crashes (accessed on 16 August 2021).
112. Katrakazas, C.; Michelaraki, E.; Sekadakis, M.; Yannis, G. A descriptive analysis of the effect of the COVID-19 pandemic on driving behavior and road safety. *Transp. Res. Interdiscip. Perspect.* **2020**, *7*, 100186. [CrossRef]
113. Budd, L.; Ison, S. Responsible transport: A post-COVID agenda for transport policy and practice. *Transp. Res. Interdiscip. Perspect.* **2020**, *6*, 100151. [CrossRef]
114. Kolesov, V.I. Dynamic characteristics of the innovation process based on the generalized golden section. In *Innovations in the Management of Regional and Sectoral Development*; TIU: Tyumen, Russia, 2019; pp. 121–127. (In Russian)
115. Soroko, E.M. *Structural Harmony of Systems*; Science and Technology: Minsk, Belarus, 1984; 264p. (In Russian)
116. Soroko, E.M. *The Criterion of Harmony of Self-Organizing Socio-Natural Systems*; Scientific Report; Institute of the Noosphere of the Far Eastern Branch of the USSR Academy of Sciences: Vladivostok, Russia, 1989; 83p. (In Russian)

117. Kolesov, V.I. Criterion of system harmony. In *New Information Technologies in the Oil and Gas Industry and Education*; TIU: Tyumen, Russia, 2019; pp. 206–212. (In Russian)
118. Shastova, G.A. *Choice and Optimization of the Structure of Information Systems*; Energia: Moscow, Russia, 1972; 256p. (In Russian)
119. Prangishvili, I.V. Problems of effective management of complex socio-economic and organizational systems. *Prop. Relat. Russ. Fed.* **2006**, *11*, 82–86. (In Russian)
120. Ivanus, A.I. *Fundamentals of Harmonious Management (the Concept of F-Technology)*; V.A. Trapeznikov's Institute of Management Problems, RAS: Moscow, Russia, 2004; 82p. (In Russian)
121. Kornai, Y. System paradigm. *Soc. Econ.* **1999**, *3–4*, 85–96. (In Russian)
122. Stepin, V.S. Self-developing systems and post-non-classical rationality. *Quest. Philos.* **2003**, *8*, 5–17. (In Russian)
123. Kleiner, G.B. System paradigm and system management. *Russ. J. Manag.* **2008**, *6*, 27–50. (In Russian)
124. Kolesov, V.I. Reference systems in the metric of the generalized golden s-section. In *New Information Technologies in the Oil and Gas Industry and Education*; TIU: Tyumen, Russia, 2020; pp. 11–17. (In Russian)
125. Popov, S.A. *The Concept of Actual Strategic Management for Modern Russian Companies*; Yurayt Publishing House: Moscow, Russia, 2020; 223p. (In Russian)
126. Drucker, P.F. The theory of business. *Harv. Bus. Rev.* **1994**, *72*, 95–104.
127. Krutov, V.I.; Glushko, I.M.; Popov, V.V. *Fundamentals of Scientific Research*; Higher School: Moscow, Russia, 1989; 400p. (In Russian)

*Article*

# Impact of COVID-19 on the Robustness of the Probability of Default Estimation Model

Ming-Chin Hung [1,*], Yung-Kang Ching [2] and Shih-Kuei Lin [3]

1 Department of Financial Engineering and Actuarial Mathematics, Soochow University, Taipei 100, Taiwan
2 Risk Management Development, China Development Financial Holding, Taipei 105, Taiwan; stevenching0729@gmail.com
3 Department of Money and Banking, National Chengchi University, Taipei 116, Taiwan; square@nccu.edu.tw
* Correspondence: nhungg@scu.edu.tw

**Abstract:** Probability of default (PD) estimation is essential to the calculation of expected credit loss under the Basel III framework and the International Financial Reporting Standard 9. Gross domestic product (GDP) growth has been adopted as a key determinant in PD estimation models. However, PD models with a GDP covariate may not perform well under aberrant (i.e., outlier) conditions such as the COVID-19 pandemic. This study explored the robustness of a PD model with a GDP determinant (the test model) in comparison with that of a PD model with a credit default swap index (CDX) determinant (the alternative model). The test model had a significantly greater ratio of increase in Akaike information criterion than the alternative model in comparisons of the fit performance of models including 2020 data with that of models excluding 2020 data (i.e., that do not cover the COVID-19 pandemic). Furthermore, the Cook's distance of the 2020 data of the test model was significantly greater than that of the alternative model. Therefore, the test model exhibited a serious robustness issue in outlier scenarios, such as the COVID-19 pandemic, whereas the alternative model was more robust. This finding opens the prospect for the CDX to potentially serve as an alternative to GDP in PD estimation models.

**Keywords:** Anscombe's quartet; Cook's distance; default rate; expected credit loss; gross domestic product

**Citation:** Hung, M.-C.; Ching, Y.-K.; Lin, S.-K. Impact of COVID-19 on the Robustness of the Probability of Default Estimation Model. *Mathematics* **2021**, *9*, 3087. https://doi.org/10.3390/math9233087

Academic Editors: Lina Novickytė, Jolanta Drozdz, Radosław Pastusiak and Michał Soliwoda

Received: 7 November 2021
Accepted: 27 November 2021
Published: 30 November 2021

**Publisher's Note:** MDPI stays neutral with regard to jurisdictional claims in published maps and institutional affiliations.

**Copyright:** © 2021 by the authors. Licensee MDPI, Basel, Switzerland. This article is an open access article distributed under the terms and conditions of the Creative Commons Attribution (CC BY) license (https://creativecommons.org/licenses/by/4.0/).

## 1. Introduction

Credit risk is generally understood as the potential that a borrower or counterparty will fail to meet its contractual obligations. Banks need to estimate the probability of such events occurring and set aside capital to absorb contingent losses. Loan loss provision estimates are constantly updated based on the bank's potential customer defaults. These estimates are usually calculated based on a probability of default (PD) model, as applied to historical default data. Credit risk evaluation is crucial not only for internal credit decisions but also for regulatory purposes (BCBS [1,2]). In July 2014, the International Accounting Standards Board (IASB) issued the final version of the International Financial Reporting Standard 9 (IFRS 9)—Financial Instruments. The IFRS 9 introduced an expected credit loss (ECL) framework concerning how banks should recognize and manage potential credit losses for financial statement–reporting purposes. IFRS 9 defines principles but grants freedom in choosing which models and approaches banks use to estimate their potential losses. These estimates are then used to determine how much capital is to be set aside as buffers against loss. This ECL practice is aligned with internal ratings–based regulatory practices for determining financial institutions' regulatory capital requirements in Basel III.

Effective from 1 January 2018, the IFRS 9 mandates for the measurement of impairment loss allowances to be based on a forward-looking ECL accounting model rather than on an incurred loss accounting model. The ECL model, which incorporates current and predicted macroeconomic factors, such as expectations in changes in the GDP growth rate, is designed to yield more accurate predictions of credit losses. As a standard of financial reporting purposes, however, the ECL model can result in volatile credit loss estimation following unexpected events, such as the COVID-19 pandemic.

The income information statement from the Barclays Group 2nd Quarter Financial Report provides an example of this (Figure 1). It stated that a total of £1097 million in profit in Q419 decreased to £359 million in Q220. Conversely, the credit impairment charge increased more than fourfold, from £523 million, in Q419, to £2115 million, in Q120. In Q220, it remained substantially higher than that at Q419, at £1623 million. After Q220, the amount accrued decreased back to £608 million in Q320 and £492 million in Q420. Moreover, due to the economic recovery from the COVID-19 pandemic, £797 million of credit impairment was released in Q221 and the single-quarter profit thus increased to £2580 million. The point-in-time characteristics of forward-looking ECL estimation resulted in great volatility in the bank's profit data.

### Barclays Group

| Income statement information | Q221 £m | Q121 £m | Q420 £m | Q320 £m | Q220 £m | Q120 £m | Q419 £m | Q319 £m |
|---|---|---|---|---|---|---|---|---|
| Net interest income | 2,052 | 1,851 | 1,845 | 2,055 | 1,892 | 2,331 | 2,344 | 2,445 |
| Net fee, commission and other income | 3,363 | 4,049 | 3,096 | 3,149 | 3,446 | 3,952 | 2,957 | 3,096 |
| Total income | 5,415 | 5,900 | 4,941 | 5,204 | 5,338 | 6,283 | 5,301 | 5,541 |
| Credit impairment releases/(charges) | 797 | (55) | (492) | (608) | (1,623) | (2,115) | (523) | (461) |
| Net operating income | 6,212 | 5,845 | 4,449 | 4,596 | 3,715 | 4,168 | 4,778 | 5,080 |
| Operating costs | (3,587) | (3,545) | (3,480) | (3,391) | (3,310) | (3,253) | (3,308) | (3,293) |
| UK bank levy | — | — | (299) | — | — | — | (226) | — |
| Litigation and conduct | (66) | (33) | (47) | (76) | (20) | (10) | (167) | (1,568) |
| Total operating expenses | (3,653) | (3,578) | (3,826) | (3,467) | (3,330) | (3,263) | (3,701) | (4,861) |
| Other net income/(expenses) | 21 | 132 | 23 | 18 | (26) | 8 | 20 | 27 |
| Profit before tax | 2,580 | 2,399 | 646 | 1,147 | 359 | 913 | 1,097 | 246 |
| Tax charge | (263) | (496) | (163) | (328) | (42) | (71) | (189) | (269) |
| Profit/(loss) after tax | 2,317 | 1,903 | 483 | 819 | 317 | 842 | 908 | (23) |
| Non-controlling interests | (15) | (4) | (37) | (4) | (21) | (16) | (42) | (4) |
| Other equity instrument holders | (194) | (195) | (226) | (204) | (206) | (221) | (185) | (265) |
| Attributable profit/(loss) | 2,108 | 1,704 | 220 | 611 | 90 | 605 | 681 | (292) |

**Figure 1.** Barclays Group 2nd quarter income statement information at 30 June 2021 [3]. Data source: Barclays Group Quarterly result summary of 2nd quarter Financial report at 30 June 2021.

Barclays' credit cost percentage, which is defined as the credit impairment cost divided by total income, is illustrated in Figure 2. Between Q319 and Q221, the credit cost percentage changed considerably, with a high of 34% ($\approx 2115/6283$), in Q120, and a low of $-15\%$ ($\approx -797/5415$), in Q221. The ECL method was designed to improve the accuracy of credit cost predictions. However, when one considers the accounting principle of matching cost with revenue, excessive change in the credit cost percentage can confound inter-period analysis and confuse investors.

**Figure 2.** Barclays Group credit cost percentage (credit impairment cost divided by total income), Q319 to Q221.

Motivated by observing the fluctuated credit impairment estimation and credit cost percentage exhibited in Figures 1 and 2, the main aim of this paper is to explore the robustness of the PD model with a GDP determinant. ECL is generally calculated as the PD-weighted average of credit losses, specifically ECL = PD × (exposure at default) × (loss given default). A key factor generally adopted in a PD model is GDP growth. However, this approach may lead to dramatic changes in accounting or financial profit and loss and, thus, result in excessive fluctuations in ECL estimates. As noted, this phenomenon was especially evident during the COVID-19 pandemic in 2020. In this paper, we also explore the usage of a credit default swap index (CDX) determinant in a PD model in place of a GDP determinant to reach a less volatile credit loss estimation. The remainder of this paper is structured as follows: Section 2 reviews the literature on the PD model. Section 3 describes the empirical results of PD models with versus without the COVID-19 data. Section 4 concludes the paper.

## 2. Literature Review

The Basel III framework and the IFRS 9 were introduced following the financial crisis and European debt crisis. Basel III regulates bank capital, whereas IFRS 9 specifies how banks should classify their assets and estimate their future credit losses. Under IFRS 9, as a part of lifetime ECL calculations for stage 2 credit assets, banks must estimate multiperiod lifetime PDs. Under the Basel accord, PDs are commonly estimated as through-the-cycle to neutralize economic fluctuations and achieve lower volatility in credit risk capital requirements. Conversely, under the IFRS 9, PD estimates should be point-in-time and include forward-looking information, especially for macroeconomic forecasts [4,5]. The COVID-19 pandemic is the first stressful economic scenario since the implementation of IFRS 9 in 2018. In this study, we focus on the effect of COVID-19 on the robustness of PD estimation.

### 2.1. Logistic Regression PD Model

PDs are of interest to practitioners in financial institutions, as well as to regulators. Logistic regression has been widely adopted for PD models because of its simplicity and amenability to intuition and explanation (Crook et al. [6]). For example, one of the most popular credit risk models is the credit portfolio view model, which is analyzed using logistic regression and contains macroeconomic factors, such as the GDP, as the systematic explanatory variables.

Logistic regression is a common classification method when the response variable is binary, such as whether a default or nondefault occurs. A sound logistic regression model should feature high interpretability, high predictive power, and robustness to data outliers and default sparsity. Given a binary response variable $L$ and a set of covariates $x$, the basic setup of the logistic regression model is as follows: Conditional on $x$, the response variable $L$ is assumed to be Bernoulli distributed; that is, $L|x \sim Bernoulli\ (p)$ for some $p \in [0,1]$. The goal of logistic regression is to fit a predictive model for the binary response variable. Let the random variable $L_{i,t}$ be defined as:

$$L_{i,t} = \begin{cases} 1, & \text{default in } i^{\text{th}} \text{ loan at year } t \\ 0, & \text{no default in } i^{\text{th}} \text{ loan at year } t \end{cases}$$

and the PD for a rating class in the same year is assumed to be constant. The observation of $n_t$ credit exposures can be written as

$$L_t \equiv (L_{1,t}, \cdots, L_{i,t}, \cdots, L_{n_t,t}) \text{ with } L_{i,t}|x_t \sim Bernoulli(1; p_t),\ i = 1, \cdots, n_t.$$

In the case of binomial data, the random variables $L_{1,t}, \cdots, L_{i,t}, \cdots, L_{n_t,t}$ are assumed to be independent and $Y_t$, the number of defaults observed, is defined as:

$$Y_t \equiv L_{1,t} + L_{2,t} + \cdots + L_{n_t,t}.$$

As $L_{1,t}, \cdots, L_{i,t}, \cdots, L_{n_t,t}$ are $n_t$ independent and identically distributed trials, it can be inferred that, conditional on $x_t$, $Y_t$ follows the binomial distribution

$$Y_t|x_t \sim binomial(n_t; p_t), \quad t = 1, \cdots, T,$$

where $T$ is the number of years in the default data set. By utilizing the logit relationship

$$logit(p_t) = \ln \frac{p_t}{1-p_t} = \beta' x_t,$$

in terms of the logistic density function, the conditional probability of default number at year $t$ is

$$\begin{aligned} P(Y_t = y | x_t; \beta) &= \binom{n_t}{y} p_t^y (1-p_t)^{n_t-y} \\ &= \binom{n_t}{y} \left(\frac{1}{1+e^{-\beta' x_t}}\right)^y \left(1 - \frac{1}{1+e^{-\beta' x_t}}\right)^{n_t-y} \end{aligned} \quad (1)$$

The likelihood function, assuming that all the observations $(Y_1, Y_2, \cdots, Y_T)$ are independent and binomially distributed, is defined as

$$Lik(\beta|y;x) = \prod_{t=1}^{T} P(y_t|x_t;\beta),$$

and the log-likelihood function that is defined as

$$\ell(\beta|y;x) \equiv \log Lik(\beta|y;x) = \sum_{t=1}^{T} P(y_t|x_t;\beta) \quad (2)$$

is maximized using various optimization techniques, such as the gradient descent method. Furthermore, the associated Akaike information criterion (AIC) is defined as

$$AIC = 2k - 2 \log \hat{Lik}(\cdot), \quad (3)$$

where $k$ is the number of model parameters and $\log \hat{Lik}(\cdot)$ is the maximum value of the log-likelihood function in Equation (2). As the equation expresses a property of the penalty (negative) function, a smaller AIC value suggests a better fit.

### 2.2. PD Model with a GDP Determinant

This study primarily aimed to explore the robustness of a PD model with a GDP covariate versus that of a PD model with a CDX covariate. Estimating PDs is challenging due to the limited availability of data and the sparsity of defaults. We explored the logit model with GDP growth as a macroeconomic parameter. The relationship between PD and various macroeconomic variables has been modeled in many applications. Most of the papers discussed in this subsection have demonstrated that GDP growth is significantly related to the default rate (DR).

For the banking sector, Jabra [7] used a binomial logit model and demonstrated how much bank default in the European banking system can be explained, not only by CAMELS (capital adequacy, asset quality, management quality, earnings potential, liquidity, and sensitivity to market risk) variables, but also by GDP growth. Bonjini et al. [8] discovered that bank defaults in developing countries increase with the severity of macroeconomic shocks. Arena [9] and Männasoo and Mayes [10] demonstrated that increased GDP growth (as a macroeconomic indicator) significantly reduced bank PD. Ortolano and Angelini [11] noted that the highest correlation between PD and various adopted GDP covariates was $-24\%$. The negative value corroborated the finding of a relationship between GDP and banking credit risk assessment reported by Jabra, Mighri, and Mansouri [12].

With regard to the corporate sector, Simons and Rolwes [13] provided robust evidence for a relationship between macroeconomic variables and GDP growth in the default behavior of Dutch firms. This observation led to the implementation of econometric models that describe PD in terms of macroeconomic variables. Couderc and Renault [14] demonstrated that GDP growth is a significant macroDR of firms listed in the Standard and Poor's 500 index and Jakubik [15] demonstrated the same for Finnish firms in 1988–2003 in addition to reporting that interest rate was a nonsignificant macroeconomic variable. By studying the relationship between the credit cycle and macroeconomic variables using data on the rating changes and defaults of US corporations, Koopman et al. [16] demonstrated that many of the variables that were conventionally thought to explain the credit cycle were nonsignificant, with the exception of GDP growth. Virolainen [17] used Finnish data and reported a significant relationship between corporate sector DR and several macroeconomic factors, including GDP. Using data on nonfinancial corporate bond DRs over 150 years, Giesecke et al. [18] studied the relationship between credit default and macroeconomic variables and determined that change in GDP is a strong predictor of DR. Penikas [19] reported that default correlation tends to align with systemic factors, such as the GDP growth rate.

## 2.3. Robustness of a Model

Anscombe [20] constructed four data sets that yielded the exact same linear regression outputs, namely, the number of observations, mean of the independent variable, mean of the dependent variable, estimated regression coefficient, regression sum of squares, residual sum of squares, estimated standard error of the regression coefficient, and coefficient of determination. However, the four data sets had different characteristics due to the presence of various types of outliers. Intuitively, an outlier is an observation that appears to be "different" from other observations in a data set. An outlier can come in one of three forms: (a) outlier with respect to the dependent variable; (b) outlier with respect to the independent variable (a leverage point); and (c) outlier with respect to both the dependent and independent variables. An outlier can be influential or not influential. An influential observation is an observation whose inclusion in the data set would greatly change the analytical result.

To measure the degree of influence the $i$th data point has on the analytical result, a natural step is to compute the difference in the fitted results when the $i$th data point is included and when it is excluded. Cook's distance [21] is based on such an idea for a generalized linear model. An approximation of Cook's distance measure of influence has also been also formulated (Fox [22]). Outliers can distort estimates of binary logit models and linear regression models. In this study, logistic regression diagnostics were performed using the statsmodels package [23] in Python [24]. This measure was computed based on a one-step approximation of the results after one observation was deleted. The diagnostic analytics can also be conducted by means of the local influence method [25].

## 2.4. CDX as a Determinant in the PD Model

All the studies reviewed in Section 2.2 demonstrated a significant negative relationship between DR and GDP growth. However, using an estimation framework presentation of lifetime PD in accordance with the IFRS 9, Đurović [26] reported that the state of the macroeconomy had a small effect on PD development. He argued that PD development is mainly affected by a rapidly changing marketplace and a constant increase in the number of market participants. Obeid [27] examined data from 40 commercial banks in the Arab world and reported a nonsignificant effect of GDP on bank defaults. Chortareasab et al. [28] performed a meta-analysis of 56 empirical studies on the effect of GDP on nonperforming loans. Their results revealed that GDP performance does not have a predictable effect on credit quality.

Using a regime-switching model, Giesecke et al. [18] reported that change in GDP is a strong predictor of DRs. Surprisingly, however, they also reported that credit spreads do not adjust to current DRs or macroeconomic conditions. Conversely, in studying the effect of credit default swap (CDS) spread determinants on the probability of default, Ortolano and Angelini [11] demonstrated that the price of CDSs is a sound indicator of banks' creditworthiness. By contrast, Collin-Dufresne et al. [29] demonstrated that credit spreads are driven by factors that are difficult to explain using a standard credit model. Fu et al. [30] revealed that firm performance and macroeconomic conditions play a significant role in explaining CDS spreads.

In studying the fit performance of a PD model, Hu et al. [31] concluded that high-rated companies exhibit a greater need to use market-traded information, such as the CDX, to capture changes in the DR. The similarities and differences between this paper and that of Hu et al. [31] are as follows. A logistic regression model was used as the underlying PD model in both papers. In addition, Moody's DR and the IMF's GDP datasets were used in both papers with different time periods. The paper from Hu et al. [31] was motivated by observing the poorly fitted results of the PD model with GDP determinants, whereas this paper is motivated by observing the extreme mismatch between the behaviour of GDP and DR over 2020. The main criteria of model comparison used by Hu et al. [31] were $p$ values and AIC, whereas we primarily use Cook's distance and AIC increasing ratio (see Section 3.2). The empirical results registered by Hu et al. [31] related to goodness-of-fit, especially for the companies from higher rated classes, whereas we, mainly, have determined the impact on PD and, thus, ECL estimation through outlier observation. In other words, the results of the PD model (with GDP determinant) revealed a serious lack of robustness in the 2020 data originating from COVID-19.

To explore the robustness of the PD model with a GDP determinant, we compared the fitted results and influence measures of a PD model using a GDP covariate to that of a PD model using a CDX covariate in the following empirical study.

## 3. Data and Empirical Results

### 3.1. Data Descriptions

This study used GDP growth data from the International Monetary Fund (IMF) and corporate DRs by letter rating from a data set of Moody's for 2004–2020. The index of investment grade (Baa and higher) credit default swaps (CDX.NA.IG) starts from 2004, whereas the index of high yield (Ba and lower) credit default swaps (CDX.NA.HY) starts from 2006. To compare the PD fit performance, the same data period were used for both the GDP and CDX explanatory variables. In addition, because defaults are rare among the highest-rated credit entities, the analysis was restricted to the rating classes $r$ = [A, Baa, Ba, B].

The descriptive statistics and kernel density estimates of DRs and GDP growth are illustrated in Table 1 and Figure 3. GDP growth, in Table 1 and the left panel of Figure 3, indicates left-skewed distributions with significant negative skew-test statistics and $p$ values of 0.001. Conversely, the DRs of all ratings in the right panel of Figure 3 are all positive, right-skew-distributed with $p$ values close to zero. This phenomenon aligns with the reverse relationship between macroeconomic factors (such as GDP) and DRs.

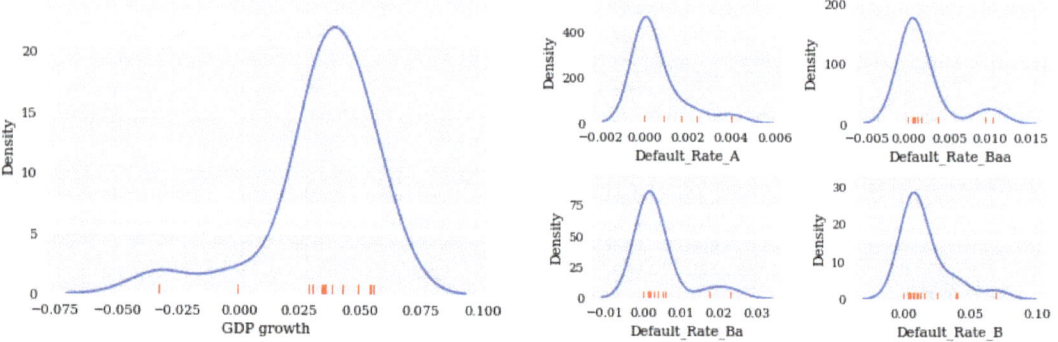

**Figure 3.** Kernel density estimates of GDP growth rate (**left panel**) and default rates (**right panel**) for ratings A, Baa, Ba, and B.

**Table 1.** Descriptive statistics of GDP and default rates for ratings A, Baa, Ba, and B.

| Rating (GDP) | A [1] | Baa | Ba | B | GDP-gr [2] |
|---|---|---|---|---|---|
| Count | 17 | 17 | 17 | 17 | 17 |
| Mean | 0.0006 | 0.0018 | 0.0040 | 0.0157 | 0.0344 |
| Std | 0.0011 | 0.0032 | 0.0065 | 0.0180 | 0.0220 |
| Min | 0.0000 | 0.0000 | 0.0000 | 0.0000 | −0.0330 |
| 25% | 0.0000 | 0.0000 | 0.0000 | 0.0049 | 0.0343 |
| (Median) | 0.0000 | 0.0007 | 0.0014 | 0.0081 | 0.0359 |
| 75% | 0.0009 | 0.0012 | 0.0038 | 0.0157 | 0.0491 |
| Max | 0.0040 | 0.0103 | 0.0232 | 0.0687 | 0.0556 |
| Skew | 2.20 | 2.26 | 2.38 | 2.00 | −2.08 |
| Skew_test | 3.42 | 3.49 | 3.62 | 3.19 | −3.28 |
| $p$-value of skew test | 0.0006 | 0.0005 | 0.0003 | 0.0014 | 0.0010 |

Data sources: [1] Moody's Default Reports [32]; [2] IMF, real GDP growth [33].

As illustrated in Figure 4, GDP (red line) was slightly negatively correlated with DR. Two of the most liquid CDX indices were the CDX.NA.IG and CDX.NA.HY. The daily data of the CDX.NA.IG (since 2004) and CDX.NA.HY (since 2006) are displayed in Figure 5, and the trends for the two indexes run in opposite directions. This was because high-yield CDS indices (dotted red line) are conventionally quoted in prices, whereas investment-grade equivalents are quoted in spread basis points.

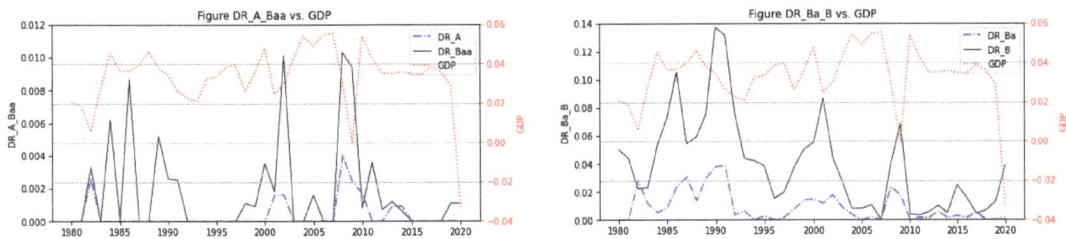

**Figure 4.** Time series of GDP (see **right** y-axis) and DRs (see **left** y-axis) for ratings A and Baa (**left panel**) and for ratings Ba and B (**right panel**).

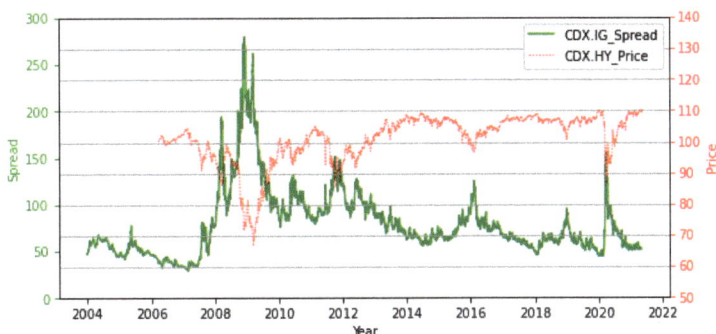

**Figure 5.** CDX.NA.IG (spread) and CDX.NA.HY (price). Data sources: Datastream database and Bloomberg.

## 3.2. Empirical Results

Figures 6–9 present the fitted curves (left panels) and Cook's distances (right panels) of the binomial logistic regression for ratings A, Baa, Ba, and B, respectively. For both the left and right panels in Figures 6–9, the left subplots (a) and (c) illustrate the PD model with the GDP covariate (the test model), whereas the right subplots (b) and (d) illustrate the PD model with the CDX covariate (alternative model). To explore the robustness of PD estimation following the COVID-19 pandemic in 2020, we fitted the PD model and calculated the AIC (displayed in the left panel as a legend) and influence measures (displayed in the right panel) for the regression of DR on GDP and on CDX with two data sets, both excluding the 2020 data point (subplots (a) and (b)) and including the 2020 data point (subplots (c) and (d)). We fitted the DRs of the investment rating classes [A, Baa] on the CDX.NA.IG index and fit the DRs of the noninvestment ratings [Ba, B] on the CDX.NA.HY index. For demonstrative purposes and due to data limitations, we used the CDX annual average to fit Moody's annual DRs.

Starting from the probability density function in Equation (1), we used maximum likelihood estimation (MLE) and the associated AIC in Equation (3) to select the best-fitting logistic regression model for historical DRs. The results were obtained using MLE and the expectation–maximization algorithm, as implemented in the statsmodels fitting procedure in Python.

### 3.2.1. Comparison of Fitted Curves in the Left Panels and Cook's Distance in the Right Panels

As evident in the left panels of Figures 6–9, the fitted curve in subplot (a) flattened to a near-horizontal curve in subplot (c). In other words, compared with the fit in subplot (a) of Figures 6–9, the marked 2020 data point was dominant and flattened the fitted curve in the lower-left subplot (c). This demonstrates that the PD model with a GDP determinant was not robust for data after the COVID-19 pandemic. The 2020 data point, illustrated in the left panels of Figures 6–9, was an outlier due to its negative value (−3.3%) and was an influential observation (having a high leverage point). This phenomenon occurs in one of the outlier cases in Anscombe's quartet. Conversely, such non-robustness was not evident in the alternative models illustrated in subplots (b) and (d).

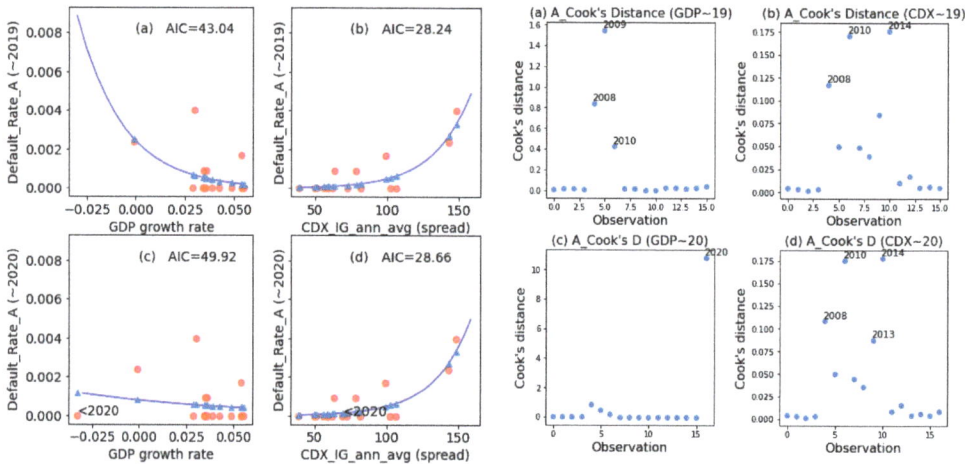

**Figure 6.** Fitted logistic regression models (**left panel**) and Cook's distances (**right panel**) of default rate in relation to (**a**) GDP in 2004–2019 data; (**b**) CDX.NA.IG in 2004–2019 data; (**c**) GDP in 2004–2020 data; and (**d**) CDX.NA.IG in 2004–2020 data (spread) for A class ratings.

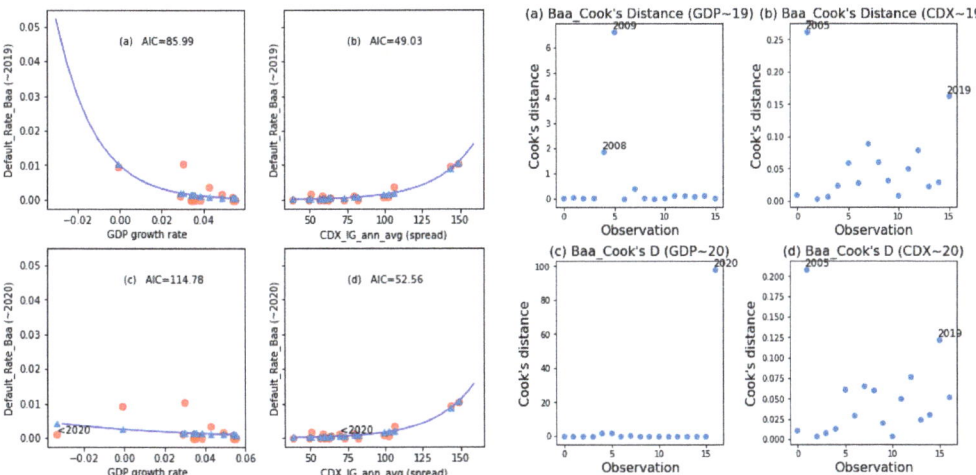

**Figure 7.** Fitted logistic regression models (**left panel**) and Cook's distances (**right panel**) of default rate in relation to (**a**) GDP in 2004–2019 data; (**b**) CDX.NA.IG in 2004–2019 data; (**c**) GDP in 2004–2020 data; and (**d**) CDX.NA.IG in 2004–2020 data (spread) for Baa class ratings.

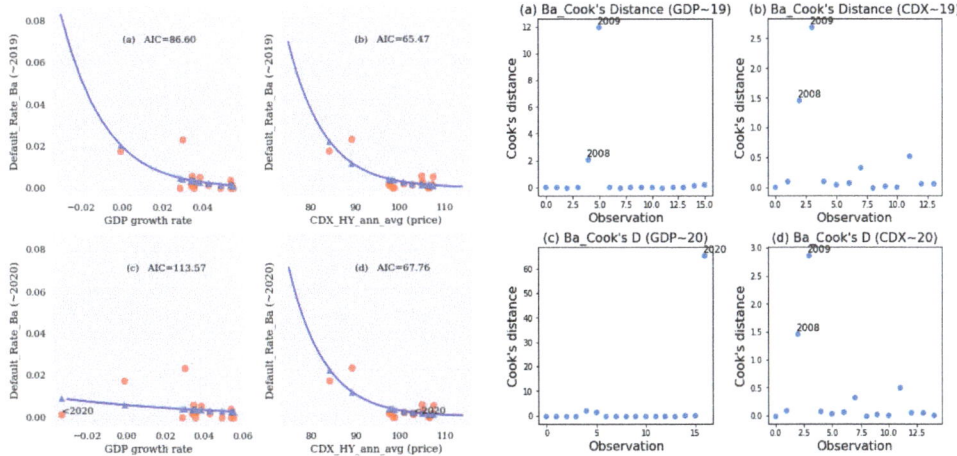

**Figure 8.** Fitted logistic regression models (**left panel**) and Cook's distances (**right panel**) of default rate in relation to (**a**) GDP in 2006–2019 data; (**b**) CDX.NA.HY in 2006–2019 data; (**c**) GDP in 2006–2020 data; and (**d**) CDX.NA.HY in 2006–2020 data (price) for Ba class ratings.

For Figures 6–9, the fitted curve of subplot (c), in the left panel, echoes the high Cook's distance of that 2020 data point in the upper right corner of subplot (c), in the right panel. Note that, in the right panel of Figures 6–9, the scales substantially differ between subplots (a) and (c). As an example, consider rating A in Figure 6. The y-axis range in subplot (a) for GDP (data through 2019) is narrow at (0, 1.6) in contrast to the wide range of (0, 10) for GDP (data through 2020) in subplot (c). For the test model, the 2020 data point (located in the upper right corner of subplot (c) in the right panel) had an influence value of 11. By contrast, the 2020 data point in subplot (d) for the alternative model only had an influence number of 0.0083, which is not influential in the model fitting process. A similar pattern could be observed for the ratings Baa, Ba, and B.

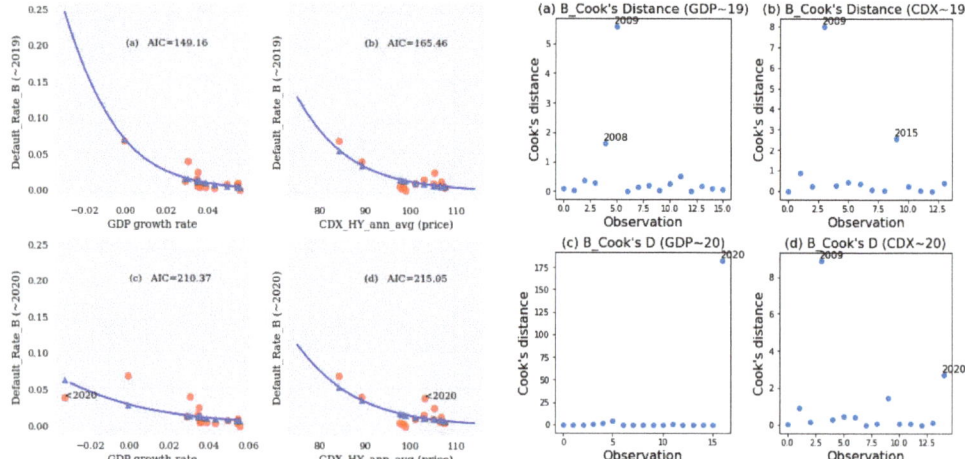

**Figure 9.** Fitted logistic regression models (**left panel**) and Cook's distances (**right panel**) of default rate in relation to (**a**) GDP in 2006–2019 data; (**b**) CDX.NA.HY in 2006–2019 data; (**c**) GDP in 2006–2020 data; and (**d**) CDX.NA.HY in 2006–2020 data (price) for B class ratings.

3.2.2. Comparison of Ratio of Increase of AIC

The property of the penalty function implies that a smaller AIC value indicates a better fit. Furthermore, the length of time covered by the data (sample size) affects the calculation of the likelihood function and AIC values. The associated AIC value for the fit of each model is displayed as a legend in each subplot of the left panel in Figures 6–9. To compare the robustness between the test and alternative model following the COVID-19 pandemic, we used the concept of the (negative) rate of return in finance and defined the $\Delta AIC$ and $AIC_{increasing}$ ratio as

$$\Delta AIC = AIC_{including\ 2020\ data} - AIC_{excluding\ 2020\ data}$$

and

$$AIC_{ir} = \frac{AIC_{including\ 2020\ data} - AIC_{excluding\ 2020\ data}}{AIC_{excluding\ 2020\ data}}$$

Correspondingly, the more $AIC_{ir}$ increases from the addition of a data point to a data set, the less the robustness of the model with respect to that data point. For example, consider the GDP versus CDX determinant for the A rating in Figure 6. $AIC\_ir\_GDP\_A = (49.92 - 43.04)/43.04 = 0.16$ and $AIC\_ir\_CDX\_A = (28.66 - 28.24)/28.24 = 0.01$, which demonstrate that the alternative model is much more robust than the test model.

Table 2 contains the results for the $AIC_{ir}$ and $\Delta AIC$ of the test model versus the alternative model for ratings A, Baa, Ba, and B. Every $AIC_{ir}$ and $\Delta AIC$ of the test model, for each rating, was significantly higher than that of the alternative model. That is, the alternative model was more robust than the test model for all ratings, especially for the higher-rated classes, namely A, Baa, and Ba. As the DR of rating B in 2020 remained at the high level of 3.87% (see subplots (c,d) of the left panel of Figure 9), the difference of the ratio of increase in AIC between these two models (0.41 vs. 0.30) was not highly significant relative to the higher-rated classes. This phenomenon may be because the target to buyback from the quantitative easing (QE) policy primarily centers on higher-rated bonds.

**Table 2.** $AIC_{ir}$ and $\Delta AIC$ for the PD model with a GDP determinant versus the PD model with a CDX determinant.

| Determinants in PD Model Ratings | $AIC_{ir}$ | | $\Delta AIC$ | |
|---|---|---|---|---|
| | GDP | CDX | GDP | CDX |
| A | 0.16 | 0.01 | 6.88 | 0.42 |
| Baa | 0.33 | 0.07 | 28.79 | 3.53 |
| Ba | 0.31 | 0.03 | 26.97 | 2.29 |
| B | 0.41 | 0.30 | 61.21 | 49.59 |

## 4. Conclusions and Remarks

Overall, the test model functioned well for normal economic conditions (with data through 2019) but was less robust following the COVID-19 pandemic. The test model had a considerably greater ratio of increase in the AIC than the alternative model in comparisons of fit performance when the 2020 data point (representing the onset of the COVID-19 pandemic) was included versus when it was excluded. Furthermore, the Cook's distance of the 2020 data point of the test model was significantly greater than that of the alternative model. In conclusion, the test model exhibited serious problems with robustness in terms of outliers, such as a global pandemic, especially for high-rated classes, whereas the alternative model was much more robust. These findings echo those of a recent IMF working paper (Roch and Roldán [34]) that examined why countries have issued sovereign state–contingent bonds on only a modest scale and traded them at a large discount, despite the well-known benefits discussed in the literature. They discovered that, for state-contingent bond structures such as the GDP-linked bond issued by Argentina in 2005, a model lacking robustness generates ambiguity premia in bond spreads that are labeled as novelty premia. Their findings rationalize the scarcity of state-contingent debt instruments in practice. A PD model of sovereign default with robustness is required to avoid the novelty premium and increase market liquidity.

The impact of the 2020 data point in this analysis is similar to that of a case introduced in Anscombe's Quartet [20], which indicates that a model fit is predominantly determined by an influential data point. In the present case, we determined that the PD model based on GDP growth was non-robust after the COVID-19 pandemic's commencement on the basis of an additional data point in 2020 (applied to each rating group). However, in the theoretical sense, the 2020 data point involved an observation of a binomial distribution with parameters $(n_t; p_t)$, which was formed from $n_t$ Bernoulli trials (default or nondefault) with $n_t$ as the number of the rated companies in 2020 for each rating class. From a practical perspective, on the other aspect, the ECL estimation occurred on both monthly and quarterly bases (e.g., see Figure 1). However, in this paper, the reported results were based only on the yearly observations due to the data availability constraints of the DRs. The DRs in 2020 were presumably lower than they would have been if governments had not intervened. Therefore, the 2020 DRs may not reflect the true economic situation indicated by the GDP drop. The problem is that whether (and if so, when) government support programs, such as QE, will intervene in the market is unknown.

One limitation of this study is the use of a single-factor model instead of a multi-factor model because our main purpose was to illustrate the robustness of using a GDP versus CDX determinant in a PD model. Furthermore, the analyzed data represented default only as a binary variable (default or nondefault). However, especially within the Basel framework, banks use rating systems with multiple rating grades. Using multiple rating grades would force the adjustment of default probabilities as well as the consideration of the transition probabilities between rating grades. Therefore, future studies can use Markov chains to capture this phenomenon. Furthermore, our PD estimation was based on realized GDP growth. However, the difference between predicted and realized GDP growth may lead to greater fluctuation in the estimation of credit loss. For example,

IMF-predicted 2020 GDP growth was less than −5%, in contrast to the realized −3.3% used in this study. The use of the predicted value in estimating ECL would have caused more serious robustness issue of the PD model. Hence, we argue that some market-based index should be introduced into the PD model. Accordingly, the fluctuating ECL scenario exhibited in Figures 1 and 2 may be at least partially resolved.

**Author Contributions:** Conceptualization, M.-C.H. and Y.-K.C.; methodology, M.-C.H. and S.-K.L.; validation, S.-K.L. and Y.-K.C.; formal analysis, Y.-K.C. and M.-C.H.; writing—original draft preparation, M.-C.H.; writing—review and editing, M.-C.H. and S.-K.L. All authors have read and agreed to the published version of the manuscript.

**Funding:** This research received no external funding.

**Institutional Review Board Statement:** Not applicable.

**Informed Consent Statement:** Not applicable.

**Data Availability Statement:** Dataset used in this study include (a) Historical default rates and GDP data are publicly available from Moody's and IMF, respectively (b) CDX.NA.IG/HY are retrieved from Datastream and Bloomberg.

**Acknowledgments:** The authors like to thank the two anonymous reviewers for their constructive comments which led to improve the manuscript.

**Conflicts of Interest:** The authors declare no conflict of interest.

## References

1. BCBS. *Consultative Document Guidelines—Guidance on Accounting for Expected Credit Losses*; 2015. Available online: https://www.bis.org/bcbs/publ/d350.pdf (accessed on 21 April 2021).
2. Skoglund, J.; Chen, W. The application of credit risk models to macroeconomic scenario analysis and stress testing. *J. Credit. Risk* **2016**, *12*. [CrossRef]
3. Barclays PLC Interim Results Announcement. 2021. Available online: https://home.barclays/content/dam/home-barclays/documents/investor-relations/ResultAnnouncements/H12021/20210728-BPLC-H12021-ResultsAnnouncement.pdf (accessed on 6 July 2021).
4. Novotny-Farkas, Z. The Significance of IFRS 9 for Financial Stability and Supervisory Rules. A Study from the European Parliament's Committee on Economic and Monetary Affairs. 2015. Available online: https://www.europarl.europa.eu/RegData/etudes/STUD/2015/563461/IPOL_STU%282015%29563461_EN.pdf (accessed on 6 July 2021).
5. Ewanchuk, L.; Frei, C. Recent Regulation in Credit Risk Management: A Statistical Framework. *Risks* **2019**, *7*, 40. [CrossRef]
6. Crook, J.N.; Edelman, D.B.; Thomas, L.C. Recent developments in consumer credit risk assessment. *Eur. J. Oper. Res.* **2007**, *183*, 1447–1465. [CrossRef]
7. Jabra, W.B. The fundamental determinants of bank default for european commercial banks. *Int. J. Res. Commer. Manag. Stud.* **2021**, *3*, 1–23.
8. Bongini, P.; Claessens, C.; Ferri, G. The Political Economy of Distress in East Asian Financial Institutions. *J. Financ. Serv. Res.* **2001**, *19*, 5–25. [CrossRef]
9. Arena, M. Bank failures and bank fundamentals: A comparative analysis of Latin America and East Asia during the nineties using bank-level data. *J. Bank. Financ.* **2008**, *32*, 299–310. [CrossRef]
10. Männasoo, K.; Mayes, D.G. Explaining bank distress in Eastern European transition economies. *J. Bank. Financ.* **2009**, *33*, 244–253. [CrossRef]
11. Ortolano, A.; Angelini, E. Do CDS Spread Determinants Affect the Probability of Default? A Study on the EU Banks. Bank I Kredyt 2020. pp. 1–32. Available online: https://bankikredyt.nbp.pl/content/2020/01/BIK_01_2020_01.pdf (accessed on 6 April 2021).
12. Ben Jabra, W.; Mighri, Z.; Mansouri, F. Determinants of European bank risk during financial crisis. *Cogent Econ. Financ.* **2017**, *5*, 2017. [CrossRef]
13. Simons, D.; Rolwes, F. Macroeconomic Default Modeling and Stress Testing. 2009. Available online: https://www.ijcb.org/journal/ijcb09q3a6.pdf (accessed on 6 July 2021).
14. Couderc, F.; Renault, O. Times-to-Default: Life Cycles, Global and Industry Cycle Impact. *FAME Res. Pap. Ser.* **2005**, *142*. Available online: https://www.researchgate.net/profile/Olivier-Renault-3/publication/5021538_Times-To-DefaultLife_Cycle_Global_and_Industry_Cycle_Impact/links/5632213208ae13bc6c3779c8/Times-To-DefaultLife-Cycle-Global-and-Industry-Cycle-Impact.pdf (accessed on 6 July 2021).
15. Jakubik, P. *Does Credit Risk Vary with Economic Cycles? The Case of Finland*; IES Working Paper No. 2006/11; Charles University Prague, Faculty of Social Sciences, Institute of Economic Studies: Prague, Czechia, 2006.

16. Koopman, S.J.; Kraussl, R.G.W.; Lucas, A.; Monteiro, A. Credit Cycles and Macro Fundamentals. Tinbergen Institute Discussion Paper. No. 06-023/2. 2006. Available online: https://papers.tinbergen.nl/06023.pdf (accessed on 14 July 2021).
17. Virolainen, K. Macro Stress Testing with a Macroeconomic Credit Risk Model for Finland, Bank of Finland Discussion Papers. 2004. Available online: https://papers.ssrn.com/sol3/papers.cfm?abstract_id=622682 (accessed on 20 April 2021).
18. Giesecke, K.; Longstaff, F.A.; Schaefer, S.; Strebulaev, I. Corporate bond default risk: A 150-year perspective. *J. Financ. Econ.* **2011**, *102*, 233–250. [CrossRef]
19. Penikas, H. Why the Conservative Basel III Portfolio Credit Risk Model Underestimates Losses. Available online: http://ceur-ws.org/Vol-2795/paper7.pdf (accessed on 20 April 2021).
20. Anscombe, F.J. Graphs in Statistical Analysis. *Am. Stat.* **1973**, *27*, 17–21. [CrossRef]
21. Cook, R.D. Detection of Influential Observation in Linear Regression. *Technometrics* **1977**, *19*, 15. [CrossRef]
22. Millar, P.; Fox, J. An R and S-Plus Companion to Applied Regression. *Can. J. Sociol. Cah. Can. Sociol.* **2003**, *28*, 110. [CrossRef]
23. Python Statsmodels Package. Available online: https://www.statsmodels.org/stable/index.html (accessed on 25 April 2021).
24. Pregibon, D. Logistic Regression Diagnostics. *Ann. Stat.* **1981**, *9*, 705–724. [CrossRef]
25. Liu, Y.; Mao, G.; Leiva, V.; Liu, S.; Tapia, A. Diagnostic Analytics for an Autoregressive Model under the Skew-Normal Distribution. *Mathematics* **2020**, *8*, 693. [CrossRef]
26. Đurović, A. Macroeconomic Approach to Point in Time Probability of Default Modeling—IFRS 9 Challenges. *J. Cent. Bank. Theory Pr.* **2019**, *8*, 209–223. [CrossRef]
27. Obeid, R. Bank Failure Prediction in the Arab Region Using Logistic Regression Model. 2021. Available online: https://www.researchgate.net/publication/351308263_Bank_Failure_Prediction_in_the_Arab_Region_Using_Logistic_Regression_Model (accessed on 20 April 2021).
28. Chortareasab, G.; Magkonisc, G.; Zekented, K.M. Credit Risk and the Business Cycle: What Do We Know? International Review of Financial Analysis. January 2020, Volume 67. Available online: https://www.sciencedirect.com/science/article/abs/pii/S1057521918307579 (accessed on 6 November 2021).
29. Collin-Dufresne, P.; Goldstein, G.S.; Martin, J.S. The Determinants of Credit Spread Changes. *J. Financ.* **2001**, *56*, 2177–2207. [CrossRef]
30. Fu, X.; Li, M.C.; Molyneux, P. Credit default swap spreads: Market conditions, firm performance, and the impact of the 2007–2009 financial crisis. *Empir. Econ.* **2021**, *60*, 2203–2225. [CrossRef]
31. Hu, K.-H.; Lin, S.-K.; Ching, Y.-K.; Hung, M.-C. Goodness-of-Fit of Logistic Regression of the Default Rate on GDP Growth Rate and on CDX Indices. *Mathematics* **2021**, *9*, 1930. [CrossRef]
32. Moody's Corporation. Annual Default Study: Corporate Default and Recovery Rates, Moody's Investor Service. 2021. Available online: The-performance-of-Moodys-corporate-debt-ratings-Q1-2021-Excel-Supplement-30Apr21.xlsx (accessed on 10 May 2021).
33. IMF. Real GDP Growth. Available online: https://www.imf.org/external/datamapper/NGDP_RPCH@WEO/OEMDC/ADVEC/WEOWORLD (accessed on 10 May 2021).
34. Roch, F.; Roldán, F. Uncertainty Premia, Sovereign Default Risk, and State-Contingent Debt. *IMF Work. Pap.* **2021**, *47*. [CrossRef]

Article

# Fundamentals vs. Financialization during Extreme Events: From Backwardation to Contango, a Copper Market Analysis during the COVID-19 Pandemic

Juan Antonio Galán-Gutiérrez and Rodrigo Martín-García *

Department of Business and Accounting, Universidad Nacional de Educación a Distancia (UNED), Paseo Senda del Rey, 28040 Madrid, Spain; jgalan211@alumno.uned.es
* Correspondence: rmarting@cee.uned.es; Tel.: +34-91-3988463

**Abstract:** The COVID-19 pandemic has shocked commodities markets in general and base metals markets in particular. The market turmoil made it very difficult to act in the physical market, given the impossibility of establishing or maintaining physical and/or financial positions in a context of high uncertainty. This has happened both in different moments of the development of the pandemic and in geographically different frames. That is why this contribution tries to explain the evolution of warehouses and copper price structure and its utility for hedging in the context of an extreme event. To that end, Granger causality has been used to test whether, during the COVID-19 first wave, the pandemic evolution is cointegrated on one hand with copper futures price structure and, on the other, with the incremental levels of copper stocks. Using 102 official copper prices on London Metal Exchange (LME) trading days, between 13 January 2020 and 5 June 2020 (once the most severe effects of the first wave had been overcome), it was demonstrated that, during the first COVID-19 wave in Europe, the weekly death index variation was cointegrated with the copper future price structure. It has been proven that, in this timelapse, contango in futures price structure has increased its value, and the incremental levels of stock in copper LME warehouses are linked with a stable contango structure. In short, we find that fundamental market effects predominate, in a context in which commodities used to be more financialized. This leads market players, such as traders, miners, and transformers, to move exposures in their hedging structures, under such extreme event situations, in favor of or against either contango or backwardation, so as to derive value from them.

**Keywords:** COVID-19; commodities; structure of copper futures prices; cointegration; contango; backwardation; extreme event contexts

## 1. Introduction

The COVID-19 pandemic started as an epidemic, with China being the first country reporting the disease. It was only 100 days until the declaration of the pandemic. After that, governments in every country implemented different measures to control the crisis, with a common structure: social distancing, lockdowns, stay-at-home orders, and travel restrictions, all of which had economic impacts. The whole world experienced a period in which the economy was not running efficiently, causing some businesses to collapse.

The recovery after the emergence of the pandemic evolved differently depending on the country and the sanitary situation, causing a global disruption in the commerce interchange and affecting the full value-added chain.

Commodities market prices reached their lowest level in decades, such as, for example, the crude oil and natural gas markets [1]. Other commodities traded in futures exchanges, such as soft commodities and metals, also reacted sharply to this global crisis, with a vast shift in prices [2], and the historical refuges of these stock markets also being affected [3]. Copper, in particular, underwent a price decrease of almost 25%, from EUR 6200 at the beginning of 2020 to EUR 4627 per metric ton only 3 months after, with a lack of interest in

the buying market and with most of the players trying to liquidate their long-held positions in official warehouses.

This COVID-19 pandemic has had by far the biggest influence on every market in recent times when base metals prices on commodities exchanges have been influenced by macroeconomic and microeconomic events. Each of these base metals shows different behaviors depending on its supply–demand situation, and how financialized each is.

Microeconomic and macroeconomic events have influenced commodities' behaviors in different exchanges. Some of these macroeconomics variables, such as Gross Domestic Product (GDP), have been used to determine the effects on the 27 commodity futures traded on the Commodity Research Bureau (CRB) [4], and the effect on the S&P 500 index has been tested using commodity price indexes [5]. It is also informative to study currency volatility and the link between currency rates for 17 soft and hard commodities [6]. Crude oil prices have also been analyzed by some authors, who found a vast range of variables affecting prices, such as the COVID-19 outbreak, the USD index, and Pacific Investment Management Company (PIMCO) Investment Grade Corporate bond index [7], and US and BRICS (Brazil, Russia, India, China and South Africa) equities [8]. Globally, it has been demonstrated that price cycles are affected by macroeconomic variables [9].

The increase in financialization on the commodity market has been observable for a while [10,11], with commodities in general and base metals in particular being a refuge for investors trying to hedge their global exposure. In this regard, 2004 was pinpointed by some authors [12] as the year in which financialization became more present, ultimately achieving inflows of up to USD 450 billion seven years later in 2011 [13].

Specifically, we find that copper and aluminum are the two most highly financialized base metals, following the LME's (London Metal Exchange) Commitment of Traders Report (see Figure 1).

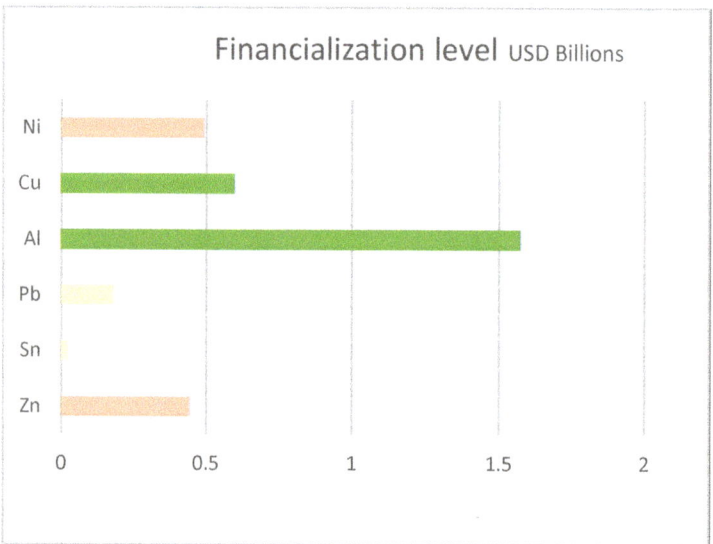

**Figure 1.** Financialization level per metal, financial institutions holdings on LME. Note: Ni (nickel), Cu (copper), Al (aluminum), Pb (lead), Sn (tin), Zn (zinc).

The so-called "normal backwardation" theory links the fundamental scarcity level of a commodity (physical supply and demand) with the appearance of a higher price in the short term than in the long term. This was first studied by [14], looking generally at commodities [15] and specifically at certain metals such as zinc [16], and some have recently assessed financialization factors [17]. Several trends in the data also reflect the disappearance of "normal backwardation" in specific periods of study and in different commodities [18,19].

The theory of normal backwardation is also established through the theory of storage and is related to the cost of carry (COC) model, as shown in [20], where it was shown that risk premium could be used to determine a long-term pricing model. This theory of storage was used to study the levels of stocks in warehouses in different exchanges, which has always been one of the main factors of the fundamentals-based movements of contango and backwardation. The literature addressing this theory is broad [21–23], and a model combining backwardation and storage has even been considered [24]. We can also find evidence of normal backwardation in oil price curves [24–26].

"Normal backwardation" is a theoretical framework that studies the futures price structure, whether it be backwardation or contango, wherein the fundamentals are the main drivers of prices in the short term. Said structure is also linked to several factors, such as the combination of lack of demand and excess of offer, indicating contango, and an absence of offer with a surplus of demand, indicating backwardation.

In this paper, the purpose is to follow and to check the link between the increase of LME warehouses' stock and a high contango value on copper prices, which is evidence of the normal backwardation theory, related to an extreme event, such as COVID-19. This recent crisis has shocked the metals market, causing the whole value-added chain to slow down in the period immediately after the declaration of the pandemic. This slowing forced some market participants to increase their efforts to finance their sales to official warehouses. In the case of commodity sellers, the goods were directly moved to LME warehouses. Therefore, an increase in the stocks in warehouses was achieved at the same time as the pause in commerce, and the copper market futures prices developed into contango structure. Thus, we have analyzed prices and stocks data obtained from LME, and the number of deaths due to COVID-19 by geographical area, obtained from the World Health Organization (WHO), building data series to assess stationarity. Stationary tests have demonstrated stationarity or same level of non-stationarity, performing ADF (augmented Dickey–Fuller) [27], PP (Phillips Perron) [28], and KPSS (Kwiatkowski Phillips Schmidt Shin) tests [29]. Subsequently, the cointegration between prices and deaths on the one hand, and contango structure and level of stocks in warehouses on the other hand, can be obtained by the Johansen approximation [30] of the Engle and Granger causality theory.

The aim of this work is to clearly show that copper is a market linked to fundamentals, and is not only a refuge of investors, traders, and speculators—it is, for instance, a financialized market. The importance of copper to our daily lives makes the influences on offer and demand extremely important, and the situation during the first waves of COVID-19 in Europe offers evidence of this.

The contributions of this research include the findings of co-movements between the COVID-19 index of weekly deaths and the copper futures price structure during the first wave of contagions in Europe, and of evidence of normal backwardation with the development of such a futures price structure and the increase in stocks in official LME warehouses.

More specifically, we have completed an analysis of the development of contango in crisis situations and not only of the effects on prices (as in [31]), which opposes the findings of some other authors (such as [32,33], which continued to see financialization throughout the COVID-19 crisis and other references such as [17] that really focus on the paper of Financialization against Normal Backwardation).

A better illustration of how COVID-19 has shocked the copper market in particular is offered by the descriptive change in tendency in the first half of 2020 (during the first wave of COVID-19 contagions in Europe) (see Figure 2). The figure shows LME copper market evolution, in reference to its official historical price structure, and it can be seen, too, how the market had been in a negative ($-0.0102$) trend, then in a positive one ($+0.0362$), in both cases, using a linear regression approach.

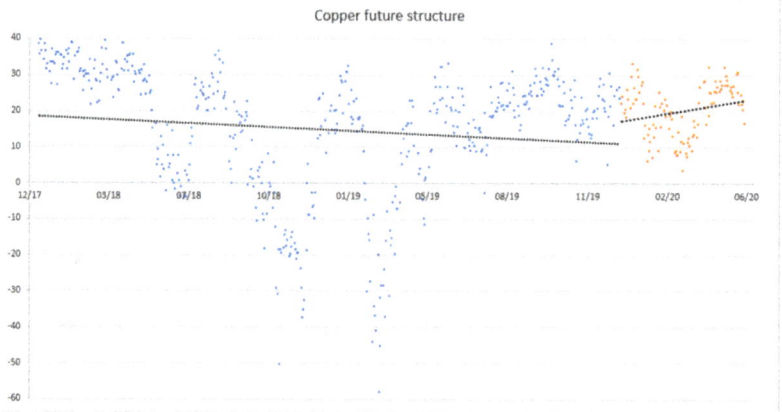

**Figure 2.** Copper futures structure from January 2018 to June 2020.

An additional illustration of the influence of the situation on stocks in the first half of 2020 is given by Figure 3, representing the average levels of stocks in warehouses.

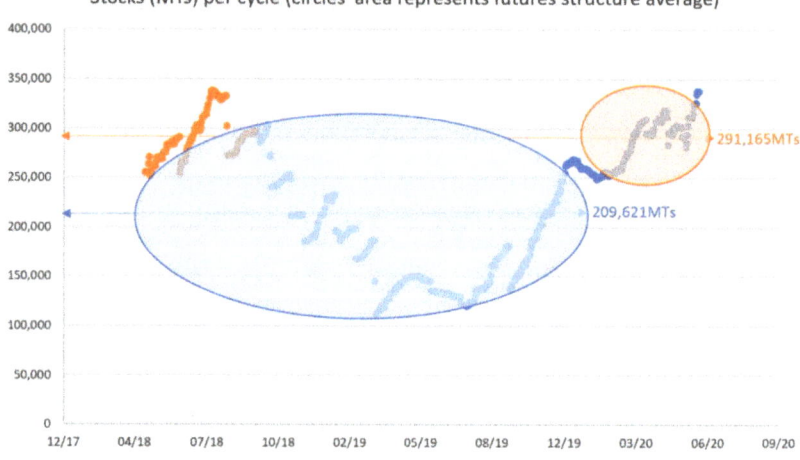

**Figure 3.** Average value of stocks in warehouses in different frames.

Copper stocks significantly changed, as volume went from 209,621 MTs, on average, during 2018–2019, to 291,165 MTs, on average, during the first half of 2020, which represents a 39% increase.

The remainder of this paper is organized as follows. Section 2 reviews the relevant literature on cointegration, co-movements, copper, and the COVID-19 crisis. The data and methodology are reviewed in Section 3. A description of the results and an analytical review are presented in Section 4. Finally, conclusions and recommendations are discussed in Section 5.

## 2. Literature Review

The main aim of this study is to prove the appearance of "normal backwardation" under the conditions of a critical event, such as the COVID-19 pandemic. For this purpose, we have assessed the literature on co-movements and the COVID-19 pandemic.

## 2.1. Cointegration and Co-Movements: Copper

The influence of different variables on time series fluctuations has been a matter of global study within several economic environments and, specifically, in commodity markets, as has been assessed by [34,35] and, more recently, [36–39].

Some commodities' prices move together, which is referred to as co-movement, such as in the energy markets [40,41] and oil markets [42], and between different metals [43–46] and in metal exchanges [47].

Interest in cointegration and causality has also been present in topics such as cryptocurrencies [48] and Brexit [49].

Copper has been chosen for this study for many reasons. First, it is one of the most financialized base metals priced on the Shanghai Futures Exchange (SHFE), the London Metal Exchange (LME), and the New York Commodity Exchange (COMEX), which are commonly used for speculative strategies [50]. Second, it has a large influence at different economic levels, for example in rich economies, such as Chile's, and in the development of many others [51]. Third, it is one of the metals that are taking over the incipient metal super-cycle, due to the increase in needs and consumption related to the appearance of electric vehicles [52], the increase in renewable energies, and the use of electric applications in general. Given all these factors, authors such as [53] have identified a high probability of a lack of copper in the short term. This battle between the influence of fundamentals and financialization on copper markets has also been studied by [54]. In addition, cointegration and co-movements in the copper market have been a matter of study for authors such as [55], assessing not only copper but also another 43 commodities; [56], assessing efficiency in the structure of prices; [57], studying the cointegration of copper prices with China's activity and stock returns, and finally [58], looking at cointegration in certain time periods between future prices and cash prices.

## 2.2. COVID-19 Influence on Markets

COVID-19 has been the biggest macroeconomic influence in recent history, affecting the global economy, the flow of trade, and human beings in general. Although this is a relatively recent matter, the numbers of studies and authors that have concentrated their efforts on investigating and rationalizing each step of this process has been extremely important. The economic effect of COVID-19 is obvious, as Appendix A shows. Table 1 shows a compendium of articles showing COVID-19's influences on the commodities market.

Therefore, the effects of co-movements on commodities in general and on copper in particular have been studied in depth in the literature. Finding are, in general, there is a dependence between the behaviors of the prices of these commodities and different factors, such as microeconomic and macroeconomic events. In this regard, COVID-19 is the recent event that has most strongly affected the whole structure of exchange markets, shaking the entire market's structure in different sectors.

**Table 1.** Articles concerning COVID-19's influence on the commodities market.

| Doc. | Topic/Theme | Context | Purpose | Key Findings |
|---|---|---|---|---|
| [59] | Co-movements in energy counterparties' parameters under extreme conditions | COVID-19 crisis and West Texas Intermediate (WTI) oil future prices showing negative prices | To study transmissions and contagion in the energy sector | Existence of spillovers and co-movements among these energy-focused corporations |
| [60] | Connectedness in energy commodities after COVID-19 pandemic beginning | First two months of the COVID-19 outbreak | To look into the financial impact on COVID-19, concentrated on the energy sector | Dependence among energy commodities increases |

Table 1. *Cont.*

| Doc. | Topic/Theme | Context | Purpose | Key Findings |
|---|---|---|---|---|
| [1] | Effect of the pandemic on the connectedness amongst the commodities market | US and worldwide COVID-19 pandemic effect | To explore the risk transmission in commodity and financial markets during the COVID-19 pandemic | Volatility connectedness between commodities and financial markets |
| [61] | Commodity price returns during the pandemic | COVID-19 Global Fear Index (GFI) rising | To examine how GFI is linked to commodity price returns | Commodity prices' linkage with global COVID-19 fear index |
| [62] | Alternative markets study | COVID-19 beginning up to March 2020 and the safe haven assets | To study the effectiveness of safe haven markets under the COVID-19 crisis | The safe havens of gold and soybean |
| [63] | Study of some commodities' market volatilities | Price prediction model changes during the COVID-19 crisis | To readapt the existing price prediction models to the variations caused by COVID-19 | Volatility of commodity prices |
| [32] | Speculation on commodities | No speculation increase caused by other critical financial effects | To evidence the increase in the speculation of commodities (energy, soft and precious metals) in the presence of COVID-19 effects | Different influences on soft and hard commodities |
| [64] | Overreactions in commodities prices | Intraday price changes (changes of prices followed by proportional price reversals) | To identify how 20 different commodities react to COVID-19 effect on intraday prices | Commodity price overreactions in this period |
| [65] | Volatility connectedness among assets peaked during the outbreak | US ETFs, before COVID-19 and during the first wave (up to 29 May 2020) | Changes in the structure and time-varying patterns of volatility connectivity between stocks and major commodities (oil, gold, silver, and natural gas) | Volatility connectedness peaked during the COVID-19 pandemic |
| [66] | The influence of the COVID-19 pandemic on commodity prices | International commodity (metal and agricultural) prices (2 December 2019–1 October 2020) | To show, in the context of the COVID-19 pandemic, the impacts of oil supply and global demand shocks on metal and agricultural commodity prices | The pandemic represents a mix of supply, demand, and uncertainty shocks, and the result is that price indices have significantly declined as it continues to disrupt global supply and demand chains |
| [67] | Comparative commodity (oil and metals) prices | The COVID-19 outbreak generated price declines in precious and industrial metals, although drops were lower than in oil prices | To comprehensively address the potential impacts of the COVID-19 outbreak on commodity markets | Drop in oil market prices and metal prices, particularly in copper |

Table 1. Cont.

| Doc. | Topic/Theme | Context | Purpose | Key Findings |
|---|---|---|---|---|
| [17] | Since the correlations between stocks, bonds, and commodity futures returns are likely to change over time, the weight of commodity futures in optimal portfolios could also be time-varying | Commodity futures have traditionally shown low correlations with stocks and bonds | Normal backwardation in commodity markets no longer works | End of normal backwardation in recent times and the difficulty of hedging in the present scenario |
| [31] | Trend-following strategies create significant abnormal returns in futures markets | A paired trading market–neutral strategy is used (through machine learning algorithms), involving long and short positions in two different future contracts with similar time series price trends | To show that normal backwardation and contango do not consistently characterize futures markets, but each futures market exhibits unique prevailing price trends | Algorithm of trading pairs in futures price structures and the effect on hedging strategies during the COVID-19 crisis |

## 3. Data and Methodology

### 3.1. Data

The copper price data were obtained from the London Metal Exchange and have been used to establish the price structure upon official daily close of the market. The database includes 102 official LME calendar trading days, stretching between 13 January 2020 (day 44 of the pandemic, following [68], with the first case identified in China) and 5 June 2020 (day 188, when the first wave in Europe was considered under control), as used for a descriptive analysis of the first wave of contagions in Europe as the growth rate moved to zero (this interval has also been used by some other authors [69]). The COVID-19 data index we used was composed of the accumulated deaths collected each week in different regions of the world, according to the data published by the WHO, evaluating the number of cumulative deaths (weekly summarized) per population (10,000 habitants' ratio) as per the United Nations World Populations Prospects 2019. These COVID-19 data were segmented by Date/Country/WHO_region/New_cases/Cumulative_cases/New_deaths/Cumulative deaths, and the different regions are shown in Table 2 below.

Table 2. Regions as per WHO.

| | |
|---|---|
| European Region | EURO |
| Eastern Mediterranean Region | EMRO |
| Western Pacific Region | WPRO |
| African Region | AFRO |
| Region of the Americas | PAHO |
| South-East Asia Region | SEARO |

3.1.1. WHO Weekly Mortality Index

We have used the percentage of increase in cumulative deaths, measured weekly as a percentage per 100,000 habitants, as cases detected during the first wave were not measured in the same diametric manner in every country (due to the different capacities to do so) and weekend data were usually not published on time by every country. The availability of tests and the differences in how countries report their figures have been amongst the biggest limitations to our data.

The figures show the data on the biggest countries in each WHO region to perform a descriptive analysis of the information available.

The COVID-19 weekly mortality index (represented by the time series COVIDt) was obtained through arithmetic assessments of the data given every Monday by WHO, focusing on the difference in cumulative deaths between one reference and that from the previous week. The percentage of growth shown by one reference over this period is the focus of our study. These data have been assessed for the number of inhabitants in every region. As such, we can establish:

Day 1 Cumulative deaths 1 Mortality assessed 1
Day 8 Cumulative deaths 2 Mortality assessed 2

$$INDEX = (Cumulative\ deaths\ 2 - Cumulative\ deaths\ 1) * 100 / Number\ of\ inhabitants \quad (1)$$

Cumulative deaths data from Monday to Sunday were calculated through the sum of daily deaths that were published. Even though Europe alone is the subject of our investigation, we display the results for the six areas (see Figures 4–9).

Low values were found in African and West Pacific regions during the first wave of contagions in Europe, and these are mainly related to the low ages of the populations in the main countries in the African area and to the heavy measures taken to control the pandemic in the West Pacific region.

Eastern Mediterranean, South-Eats Asia and Europe regions have shown constant increases, but Europe has shown a very significant constant increase in the seven days mortality index.

The American region has shown a constantly increasing ratio indicating an uncontrolled pandemic situation followed by a period of apparent control, with a substantial drop in the percentage of increase in deaths due to COVID-19; the reality, however, is that the increase was so big (achieving values of more than 500%) that the decrease appears as 200%.

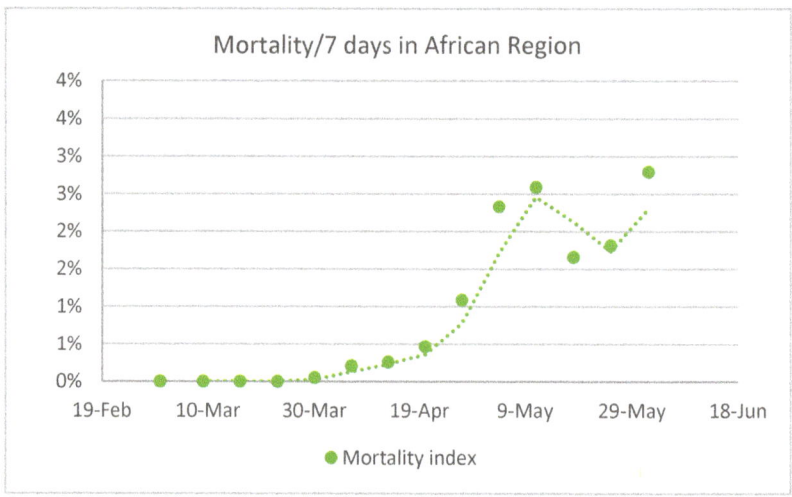

**Figure 4.** COVID-19 weekly mortality index in Africa.

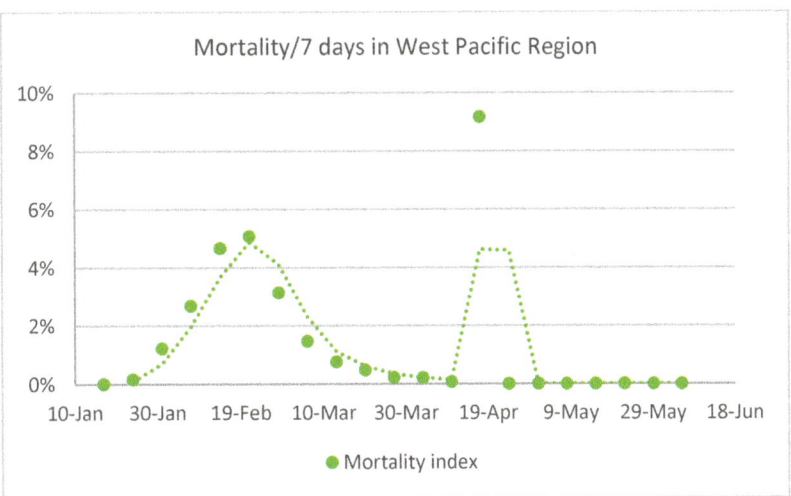

**Figure 5.** COVID-19 weekly mortality index in the West Pacific.

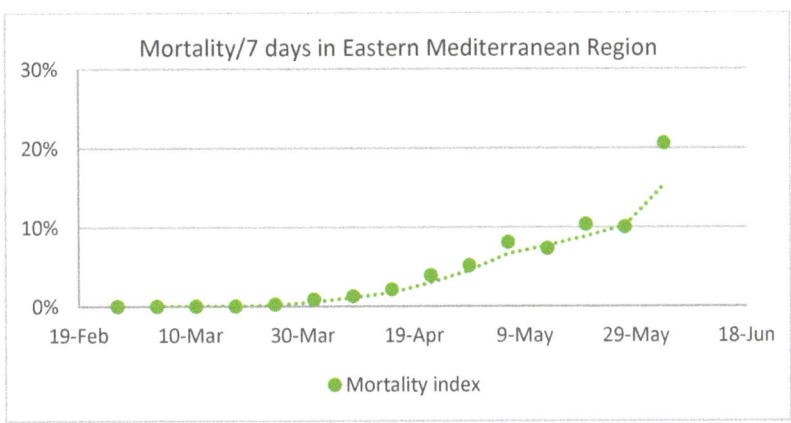

**Figure 6.** COVID-19 weekly mortality index in the East Mediterranean region.

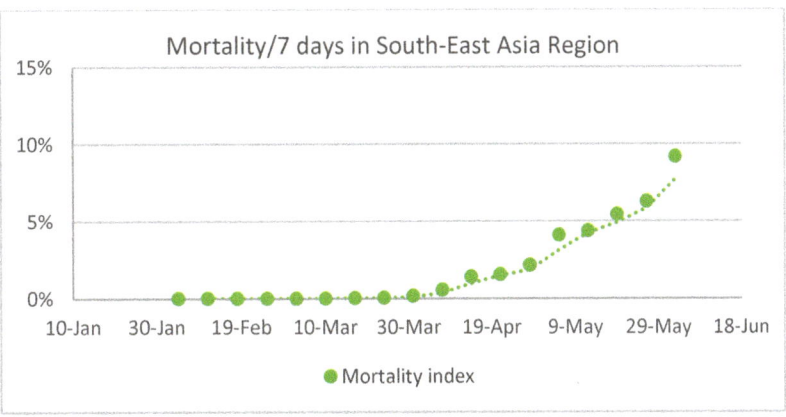

**Figure 7.** COVID-19 weekly mortality index in the East Asia region.

**Figure 8.** COVID-19 weekly mortality index in Europe.

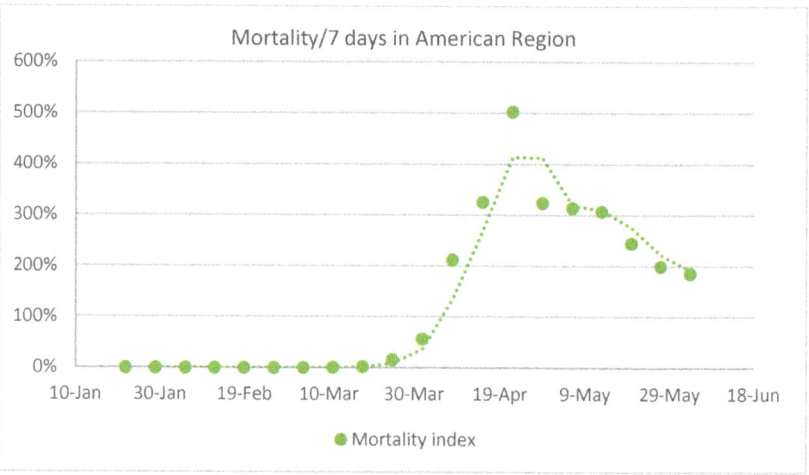

**Figure 9.** COVID-19 weekly mortality index in the American region.

3.1.2. LME Data: Prices and Warehouses' Stocks

The allocation of the futures price structure is derived from the difference between the 3-month control reference and the cash or spot price. The 3-month basis is a liquid position [70] and is that to which the whole market refers a large part of its operations; therefore, this metal's structure refers to this difference, whereby a positive difference indicates contango and a negative one indicates backwardation.

The most common market structure should be contango, as the warehousing system is a regulator. Backwardation should only arise in a forced market, related to a lack of offer, an excess of demand, or a speculative global fund trading position. Nevertheless, this situation is becoming more and more frequent, with long periods of backwardation arising due to the developing super-cycle of metals [71,72].

The copper futures price structure data were taken from the LME and warehouses stock for the same period; the LME uses a worldwide warehouse system to normalize different levels of metal demand and offers. Producers and traders can place large amounts of metal into these warehouses if its brand and quality are assured by the LME's standards;

this can be done through brokers, who also need to be listed under the LME's standards. As the premium for introducing a metal into an LME warehouse is null, producers prefer to sell directly to the market so as to achieve a premium; therefore, it is usually only when the direct consumer market is not active or is sparse that metals arrive at these warehouses. Traders can also perform this type of operation to manipulate the structure of the prices or the forward curve in favor of their short- or long-term global positions. The levels of copper in LME's warehouses and the structure of the copper futures prices are shown in Figure 10.

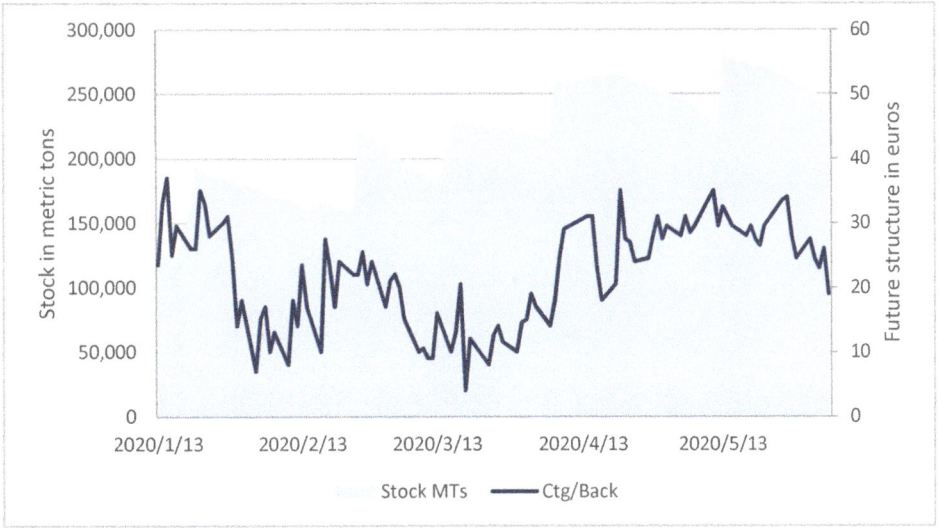

**Figure 10.** Stocks in LME warehouses (STOCK$_t$) and copper futures price ($stru_t$) over the period studied.

European data were chosen for this analysis for three reasons. First, Europe is one of the major economies outside of China; second, it is where the LME warehouses have been established; third, its markets are mostly based on fundamentals. Additionally, descriptive analysis also supports the strategy of using Europe as the basis of this study, as the same trends are shown in their COVID-19 indexes as in the changes in LME warehouses.

Both data series—the COVID-19 index in Europe and the LME copper futures price structure—are represented in Figure 11.

*3.2. Methodology*

Unit root tests have been performed to ensure that the time series do not follow a random walk structure, ensuring that they are stationary and that causality tests can be used. In this regard, our aim was to identify the situation wherein series bind together, with no deviation from equilibrium in the long run.

In these types of unit root tests, the null hypothesis can be linked with the stationarity of the time series, as in the ADF and PP tests, as well as in different ones, such as KPSS tests.

Because the time series addressed in this study were non-stationary and exhibited non-constant variance, they were analyzed with the augmented Dickey–Fuller (ADF) [27] unit root test, as recently deployed by [73] and [74].

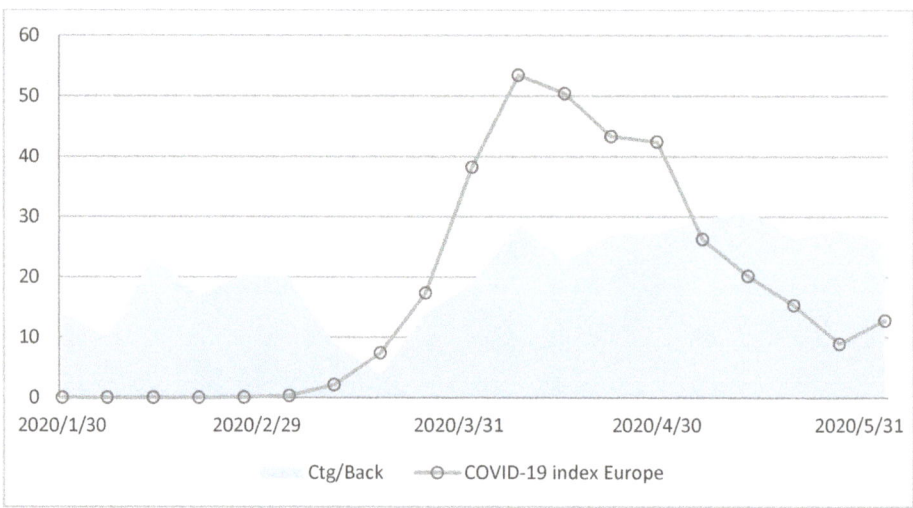

**Figure 11.** Copper futures price structure ($stru_t$) and COVID-19.

The three regression models for ADF are set out below:

$$\Delta y_t = \psi_{ADF} y_{t-1} + \sum_{i=1}^{p-1} \psi_i \Delta y_{t-1} + u_t; \ u_t \approx IID\left(0, \sigma^2\right); \ t = 1, 2, \ldots, \quad (2)$$

$$\Delta y_t = \psi_{ADF} y_{t-1} + \sum_{i=1}^{p-1} \psi_i \Delta y_{t-1} + \mu + u_t; \ u_t \approx IID\left(0, \sigma^2\right); \ t = 1, 2, \ldots, \quad (3)$$

$$\Delta y_t = \psi_{ADF} y_{t-1} + \sum_{i=1}^{p-1} \psi_i \Delta y_{t-1} + \mu + \gamma t + u_t; \ u_t \approx IID\left(0, \sigma^2\right); \ t = 1, 2, \ldots, \quad (4)$$

In these equations, the difference between two time values is a function of non-constant variance $u_t$, with or without constant drift, $\mu$, and a trend term, $\gamma_t$.

The symbols in the above expressions are defined below.

$\Psi_{ADF}$, parameter determining the fulfilment or otherwise of the null hypothesis.

$\sum_{i=1}^{p-1} \psi_i \Delta y_{t-1}$, sum of differentials in the value series multiplied by $\Psi$ in $p-1$ iterations.

$p$, maximum regression delay.

$\mu$, constant.

$\gamma_t$, trend.

$u_t$, process error, a function of the variance series.

The ADF and Phillips–Perron test that there is a unit root for a times series as a null hypothesis. The existence of a unit root implies that the process is non-stationary. KPSS tests the null hypothesis that there is stationarity in the series [75].

Engle and Granger causality-based cointegration tests [33] were performed on the transformed series. The latter yield the order of autoregressive vectors (VAR) [76] and a basis for calculating $\lambda_{max}$ using Johansen's approximation, which is used to find at least one cointegration relationship between the two series.

The Granger causality theory (Johansen approximation [30]) was used to analyze the relationship between the series $(y_t)_{t=1}^N$.

$$\text{Structure of copper futures prices, } (y_t)_{t=1}^N: \quad (stru_t)_{t=05-06-2020}^{13-01-2020} \quad (5)$$

$$\text{Stocks in warehouses, } (z_t)_{t=1}^N: \quad (STOCK_t)_{t=05-06-2020}^{13-01-2020} \quad (6)$$

On the other hand,

$$\text{Structure of copper futures prices, } (y_t)_{t=1}^{N}: \quad (stru_t)_{t=05-06-2020}^{13-01-2020} \quad (7)$$

$$\text{COVID} - 19 \text{ weekly deaths index, } (z_t)_{t=1}^{N}: \quad (COVID_t)_{t=05-06-2020}^{13-01-2020} \quad (8)$$

To resolve the equations shown below ((9)–(12)), Engle and Granger cointegration tests were conducted by applying ordinary Least Squares (OLS) to the transformed data series:
On the one hand,

$$stru_t = \alpha_0 + \alpha_1 \, stru_{t-1} + \ldots + \alpha_1 \, stru_{t-d} + \beta_1 \, stru_{t-1} + \ldots + \beta_1 \, stock_{t-d} + \varepsilon_t \quad (9)$$

$$stock_t = \alpha_0 + \alpha_1 \, stock_{t-1} + \ldots + \alpha_1 \, stock_{t-d} + \beta_1 \, stock_{t-1} + \ldots + \beta_1 \, stru_{t-d} + u_t \quad (10)$$

where d is the number of delays used, $stru_t$ and $stock_t$ are the time series for which cointegration was to be determined, $\alpha$ and $\beta$ are the parameters to be studied, and $\varepsilon_t$ and $u_t$ are the errors or random disturbance, which are normally uncorrelated. It is necessary to fit a vector autoregressive (VAR) model to obtain the optimum lag model [76].

On the other hand,

$$stru_t = \alpha_0 + \alpha_1 \, stru_{t-1} + \ldots + \alpha_1 \, stru_{t-d} + \beta_1 \, stru_{t-1} + \ldots + \beta_1 \, COVID_{t-d} + \varepsilon_t \quad (11)$$

$$COVID_t = \alpha_0 + \alpha_1 \, COVID_{t-1} + \ldots + \alpha_1 \, COVID_{t-d} + \beta_1 \, COVID_{t-1} + \ldots + \beta_1 \, stru_{t-d} + u_t \quad (12)$$

for the other pair of data series studied.

Finally, a robustness test was done, studying cointegration between the independent variables of the above analysis: $COVID_t$ and $STOCK_t$.

From a methodological point of view, once the series are transformed enough times to obtain stationarity, these series can be represented as a set of p iterations with consecutive values, as follows:

$$y_t = c + A_1 \, y_{t-1} + A_2 \, y_{t-2} + \ldots + + A_p \, y_{t-p} + e_t \quad (13)$$

in which the values are corrected by a series of constants, such as $A_i$, where $i = 1, \ldots, n$; the input constant is $c$, and the error vector is $e_t$.

The p-value of Equation (13) defines the VAR order of the series [77]. Here, it was found with the Schwarz or Bayesian (BIC) and Akaike information criteria (AIC), as defined by [78]:

$$\text{Akaike (AIC)}: \quad AIC \equiv -\frac{2L^*}{n} + \frac{2m}{n} \quad (14)$$

$$\text{Schwarz or Bayesian (BIC)}: \quad BIC \equiv -\frac{2L^*}{n} + \frac{m \ln(n)}{n} \quad (15)$$

where $L^*$ is the Napierian logarithm of the likelihood function; $n$ is the number of observations, and $m$ is the number of estimated parameters.

The Johansen approximation yields $\alpha$ and $\beta$ as the vectors:

$$\alpha = |p,r| \text{ and } \beta = |m,r| \quad (16)$$

where r is the number of cointegrating vectors, and p and m are the series vector components.

The premise underlying the maximum lambda and trace tests was described by [79] as follows: "The maximum likelihood theory of systems of potentially cointegrated stochastic variables presupposes that the variables are integrated of order 1, or I(1), and that the data-generating process is a Gaussian vector autoregressive model of finite order l, or VAR(l), possibly including some determinant components". The trace test is defined in the following terms:

$$Trace = -T \sum_{i=r+1}^{p} \log(1 - \lambda_i) \quad (17)$$

where $\lambda_i$ are the eigenvalues in ascending order that deliver the solution to the "reduced rank regression problem", and $r$ and $p$ form parts of values $\alpha$ and $\beta$, as above.

The test is run consecutively for $r$ values of $r = p - 1, \ldots, 0$ or $r = 0, \ldots, p - 1$, up to the value at which the null hypothesis is first rejected, or to the end of the series if it is not rejected.

Instead of $r$, the validity of the null hypothesis may also be determined from $r + 1$, which constitutes the $\lambda_{max}$ test, which is the one used here:

$$\lambda_{max} = -T \log(1 - \lambda_{r+1}) \tag{18}$$

which is identical to the trace test when $p - r = 1$.

Finally, it is necessary to determine whether one variable "Granger-causes" another. One variable causes the other if the past values of one are useful for predicting the other. See Appendix B for an extensive explanation of the application of this methodology in different markets.

The residuals of the linear regressions built from the different data series are a matter of study in this paper, as assessed through the Durbin–Watson approach [80–82].

Under this theory, the errors complete the definition of each time series, defined as $\varepsilon_t$, and taking in this formula, the definition of the statistic D can be given as

$$D = \frac{\sum_{t=2}^{n} (\varepsilon_t - \varepsilon_{t-1})^2}{\sum_{t=1}^{n} \varepsilon_t^2}$$

where $t$ refers to the different observations of the time series.

The null and alternative hypotheses of this test are H0, where the errors are not correlated, and H1, where they are. With a $p$-value below the significance level, we can certify that the residuals are sufficient to use in the following tests on the time series.

## 4. Results

In this section, we give the relations between the structure of copper futures, the LME copper warehouses' level, and the COVID-19 weekly mortality index during the first wave of contagions in Europe. We have also seen, in general, how extreme events are linked with big effects on the future price in comparison with the cash price, ultimately developing a contango structure, evidencing the theoretical background of so-called "normal backwardation".

### 4.1. Relationship between LME Copper Warehouses' Level and the Structure of Copper Futures Prices

Both series $STOCK_t$ and $stru_t$ have been shown to be non-stationary, even after Box–Cox [83] transformations, and we also found non-stationarity at the following levels of both series. We confirmed this via ADF, PP, and KPSS tests to check the non-stationary of the two series, $STOCK_t$ and $stru_t$, as can be seen in Table 3, finding that both series are non-stationary to the same degree. In regard to causality, Johansen's approximation of the cointegration test of Engel and Granger was performed (see Table 4), obtaining cointegration between the $STOCK_t$ and $stru_t$ series in the time frame studied. This means that increases in contango and stocks are linked, giving evidence for the theory of normal backwardation.

Table 3. Stationary tests for STOCK$_t$ and $stru_t$.

| Data Series | | p-Value | | |
|---|---|---|---|---|
| | | ADF | PP | KPSS |
| Stock MTs | I(0) | 0.893 | 0.893 | <0.0001 |
| $stru_t$ | I(0) | 0.177 | 0.177 | 0.008 |
| Stock MTs | I(1) | 0.833 | 0.435 | <0.0001 |
| $stru_t$ | I(1) | 0.218 | 0.218 | 0.004 |

Table 4. Johansen's approximation tests for causality STOCK$_t$ and $stru_t$.

| Data Series | p-Value | | |
|---|---|---|---|
| | Lambda Max | Trace Test | VAR Estimation (AIC) |
| Stock MTs $stru_t$ | 0.048 ** | 0.072 * | 2 (21,988) |

** Rejection of the null hypothesis at the 5% significance level. * Rejection of the null hypothesis at the 10% significance level.

This means that, under strongly adverse conditions in the consumption market, because of economic crises, sanitary catastrophes, low demand, or other extreme events, economic players, such as producers or traders, are forced to allocate their units to official warehouses instead of to final consumption markets. From a practical point of view, this means that copper producers cannot easily alter their volumes to adapt to rapid decreases in market consumption. This is also a characteristic of the commodity market, wherein a complex global system of warehouses is established specifically "to regulate the inflows with the outflows". The specific definition of backwardation based on fundamentals refers to the lack of availability of metal on the market, and in general, to the feeling of scarcity; therefore, contango means the opposite, that is, the excess of availability. Our findings definitely support this fundamentals-based definition of contango, as under the conditions of a sanitary crisis, with a lack of consumption and the same production model, market inflows are higher than outflows, with a strongly positive offer–demand balance, excess being allocated to the official warehouses.

This theory can be used by market players when establishing their positions in favor of contango when such market disruptions are about to occur.

*4.2. Relationship between COVID-19 Mortality Index and the Structure of Copper Futures Prices*

As in the previous assessment of the series, we have also checked the stationarity of $stru_t$, this being the futures copper price structure data series, finding (see Table 5) that for both series (this one and the COVID-19 mortality data index), non-stationary conditions were achieved. After Box–Cox transformations, we also found non-stationarity in the following levels of both series.

Table 5. Stationary tests for COVID-19 index and $stru_t$.

| Data Series | | p-Value | | |
|---|---|---|---|---|
| | | ADF | PP | KPSS |
| COVID-19 index | I(0) | 0.459 | 0.459 | 0.048 |
| $stru_t$ | I(0) | 0.177 | 0.177 | 0.008 |
| COVID-19 index | I(1) | 0.459 | 0.459 | 0.048 |
| $stru_t$ | I(1) | 0.218 | 0.218 | 0.004 |

Both data series, before and after being transformed, showed the same levels of non-stationarity, making it appropriate to use Johansen's approximation of the Engel and

Granger cointegration test to obtain co-movements between the COVID-19 index and the future price structure of copper (see Table 6).

**Table 6.** Johansen's approximation tests for causality COVID-19 index and $stru_t$.

|  | *p*-Value | | |
| --- | --- | --- | --- |
| **Data Series** | **Lambda Max** | **Trace Test** | **VAR Estimation (AIC)** |
| COVID-19 index $stru_t$ | 0.003 *** | 0.001 *** | 5 (7.088) |

*** Rejection of the null hypothesis at the 1% significance level.

These results show that an event with a strong impact on demand (such as the increase in COVID-19 mortality rate) can cause market scarcity to disappear; in fact, it could generate a feeling of oversupply, thus developing a contango structure.

A producer that is starting to feel a lack of consumption interest from their customers due to a macro event, such as an incipient economic crisis or a sanitary emergency, could easily reassert their hedge position by selling their units using future due date prices instead of short-term prices. A good example of this has been the appearance of new variants of COVID-19, as a result of which the market could be preparing to restructure into a consistent contango. This approach, as others, is speculative by nature, so what is offered here is a better chance to prepare a strategy, as the market could have opposing drivers that would make the structures of copper futures prices fall into backwardation.

Relative to the joint evolution of COVIDt and LME warehouses stock series, as a robustness test, we have found that they are cointegrated. See Figure 12 and Table 7, showing *p*-values of Engle and Granger test:

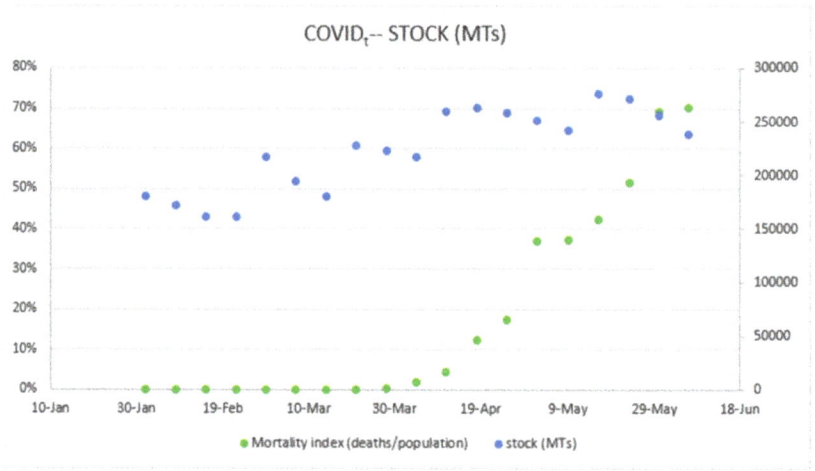

**Figure 12.** $COVID_t$ versus LME warehouses stock during the first wave of contagions of COVID-19 in Europe.

Table 7. Engle and Granger through Johansen's approximation values on cointegration.

| Data Series | p-Value | | |
| --- | --- | --- | --- |
| | Lambda Max | Trace Test | VAR Estimation (AIC) |
| $COVID_t$ stock | 0.011 ** | 0.006 *** | 5 (13,645) |

*** Rejection of the null hypothesis at the 1% significance level. ** Rejection of the null hypothesis at the 5% significance level.

Finally, we tested the null hypothesis that residuals of the model are autocorrelated. Time series' residuals have been checked via the Durbin–Watson test, trying to certify that these residuals are autocorrelated and the tendency is consistent. The results show (see Table 8) that, in the case of the series: warehouse stocks, structure of daily dataset, and futures price structure, the p-value is less than the 1% and, in the case of the COVID-19 series, the *p*-value is lower than the 5%, so the null hypothesis can be rejected.

Table 8. The *p*-value of Durbin–Watson tests performed on different time series.

| Time Series | Warehouse Stocks | Structure of Daily Dataset | COVID-19 Index | Futures Price Structure on Weekly Dataset |
| --- | --- | --- | --- | --- |
| *p*-value | <0.0001 *** | <0.0001 *** | 0.029 *** | <0.0001 *** |

*** Rejection of the null hypothesis at the 1% significance level.

## 5. Conclusions and Recommendations

The COVID-19 pandemic has thrown the world economy into turmoil, and commodity markets have lived through a tsunami since its beginning; its implications have led to a situation of strong normal backwardation.

This paper shows that the levels of stocks in warehouses are linked with the development of the commodity forward price (contango or backwardation). We proved that, in a multi-country lockdown scenario due to the first wave of COVID-19 infections in Europe, in a long-term backwardated context, copper stocks rose, and a contango structure appeared, indicating a cointegration between the data series representing these stocks and the contango structure.

In the same context, under the influence of macroeconomic events affecting commodity prices, the present findings confirm the existence of a relationship between COVID-19's impact and the structure of copper futures prices, measured on the grounds of COVID-19 weekly mortality data.

In recent times, the financialization of commodities, especially copper, has been a matter of close study and investigation, as explored in the Introduction section, and we are finding that fundamentals are also interfering in the forward price compared with spot prices. Times are approaching where analyses and statistics are suggesting there will be a lack of copper units [52,53], so we can expect this commodity to be driven increasingly by fundamentals. The development of the EV (electric vehicle) and its higher level of copper usage for fabrication, the electrification of charging points, and the development of renewable energies are causing increases in optimism and a feeling that, again, fundamentals are playing an increasingly definitive role.

In this context, some highlights can be selected as policy recommendations, when market agents follow price structure strategies. Under normal backwardation theory, backwardation is the long-term trend; that implies that the spot price is higher than the 3-month price, so, depending on the position players have (short or long), they can try to move in favor of backwardation. However, an extreme event like COVID-19, that turned it into a contango, makes spot prices lower. This way, as contango appears, players should, then, set long term positions to optimize results.

Market players can benefit from changes in tendency and extreme events, such as the recent one studied here, related to the change from structural backwardation to contango. This fact can be used by volatility-based players to increase the weight of positions supported by extreme events, not only in terms of short-term contango or short-term backwardation, but also to set up a contango/backwardation structure change-based strategy. We have experienced, during the COVID-19 pandemic, different scenarios within the commodities market, showing the strongest contangos ever during the first phase of worldwide lockdowns, followed by several ups and downs in the future structure of base metals in particular, as related to extreme events (in our recent context, COVID-19): the arrival of a vaccine, the acceleration of the vaccination process, the appearance of new variants, countries' herd immunity, new variants evading the protection of vaccines, new vaccines, new contagion waves, cross-relations between the variables under study, relations with other assets such as those in [69], etc. There is no doubt that the analysis of the commodities market's behavior in general, and that of copper's in particular, under all these scenarios opens up a new line of research and constitutes the basis of new papers. Additionally, the relation between data from the WHO regions and aggregated data from around the world could be a new research focus, even if it would be a huge challenge to measure the integrity of the data given the speed of communication between each country.

**Author Contributions:** J.A.G.-G.: conceptualization, data curation, formal analysis, investigation, methodology, validation, visualization, writing—original draft, writing—review and editing. R.M.-G.: conceptualization, formal analysis, investigation, methodology, supervision, validation, visualization, writing—review and editing. All authors have read and agreed to the published version of the manuscript.

**Funding:** This research received no external funding.

**Institutional Review Board Statement:** Not applicable.

**Informed Consent Statement:** Not applicable.

**Data Availability Statement:** Covid data can be downloaded from https://covid19.who.int/info/. Copper data can be downloaded from: https://www.lme.com/en/Metals/Non-ferrous/LME-Copper#Historical+data, accessed on 28 December 2021.

**Conflicts of Interest:** The authors declare no conflict of interest.

## Appendix A

Table A1 shows some papers that evidence the effect on the economy of the COVID-19 pandemic.

**Table A1.** COVID-19 effect on global economy.

| Doc. | Influence | Geographic Frame |
| --- | --- | --- |
| [84] | 5% Global GDP decrease | 140 regions |
| [85] | Electronic trade decrease (13–53%) and automobiles (2–49%) | China, Europe, and USA, and global |
| [86] | Readaptation of the supply chains to the lack of products | China based |
| [87] | Different approaches of different economies to the economic pandemic effect | Australia, Brazil, China, Germany, Italy, South Africa, Sweden, and USA |
| [88] | Big effect on GDP of Spain, Greece, and Portugal | Spain, Greece, and Portugal |
| [89] | 90% closure of export production units in China | China-based |
| [90] | Loss of investments and fluctuations in international trade | Global studies |
| [91] | Investor sentiment change | Global trades |

Table A1. *Cont.*

| Doc. | Influence | Geographic Frame |
|---|---|---|
| [92] | Concerns about food security | Vietnam and Kazakhstan on one hand and ex-China on the other |
| [93] | Possible hoardings, lack of pesticides | Worldwide |
| [94] | Supply chain shocks | Global aerospace companies |
| [95] | Government economic stimulus and its influence | G-7 countries |

## Appendix B

The following are applications of Granger causality related the case study.

Table A2. Granger causality in the literature.

| Reference | Market Sector | Specific Methodology |
|---|---|---|
| [48] | Bitcoin | GARCH regression and Granger causality |
| [43] | Precious metals | GJR-GARCH and causality models |
| [96] | Exchange rates, short-interest rate and Bursa Malaysia | Johansen–Juselius cointegration test |
| [97] | Liquid milk and powdered milk in Malawi | Johansen's cointegration procedure, TVAR, and TVCEM |
| [98] | Economic growth in the ASEAN-5 countries (Association of Southeast Asian Nations) | Johansen cointegration test, vector error correction model (VECM), and dynamic analysis |
| [99] | Bitcoin | VAR system and Granger causality |
| [100] | Oil and stock markets returns | Bivariate BEKK-GARCH model |
| [101] | Cryptocurrencies and stock market indices | Fractional integration and cointegration |
| [102] | Animal production processes (Veal) | VECM model and Johansen cointegration test |
| [49] | Brexit and base metals | Johansen cointegration test and Var model |
| [103] | Oil and stock markets | Wavelet coherence and BK frequency connectedness method |
| [104] | Climate variability | Mann–Kendell (MK) trend test, Sen's Slope (SS) test and Cox and Stuart (CS) test |
| [105] | Bitcoin | GSADF tests |
| [106] | Work accidents | Johansen cointegration and Granger causality test |

## References

1. Adekoya, O.B.; Oliyide, J.A. How COVID-19 drives connectedness among commodity and financial markets: Evidence from TVP-VAR and causality-in-quantiles techniques. *Resour. Policy* **2021**, *70*, 101898. [CrossRef] [PubMed]
2. Ahmed, M.Y.; Sarkodie, S.A. COVID-19 pandemic and economic policy uncertainty regimes affect commodity market volatility. *Resour. Policy* **2021**, *74*, 102303. [CrossRef] [PubMed]
3. Lahiani, A.; Mefteh-Wali, S.; Vasbieva, D.G. The safe-haven property of precious metal commodities in the COVID-19 era. *Resour. Policy* **2021**, *74*, 102340. [CrossRef]
4. Ge, Y.; Tang, K. Commodity prices and GDP growth. *Int. Rev. Financ. Anal.* **2020**, *71*, 101512. [CrossRef]
5. Creti, A.; Joëts, M.; Mignon, V. On the links between stock and commodity markets' volatility. *Energy Econ.* **2013**, *37*, 16–28. [CrossRef]
6. Liu, L.; Tan, S.; Wang, Y. Can commodity prices forecast exchange rates? *Energy Econ.* **2020**, *87*, 104719. [CrossRef]
7. Bouri, E.; Cepni, O.; Gabauer, D.; Gupta, R. Return connectedness across asset classes around the COVID-19 outbreak. *Int. Rev. Financ. Anal.* **2021**, *73*, 101646. [CrossRef]

8. Ji, Q.; Bouri, E.; Roubaud, D. Dynamic network of implied volatility transmission among US equities, strategic commodities, and BRICS equities. *Int. Rev. Financ. Anal.* **2018**, *57*, 1–12. [CrossRef]
9. Agnello, L.; Castro, V.; Hammoudeh, S.; Sousa, R.M. Global factors, uncertainty, weather conditions and energy prices: On the drivers of the duration of commodity price cycle phases. *Energy Econ.* **2020**, *90*, 104862. [CrossRef]
10. Batten, J.A.; Ciner, C.; Lucey, B.M. The macroeconomic determinants of volatility in precious metals markets. *Resour. Policy* **2010**, *35*, 65–71. [CrossRef]
11. Chen, M.H. Understanding world metals prices—Returns, volatility and diversification. *Resour. Policy* **2010**, *35*, 127–140. [CrossRef]
12. Adams, Z.; Collot, S.; Kartsakli, M. Have commodities become a financial asset? Evidence from ten years of Financialization. *Energy Econ.* **2020**, *89*, 104769. [CrossRef]
13. Bicchetti, D.; Maystre, N. The synchronized and long-lasting structural change on commodity markets: Evidence from high frequency data. *Algorithmic Financ.* **2013**, *2*, 233–239. [CrossRef]
14. Keynes, J.M. *Treatise on Money: Pure Theory of Money*; Macmilian and Co.: London, UK, 1930; Volume 1A.
15. Anderson, R.W.; Danthine, J.P. Hedger diversity in futures markets: Backwardation and the coordination of plans. *Econ. J.* **1983**, *93*, 370–389. [CrossRef]
16. Peterson, P.E. Contango and backwardation as predictors of commodity price direction. In Proceedings of the NCCC-134 Conference on Applied Commodity Price Analysis, Forecasting, and Market Risk Management, St. Louis, MO, USA, 20–21 April 2015. Available online: http://www.farmdoc.illinois.edu/nccc134 (accessed on 27 December 2021).
17. Güntner, J.; Karner, B. *Hedging with Commodity Futures and the End of Normal Backwardation Working Paper (No. 2020–21)*; Johannes Kepler University of Linz: Linz, Austria, 2020.
18. Rouwenhorst, K.G.; Tang, K. Commodity investing. *Annu. Rev. Financ. Econ.* **2012**, *4*, 447–467. [CrossRef]
19. Mishra, V.; Smyth, R. Are natural gas spot and futures prices predictable? *Econ. Modell.* **2016**, *54*, 178–186. [CrossRef]
20. Watkins, C.; McAleer, M. Cointegration analysis of metals futures. *Math. Comput. Simul.* **2002**, *59*, 207–221. [CrossRef]
21. Arseneau, D.M.; Leduc, S. Commodity price movements in a general equilibrium model of storage. *IMF Econ. Rev.* **2013**, *61*, 199–224. [CrossRef]
22. Ap Gwilym, R.; Ebrahim, M.S. Can position limits restrain 'rogue' trading? *J. Bank. Financ.* **2013**, *37*, 824–836. [CrossRef]
23. Sockin, M.; Xiong, W. Informational frictions and commodity markets. *J. Financ.* **2015**, *70*, 2063–2098. [CrossRef]
24. Ekeland, I.; Lautier, D.; Villeneuve, B. Hedging pressure and speculation in commodity markets. *Econ. Theory* **2019**, *68*, 83–123. [CrossRef]
25. Lembarki, S. Price dynamics of crude oil in the short and long term. *Int. J. Econ. Financ. Issues* **2018**, *8*, 103.
26. Ames, M.; Bagnarosa, G.; Matsui, T.; Peters, G.W.; Shevchenko, P.V. Which risk factors drive oil futures price curves? *Energy Econ.* **2020**, *87*, 104676. [CrossRef]
27. Dickey, D.A.; Fuller, W.A. Distribution of the estimators for autoregressive time series with a unit root. *J. Am. Stat. Assoc.* **1979**, *74*, 427–431. [CrossRef]
28. Phillips, P.C.; Perron, P. Testing for a unit root in time series regression. *Biometrika* **1988**, *75*, 335–346. [CrossRef]
29. Kwiatkowski, D.; Phillips, P.C.; Schmidt, P.; Shin, Y. Testing the null hypothesis of stationarity against the alternative of a unit root: How sure are we that economic time series have a unit root? *J. Econom.* **1992**, *54*, 159–178. [CrossRef]
30. Johansen, S. A representation theory for a class of vector autoregressive models for fractional processes. *Econom. Theory* **2008**, *24*, 651–676. [CrossRef]
31. Baek, S.; Glambosky, M.; Oh, S.H.; Lee, J. Machine learning and algorithmic pairs trading in futures markets. *Sustainability* **2020**, *12*, 6791. [CrossRef]
32. Sifat, I.; Ghafoor, A.; Mand, A.A. The COVID-19 pandemic and speculation in energy, precious metals, and agricultural futures. *J. Behav. Exp. Financ.* **2021**, *30*, 100498. [CrossRef]
33. Farid, S.; Kayani, G.M.; Naeem, M.A.; Shahzad, S.J.H. Intraday volatility transmission among precious metals, energy and stocks during the COVID-19 pandemic. *Resour. Policy* **2021**, *72*, 102101. [CrossRef]
34. Engle, R.F.; Granger, C.W. Co-integration and error correction: Representation, estimation, and testing. *Econometrica* **1987**, *55*, 251–276. [CrossRef]
35. Golosnoy, V.; Rossen, A. Modeling dynamics of metal price series via state space approach with two common factors. *Empir. Econ.* **2018**, *54*, 1477–1501. [CrossRef]
36. Lim, K.G.; Nomikos, N.K.; Yap, N. Understanding the fundamentals of freight markets volatility. *Transp. Res. E Logist. Transp. Rev.* **2019**, *130*, 1–15. [CrossRef]
37. Fasanya, I.O.; Awodimila, C.P. Are commodity prices good predictors of inflation? the African perspective. *Resour. Policy* **2020**, *69*, 101802. [CrossRef]
38. Mandacı, P.E.; Cagli, E.Ç.; Taşkın, D. Dynamic connectedness and portfolio strategies: Energy and metal markets. *Resour. Policy* **2020**, *68*, 101778. [CrossRef]
39. Ding, S.; Zhang, Y. Cross market predictions for commodity prices. *Econ. Model.* **2020**, *91*, 455–462. [CrossRef]
40. Boako, G.; Alagidede, I.P.; Sjo, B.; Uddin, G.S. Commodities price cycles and their interdependence with equity markets. *Energy Econ.* **2020**, *91*, 104884. [CrossRef]

41. Ma, Y.R.; Ji, Q.; Wu, F.; Pan, J. Financialization, idiosyncratic information and commodity co-movements. *Energy Econ.* **2021**, *94*, 105083. [CrossRef]
42. Mensi, W.; Rehman, M.U.; Vo, X.V. Spillovers and co-movements between precious metals and energy markets: Implications on portfolio management. *Resour. Policy* **2020**, *69*, 101836. [CrossRef]
43. Madaleno, M.; Pinho, C. Wavelet dynamics for oil-stock world interactions. *Energy Econ.* **2014**, *45*, 120–133. [CrossRef]
44. Qadan, M. Risk appetite and the prices of precious metals. *Resour. Policy* **2019**, *62*, 136–153. [CrossRef]
45. Al-Yahyaee, K.H.; Rehman, M.U.; Al-Jarrah, I.M.W.; Mensi, W.; Vo, X.V. Co-movements and spillovers between prices of precious metals and non-ferrous metals: A multiscale analysis. *Resour. Policy* **2020**, *67*, 101680. [CrossRef]
46. Sharma, C. Exchange rate volatility and exports from India: A commodity-level panel data analysis. *J. Financ. Econ. Policy* **2019**, *12*, 23–44. [CrossRef]
47. Karabiyik, H.; Westerlund, J.; Narayan, P. Panel data measures of price discovery. *Econom. Rev.* **2021**, 1–28. [CrossRef]
48. Rutledge, R.W.; Karim, K.; Wang, R. International copper futures market price linkage and information transmission: Empirical evidence from the primary world copper markets. *J. Int. Bus. Res.* **2013**, *12*, 113.
49. Eross, A.; McGroarty, F.; Urquhart, A.; Wolfe, S. The intraday dynamics of bitcoin. *Res. Int. Bus. Financ.* **2019**, *49*, 71–81. [CrossRef]
50. Galán-Gutiérrez, J.A.; Martín-García, R. Cointegration between the structure of copper futures prices and Brexit. *Resour. Policy* **2021**, *71*, 101998. [CrossRef]
51. Shao, L.G.; Zhu, X.H.; Huang, J.B.; Li, H.S. Empirical study of speculation roles in international copper price bubble formation. *Trans. Nonferrous Met. Soc. China* **2013**, *23*, 2475–2482. [CrossRef]
52. Pedersen, M. The impact of commodity price shocks in a copper-rich economy: The case of Chile. *Empir. Econ.* **2019**, *57*, 1291–1318. [CrossRef]
53. Jones, B.; Elliott, R.J.; Nguyen-Tien, V. The EV revolution: The road ahead for critical raw materials demand. *Appl. Energy* **2020**, *280*, 115072. [CrossRef]
54. Sverdrup, H.U.; Ragnarsdottir, K.V.; Koca, D. On modelling the global copper mining rates, market supply, copper price and the end of copper reserves. *Resour. Conserv. Recycl.* **2014**, *87*, 158–174. [CrossRef]
55. Guzmán, J.I.; Silva, E. Copper price determination: Fundamentals versus non-fundamentals. *Miner. Econ.* **2018**, *31*, 283–300. [CrossRef]
56. Cashin, P.; Céspedes, L.F.; Sahay, R. Commodity currencies and the real exchange rate. *J. Dev. Econ.* **2004**, *75*, 239–268. [CrossRef]
57. Park, J.; Lim, B. Testing efficiency of the London metal exchange: New evidence. *Int. J. Financ. Stud.* **2018**, *6*, 32. [CrossRef]
58. Guo, J. Co-movement of international copper prices, China's economic activity, and stock returns: Structural breaks and volatility dynamics. *Glob. Financ. J.* **2018**, *36*, 62–77. [CrossRef]
59. Yu, H.; Ding, Y.; Sun, Q.; Gao, X.; Jia, X.; Wang, X.; Guo, S. Multi-scale co-movement of the dynamic correlations between copper futures and spot prices. *Resour. Policy* **2021**, *70*, 101913. [CrossRef]
60. Corbet, S.; Goodell, J.W.; Günay, S. Co-movements and spillovers of oil and renewable firms under extreme conditions: New evidence from negative WTI prices during COVID-19. *Energy Econ.* **2020**, *92*, 104978. [CrossRef]
61. Lin, B.; Su, T. The impact of COVID-19 on the connectedness in energy commodities: A pandora's box or sudden event? *Res. Int. Bus. Financ.* 2020, 10, p. 1360. Available online: https://www.sciencedirect.com/science/article/pii/S0275531920309685?via%3Dihub (accessed on 27 December 2021).
62. Salisu, A.A.; Akanni, L.; Raheem, I. The COVID-19 global fear index and the predictability of commodity price returns. *J. Behav. Exp.* **2020**, *27*, 100383. [CrossRef]
63. Ji, Q.; Zhang, D.; Zhao, Y. Searching for safe-haven assets during the COVID-19 pandemic. *Int. Rev. Financ. Anal.* **2020**, *71*, 101526. [CrossRef]
64. Kamdem, J.S.; Essomba, R.B.; Berinyuy, J.N. Deep learning models for forecasting and analyzing the implications of COVID-19 spread on some commodities markets volatilities. *Chaos Solit. Fractals* **2020**, *140*, 110215. [CrossRef]
65. Borgards, O.; Czudaj, R.L.; Van Hoang, T.H. Price overreactions in the commodity futures market: An intraday analysis of the Covid-19 pandemic impact. *Resour. Policy* **2021**, *71*, 101966. [CrossRef]
66. Ezeaku, H.C.; Asongu, S.A.; Nnanna, J. Volatility of international commodity prices in times of COVID-19: Effects of oil supply and global demand shocks. *Extr. Ind. Soc.* **2021**, *8*, 257–270. [CrossRef]
67. Rajput, H.; Changotra, R.; Rajput, P.; Gautam, S.; Gollakota, A.R.; Arora, A.S. A shock like no other: Coronavirus rattles commodity markets. *Environ. Dev. Sustain.* **2020**, *23*, 6564–6575. [CrossRef]
68. Allam, Z. *Surveying the COVID-19 Pandemic and Its Implications: Urban. Health, Data Technology and Political Economy*; Elsevier: Amsterdam, The Netherlands, 2020.
69. Drożdż, S.; Kwapień, J.; Oświęcimka, P.; Stanisz, T.; Wątorek, M. Complexity in economic and social systems: Cryptocurrency market at around COVID-19. *Entropy* **2020**, *22*, 1043. [CrossRef] [PubMed]
70. Otto, S. A speculative efficiency analysis of the London Metal Exchange in a multi-contract framework. *Int. J. Financ. Econ.* **2011**, *3*, 3–16. [CrossRef]
71. Wellenreuther, C. Economic headline: Commodity prices: Supercycle or upswing? *Wirtschaftsdienst (Hambg. Ger. 1949)* **2021**, *101*, 663–664. [CrossRef]
72. Marañon, M.; Kumral, M. Empirical analysis of Chile's copper boom and the Dutch Disease through causality and cointegration tests. *Resour. Policy* **2021**, *70*, 101895. [CrossRef]

73. De Souza Ramser, C.A.; Souza, A.M.; Souza, F.M.; da Veiga, C.P.; da Silva, W.V. The importance of principal components in studying mineral prices using vector autoregressive models: Evidence from the Brazilian economy. *Resour. Policy* **2019**, *62*, 9–21. [CrossRef]
74. Khalfaoui, R.; Sarwar, S.; Tiwari, A.K. Analysing volatility spillover between the oil market and the stock market in oil-importing and oil-exporting countries: Implications on portfolio management. *Resour. Policy* **2019**, *62*, 22–32. [CrossRef]
75. Michalak, A.; Wyłomańska, A.; Wodecki, J.; Zimroz, R. Integration approach for local damage detection of vibration signal from gearbox based on KPSS test. In *Advances in Condition Monitoring of Machinery in Non-Stationary Operations, Proceedings of the International Conference on Condition Monitoring of Machinery in Non-Stationary Operation*; Santander, Spain, 20–22 June 2018; Springer: Cham, Switzerland, 2018; Volume 15, pp. 330–339. [CrossRef]
76. Hatemi-j, A. A new method to choose optimal lag order in stable and unstable VAR models. *Appl. Econ.* **2003**, *10*, 135–137. [CrossRef]
77. Scott Hacker, R.; Hatemi, J.A. Optimal lag-length choice in stable and unstable VAR models under situations of homoscedasticity and ARCH. *J. Appl. Stat.* **2008**, *35*, 601–615. [CrossRef]
78. Mauricio, J.A. Exact maximum likelihood estimation of partially nonstationary vector ARMA models. *Comput. Stat. Data Anal.* **2006**, *50*, 3644–3662. [CrossRef]
79. MacKinnon, J.G.; Haug, A.A.; Michelis, L. Numerical distribution functions of likelihood ratio tests for cointegration. *J. Appl. Econom.* **1999**, *14*, 563–577. [CrossRef]
80. Durbin, J.; Watson, G.S. Testing for serial correlation in least squares regression: I. *Biometrika* **1950**, *37*, 409–428. [PubMed]
81. Durbin, J.; Watson, G.S. Testing for serial correlation in least squares regression. II. In *Breakthroughs in Statistics*; Springer: New York, NY, USA, 1992; pp. 260–266.
82. Durbin, J.; Watson, G.S. Testing for serial correlation in least squares regression. III. *Biometrika* **1971**, *58*, 1–19. [CrossRef]
83. Box, G.E.; Cox, D.R. An analysis of transformations. *J. R. Stat. Soc. Ser. B (Methodol.)* **1964**, *26*, 211–243. [CrossRef]
84. Zeshan, M. Double-hit scenario of Covid-19 and global value chains. *Environ. Dev. Sustain.* **2021**, *23*, 8559–8572. [CrossRef]
85. Guan, D.; Wang, D.; Hallegatte, S.; Davis, S.J.; Huo, J.; Li, S.; Bai, Y.; Lei, T.; Xue, Q.; Coffman, D.; et al. Global supply-chain effects of COVID-19 control measures. *Nat. Hum. Behav.* **2020**, *4*, 577–587. [CrossRef]
86. Zhang, J. Five basic insights into the economic impact of the COVID-19 outbreak. *Front. Econ. China* **2020**, *15*, 167–178. [CrossRef]
87. Perasolo, L.; Schaller, D.; Stitteneder, T.; Valeyatheepillay, M. Covid-19: Economic policy interventions across continents. In *CESifo Forum*; Ifo Institut-Leibniz-Institut für Wirtschaftsforschung an der Universität München: München, Germany, 2020; Volume 21, pp. 49–57.
88. Fernandes, N. Economic Effects of Coronavirus Outbreak (COVID-19) on the World Economy 2020. Available online: https://ssrn.com/abstract=3557504 (accessed on 27 December 2021).
89. Sohrabi, C.; Alsafi, Z.; O'neill, N.; Khan, M.; Kerwan, A.; Al-Jabir, A.; Iosifidis, C.; Agha, R. World Health Organization declares global emergency: A review of the 2019 novel coronavirus (COVID-19). *Int. J. Surg.* **2020**, *76*, 71–76. [CrossRef]
90. Ozili, P.K.; Arun, T. Spillover of COVID-19: Impact on the Global Economy 2020. Available online: https://ssrn.com/abstract=3562570 (accessed on 27 December 2021).
91. Maghyereh, A.; Abdoh, H. The tail dependence structure between investor sentiment and commodity markets. *Resour. Policy* **2020**, *68*, 101789. [CrossRef]
92. Glauber, J.; Laborde Debucquet, D.; Martin, W.; Vos, R. COVID-19: Trade restrictions are worst possible response to safeguard food security. In *COVID-19 and Global Food Security IFPRI Book Chapters*; IFPRI: Washington, DC, USA, 2020; pp. 66–68.
93. Schmidhuber, J.; Pound, J.; Qiao, B. COVID-19: Channels of transmission to food and agriculture. *Covid* **2020**, *19*.
94. Belhadi, A.; Kamble, S.; Jabbour, C.J.C.; Gunasekaran, A.; Ndubisi, N.O.; Venkatesh, M. Manufacturing and service supply chain resilience to the COVID-19 outbreak: Lessons learned from the automobile and airline industries. *Technol. Forecast. Soc. Chang.* **2021**, *163*, 120447. [CrossRef] [PubMed]
95. Narayan, P.K.; Phan, D.H.B.; Liu, G. COVID-19 lockdowns, stimulus packages, travel bans, and stock returns. *Financ. Res. Lett.* **2021**, *38*, 101732. [CrossRef] [PubMed]
96. Hadi, A.R.A.; Yap, E.T.H.; Zainudin, Z. The effects of relative strength of USD and overnight policy rate on performance of Malaysian stock market—Evidence from 1980 through 2015. *Contemp. Econ.* **2019**, *13*, 175–187.
97. Chalmers, N.; Revoredo-Giha, C.; Jumbe, C. Measuring the degree of integration in the dairy products market in Malawi. *Soc. Sci.* **2019**, *8*, 66. [CrossRef]
98. Samsi, S.M.; Cheok, C.K.; Yusof, Z. Financial crisis, stock market and economic growth. *J. Southeast Asian Econ.* **2019**, *36*, 37–56. [CrossRef]
99. Su, C.W.; Qin, M.; Tao, R.; Umar, M. Financial implications of fourth industrial revolution: Can bitcoin improve prospects of energy investment? *Technol. Forecast. Soc. Chang.* **2020**, *158*, 120178. [CrossRef]
100. Sarwar, S.; Tiwari, A.K.; Tingqiu, C. Analyzing volatility spillovers between oil market and Asian stock markets. *Resour. Policy* **2020**, *66*, 101608. [CrossRef]
101. Gil-Alana, L.A.; Abakah, E.J.A.; Rojo, M.F.R. Cryptocurrencies and stock market indices. Are they related? *Res. Int. Bus. Financ.* **2020**, *51*, 101063. [CrossRef]
102. Mat, B.; Arikan, M.S.; Çevrimli, M.B.; Akin, A.C.; Tekindal, M.A. Causality analysis of the factors affecting the consumer price of veal: The case of Turkey. *Sustainability* **2020**, *12*, 6257. [CrossRef]

103. Cui, J.; Goh, M.; Li, B.; Zou, H. Dynamic dependence and risk connectedness among oil and stock markets: New evidence from time-frequency domain perspectives. *Energy* **2021**, *216*, 119302. [CrossRef]
104. Syed, A.; Liu, X.; Moniruzzaman, M.; Rousta, I.; Syed, W.; Zhang, J.; Olafsson, H. Assessment of climate variability among seasonal trends using in situ measurements: A case study of Punjab, Pakistan. *Atmosphere* **2021**, *12*, 939. [CrossRef]
105. Li, Y.; Wang, Z.; Wang, H.; Wu, M.; Xie, L. Identifying price bubble periods in the Bitcoin market-based on GSADF model. *Qual. Quant.* **2021**, *55*, 1829–1844. [CrossRef]
106. Ivascu, L.; Sarfraz, M.; Mohsin, M.; Naseem, S.; Ozturk, I. The causes of occupational accidents and injuries in Romanian firms: An application of the Johansen Cointegration and Granger Causality Test. *Int. J. Environ.* **2021**, *18*, 7634. [CrossRef] [PubMed]

*Article*

# Amid COVID-19 Pandemic, Entrepreneurial Resilience and Creative Performance with the Mediating Role of Institutional Orientation: A Quantitative Investigation Using Structural Equation Modeling

Alaa M. S. Azazz [1,2,3] and Ibrahim A. Elshaer [1,4,5,*]

1. The Saudi Investment Bank Chair for Investment Awareness Studies, The Deanship of Scientific Research, The Vice Presidency for Graduate Studies and Scientific Research, King Faisal University, Al-Ahsa 31982, Saudi Arabia; aazazz@kfu.edu.sa
2. Department of Tourism and Hospitality, Arts College, King Faisal University, Al-Ahsa 31982, Saudi Arabia
3. Tourism Studies Department, Faculty of Tourism and Hotels, Suez Canal University, Ismailia 41522, Egypt
4. Department of Management, School of Business, King Faisal University, Al-Ahsa 31982, Saudi Arabia
5. Hotel Studies Department, Faculty of Tourism and Hotels, Suez Canal University, Ismailia 41522, Egypt
* Correspondence: ielshaer@kfu.edu.sa

**Abstract:** As a result of the spread of the coronavirus (COVID-19), thousands of small companies around the world have been severely disrupted. Many business professionals, particularly entrepreneurs, suffer from the unprecedented magnitude of the lockdown of social activities, which is combined with limits on individual mobility. This study investigates the resilience of entrepreneurs—which is characterized by hardiness, resourcefulness, and optimism—as well as the relationship between resilience and creative performance. Additionally, the mediating role of institutional orientation is investigated in order to highlight how contextual factors influence this relationship. Using a quantitative study approach and structural equation modeling data analysis technique, 390 entrepreneurs were investigated, and the analyzed data demonstrate that entrepreneurs' ability to persevere in the face of adversity is strongly related to their ability to innovate, with institutional orientation serving as a partial mediating variable. Implications and future research opportunities are also explored in the paper.

**Keywords:** entrepreneurial resilience; creative performance; institutional orientation; SEM

**MSC:** 91Cxx

## 1. Introduction

The novel coronavirus (COVID-19) is causing a prolonged crisis for the majority of entrepreneurs, which is likely threatening their business performance. However, despite the hardships, earlier research has shown that entrepreneurs who have a resilience capacity that allows them to face reality, empower their employees, and adapt their performance to changed situations are likely best prepared to recover [1–3]. Cooper et al. [4] argued that resilient entrepreneurs are confident, adaptable, and sociable, which helps them to build external and internal support networks. Therefore, resilience in entrepreneurs is widely regarded as a crucial factor for the continued existence of businesses and their continued success despite adverse conditions [3,5]—with a high-quality institutional setting, entrepreneurs are able to survive and succeed [6].

An inspection of the current literature [4,7,8] suggests that resilience in organizations arises as a result of the interaction of proactive factors such as individual characteristics and efforts, interrelationships within the organizational environment, and dynamic processes. Current research [4,7,8] proposes that organizational resilience results from the accumulation of proactive variables such as people traits and efforts, business environment interdependencies, and continuously changing processes. This emphasizes the need to investigate the resilience of entrepreneurs as a dynamic capability impacted by its external environment and disheartened or promoted over time. Although the number of studies exploring the resilience concept in business organizations is growing, resilience research in the field of entrepreneurship is extremely scarce [9].

The Disaster Resilience Framework (DRF) identifies adaptability and communications with government institutions as the most important business resilience enablers [10]. Moreover, the institutional theory indicates that the institutional environment plays a crucial role in shaping the behavior and decisions of humans [11] and therefore the behavior inside organizations and corporate performance [12].

Consistent with the DRF, human resources are believed to be a key factor in failure resilience. This explains the knowledge, skills, and competencies that entrepreneurs possess [10]. The ability to continue to look to the future despite adversity is essential to an entrepreneur's success [3,4]. A recent study of the restaurant industry, for instance, shows that resilient entrepreneurs were more capable of generating new ideas and innovating alternative solutions to market disruptions and adversity, thereby enhancing their business's creative performance [13].

There have been repeated calls for empirical research to examine the institutional context as one of the main dimensions that can affect the success or failure of entrepreneurs [14,15]. Based on the Disaster Resilience Framework (DRF) developed by Brown et al. [10] and the institutional theory introduced by Scott [11], this study attempts to find answers to a research question on how entrepreneurial resilience can generate creative performance through the mediating role of institutional orientation in the context of the COVID-19 pandemic in the Kingdom of Saudi Arabia (KSA).

This paper offers several implications for how entrepreneurs of small-size businesses can survive amid the COVID-19 pandemic and how to be innovative when investing in such businesses while considering some contextual factors, such as the institution's orientation toward customers, the market, and the environment, among other things. The paper is structured as follows: a literature review is extensively discussed to create the research framework and hypotheses; then, the methods and data analysis techniques are discussed, followed by writing the research findings and discussion; and finally, the implications and conclusions are explained along with the limitations and further study opportunities.

## 2. Literature Review and Hypotheses Development

### 2.1. Entrepreneurs' Resilience and Creative Performance

Resilience is the capacity of an organization's people, groups, and systems to respond to a significant unexpected disturbance that can alter the organization's expected performance model [16]. It is the capacity of a business to obtain a commanding position and transformative practices when confronted with unforeseen circumstances that threaten its existence [7]. Highly resilient businesses, according to Kobasa et al. [17], establish a robust fit with the new troublesome circumstances without suffering from long-term dysfunctional performance. Staying resilient does not merely entail returning the business to its normal practices; it also entails creating and developing existing resources to continue operations in adverse environments and yet generate new prospects [18]. People with a high level of resiliency are deemed to be thriving due to their capacity to profit from unforeseen obstacles [7]. Resilience in people allows businesses confronting turbulence to creatively solve challenges, mitigate threats, and foster creative performance [19].

Regarding the resilience structure, Martin et al. [20], proposed that it is a multidimensional concept comprised of an assortment of positive attitudes and behaviors. Nevertheless, these attitudes and behaviors are challenging to identify [21]. Some scholars contend that hardiness, resourcefulness, and optimism are predictors of entrepreneurial resilience [3,22,23]. Hardiness defines a person's degree of self-control and willingness to accept change as a challenge [17]. Entrepreneurs with a high level of hardiness are especially determined to succeed when confronted with a traumatic circumstance [24]. In addition, their resilience prevents them from adhering to short-term activities and compels them to adhere tenaciously to creativity, high performance, and business sustainability [23].

Entrepreneurs' resourcefulness contains the collection of abilities, skills, and resources that give them confidence in their competence to manage and control the result of adverse conditions [3]. The high performance of resourceful business owners is a result of their effective response to ambiguous or dire circumstances and their view of adversity as an opportunity [9]. Additionally, resourcefulness is associated with the capacity of entrepreneurs to adopt innovative solutions and enhance their creative performance [23].

Optimism defines the capacity to sustain a positive position in the face of adversity, to be more enthusiastic and accurately assess the business process, to correct the business performance, and to learn from past mistakes [8,9]. Optimism encourages entrepreneurs to pursue long-term objectives [23]. In summary, entrepreneurs who excel in hardiness, resourcefulness, and optimism are regarded as resilient as they possess sufficient ability to stick to corporate goals, better adapt to adverse circumstances, have the ability to extract opportunities from threats, and therefore evolve the ability for business survival and creativity.

Creative performance is defined as an individual or group's problem-solving behavior that creates creative ideas/solutions for tasks, procedures, products, services, and strategies [25]. It is a key indicator of an organization's ability to prepare for, respond to, and recover from hazardous issues [26]. It is motivated by the business's need to endure and survive despite adversity. According to Ayala and Manzano [3] and Prayag et al. [27], resilient entrepreneurs and middle managers are skilled in implementing creative knowledge in new ways and employing competencies they frequently did not know they had, which significantly benefits the organizations. This is in line with the suggestions introduced by Luthans et al. [21] that individuals who are resilient have the ability to survive in the face of unpredicted changes that require innovative problem-solving methods. For instance, entrepreneurs who possess hardiness and resourcefulness characteristics are likely to create a variety of untraditional means to overcome the consequences of disaster, while optimistic entrepreneurs are encouraged to believe in their ability to achieve the organization's goals. According to Hannah et al. [28], hardiness and optimism have a positive impact on people's perceptions of hard consequences and their capability to cope with them, resulting in enhanced actual organization performance, which can assist in mitigating the threat. Sweetman et al. [29] made a similar deduction, indicating that staff resilience that is derived from a positive and optimistic evaluation of unpredicted hard situations is associated with the idea-generation stage of creativity. Consequently, the subsequent hypotheses (as shown in Figure 1)are proposed:

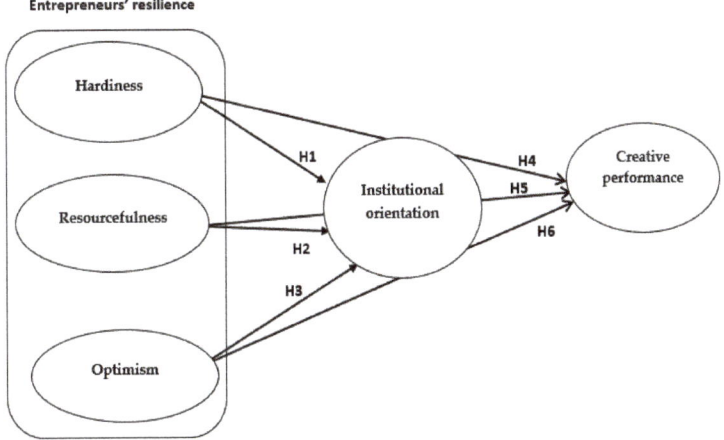

**Figure 1.** Research framework.

**Hypothesis 1 (H1).** *Hardiness (as a dimension of entrepreneurs' resilience) has a positive significant impact on creative performance.*

**Hypothesis 2 (H2).** *Resourcefulness (as a dimension of entrepreneurs' resilience) has a positive significant impact on creative performance.*

**Hypothesis 3 (H3).** *Optimism (as a dimension of entrepreneurs' resilience) has a positive significant impact on creative performance.*

*2.2. Institutional Orientation as a Mediator between Entrepreneurs' Resilience and Creative Performance*

Previous research has demonstrated that the institutional environment plays a significant role in fostering or hindering the survival of entrepreneurs [30]. Furthermore, there is a common prominence of the impact of informal institutions on business performance, particularly in promising markets, where conventions and norms prevail [31,32]. The previous argument is supported by empirical evidence that has highlighted the significant impact of a high and low standard of the institutional environment on the entrepreneurial ability to survive and succeed [6,33]. On the other hand, Lawal et al. [34] argued that the institutional environment alone cannot explain the success or failure of operations. Entrepreneurs who struggle for the survival of their operations typically participate in practices that permit them to recognize the complications of the institutional context and work in partnership with the local government and stakeholders [34]. Despite the key role of adapting and adopting within the institutional environment in entrepreneurial business survival and success [30], the elements of this mechanism are still unclear [35].

According to the institutional theory, institutional alignment offers a persuasive justification for the direction that entrepreneurs can adapt to the continuously changing institutional environment [36,37]. Institutional alignment is the commitment of the company founder and administrative staff to create and sustain positive connections with their main customers, policymakers, rivals, and other stakeholders in the unstable external environment [37].

Chaney et al. [38], propose three aspects of institutional orientation: market legitimacy, institutional embeddedness, and the key institutional customer concept. Institutional embeddedness is the ability to understand and accept the external environment's rules and conventions [39]. Institutional embeddedness allows the business originators to map the powerful players (i.e., policymakers), assess their impacts on their business, and inspire mutual relations to affect and manage the unstable environment [38].

The concept of key institutional customers entails that the business creators prioritize business-to-business (B2B) customers, especially those with a significant impact on the institutional local environment. Having extensive connections with valuable customers gives businesses greater market access and referral opportunities [30]. Market legitimacy is the widespread awareness of all key players in the company's external environment that the organization's actions comply with the government rules and regulations [40]. Obtaining market legitimacy allows organizations to conquer disputes with stakeholders, which can be legislative, social, financial, or political challenges [38].

This study suggests that institutional orientation mediates the effect of entrepreneurs' resiliency (hardiness, resourcefulness, and optimism) on creative performance. Previous empirical evidence from the European Union (EU) context showed that market orientation allowed resilient entrepreneurs to make a smooth market entry, compared to other entrepreneurs who suffered from bankruptcy or did not survive [41,42]. The wide connections with external organizations have also been shown to accelerate resilient adoptability to environmental uncertainty and complexity [7,43]. Other research on resilient entrepreneurs in the retail industry found that pre-disaster solid connections with stakeholders (i.e., suppliers and consumers) facilitated a business's ability to survive and foster creative performance [44]. Furthermore, Vlasov et al. [45] stated that embeddedness in business allowed entrepreneurs to create a social added value to the local community and obtain access to local business resources such as the information about business threats and their pragmatic explanations in addition to gaining legitimacy. Consequently, institutional orientation exemplified by legitimacy, key customer relationships, and embeddedness is more likely to accelerate the recovery of businesses during and after disaster and foster creative performance that enhances an organization's ability to endure during times of crisis. Therefore, we hypothesize the following:

**Hypothesis 4 (H4).** *Institutional orientation positively mediates the relationship betweenhHardiness (as a dimension of entrepreneurs' resilience) and creative performance.*

**Hypothesis 5 (H5).** *Institutional orientation positively mediates the impact of resourcefulness (as a dimension of entrepreneurs' resilience) on creative performance.*

**Hypothesis 6 (H6).** *Institutional orientation positively mediates the relationship between optimism (as a dimension of entrepreneurs' resilience) and creative performance.*

## 3. Methods
*3.1. Sampling, Measures, and Instrument Development*

The study population consists of all entrepreneurs in micro and small businesses (i.e., restaurants, travel agents, estate management owners, mobile phone accessories owners, and food truck owners) in KSA. Micro and small entrepreneurs were selected based on their self-funding and direct management of the operations [46], with no more than 5 full-time employees for micro-business and 6 to 49 full-time workers for small businesses. The accurate total number of micro and small businesses in KSA is not available; however, according to Monshaat (The Small and Medium Enterprises General Authority) 2021 report, the number of micro and small businesses in the Eastern Province is around 600 enterprises that provide services in food and beverages, mobile phone accessories, estate management, and travel agents. Forty enumerators with Bachelor's degrees were recruited to gather data from Al Ahsa governorate entrepreneurs (the largest governorate in the Eastern Province of KSA). This strategy was employed to circumvent the typical weak response rate of usual mail or online surveys [47,48]. Enumerators took precautionary procedures to protect all involved parties from the risk of infection amid the data gathering process.

Respondents signed a consent letter before proceeding with the survey. Enumerators were trained to read the questionnaire in a clear language and fill in the answers from the respondents. The study targeted 400 entrepreneurs for analysis, and 390 responses were collected and valid for analysis. Data were collected during the first three weeks of February 2022.

The standard procedures for the development of psychometric measures were used to create the study scales. All measurements were derived from formerly widely used scales with reflective variables for all employed multi-item dimensions [49]. To measure the resilience of entrepreneurs, the Connor–Davidson Resilience Scale (CD-RISC) developed by Connor and Davidson [50] was adopted. The scale had three primary reflective dimensions: hardiness (9 variables, $a = 0.963$)), resourcefulness (7 variables, $a = 0.966$), and optimism (9 variables, $a = 0.968$). Similarly, three items were obtained from Chaney, Carrillat, and Zouari's [38] study to operationalize institutional orientation ($a = 0.939$): variable number one explains customer perception of institutional orientation, variable two reveals the organizational embeddedness, and variable number three explains the market legitimacy. Lastly, creative performance was measured by six items ($a = 0.945$) derived from the work of Wang and Netemeyer [51]. Sample items include "I come up with new ideas for satisfying customer needs".

Due to the fact that all employed measures were collected from the same participants, the problem of common method variance (CMV) may arise. According to Podsakoff, MacKenzie, and Podsakoff [52], four proactive steps are effective in addressing this anticipated problem (CMV). First, all participating entrepreneurs were assured that their responses would remain completely anonymous and confidential. Second, the scale-dependent related questions were designed to be located before the independently related questions [53]. Third, experts translated the study questionnaire from English to Arabic, pre-tested it with 15 entrepreneurs and 15 business school professors, and purified it subsequently. Finally, "Harman's Single-Factor Test" was employed [52]. The first constrained dimension was able to explain only 27% of all variances that occurred. When considering all the previous steps, we can argue that CMV is not a problem in this paper.

A 10 point continuous scale was employed in designing the questionnaire, where 10 indicates "strongly agree" and 1 means "strongly disagree". As depicted in Table 1, the mean values for all questions ranged from 3.80 to 5.30, while the standard deviation (S.D.) scores were found to range from 0.788 to 1.927 which revealed that the collected primary data are normally spread and less condensed all around the mean scores [54].

Table 1. SEM GoF metrics.

| Metrics | Meaning | Formula | Cutoff Point | Refs. |
|---|---|---|---|---|
| 1- "Absolute fit measures." | | | | |
| Chi-square/df | Chi-square/degree of freedom | "The differences between the observed and estimated covariance matrix." | ≤5.0 | Hair et al. [55] and Tabachnic and Fidell [56] |
| SRMR | Standardized Root Mean Residual | "Average of the residuals between observed and estimated input metrics but standardized to be between 0 to 1." | ≤0.05 | |
| RMSEA | Root Mean Square Error of Approximation | "The discrepancy per degree of freedom, yet measures discrepancy in terms of the population, not just the sample used for estimation." | ≤0.05 | |
| 2- "Incremental fit measures." | | | | |
| CFI | Comparative Fit Index). | "The relative improvement in fit of the hypothesized model over the null model, CFI provides an unbiased estimate of its corresponding population value and is less sensitive to the sample size." | ≥0.90 | Hair et al. [57] and Tabachnic and Fidell [56] |
| NFI | Normed fit index | "A relative comparison of the proposed model to the null model." | ≥0.90 | |
| 3- "Parsimonious fit measures." | | | | |
| PNFI | Parsimony Normed Fit Index | An extension of NFI by multiplying it by the parsimony ratio or PR (the ratio of degrees of freedom used by a model to the total degrees of freedom available) | >0.5 | Hair et al. [57] and Tabachnic and Fidell [56] |
| PCFI | Parsimony Comparative Fit Index | "Adjusts the CFI using PR." | >0.5 | |

3.2. Data Analysis Techniques

To analyze the study data, multiple sequential steps were taken. First, descriptive analysis was conducted to observe the profile of the respondents. To assess reliability, the composite reliabilities (CR = "Squared sum of factor loadings for construct items/Squared sum of factor loadings for construct items + sum of estimation error variance of a construct") and Cronbach's alphas were computed for each dimension. Following the two-step method suggested by Anderson and Gerbing [58], the convergent and discriminant validity of the employed measurement model was assessed using first-order confirmatory factor analysis (CFA) with MLE (Maximum Likelihood Estimation). The hypothesized structural model was subsequently evaluated using structural equation modeling (SEM). The structured model fit compares the hypothesized theory to real collected data. To provide an estimation of model fit, the expected covariance matrix (k) is statistically linked to the real examined covariance matrix (S). The closer the scores of these two matrices are to one another, the better the model fit [57].

Following suggestions from Bryne [59]; Hair Black, Babin, and Anderson [57], and Tabachnick and Fidell [56], several goodness of fit (GoF) metrics were employed to test the model's goodness of fit to the data, as shown in Table 1. In the whole development of data analysis, SPSS vs. 24 and AMOS vs. 24 software was utilized.

## 4. Results

*4.1. Entrepreneur Profiles and Business Demographics*

As shown in Figure 2 and Table 2, the majority (75%) of entrepreneurs who participated in this study had less than 5 employees in their business, while 25% had from 5 to 49 employees. Half of the entrepreneurs (50%) had 6 to 15 years of experience in their operations, while 30% had less than 5 years of experience. The numbers of entrepreneurs who owned and ran food trucks (30%) amounted to more than those who ran restaurants (20%), followed by travel agents' managers (18%), as shown in Table 2. The vast majority (92%) of the participating entrepreneurs were male, married (75%), and aged between 22 to 45 (41%). The majority (60%) of entrepreneurs involved in the study sample were university educated, while only 9% had an MBA degree. Table 2 introduces a review of the profiles of the investigated entrepreneurs and their business categories.

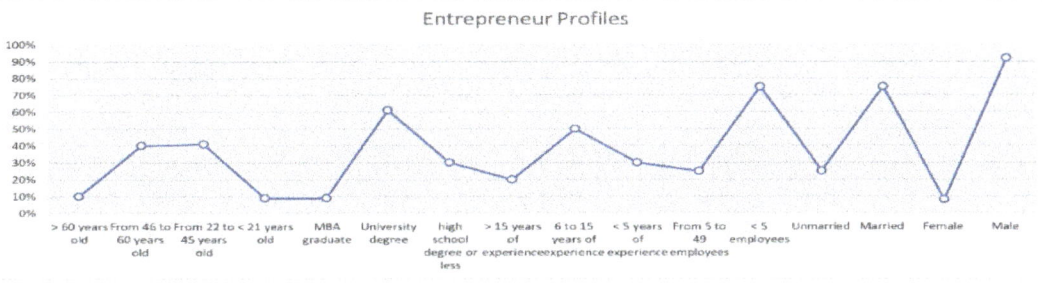

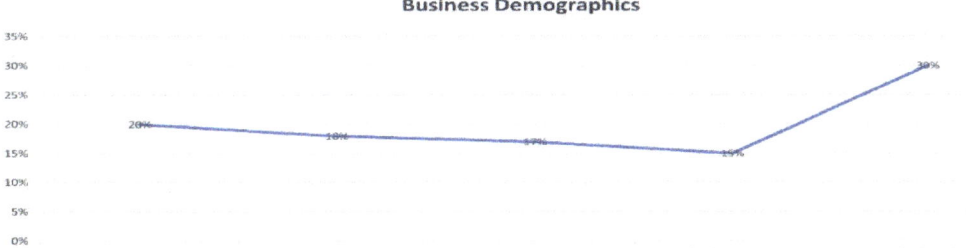

**Figure 2.** Entrepreneur profiles and business demographics. Source: Developed by authors.

**Table 2.** Entrepreneurs profile.

|  |  | N = 390 | % | Groups | N = 390 | % |
|---|---|---|---|---|---|---|
| Gender | Male | 359 | 92% | Restaurants | 78 | 20% |
|  | Female | 31 | 8% | Travel agents | 70 | 18% |
| Marital status | Married | 293 | 75% | Estate management | 66 | 17% |
|  | Unmarried | 97 | 25% | Mobile phone accessories | 59 | 15% |
| Age | <21 years old | 35 | 9% | Food truck | 117 | 30% |
|  | From 22 to 45 years old | 160 | 41% |  |  |  |
|  | From 46 to 60 years old | 156 | 40% |  |  |  |
|  | >60 years old | 39 | 10% |  |  |  |
| Education level | high school degree or less | 117 | 30% |  |  |  |
|  | University degree | 238 | 61% |  |  |  |
|  | MBA graduate | 35 | 9% |  |  |  |
| Number of employees | <5 employees | 293 | 75% |  |  |  |
|  | From 5 to 49 employees | 97 | 25% |  |  |  |
| Years in operation | <5 years of experience | 117 | 30% |  |  |  |
|  | 6 to 15 years of experience | 195 | 50% |  |  |  |
|  | >15 years of experience | 78 | 20% |  |  |  |

Source: Developed by authors.

*4.2. Measurement Model*

For the purpose of testing the validity and reliability of the employed measurement model, a confirmatory factor analysis (CFA) with the Amos vs24 program was conducted. As depicted in Table 3, the model had a good fit to the data: $\chi^2$ (517, N = 390) = 1556.17, $p < 0.001$, normed $\chi^2$ = 3.010, RMSEA = 0.038, SRMR = 0.021, CFI = 0.987, TLI = 0.966, NFI = 0.988, PCFI = 0.809, and PNFI = 0.709 (see Table 1).

**Table 3.** Results of first-order CFA M and standard deviation.

| | Factors and Items | SFL | *t*-Value | M | S.D |
|---|---|---|---|---|---|
| \multicolumn{6}{c}{Entrepreneurs' Resilience (Optimism) Connor & Davidson [50] (a = 0.968) (CR = 0.986, AVE = 0.887, MSV = 0.145)} | | | | | |
| Optmsm1 | Things happen for a reason | 0.919 | F | 3.35 | 1.037 |
| Optmsm2 | I can handle unpleasant feelings | 0.931 | 33.732 | 3.36 | 1.031 |
| Optmsm3 | I have to act on a hunch | 0.942 | 35.186 | 3.36 | 1.034 |
| Optmsm4 | I have a strong sense of purpose | 0.921 | 32.564 | 3.35 | 1.031 |
| Optmsm5 | I see the humorous side of things | 0.944 | 35.500 | 3.37 | 1.025 |
| Optmsm6 | I tend to bounce back after a hardship or illness | 0.928 | 33.430 | 3.36 | 1.026 |
| Optmsm7 | Coping with stress strengthens me | 0.979 | 41.202 | 3.38 | 1.009 |
| Optmsm8 | I give my best effort, no matter what | 0.947 | 35.885 | 3.36 | 1.032 |
| Optmsm9 | Sometimes fate or God can help | 0.965 | 38.631 | 3.37 | 1.032 |

Table 3. Cont.

| | Factors and Items | SFL | t-Value | M | S.D |
|---|---|---|---|---|---|
| | Entrepreneurs' resilience (Hardiness) Connor & Davidson [50] (a = 0.963) (CR = 0.970, AVE = 0.819, MSV = 0.396) | | | | |
| Hardns1 | Under pressure, I focus and think clearly | 0.917 | F | 5.30 | 1.740 |
| Hardns2 | When things look hopeless, I don't give up | 0.878 | 27.895 | 5.07 | 1.834 |
| Hardns3 | I can deal with whatever comes my way | 0.940 | 34.262 | 5.16 | 1.744 |
| Hardns4 | I can make unpopular or difficult decisions | 0.898 | 29.708 | 5.09 | 1.673 |
| Hardns5 | I prefer to take the lead in problem-solving | 0.872 | 27.432 | 5.25 | 1.834 |
| Hardns6 | I think of myself as a strong person | 0.896 | 29.489 | 5.20 | 1.671 |
| Hardns7 | I am not easily discouraged by failure | 0.889 | 28.864 | 5.15 | 1.784 |
| Hardns8 | I like challenges | 0.892 | 29.148 | 5.09 | 1.843 |
| Hardns9 | I work to attain my goals | 0.960 | 37.024 | 5.18 | 1.781 |
| | Entrepreneurs' resilience (Resourceful.) Connor & Davidson [50] (a = 0.966) (CR = 0.948, AVE = 0.776, MSV = 0.216) | | | | |
| Resrorflns1 | I take pride in my achievements | 0.914 | F | 4.74 | 1.824 |
| Resrorflns2 | I have close and secure relationships | 0.961 | 32.802 | 4.72 | 1.795 |
| Resrorflns3 | I know where to turn for help | 0.910 | 39.410 | 4.76 | 1.798 |
| Resrorflns4 | Past success gives me confidence for new challenges | 0.900 | 39.066 | 4.66 | 1.875 |
| Resrorflns5 | I can achieve my goals | 0.930 | 25.617 | 4.61 | 1.868 |
| Resrorflns6 | I can adapt to change | 0.852 | 18.334 | 4.45 | 1.927 |
| Resrorflns7 | I feel in control of my life | 0.851 | 18.198 | 4.46 | 1.915 |
| | Creative performance Wang & Netemeyer [51] (a = 0.945) (CR = 0.950, AVE = 0.761, MSV = 0.145) | | | | |
| Cr_Perf_1: | I carry out my routine tasks in inventive ways | 0.899 | F | 3.63 | 0.871 |
| Cr_Perf_2: | I come up with new ideas for satisfying customer needs | 0.878 | 26.004 | 3.59 | 1.059 |
| Cr_Perf_3 | I generate and evaluate multiple alternatives for novel customer problems | 0.806 | 21.686 | 3.58 | 1.186 |
| Cr_Perf_4 | I have fresh perspectives on old problems | 0.905 | 27.945 | 3.57 | 0.788 |
| Cr_Perf_5 | I improvise methods for solving a problem when an answer is not apparent | 0.850 | 24.149 | 3.39 | 0.928 |
| Cr_Perf_6: | I generate creative ideas for service delivery | 0.892 | 26.949 | 3.41 | 0.910 |
| | Institutional orientation Chaney et al. [38] (a = 0.939) (CR = 0.939, AVE = 0.838, MSV = 0.396) | | | | |
| Cus_Orint | We are primarily focused on the customers with institutional power | 0.920 | F | 4.63 | 2.114 |
| Embedness | We foster institutional and political relationships to influence and control the organization's environment | 0.928 | 30.754 | 4.66 | 1.940 |
| Legitmcy | Our organization is seen as well-established in the market and effectively performs institutional work | 0.898 | 28.426 | 4.62 | 2.043 |

Results of CFA model fit: ($\chi^2$ (517, N = 390) = 1556.17, $p < 0.001$, normed $\chi^2$ = 3.010, RMSEA = 0.038, SRMR = 0.021, CFI = 0.987, TLI = 0.966, NFI = 0.988, PCFI = 0.809 and PNFI = 0.709).

SFL: standardized factor loadings; M: mean; S.D: standard deviation; F: fixed value to run the model. **Source**: developed by authors based on Connor & Davidson [50]; Wang & Netemeyer [51], and Chaney et al. [38].

All of the study dimensions' Cronbach's alphas (a) and CR "composite reliability" scores were higher than the cutoff value of 0.80 [60], which indicates a satisfactory level of internal reliability, as shown in Table 3. All standardized factor loadings for all the reflective items were between 0.80 and 0.98, surpassing the desirable level of 0.7, with t-values beyond 18.198 [58] (see Table 3). This indicates a statistically positive and significant interrelationship between the variables that measure the study dimensions (see Figure 3). Consequently, convergent validity is achieved. The Average Variance Extracted (AVE) scores for all reflective dimensions—optimism (0.887), hardiness (0.819), resourcefulness (0.776), institutional orientation (0.838), and creative performance (0.761)—exceeded the recommended threshold of 0.50 [60], further verifying the scale convergent validity.

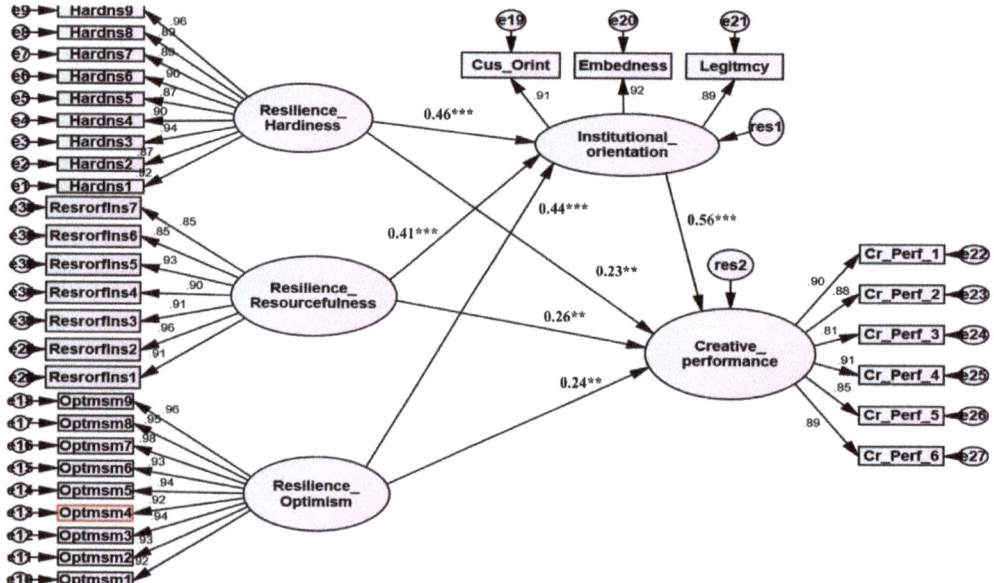

**Figure 3.** The results of the structural model from the Amos output. **Source:** Developed by authors. ***: significant level is below 0.001; **: significant level is below 0.01.

In terms of testing the scale discriminant validity, two statistical methods are extensively employed. First, the AVE square root (AVE √) for every single dimension should exceed the values of the shared correlations with other dimensions [60]. As depicted in Table 4, the AVE square roots in bold diagonal values exceeded the shared correlations below the diagonal values, showing a good discriminant validity. Second, Hair et al. [57] proposed that, for good discriminant validity, the AVE values should surpass the maximum shared value (MSV) scores for each dimension. As displayed in Table 3, all the AVEs scores are higher than the MSV scores, which indicates that all items loaded on their dimension more greatly than on any other dimension, further confirming the discriminant validity of the employed scale. In other words, the results showed a satisfactory psychometric property of the employed measurement model.

**Table 4.** Discriminant validity based on Fornell–Larcker criterion analysis.

|  | 1 | 2 | 3 | 4 | 5 |
|---|---|---|---|---|---|
| 1—Entrepreneurs' resilience (optimism) | 0.942 | | | | |
| 2—Entrepreneurs' resilience (hardiness) | 0.055 | 0.905 | | | |
| 3—Entrepreneurs' resilience (resourcefulness) | 0.104 | 0.431 | 0.852 | | |
| 4—Creative performance | 0.381 | 0.069 | 0.036 | 0.872 | |
| 5—Institutional orientation | 0.126 | 0.629 | 0.431 | 0.206 | 0.915 |

Note: Bold diagonal numbers represent the square root of Average Variance Extracted (AVEs) for the related dimension; Source: Developed by authors.

*4.3. Structural Model*

The causal complexed interrelations in the research model were examined by structural equation modeling (SEM), which was accompanied by an estimation based on the maximum likelihood approximation. The structural equation model (SEM) is an adequate method for data analysis in this study because it enables simultaneous and comprehensive assessments of the whole relationships at the same time [56]. Overall, the GoF metrics for the structural model ($\chi^2$ (520, N = 390) = 1960.4, $p < 0.001$, normed $\chi^2$ = 3.770, RMSEA = 0.029, SRMR = 0.022, CFI = 0.981, TLI = 0.956, NFI = 0.968, PCFI = 0.831 and PNFI = 0.819) showed a perfect model fit to the primary data (as shown in Table 5). Moreover, the structural model suggests a reasonable explanatory power as the SMC "squared multiple correlations" explained 51% of the entrepreneur's creative performance.

**Table 5.** The results of the structural model.

| | Hypotheses | | | Beta (β) | C-R (t-Value) | $R^2$ | Hypotheses Results |
|---|---|---|---|---|---|---|---|
| H1 | Hardiness | → | Creative performance | 0.23 ** | 2.369 | | Supported |
| H2 | Resourcefulness | → | Creative performance | 0.26 ** | 3.754 | | Supported |
| H3 | Optimism | → | Creative performance | 0.24 ** | 3.818 | | Supported |
| H4 | Hardiness → Institutional orientation → Creative Performance | | | Path 1 β = 0.46 *** and Path 2: β = 0.56 *** | Path 1 t-value = 8.011 and Path 2: t-value = 9.797 | | Supported |
| H5 | Resourcefulness → Institutional orientation → Creative Performance | | | Path 1 β = 0.41 *** and Path 2: β = 0.56 *** | Path 1 t-value = 7.629 and Path 2: t-value = 9.797 | | Supported |
| H6 | Optimism → Institutional orientation → Creative Performance | | | Path 1 β = 0.44 *** and Path 2: β = 0.56 *** | Path 1 t-value = 7.499 and Path 2: t-value = 9.797 | | Supported |
| Creative performance | | | | | | 0.51 | |

Model fit: ($\chi^2$ (520, N = 390) = 1960.4, $p < 0.001$, normed $\chi^2$ = 3.770, RMSEA = 0.029, SRMR = 0.022, CFI = 0.981, TLI = 0.956, NFI = 0.968, PCFI = 0.831 and PNFI = 0.819). ***: significant level is below 0.001; ** significant level is below 0.01; Source: Developed by authors.

Table 5 and Figure 3 explain the direct and indirect effects of the research variables. The SEM-analyzed data provide evidence that the three dimensions of an entrepreneur's resilience (hardiness, optimism, and resourcefulness) have direct and positive impacts on creative performance, but with different effect sizes. Resourcefulness was found to have the highest impact size (β 0.26, t-value = 3.754, $p < 0.01$) on creative performance, followed by optimism (β 0.24, t-value = 3.818, $p < 0.01$) and hardiness (β 0.23, t-value = 2.369, $p < 0.01$); accordingly, hypotheses $H_1$, $H_2$, and $H_3$ were supported.

To examine the mediation effects, all path coefficients in the Amos output were evaluated following the recommendations from (1) Kelloway [61] for full and partial mediation conditions, (2) Zhao et al. [62] for complementary mediation and competitive mediation, and (3) SEM-specific standardized indirect path effects.

Kelloway [61] argued that for full mediation, indirect effects only should be significant and direct effects (from the independent variable to the final dependent variable) should be insignificant, while if both direct and indirect effects were found to be significant, only partial mediation could be supported. Zhao et al. [62] went further to differentiate between cases when the significant effects were found to be positive or negative. In other words, if all paths (direct and indirect) were found to be significant with the same signs, then complementary mediation should be supported, while if different significant signs (positive and negative) emerged in the model, then competitive mediation should be supported.

As depicted in Figure 3 and Table 5, all the direct and indirect path coefficients were found to be positive and significant in the model; therefore, partial [61] complementary mediation [62] can be supported, thus supporting Hypotheses 4, 5, and 6. More specifically, the path from hardiness to institutional orientation ($\beta$ 0.46, $t$-value = 8.011, $p < 0.001$) and the path from institutional orientation to creative performance ($\beta$ 0.56, $t$-value = 9.797, $p < 0.001$) were found to be significant with positive signs, thus supporting the partial complementary mediation of the effect of institutional orientation in the relationship between hardiness (as a dimension of entrepreneurs resilience) and creative performance and supporting Hypothesis 4. Similarly, the impact of resourcefulness on institutional orientation ($\beta$ 0.41, $t$-value = 7.629, $p < 0.001$) and the impact of institutional orientation on creative performance ($\beta$ 0.56, $t$-value = 9.797, $p < 0.001$) were found to be significant with positive signs, thus supporting the partial complementary mediation of institutional orientation in the relationship between resourcefulness (as a dimension of entrepreneurs resilience) and creative performance, and thus Hypothesis 5 was supported. Finally, the effect of optimism (as a dimension of entrepreneurs resilience) on institutional orientation ($\beta$ 0.44, $t$-value = 7.499, $p < 0.001$) and the effect of institutional orientation on creative performance ($\beta$ 0.56, $t$-value = 9.797, $p < 0.001$) were found to be significant and positive, thus supporting the partial complementary mediation of the effect of institutional orientation in the relationship between optimism and creative performance and supporting Hypothesis 6.

The previous result was supported by calculating the specific indirect estimated from the Amos output to detect the mediation effects of institutional orientation in the relations between hardiness and creative performance, in which the lower (0.269) and the upper value (0.450) produced significant ($p > 0.001$) standardized indirect estimates of 0.354, thus further supporting Hypothesis 4. Similarly, as depicted in Table 6, the specific indirect estimate from resourcefulness to creative performance through institutional orientation has a lower (0.201) and an upper value (0.420) that established a significant ($p > 0.001$) standardized indirect estimate of 0.306, thus giving more evidence to support Hypothesis 5. Finally, the specific indirect estimation from optimism to creative performance through institutional orientation has a lower (0.221) and an upper value (0.438) that formed a significant ($p > 0.001$) standardized indirect estimation of 0.329, thus further supporting Hypothesis 6.

Table 6. Specific indirect estimates calculation from Amos.

| Indirect Path | Unstandardized Estimate | Lower | Upper | $p$-Value | Standardized Estimate |
| --- | --- | --- | --- | --- | --- |
| Hardiness –> institutional orientation –> creative performance | 0.371 | 0.269 | 0.450 | 0.001 | 0.354 *** |
| Resourcefulness –> institutional orientation –> creative performance | 0.394 | 0.201 | 0.420 | 0.001 | 0.306 *** |
| Optimism –> institutional orientation –> creative performance | 0.384 | 0.221 | 0.438 | 0.001 | 0.329 *** |

***: significant level is below 0.001; Source: Developed by authors.

## 5. Discussion

This study aimed to examine the relationship between entrepreneurs' resilience and their creative performance, with institutional orientation serving as a mediator. Despite the ever-increasing research on resilience in business organizations, entrepreneurial resilience remains understudied [1,63]. As a result, this research contributes to the existing body of knowledge by analyzing the interactions between the resilient nature of entrepreneurs and the institutional orientation of small businesses in Saudi Arabia, as well as how these interactions influence the level of creative performance during the COVID-19 pandemic.

The data were obtained from 390 entrepreneurs of micro and small-sized businesses in Saudi Arabia (i.e., restaurants, travel agents, estate management owners, mobile phone accessories owners, and food truck owners). The law in Saudi Arabia states that a microbusiness can have no more than 5 full-time employees, while a small business can have anywhere from 6 to 49 full-time workers.

In accordance with findings from earlier studies [2,27,64,65], the findings of our study propose that entrepreneurs who are brave (hardy) and willing to face challenges, resourceful in offering new innovative explanations to business problems, and optimistic despite unfavorable conditions are more able to manage their feelings of uncertainty, minimize their doubts of failure, and have faith in their capability to successfully rise to hazardous situations. According to the DRFH [10], proactive and effective leadership skills enable businesses to endure and recover from adversity. Notwithstanding the COVID-19 pandemic, resilient business owners have a greater chance of survival than others. This is due to the fact that they are able to keep their feelings of pressure and uncertainty under control, conduct a rapid and accurate assessment of the intangible and tangible resources that their company possesses, and have faith in their abilities to save their company. The current study is consistent as well with that of Pourmansouri et al. [55], where it was found that enterprises should have a system in their structure to recover and adapt quickly according to the external continuously changing environment, especially with the outbreak of the COVID-19 pandemic and its consequences on the global economy.

According to the proposed hypotheses, institutional orientation acts as a mediator (partially) of the relationship between the resiliency of entrepreneurs and the creative performance of their businesses. According to the findings of our study, having an institutional orientation seems to activate the resiliency skills of entrepreneurs, which in turn decreases the entrepreneurs' feelings of uncertainty and boosts their creative performance. According to the DRF theory [10], strong relationships and connections between the enterprise, policymakers, and other stakeholders allow for productive partnership and reciprocal support to prepare for harsh conditions. Entrepreneurs with strong connections with influential market participants and key B2B partners are more able to address their anxieties about the insecure condition, obtain support from all parties, and solve problems, thus justifying their perception of uncertainty and fostering innovative performance. This is critical since insecurity during and after disruptive conditions causes entrepreneurs to feel their career progress is in jeopardy [66], prompting them to take significant decisions such as shutting their small business [67]. This finding was supported by a similar study conducted by Bai Gokarna et al. [68] that argued that institutional orientation can enhance the impact of leadership on performance. In summary, institutional orientation helps in the creation of a suitable environment in which resilient entrepreneurs feel protected in their careers through hardships, allowing small business recovery and creativity.

## 6. Implications and Conclusions

Examining the changing aspects of resilience in the context of entrepreneurship is crucial for enhancing entrepreneurs' ability to adapt to unfavorable actions. These dynamics of resilience entail a much wider scope of research. This study aims to address this gap by examining the role of entrepreneurs' resilience in generating creative performance in the face of the COVID-19 pandemic outbreak, with a focus on the impact of institutional orientation as a mediator.

In multiple ways, the study findings contribute to the management of small business literature. First, theoretically, the finding confirms the findings of prior research indicating that entrepreneurial resilience is essential for survival and creativity [3,7]. Second, the research results suggest that entrepreneurs' resilience can be established and maintained through external contextual elements of the local entrepreneurial environment. This research identifies abandoned research areas as one example of these contextual elements: institutional orientation. There is a scarcity of empirical research papers exploring the impact of the institutional perspective on entrepreneurial creative performance [15]. This study demonstrates that institutional orientation strengthens the impacts of resilience on entrepreneurs' creative performance. The data were collected from entrepreneurs of micro and small businesses in KSA who were affected by the adverse effects of the COVID-19 pandemic. Notwithstanding encouraging laws (formal legislations) supporting entrepreneurship in Saudi Arabia, having a connection with local policymakers and main performers in private business is a key informal institution in Saudi Arabia that hinders the creativity of entrepreneurs' operations. The findings indicated that strong connections and an association with local government organizations positively influence the resilience and creativity of entrepreneurs. These findings also suggest that, due to the institutional context of their businesses, some resilient micro and small business entrepreneurs are more able to adapt to and recover from hardship than others.

Two main useful practical implications stem from our research findings. First, the findings suggest that entrepreneurial resilience can be fostered and sustained. Entrepreneurs can proactively boost their resilience and creativity. Entrepreneurs gain resilience through experience and continuous learning, according to [1]. Entrepreneurs have to improve their own competencies through education and training. Business seminars, executive courses, and workshops are some available options. Entrepreneurs who improve their problem-solving and emotion-management abilities can better adapt to adverse conditions.

Second, the findings highlight institutional orientation as a significant factor influencing the creativity of an entrepreneur's business. Entrepreneurs should be institutionally focused on creating strong networks and networks with key local actors. This would help entrepreneurs to recognize the rules of the game, adapt to the local environment, gain market legitimacy, and receive financial and social aid when vulnerable.

## 7. Limitations and Further Research Opportunities

This research does have a few limitations. First, the study surveyed entrepreneurs of micro and small businesses in KSA, thus preventing the wide generalization of the study results. As a consequence of this, it would be a good idea to collect data from a variety of countries, each of which has a unique institutional setting. Second, the socio-demographic attributes of entrepreneurs could be further examined in greater depth to reflect the distinctions based on education, age, and type of business. Third, the entrepreneurs' culture can be employed in further studies as a moderator that can enhance the effect of entrepreneurial resilience and creative performance. Fourth, this research tested only institutional orientation as a contextual mediating variable, and upcoming research papers could test the impacts of other contextual elements on the relation between entrepreneurs' resilience and business creative performance, such as market orientation, proactivity, and risk-taking. Finally, the cross-sectional approach of collecting the data employed in this study is another constraint—a longitudinal research approach may be advised to allow greater inferences.

**Author Contributions:** Data curation, A.M.S.A. and I.A.E.; Methodology, A.M.S.A.; Software, I.A.E.; Writing—original draft, A.M.S.A. and I.A.E.; Writing—review & editing, A.M.S.A. and I.A.E. All authors have read and agreed to the published version of the manuscript.

**Funding:** This work was supported by the Saudi Investment Bank Chair for Investment Awareness Studies, the Deanship of Scientific Research, Vice Presidency for Graduate Studies and Scientific Research, King Faisal University, Saudi Arabia (Grant No. CHAIR29).

**Institutional Review Board Statement:** The study was conducted according to the guidelines of the Declaration of Helsinki and approved by the deanship of the scientific research ethical committee, King Faisal University (project number: CHAIR29, date of approval: 15 January 2022).

**Informed Consent Statement:** Informed consent was obtained from all subjects involved in the study.

**Data Availability Statement:** Data are available upon request from researchers who meet the eligibility criteria. Kindly contact the first author privately by e-mail.

**Acknowledgments:** The authors acknowledge the Saudi Investment Bank Chair for Investment Awareness Studies, the Deanship of Scientific Research, Vice Presidency for Graduate Studies and Scientific Research, King Faisal University, Saudi Arabia (Grant No. CHAIR29).

**Conflicts of Interest:** The authors declare no conflict of interest.

## References

1. Duchek, S. Entrepreneurial Resilience: A Biographical Analysis of Successful Entrepreneurs. *Int. Entrep. Manag. J.* **2018**, *14*, 429–455. [CrossRef]
2. Haines, H.; Townsend, D. Self-Doubt and Entrepreneurial Persistence: How Founders of High-Growth Ventures Overcome Cognitive Constraints on Growth and Persist with Their Ventures. In *Entrepreneurial Resourcefulness: Competing with Constraints*; Emerald Group Publishing Limited: Bingley, UK, 2014.
3. Ayala, J.-C.; Manzano, G. The Resilience of the Entrepreneur. Influence on the Success of the Business. A Longitudinal Analysis. *J. Econ. Psychol.* **2014**, *42*, 126–135. [CrossRef]
4. Cooper, C.L.; Flint-Taylor, J.; Pearn, M. *Building Resilience for Success: A Resource for Managers and Organizations*; Springer: Berlin/Heidelberg, Germany, 2013; Volume 8.
5. Ayala Calvo, J.C.; Manzano García, G. Established Business owners'success: Influencing Factors. *J. Dev. Entrep.* **2010**, *15*, 263–286.
6. Vorley, T.; Williams, N. Fostering Entrepreneurship and Economic Growth: Pathways to Economic Resilience in Kosovo. *World Rev. Entrep. Manag. Sustain. Dev.* **2017**, *13*, 159–177. [CrossRef]
7. Lengnick-Hall, C.A.; Beck, T.E. Adaptive Fit versus Robust Transformation: How Organizations Respond to Environmental Change. *J. Manag.* **2005**, *31*, 738–757. [CrossRef]
8. Nguyen, Q.; Kuntz, J.R.; Näswall, K.; Malinen, S. Employee Resilience and Leadership Styles: The Moderating Role of Proactive Personality and Optimism. *N. Z. J. Psychol.* **2016**, *45*, 13.
9. Bullough, A.; Renko, M.; Myatt, T. Danger Zone Entrepreneurs: The Importance of Resilience and Self–Efficacy for Entrepreneurial Intentions. *Entrep. Theory Pract.* **2014**, *38*, 473–499. [CrossRef]
10. Brown, N.A.; Orchiston, C.; Rovins, J.E.; Feldmann-Jensen, S.; Johnston, D. An Integrative Framework for Investigating Disaster Resilience within the Hotel Sector. *J. Hosp. Tour. Manag.* **2018**, *36*, 67–75. [CrossRef]
11. Scott, W.R. *Institutions and Organizations: Ideas, Interests, and Identities*; Sage Publications: New York, NY, USA, 2013.
12. Bhat, S.; Khan, R. Entrepreneurship and Institutional Environment: Perspectives from the Review of Literature. *Eur. J. Bus. Manag.* **2014**, *6*, 84–91.
13. Hallak, R.; Assaker, G.; O'Connor, P.; Lee, C. Firm Performance in the Upscale Restaurant Sector: The Effects of Resilience, Creative Self-Efficacy, Innovation and Industry Experience. *J. Retail. Consum. Serv.* **2018**, *40*, 229–240. [CrossRef]
14. Fu, H.; Okumus, F.; Wu, K.; Köseoglu, M.A. The Entrepreneurship Research in Hospitality and Tourism. *Int. J. Hosp. Manag.* **2019**, *78*, 1–12. [CrossRef]
15. Urban, B.; Kujinga, L. The Institutional Environment and Social Entrepreneurship Intentions. *Int. J. Entrep. Behav. Res.* **2017**, *23*, 638–655. [CrossRef]
16. Bhamra, R.; Dani, S.; Burnard, K. Resilience: The concept, a literature review and future directions. *Int. J. Prod. Res.* **2011**, *49*, 5375–5393. [CrossRef]
17. Kobasa, S.C.; Maddi, S.R.; Kahn, S. Hardiness and Health: A Prospective Study. *J. Personal. Soc. Psychol.* **1982**, *42*, 168. [CrossRef]
18. Jamrog, J.J.; McCann, J.E.I.; Lee, J.M.; Morrison, C.L.; Selsky, J.W.; Vickers, M. *Agility and Resilience in the Face of Continuous Change*; American Management Association: New York, NY, USA, 2006.
19. Saad, S.K.; Elshaer, I.A. Justice and Trust's Role in Employees' Resilience and Business' Continuity: Evidence from Egypt. *Tour. Manag. Perspect.* **2020**, *35*, 100712. [CrossRef]
20. Martin, A.S.; Distelberg, B.; Palmer, B.W.; Jeste, D.V. Development of a New Multidimensional Individual and Interpersonal Resilience Measure for Older Adults. *Aging Ment. Health* **2015**, *19*, 32–45. [CrossRef]
21. Luthans, F.; Youssef, C.M.; Avolio, B.J. *Psychological Capital: Developing the Human Competitive Edge*; Oxford University Press: Oxford, UK, 2007; Volume 198.
22. Singh, K.; Yu, X. Psychometric Evaluation of the Connor-Davidson Resilience Scale (CD-RISC) in a Sample of Indian Students. *J. Psychol.* **2010**, *1*, 23–30. [CrossRef]
23. Wu, W.; Wang, H.; Lee, H.-Y.; Lin, Y.-T.; Guo, F. How Machiavellianism, Psychopathy, and Narcissism Affect Sustainable Entrepreneurial Orientation: The Moderating Effect of Psychological Resilience. *Front. Psychol.* **2019**, *10*, 779. [CrossRef]
24. Franco, M.; Haase, H.; António, D. Influence of Failure Factors on Entrepreneurial Resilience in Angolan Micro, Small and Medium-Sized Enterprises. *Int. J. Organ. Anal.* **2020**, *29*, 240–259. [CrossRef]
25. Amabile, T.M.; Schatzel, E.A.; Moneta, G.B.; Kramer, S.J. Leader Behaviors and the Work Environment for Creativity: Perceived Leader Support. *Leadersh. Q.* **2004**, *15*, 5–32. [CrossRef]
26. Lee, A.V.; Vargo, J.; Seville, E. Developing a Tool to Measure and Compare Organizations' Resilience. *Nat. Hazards Rev.* **2013**, *14*, 29–41. [CrossRef]
27. Prayag, G.; Ozanne, L.K.; de Vries, H. Psychological Capital, Coping Mechanisms and Organizational Resilience: Insights from the 2016 Kaikoura Earthquake, New Zealand. *Tour. Manag. Perspect.* **2020**, *34*, 100637.

28. Hannah, S.T.; Uhl-Bien, M.; Avolio, B.J.; Cavarretta, F.L. A Framework for Examining Leadership in Extreme Contexts. *Leadersh. Q.* **2009**, *20*, 897–919. [CrossRef]
29. Sweetman, D.; Luthans, F.; Avey, J.B.; Luthans, B.C. Relationship between Positive Psychological Capital and Creative Performance. *Can. J. Adm. Sci./Rev. Can. Sci. L'adm.* **2011**, *28*, 4–13. [CrossRef]
30. Estrin, S.; Mickiewicz, T.; Stephan, U. Entrepreneurship, Social Capital, and Institutions: Social and Commercial Entrepreneurship across Nations. *Entrep. Theory Pract.* **2013**, *37*, 479–504. [CrossRef]
31. Seyoum, B. Informal Institutions and Foreign Direct Investment. *J. Econ. Issues* **2011**, *45*, 917–940. [CrossRef]
32. Kolk, A. Linking Subsistence Activities to Global Marketing Systems: The Role of Institutions. *J. Macromark.* **2014**, *34*, 186–198. [CrossRef]
33. Rios, V.; Gianmoena, L. The Link between Quality of Government and Regional Resilience in Europe. *J. Policy Modeling* **2020**, *42*, 1064–1084. [CrossRef]
34. Lawal, F.A.; Iyiola, O.O.; Adegbuyi, O.A.; Ogunnaike, O.O.; Taiwo, A.A. Modelling the relationship between entrepreneurial climate and venture performance: The moderating role of entrepreneurial competencies. *Acad. Entrep. J.* **2018**, *24*, 1–16.
35. Roxas, B.; Chadee, D. Effects of Formal Institutions on the Performance of the Tourism Sector in the Philippines: The Mediating Role of Entrepreneurial Orientation. *Tour. Manag.* **2013**, *37*, 1–12. [CrossRef]
36. Liu, C.-L.E.; Ghauri, P.N.; Sinkovics, R.R. Understanding the Impact of Relational Capital and Organizational Learning on Alliance Outcomes. *J. World Bus.* **2010**, *45*, 237–249. [CrossRef]
37. McFarland, R.G.; Bloodgood, J.M.; Payan, J.M. Supply Chain Contagion. *J. Mark.* **2008**, *72*, 63–79. [CrossRef]
38. Chaney, D.; Carrillat, F.A.; Zouari, A. Uncovering Institutional Orientation as a New Strategic Orientation in Industrial Marketing. *Ind. Mark. Manag.* **2019**, *80*, 242–250. [CrossRef]
39. Rizopoulos, Y.A.; Sergakis, D.E. MNEs and Policy Networks: Institutional Embeddedness and Strategic Choice. *J. World Bus.* **2010**, *45*, 250–256. [CrossRef]
40. Suchman, M.C. Managing Legitimacy: Strategic and Institutional Approaches. *Acad. Manag. Rev.* **1995**, *20*, 571–610. [CrossRef]
41. Lengnick-Hall, C.A.; Beck, T.E.; Lengnick-Hall, M.L. Developing a Capacity for Organizational Resilience through Strategic Human Resource Management. *Hum. Resour. Manag. Rev.* **2011**, *21*, 243–255. [CrossRef]
42. Shafi, M.; Liu, J.; Ren, W. Impact of COVID-19 pandemic on micro, small, and medium-sized Enterprises operating in Pakistan. *Res. Glob.* **2020**, *2*, 100018.
43. Elshaer, I.A. and Azazz, A.M. Amid the COVID-19 Pandemic, Unethical Behavior in the Name of the Company: The Role of Job Insecurity, Job Embeddedness, and Turnover Intention. *Int. J. Environ. Res. Public Health* **2021**, *19*, 247. [CrossRef]
44. Martinelli, E.; Tagliazucchi, G.; Marchi, G. The Resilient Retail Entrepreneur: Dynamic Capabilities for Facing Natural Disasters. *Int. J. Entrep. Behav. Res.* **2018**, *24*, 1222–1243. [CrossRef]
45. Vlasov, M.; Bonnedahl, K.J.; Vincze, Z. Entrepreneurship for Resilience: Embeddedness in Place and in Trans-Local Grassroots Networks. *J. Enterprising Communities People Places Glob. Econ.* **2018**, *12*, 374–394. [CrossRef]
46. Thomas, R.; Shaw, G.; Page, S.J. Understanding Small Firms in Tourism: A Perspective on Research Trends and Challenges. *Tour. Manag.* **2011**, *32*, 963–976. [CrossRef]
47. Kittleson, M.J. Response Rate Via The. *Health Values* **1995**, *18*, 27–29.
48. Parker, L. Collecting Data the E-Mail Way. *Train. Dev.* **1992**, *46*, 52–55.
49. Jarvis, C.B.; MacKenzie, S.B.; Podsakoff, P.M. A Critical Review of Construct Indicators and Measurement Model Misspecification in Marketing and Consumer Research. *J. Consum. Res.* **2003**, *30*, 199–218. [CrossRef]
50. Connor, K.M.; Davidson, J.R. Development of a New Resilience Scale: The Connor-Davidson Resilience Scale (CD-RISC). *Depress. Anxiety* **2003**, *18*, 76–82. [CrossRef]
51. Wang, G.; Netemeyer, R.G. Salesperson Creative Performance: Conceptualization, Measurement, and Nomological Validity. *J. Bus. Res.* **2004**, *57*, 805–812. [CrossRef]
52. Podsakoff, P.M.; MacKenzie, S.B.; Lee, J.-Y.; Podsakoff, N.P. Common Method Biases in Behavioral Research: A Critical Review of the Literature and Recommended Remedies. *J. Appl. Psychol.* **2003**, *88*, 879. [CrossRef]
53. Salancik, G.R.; Pfeffer, J. An Examination of Need-Satisfaction Models of Job Attitudes. *Adm. Sci. Q.* **1977**, *22*, 427–456. [CrossRef]
54. Bryman, A.; Cramer, D. *Quantitative Data Analysis with IBM SPSS 17, 18 & 19: A Guide for Social Scientists*; Routledge: London, UK, 2012.
55. Pourmansouri, R.; Mehdiabadi, A.; Shahabi, V.; Spulbar, C.; Birau, R. An Investigation of the Link between Major Shareholders' Behavior and Corporate Governance Performance before and after the COVID-19 Pandemic: A Case Study of the Companies Listed on the Iranian Stock Market. *J. Risk Financ. Manag.* **2022**, *15*, 208. [CrossRef]
56. Tabachnick, B.G.; Fidell, L.S.; Ullman, J.B. *Using Multivariate Statistics*; Pearson: Boston, MA, USA, 2007; Volume 5.
57. Hair, J.F.; Gabriel, M.; Patel, V. AMOS Covariance-Based Structural Equation Modeling (CB-SEM): Guidelines on Its Application as a Marketing Research Tool. *Braz. J. Mark.* **2014**, *13*, 1–12.
58. Anderson, J.C.; Gerbing, D.W. Structural Equation Modeling in Practice: A Review and Recommended Two-Step Approach. *Psychol. Bull.* **1988**, *103*, 411. [CrossRef]
59. Byrne, B.M. *Structural Equation Modeling with Mplus: Basic Concepts, Applications, and Programming*; Routledge: London, UK, 2013.
60. Fornell, C.; Larcker, D.F. Structural Equation Models with Unobservable Variables and Measurement Error: Algebra and Statistics. *J. Mark. Res.* **1981**, *18*, 382–388. [CrossRef]

61. Kelloway, E.K. Structural Equation Modelling in Perspective. *J. Organ. Behav.* **1995**, *16*, 215–224. [CrossRef]
62. Zhao, X.; Lynch, J.G., Jr.; Chen, Q. Reconsidering Baron and Kenny: Myths and Truths about Mediation Analysis. *J. Consum. Res.* **2010**, *37*, 197–206. [CrossRef]
63. Bullough, A.; Renko, M. Entrepreneurial Resilience during Challenging Times. *Bus. Horiz.* **2013**, *56*, 343–350. [CrossRef]
64. D'andria, A.; Gabarret, I.; Vedel, B. Resilience and Effectuation for a Successful Business Takeover. *Int. J. Entrep. Behav. Res.* **2018**, *24*, 1200–1221. [CrossRef]
65. Ndlovu, V.; Ferreira, N. Students' Psychological Hardiness in Relation to Career Adaptability. *J. Psychol. Afr.* **2019**, *29*, 598–604. [CrossRef]
66. Colakoglu, S.N. The Impact of Career Boundarylessness on Subjective Career Success: The Role of Career Competencies, Career Autonomy, and Career Insecurity. *J. Vocat. Behav.* **2011**, *79*, 47–59. [CrossRef]
67. Kang, J. Relationship among Leader-Member Exchange (LMX), Burnout and Career Turnover Intention in Social Workers Using SEM. *J. Korea Acad.-Ind. Coop. Soc.* **2013**, *14*, 3739–3747.
68. Bai Gokarna, V.; Mendon, S.; Thonse Hawaldar, I.; Spulbar, C.; Birau, R.; Nayak, S.; Manohar, M. Exploring the antecedents of institutional effectiveness: A case study of higher education universities in India. *Econ. Res.-Ekonomska Istraživanja* **2021**, 1–21. [CrossRef]

*Article*

# The Role of Broadband Infrastructure in Building Economic Resiliency in the United States during the COVID-19 Pandemic

Raúl Katz [1] and Juan Jung [2,*]

[1] Columbia Institute for Tele-Information, Columbia University, New York, NY 10027, USA
[2] ICADE, Facultad de Ciencias Económicas y Empresariales, Universidad Pontificia Comillas, 28015 Madrid, Spain
* Correspondence: jfjung@icade.comillas.edu; Tel.: +34-6-1696-3716

**Abstract:** The purpose of this paper is to study the role of broadband in mitigating the economic losses resulting from COVID-19 in the United States by providing a necessary infrastructure to keep economic systems operating, albeit partially. The study is based on an empirical framework underlined by a Cobb–Douglas production function and estimated within a structural multi-equation model through the three-stage least squares approach. To consider the impact of COVID-19 on the economy, we rely on two main variables: an indicator of the quantity of deaths attributed to the disease for every 100,000 inhabitants; and the Stringency Index, a metric linked to the intensity of social restrictions imposed by national and local governments. The main contribution of this article is to provide robust evidence for how the heterogeneous effects of the pandemic across states are in part explained by differences in broadband adoption. Our results indicate that those states with higher broadband adoption were able to mitigate a larger portion of their economic losses derived from the pandemic-induced lockdowns. Addressing the digital divide and ensuring universal access to broadband represent critical goals for building economic resilience to face future emergencies.

**Keywords:** telecommunications; broadband; digitization; resilience; COVID-19; pandemics

**MSC:** 91B02; 91B60; 91B99

**Citation:** Katz, R.; Jung, J. The Role of Broadband Infrastructure in Building Economic Resiliency in the United States during the COVID-19 Pandemic. *Mathematics* **2022**, *10*, 2988. https://doi.org/10.3390/math10162988

Academic Editors: Lina Novickytė, Jolanta Drozdz, Radosław Pastusiak and Michał Soliwoda

Received: 15 July 2022
Accepted: 16 August 2022
Published: 18 August 2022

**Publisher's Note:** MDPI stays neutral with regard to jurisdictional claims in published maps and institutional affiliations.

**Copyright:** © 2022 by the authors. Licensee MDPI, Basel, Switzerland. This article is an open access article distributed under the terms and conditions of the Creative Commons Attribution (CC BY) license (https://creativecommons.org/licenses/by/4.0/).

## 1. Introduction

The COVID-19 pandemic has posed a critical challenge to the global socioeconomic system, raising questions about the levels of preparedness and potential vulnerabilities of most economies to such shocks [1]. In particular, the pandemic forced populations to reexamine social practices and production systems otherwise considered normal up to the end of 2019. For example, before the launch of vaccination campaigns, governments enacted massive social distancing measures, including strict lockdowns, with abrupt declines in travelling, tourism, and all physical work interactions. In the United States, the pandemic seriously affected the performance of the daily routines of its population and the functioning of enterprises.

The Stringency Index published by Our World in Data, which measures the levels of closures of social and economic activity in response to the pandemic including school and office closures as well as travel bans among other measures, shows that the severity of lockdowns during 2020 in the United States was concentrated in the period from March to September of that year, while another period of strong restrictions was imposed beginning in November 2020. This degree of restrictions considerably affected the economic routines of the country. For example, as of June 2020, 66% of US respondents to Nielsen had started to work from home since the outbreak (Nielsen Total Audience Report, August 2020). Figure 1 shows the daily evolution of the Stringency Index.

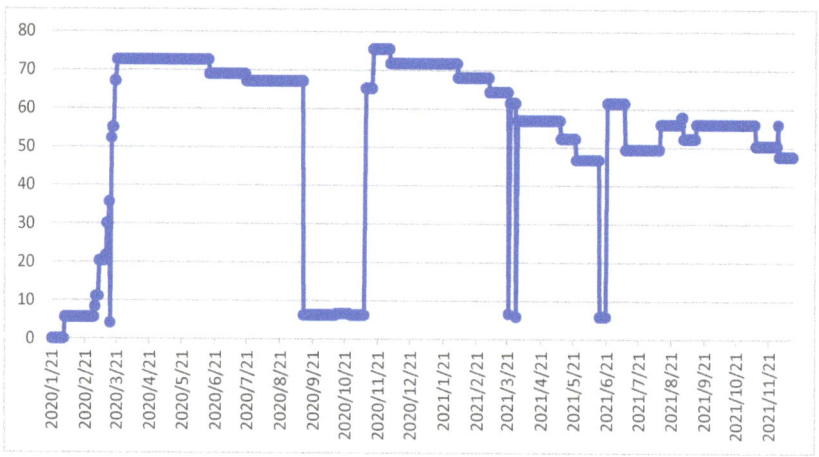

**Figure 1.** United States: Stringency Index (Source: Our World in Data).

The average national Stringency Index masks important regional differences. Figure 2 displays the index by state, indicating that the more severe lockdowns were imposed in the northeastern states, as well as Maryland, Delaware, Kentucky, New Mexico, and California.

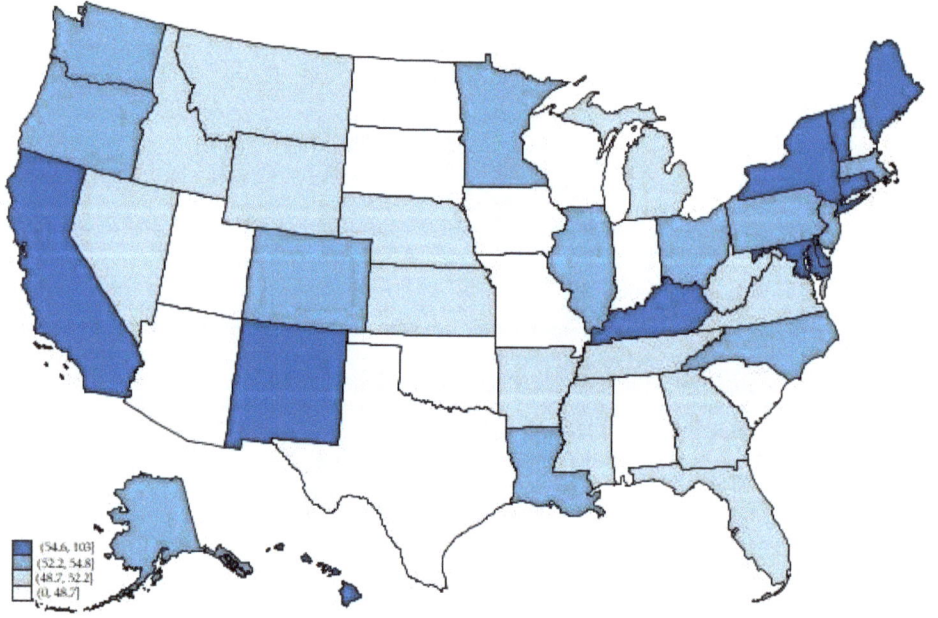

**Figure 2.** United States: Stringency Index by state (2020 average, Source: Our World in Data).

Following the strict lockdowns carried out in 2020, strong anecdotal evidence has emerged suggesting that a robust ICT (information and communication technologies) infrastructure contributed to counteracting some of the isolation measures, allowing economic systems to continue operating at least partially. In this context, the purpose of this study is to investigate the extent to which ICT adoption (more specifically, fixed broadband networks) mitigated the negative economic impacts generated by the COVID-19 crisis in the United States. The study's hypothesis is that beyond its economic contribution under normal conditions, broadband adoption was also essential in building resiliency against the economic disruption generated by the pandemic. In this respect, the main contribution of this paper lies in being, to the best of our knowledge, the first empirical research that studies the role of broadband in mitigating the economic losses resulting from COVID-19 within the United States.

This situation raises a new research imperative: If societies are transitioning to environments combining a mix of physical and virtual interactions, it is pertinent to assess how prepared they are to deal with the new conditions. What effect this could have on those regions that are less connected than others? Would we be accelerating unequal development trends? If this were to be the case, the experience of the COVID-19 disruption would be useful in providing some evidence to that effect. The implication from a policy standpoint would be self-evident: there is a critical need to accelerate the development of broadband infrastructure to be ready to deal with the "new normal" expected in the post-COVID world.

The next section of this study reviews the research literature on the impact of broadband on economic resilience in the context of health and other emergencies. Section 3 details the theoretical model proposed for testing this causality under COVID-19. Section 4 presents the dataset developed for this study along with the main descriptive statistics. Section 5 presents and discusses the results of the econometric analysis, focused on estimating the value of broadband adoption for mitigating the economic disruption driven by the pandemic. Based on the evidence presented in Section 5, we conclude in Section 6 raising some policy implications.

## 2. Research Literature Review

### 2.1. Research in the Field

Research on the economic impacts of digital technologies generated in the past decades confirms, to a large extent, that ICTs and broadband in particular have an impact on economic performance [2–14]. Some authors have expanded this insight to a broader definition of ICT: digitization, which measures not only infrastructure development but also its use.

Beyond the positive economic impact, broadband can also be critical in providing economic resiliency under emergency situations such as forced lockdowns. Broadband allows individuals to conduct many daily activities that previously required physical contact. Examples of this are the ability to access telehealth apps, shop online, learn through virtual tools, and work remotely. In addition to providing workers the possibility of teleworking, digitized supply chains and electronic distribution channels can substantially contribute to keep economic activity operating in situations in which face-to-face interactions with customers and suppliers must be avoided. Finally, ICT infrastructure can increase resiliency at the government level by allowing public institutions to continue operating and delivering public services (beyond the services that are less impacted by the level of digitization, e.g., public health and safety, it is straightforward to see that a highly digitized government has more capacity to continue providing public services without interruption).

While research on the contribution of ICT infrastructure to mitigate the economic impact of pandemics is limited, evidence exists about its positive effects in the context of emergencies. So far, the empirical evidence refers mainly to natural disasters, focusing on the capacity of ICTs to provide information for decision making or allow critical public services to continue operating under such circumstances [15–17]. Other authors have studied the role of digital technologies during the COVID-19 pandemic, such as research focused on the role of digital technologies for telemedicine purposes during the pandemic [18–20]. In addition, ref. [21] studied the role of electronic customer relationship management (e-CRM) applications on firms' innovation capabilities in the context of COVID-19, while [22] argued that the COVID-19 outbreak amplified the impact of information on human behavior, as the internet was a major channel for information and social interactions while staying at home during the pandemic.

As for quantitative empirical evidence, ref. [23] provided econometric results showing the economic losses of the 2003 SARS pandemic were not equal for every country affected. Starting with a production function, the authors introduced two different variables to capture the effect of SARS: a dummy variable to identify the countries affected by the pandemic, taking value of 1 when at least one positive case had been reported, and a continuous variable based on the number of people infected for every 100,000 inhabitants. The results indicated that: (1) Countries with more positive cases were economically affected more severely, and (2) countries with higher broadband adoption were able to counteract, to some degree, the effects of the outbreak.

Following up on their first analysis, ref. [24] provided a subsequent analysis of broadband's contribution to mitigating the economic disruption of COVID-19. By applying a structural econometric model to a 121-country panel, the authors concluded that economic damage was not uniform across countries: ceteris paribus, those economies endowed with better ICT infrastructure were able to achieve higher levels of mitigation. Countries reaching a threshold of 30% fixed broadband penetration, or 50% for mobile broadband penetration, exhibited a lower elasticity of economic impact from COVID-19, as the internet adoption levels in these countries allowed for an important part of the economy and society to continue functioning.

Another study that is close to our main hypothesis is that conducted by [25] for the case of China. The author analyzed the special role of broadband to explain economic growth during the COVID-19 pandemic using data from 31 provincial districts. The results indicate that a 10% increase in broadband penetration rate resulted in a 1.87% GDP growth rate during the first 3 months of 2020 and a 1.30% GDP growth rate during the first fourth months of that year. The author concludes by suggesting that broadband alleviated the country's economic losses during the first months of 2020 and that broadband affected China's economic growth to a larger extent during the pandemic period than under normal circumstances.

Other studies have focused on the role of broadband in mitigating the pandemic disruption in the United States in the case of specific economic variables. For example, ref. [26] explored the relationship between broadband and employment rates in rural US counties during the first half of 2020. Applying a two-stage least squares model, the authors found that rural fixed broadband availability and adoption appeared to be associated with a higher employment rate. Research has also focused on assessing the impacts of digital platforms (and consequently, broadband) for increasing the survival rates of small businesses. Using data from Uber Eats, an online food ordering and delivery digital service, ref. [27] determined that the platform was critical in driving an increase in total restaurant activity and orders following the closure of the dine-in channel. In turn, ref. [28] estimated the factors influencing changes in unemployment rates for southeastern states during the initial months of the pandemic. They found that the ability to telework was a crucial factor in changing unemployment levels, with local broadband adoption influencing this relationship. They conclude that telework had a positive impact for regions with a high broadband adoption rate in the initial months of the pandemic.

*2.2. The Opinions of the Experts*

The evidence on the positive contribution of broadband in the context of pandemics generated by empirical research coincides with the insights of industry and government policy makers. The International Telecommunications Union recently organized a series of Economic Experts Roundtables to discuss the socioeconomic and regulatory challenges that emerged from the COVID-19 pandemic and the key role of digital infrastructures under such circumstances [29].

The participant experts offered insights on the positive role of broadband for building economic resiliency in the pandemic situation. Their perspectives were based on prior studies on broadband economic impact, on digital use case impact research, and on descriptive analyses of the impact on telecommuting and online learning. While generally agreeing on broadband overall positive contribution, some experts stated divergent views regarding the impact of digital resilience at the firm level depending on economic size. While one group of experts argued that large corporations have well-established digital solutions in place to rapidly become more resilient, another group considered that small and medium enterprises are the firms that can move online more quickly and easily adapt to the new environment.

All experts agreed that the degree of resiliency is highly dependent on the sector. The roundtable participants argued that as businesses, public sector bodies and ICT providers looked to address the challenging environment, many industries accelerated digitalization and automation. This happened even in industries that were lagging in their digitization before the pandemic, e.g., the health care sector, which was slow to adopt Internet-of-Things (IoT) solutions. According to some of the experts, supply chains in advanced economies have actually adjusted remarkably quickly to the challenges of COVID-19. On the other hand, they argued that low digitization sectors, such as construction, are expected to be hard hit by the pandemic. In any case, despite the nuances, the experts concurred around the key role of digital infrastructures for economic resiliency in the pandemic.

All in all, considering the evidence presented above, we should expect that more connected regions will exhibit higher economic resiliency in the case of a pandemic disruption. This will be explored through an econometric approach for the case of the United States.

## 3. Theoretical Model

The empirical model is based on an augmented Solow framework [30], where economies produce according to a Cobb–Douglas production function (this model was used in a previous study to assess the impact of broadband on economic performance for a sample of Brazilian states [31]):

$$GDP_{it} = A_{it} K_{it}^{\alpha} L_{it}^{\beta} HK_{it}^{\gamma} \tag{1}$$

where $GDP$ represents gross domestic product, $K$ is the non-telecom physical capital stock, $L$ is labor and $HK$ denotes human capital, approximated as $HK = e^{hk}$, where $HK$ reflects the efficiency of a unit of labor, as in [32]. Subscripts $i$ and $t$ denote, respectively, states and time periods (the model will be estimated for period 2016–2020). The term $A$ represents total factor productivity (TFP), which reflects differences in production efficiency across states of the country over time. TFP is expressed as:

$$A_{it} = \Omega_i BB_{it}^{\Phi + \delta SPEED_{it}} \tag{2}$$

Accordingly, TFP depends on state-specific characteristics represented by fixed effect $\Omega_i$, a term reflecting time invariant idiosyncratic productivity effects, which may make some US states more productive per se because of unobserved characteristics (we decided to design the model with fixed effects rather than random effects as the conducted Hausman tests suggested so). As it is supposed that internet connectivity contributes to increase productivity, $A$ is assumed to depend positively on the level of broadband adoption, denoted by $BB$. Thus, we expect a positive value for $\Phi$ indicating the economic gains derived from broadband. Another important aspect that could shape the impact of broadband on state-level productivity is the existence of differences in the quality of connections. To approximate quality, following [9,33], the measure we use is the download speed of connections within each state. The moderating effect of the quality of connections in a state is hypothesized to be positive, i.e., $\delta > 0$. This means that for two US states with the same broadband penetration, we expect to observe a larger economic impact for those with faster speeds. Inserting Equation (2) into (1), we obtain:

$$GDP_{it} = \Omega_i BB_{it}^{\Phi + \delta SPEED_{it}} K_{it}^{\alpha} L_{it}^{\beta} HK_{it}^{\gamma}$$

Applying logarithms for linearization, and after some rearrangements, we get:

$$\log(GDP_{it}) = \mu_i + \alpha \log(K_{it}) + \beta \log(L_{it}) + \gamma hk_{it}$$
$$+ \Phi \log(BB_{it}) + \delta SPEED_{it} \log(BB_{it})$$

where $\mu_i = \log(\Omega_i)$ is a state-level fixed effect. Thus, we understand that the evolution of *GDP* depends on specific unobserved state characteristics, on physical capital stock, on labor, on broadband adoption and on the speed of the connections. This model is appropriate for considering the effect of broadband on *GDP* under normal circumstances, but it is still incomplete in accounting for the role of this technology in mitigating economic losses in the COVID-19 context. Thus, the pandemic should be considered an external shock, not successfully absorbed by the capital or labor evolution, and therefore requiring a specific variable to account for it. Therefore, to consider the incidence of the COVID-19 on economic output, we add on the right-hand side indicators to account for the degree of propagation of the disease, with the assumption that the more the pandemic has propagated and the stricter the isolation measures to combat it, the greater the expected economic damage. To account for the role of broadband in counteracting the economic effects generated by the pandemic, we add interaction variables between broadband connectivity and the COVID-19-related indicators. As a result, by introducing the COVID-19-related indicators (denoted generically as *COVID*) and the interaction variables, the transformed equation is:

$$\log(GDP_{it}) = \mu_i + \alpha \log(K_{it}) + \beta \log(L_{it}) + \gamma hk_{it}$$
$$+ \Phi \log(BB_{it}) + \delta SPEED_{it} \log(BB_{it}) + \mathrm{n}(COVID_{it}) \quad (3)$$
$$+ \zeta(COVID_{it}) \log(BB_{it})$$

In this equation, we expect the parameter associated with COVID-19 to present a negative sign given that the greater the incidence of the disease, the worse the economic outcome; in that case, then $\mathrm{n} < 0$. As for broadband, its economic effect under "normal circumstances" is absorbed by the parameters $\Phi$ and $\delta$, while its effect in mitigating the pandemic crisis is captured by $\zeta$.

In order to correctly interpret the signs of $\mathrm{n}$ and $\zeta$, it is useful to differentiate Equation (3) with respect to the COVID-19 variable:

$$\frac{\partial \log(GDP)}{\partial(COVID)} = \mathrm{n} + \zeta \log(BB) \quad (4)$$

As long as $\mathrm{n} + \zeta \log(BB) < 0$, an increase in the COVID-19 propagation will generate a contraction of the GDP. However, we also expect that the more connected US states will be better prepared to mitigate part of the economic damage and thus experience smaller economic contractions. Because of this, the signs expected for both coefficients are the following: $\mathrm{n} < 0$ and $\zeta > 0$, with $\mathrm{n} + \zeta \log(BB) < 0$ as the mitigating role of broadband should be partial, not total. The econometric analysis conducted will aim to identify if the parameters behave as expected above.

To control for potential endogeneity between GDP and the broadband variable, Equation (3) will be estimated in the context of a structural multi-equation model, in keeping with previous authors [7,34,35].

Following [7], a 4-Equations model will be considered, as depicted in Table 1.

**Table 1.** The system of equations for the structural model.

| | |
|---|---|
| Aggregate production equation | $GDP_{it} = f(K_{it}, L_{it}, HK_{it}, BB_{it}, SPEED_{it}, COVID_{it})$ |
| Demand equation | $BB_{it} = h(GDPpc_{it}, P_{it}, HK_{it}, URBAN_{it})$ |
| Supply equation | $REVENUE_{it} = g(P_{it}, COMPETITION_{it})$ |
| Broadband infrastructure production equation | $BB_{it} - BB_{it-1} = k(REVENUE_{it})$ |

The aggregate production function is the same as that presented in Equation (3). The demand equation endogenizes broadband penetration, stating that it is a function of income (GDP per capita), the price of the service, education level (HK), and the percentage of the population that lives in densely populated areas (URBAN). The supply equation links the industry output with prices and a measure of the number of fixed providers in a market (number of operators for every 100,000 inhabitants). In our case, we proxy sectoral output with revenue rather than investment as in [7]. The reason is that there is not a reliable state-level broadband CAPEX series estimate for the US covering the considered period. Finally, the infrastructure production equation states that the annual change in broadband penetration is a function of industry revenue. Ref. [7] also adds R&D intensity and local loop unbundling as determinants in the demand and supply equations, respectively. However, we understand that these regressors are suitable for explaining demand and supply patterns in a cross-country context, but not for regional analysis as ours, as R&D is not necessarily a suitable indicator of regional disparities and regulation is uniform within the country. The three supplementary equations (demand, supply, and infrastructure production) fulfill the roll of endogenizing broadband since these three equations involve both the demand and supply of telecom infrastructure [7,34]. All equations include state-level fixed effects, and the empirical approach followed is three-stage least squares (3SLS) simultaneous equation estimation.

## 4. Descriptive Statistics

Table 2 provides the descriptions and sources of the model variables. State-level economic variables are extracted from the US Bureau of Economic Analysis database, while broadband penetration comes from Federal Communications Commission Internet Access Services reports and the American Community Survey. Internet advertised speeds are collected from the Technology Policy Institute dataset.

**Table 2.** Variables description and sources.

| Code | Description | Source |
|---|---|---|
| | Main equation variables | |
| GDP | Gross Domestic Product in millions of current dollars | Bureau of Economic Analysis |
| K | Current-Cost Net Stock of Private Fixed Assets (excluding Broadcasting and Telecom) in billions of current dollars | Built with data from the Bureau of Economic Analysis |
| L | Total Full-Time and Part-Time Employment | Bureau of Economic Analysis |
| HK | Share of the population 25–64 with tertiary education | OECD Regional Statistics |
| BB | Fixed Broadband connections offering at least 25 Mbps down and 3 Mbps up, every 100 households | FCC Internet Access Services reports/ American Community Survey (ACS) |
| Speed | Average maximum available download speed (Mbps) | Technology Policy Institute |
| | Variables for COVID-19 analysis | |
| Pandemic Deaths | Deaths by COVID-19 every 100,000 inhabitants | U.S. Center for Disease Control and Prevention |
| Stringency Index | Composite measure based on nine response indicators including school closures, workplace closures, and travel bans, rescaled to a value from 0 to 100 (100 = strictest). | Our World in Data |
| | Variables for additional equations of the structural model | |
| Price | Average price for commercially-available residential plans offering at least 25 Mbps down | US FCC |
| Operators | Number of fixed broadband operators every 100,000 inhabitants | FCC form 477 |
| Revenue | Calculated as: average price x total broadband connections (in million USD) | Built from U.S. FCC and ACS data |
| Urban | Percentage of population living in urban areas. | U.S. Census Bureau |

To account for COVID-19 propagation, we rely on two main variables. We identify two channels through which the virus can lead to changes in production and consumption routines and thus generate a negative economic effect. We first consider an indicator of the number of deaths attributed to the disease for every 100,000 inhabitants based on data provided by the U.S. Center for Disease Control and Prevention. These data indicate important differences by state, ranging from 22.5 (Vermont) to 205 (New Jersey) in 2020. This metric should be more reliable than the infections ratio (more prone to reflect differences by state in terms of testing strategies), although there is still the risk of some misreporting of deaths if officially recorded. The second variable specifically captures the normative channel, linked to the restrictions imposed in terms of home confinement and the closure of offices, shops, and schools, among others. This is measured as the average Stringency Index during 2020. Policy responses have varied significantly by state, from the strictest (New Mexico) to the lightest (South Dakota). Naturally, as the model will be estimated for a 2016–2020 panel, the COVID variables will take a value of zero for years before 2020 as there were no COVID deaths or lockdown restrictions imposed. Adding other policy-related variables, such as the share of vaccinated population, is not possible as our data set extends only through the end of 2020, when vaccines were not yet available (the first vaccine in the US was administered in mid-December of that year).

Next, we report in Table 3 the main descriptive statistics and correlations. For brevity, we report only these indicators for the variables in the primary equation of the system (aggregate production equation), although the statistics for the complete set of variables is available upon request. The main economic variables exhibit an important variation across states, in part because of size differences. In addition, average broadband penetration is 60% of the population. The joint skewness and kurtosis test for normality rejects the null hypothesis in all cases, indicating that the variables are skewed or with non-normal kurtosis, although in the case of the broadband variable, it does so at only 10% significance. Moreover, the Jarque–Bera test indicates that broadband is the only variable in the set that follows a normal distribution, as the null hypothesis is not rejected in that case. In any case, the lack of normality should not be a concern as it was faced in previous research with similar characteristics (see for instance [36] or [37]).

Table 3. Descriptive statistics and correlations.

| | Mean | Std. Dv. | Obs. | Jarque–Bera | Skewness & Kurtosis | Correlations | | | | | | |
|---|---|---|---|---|---|---|---|---|---|---|---|---|
| | | | | | | GDP | K | L | HK | BB | Speed | Pandemic Deaths |
| GDP | 406,786.70 | 507,853.30 | 245 | 1460.00 | 128.86 | 1.000 | | | | | | |
| K | 931.77 | 1172.75 | 245 | 1386.00 | 127.69 | 0.996 | 1.000 | | | | | |
| L | 3,982,840.00 | 4,387,997.00 | 245 | 861.40 | 110.48 | 0.984 | 0.988 | 1.000 | | | | |
| HK | 43.60 | 6.57 | 245 | 28.81 | 17.04 | 0.083 | 0.061 | 0.024 | 1.000 | | | |
| BB | 59.92 | 15.23 | 245 | 3.53 | 5.84 | 0.226 | 0.225 | 0.175 | 0.625 | 1.000 | | |
| Speed | 689.78 | 231.20 | 245 | 28.03 | 21.48 | 0.158 | 0.157 | 0.118 | 0.404 | 0.679 | 1.000 | |
| Pandemic Deaths | 20.94 | 45.99 | 245 | 289.30 | 79.75 | −0.007 | 0.015 | −0.026 | 0.079 | 0.229 | 0.337 | 1.000 |
| Stringency Index | 10.27 | 20.72 | 245 | 100.80 | 46.11 | 0.025 | 0.046 | −0.006 | 0.117 | 0.256 | 0.374 | 0.895 |

For the correlations, as expected K and L are highly correlated. The lack of correlation between COVID measures and the main economic variables suggests that the former should be considered exogenous shocks unrelated to the latter. Naturally, the two COVID-19 correlate highly (0.895). In order to prevent any potential multicollinearity problems, we conduct VIF tests and perform additional checks in Section 5. No multicollinearity concerns should arise from the remaining variables.

## 5. Estimation Results

In this section, we present the econometric estimates for the model presented in Section 3. We gradually consider the COVID-related variables presented in Table 2 and their interactions with broadband in order to see how GDP is affected in each case. The results highlighted below are consistent in suggesting negative economic effects of increases in both pandemic deaths and the Stringency Index, while at the same time, they highlight the role of broadband in counteracting that economic damage.

Table 4 summarizes the econometric results for the structural model. In all estimates, all equations present excellent fit (R-squared rounding 0.90 or above), except for the broadband infrastructure production equation, where the R-squared was 0.36. In column (i), we present a baseline model without including the COVID-19-related variables, with results showing the expected coefficients and signs. GDP depends on capital and labor, while human capital is found to be not significant. In addition, broadband has a positive effect on GDP, which increases with the availability of high-speed connections (speed is introduced as a dummy variable taking the value of 1 if the average maximum download speed is above 850 Mbps and 0 otherwise). Considering potential multicollinearity problems, we conducted VIF tests and subsequently performed checks in the main equation by removing some of the highly correlated regressors, with results still verifying a non-significant coefficient for human capital and a positive and significant effect from broadband on GDP (these additional checks are available upon request). This suggests that multicollinearity should not be a concern for the purpose of this study. In column (ii), the estimate introduces both pandemic deaths and Stringency Index as regressors, without interacting them with broadband. The coefficient estimate of pandemic deaths is interpreted as the percentage of GDP variation after an increase in one unit in the quantity of COVID-19 deaths per 100,000 population. As expected, pandemic deaths have a negative and significant coefficient, highlighting the damage caused by the pandemic to the economy. This means that an increase in one death per 100,000 population is associated with a GDP contraction of $-0.01\%$. In turn, the coefficient of the Stringency Index is interpreted as the percentage change in GDP after an increase in one unit in the tightness of the restrictions. The Stringency Index also exhibits a negative and significant coefficient (at 10% level). This means that, as expected, the stricter the lockdowns, the worse the economic performance. In column (iii), we add the interaction between pandemic deaths and broadband. The interaction variable is positive and highly significant, thereby confirming our hypothesis that robust fixed broadband connectivity helped to mitigate economic damage during the first year of the pandemic in the United States. Note that in column (iii), the Stringency variable loses significance. This is because it is highly correlated with the pandemic deaths variable (as seen in Table 3), with the latter effectively capturing the economic effects from the pandemic (as this is another potential source of multicollinearity, we replicated the estimates considering a single COVID-19 variable at a time and discarding the other one, with results standing unchanged). In short, results from column (iii) indicate that an increase in pandemic deaths negatively affects economic performance but that the economic contraction is mitigated through high connectivity levels. This means that for two states facing similar death rates, we expect, ceteris paribus, that the better-connected state will experience less economic damage due its ability to keep the economy running as a result of higher broadband adoption. Next, in column (iv), we consider the Stringency Index as the only interaction with broadband. Again, the role of broadband is crucial in mitigating the economic damage, as the interaction variable presents a positive and significant coefficient. In this case, the deaths variable loses significance, as the Stringency Index captures most of the economic effects from the pandemic.

The previous estimates consider a baseline specification for the secondary equations, as represented in Table 1 above. However, the pandemic may have also impacted some of the terms of those equations. In particular, broadband demand may have also been influenced by the pandemic. Neglecting that possibility may have resulted in a biased estimate of broadband through the demand equation, affecting the results of the system. To check that concern, we replicate the previous estimates by incorporating the COVID-19-related variables as determinants of broadband demand. The results, presented in columns (v) and (vi), show a non-significant effect from both COVID variables in the demand equation, with no substantial changes arising in the main equation.

From all the estimates reported in Table 4, it seems clear that the pandemic-deaths and the Stringency Index present overlapping information, as one loses significance every time we interact the other one with broadband. As a result, we will select only one of both COVID-variables to pursue the analysis. We believe that the Stringency Index is more suitable for explaining the virus impact because it measures aspects that directly affect the daily economic activity (in terms of imposed restrictions), in contrast with the death's variable, which can be interpreted as having an indirect role. In other words, it is not the deaths per se that drive the economic recession: it is the lockdown decisions made as prophylactic measures. Therefore, we continue our analysis relying on the estimated coefficients from the specification presented in column (vi): ꞃ = −0.0041 and ζ = 0.0009.

**Table 4.** Economic Impact of Broadband—Structural model (2016–2020).

| Dep. Variable: $log(GDP)$ | (i) | (ii) | (iii) | (iv) | (v) | (vi) |
|---|---|---|---|---|---|---|
| $log(K)$ | 0.3989 *** | 0.5029 *** | 0.4575 *** | 0.4520 *** | 0.4327 *** | 0.4275 *** |
|  | [0.0323] | [0.0408] | [0.0416] | [0.0415] | [0.0410] | [0.0409] |
| $log(L)$ | 0.6063 *** | 0.3153 *** | 0.3723 *** | 0.3803 *** | 0.3748 *** | 0.3823 *** |
|  | [0.0381] | [0.0770] | [0.0773] | [0.0772] | [0.0753] | [0.0752] |
| HK | −0.0003 | 0.0009 | −0.0003 | −0.0005 | 0.0009 | 0.0007 |
|  | [0.0014] | [0.0014] | [0.0014] | [0.0015] | [0.0015] | [0.0015] |
| $log(BB)$ | 0.1387 *** | 0.1281 *** | 0.1505 *** | 0.1524 *** | 0.1570 *** | 0.1587 *** |
|  | [0.0146] | [0.0138] | [0.0146] | [0.0146] | [0.0144] | [0.0144] |
| $log(BB) * Speed > 850$ | 0.0020 *** | 0.0020 *** | 0.0017 *** | 0.0017 *** | 0.0016 ** | 0.0016 ** |
|  | [0.0007] | [0.0007] | [0.0007] | [0.0006] | [0.0006] | [0.0006] |
| Pandemic deaths |  | −0.0001 *** | −0.0014 *** | −0.0001 | −0.0014 *** | −0.0001 * |
|  |  | [0.0000] | [0.0003] | [0.0000] | [0.0003] | [0.0001] |
| Stringency Index |  | −0.0003 * | −0.0002 | −0.0042 *** | −0.0002 | −0.0041 *** |
|  |  | [0.000] | [0.0001] | [0.0009] | [0.0002] | [0.0009] |
| Pandemic deaths * $log(BB)$ |  |  | 0.0003 *** |  | 0.0003 *** |  |
|  |  |  | [0.0001] |  | [0.0001] |  |
| Sringency Index * $log(BB)$ |  |  |  | 0.0009 *** |  | 0.0009 *** |
|  |  |  |  | [0.0002] |  | [0.0002] |
| Dep. variable: $log(BB)$ |  |  |  |  |  |  |
| $log(P)$ | −0.0696 * | −0.0687 * | −0.0494 | −0.0446 | −0.0362 | −0.0314 |
|  | [0.0378] | [0.0378] | [0.0363] | [0.0363] | [0.0354] | [0.0354] |
| $log(HK)$ | 0.9870 *** | 0.9687 *** | 0.9571 *** | 0.9639 *** | 0.2485 | 0.2577 |
|  | [0.3231] | [0.3228] | [0.3198] | [0.3195] | [0.3726] | [0.3724] |
| $log(GDP\ pc)$ | 2.0219 *** | 1.9330 *** | 2.0215 *** | 2.0181 *** | 2.3143 *** | 2.3082 *** |
|  | [0.1852] | [0.1877] | [0.1847] | [0.1844] | [0.1939] | [0.1935] |
| $log(URBAN)$ | 3.7088 *** | 4.5730 *** | 4.0799 *** | 4.1248 *** | 3.1266 ** | 3.1858 ** |
|  | [1.3108] | [1.3288] | [1.2841] | [1.2786] | [1.2772] | [1.2711] |
| Pandemic deaths |  |  |  |  | 0.0005 | 0.0005 |
|  |  |  |  |  | [0.0003] | [0.0003] |
| Stringency Index |  |  |  |  | 0.0002 | 0.0002 |
|  |  |  |  |  | [0.0001] | [0.0007] |
| Dep. variable: $log(REVENUE)$ |  |  |  |  |  |  |
| $log(P)$ | 0.3723 *** | 0.3679 *** | 0.3706 *** | 0.3672 *** | 0.3714 *** | 0.3682 *** |
|  | [0.0678] | [0.0679] | [0.0678] | [0.0679] | [0.0678] | [0.0679] |
| Operators | 0.0764 | 0.0787 | 0.0730 | 0.0727 | 0.0801 | 0.0798 |
|  | [0.0717] | [0.0715] | [0.0715] | [0.0714] | [0.0716] | [0.0715] |
| Dep. variable: $log\left[\frac{BB_t}{BB_{t-1}}\right]$ |  |  |  |  |  |  |
| $log(REVENUE)$ | −0.2953 *** | −0.2882 *** | −0.2923 *** | −0.2986 *** | −0.2923 *** | −0.2996 *** |
|  | [0.0598] | [0.0592] | [0.0593] | [0.0592] | [0.0593] | [0.0592] |
| Fixed effects by State (x) | YES | YES | YES | YES | YES | YES |
| Observations | 219 | 219 | 219 | 219 | 219 | 219 |
| Estimation method | 3SLS | 3SLS | 3SLS | 3SLS | 3SLS | 3SLS |

Note: Standard errors in parenthesis. * $p < 10\%$, ** $p < 5\%$, *** $p < 1\%$. (x) State-level fixed effects included in all model equations.

With the estimated coefficients, we can calculate the 2020 growth rate attributed exclusively to the restrictions imposed, which depends on the level of penetration, as seen above in Equation (4). With this information, we can simulate the GDP for 2020 according to two different scenarios of broadband penetration: that of the state with the highest broadband adoption (Delaware, 91.4%) and that with the lowest broadband adoption (Arkansas, 39.7%). Results are presented in Figure 3 next to the actual values for 2019 and 2020 GDP.

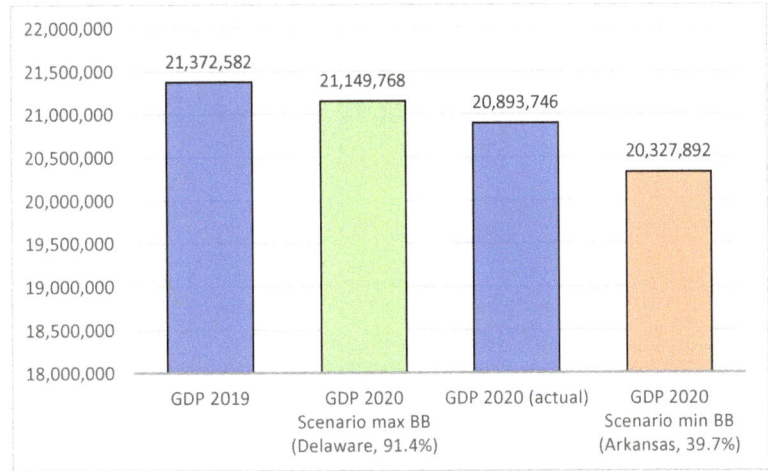

**Figure 3.** National evolution of GDP by broadband scenario.

On a national level, if the United States broadband adoption was that of Delaware (rather than the actual 2020 value of 70.5%), the GDP would have contracted only by 1% in 2020, a much lighter recession than the actual 2.2% contraction. Conversely, had broadband been below current levels, the GDP contraction would have been much more severe.

Next, we calculate the elasticity of GDP with respect to lockdown intensity as a function of the Stringency Index and broadband penetration. The elasticity to be estimated must be interpreted as how much the GDP contracts if state governments decided to tighten restrictions by 1%. By applying the estimated coefficients to Equation (4), we can derive an estimate of the elasticity between lockdown intensity and GDP:

$$\varepsilon_{(GDP,\ STRINGENCY)} = (-0.0041 + 0.0009 \log(BB)) \times (Stringency\ Index)$$

The elasticity level in this equation depends on both broadband penetration and the Stringency Index. Using the average lockdown intensity and the national-level broadband penetration in 2020, we estimate a national elasticity of $-0.014$. This means that an increase in the strictness of the restrictions by 1% above 2020 levels will result in a GDP contraction of 0.014%.

Figure 4 presents the elasticity calculations by state, using in each case their respective Stringency Index and broadband penetration. This elasticity can be thought of as a measure of how much a state's GDP was negatively affected by an increase in the Stringency Index. The largest elasticity (in absolute terms) is that of Arkansas, where an increase in 1% in the Stringency Index reduces GDP by 0.039%. On the other end of the distribution, the states that are less sensitive to lockdown intensity are those in the Northeast (Delaware, New Jersey, Rhode Island), partially because of having greater broadband adoption.

In Figure 5, we plot the elasticities by state against fixed broadband penetration levels. In the panel on the left, the elasticity calculation is plotted against the actual (real) 2020 Stringency Index by state. In the panel on the right, we replicate the calculation but leave constant the Stringency Index across states (using the national average) to isolate the specific differences in elasticity attributed to broadband penetration levels. This indicates that in states with higher broadband penetration, less economic damage occurs as a result of increasing lockdown intensity above 2020 levels.

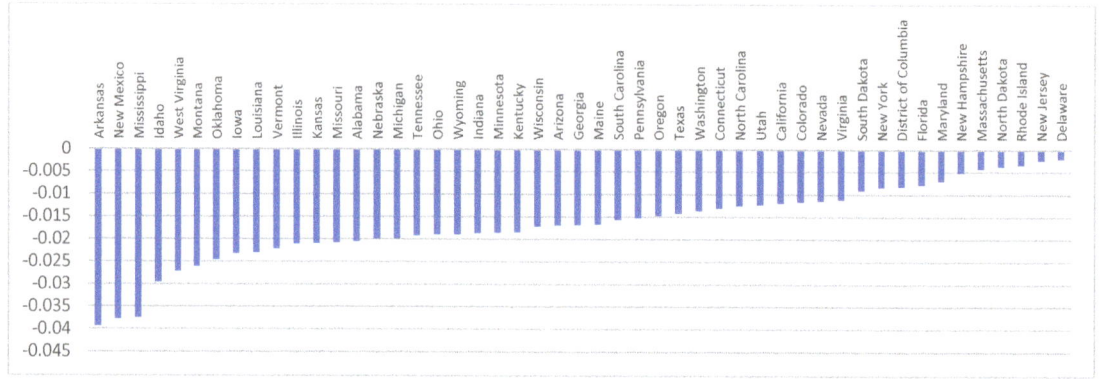

**Figure 4.** Elasticity GDP—Stringency Index.

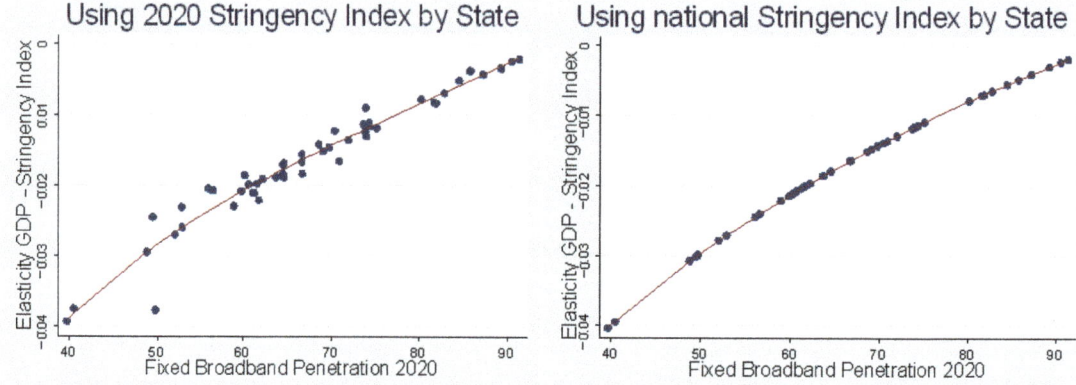

**Figure 5.** Elasticity GDP—Stringency Index by level of BB penetration.

## 6. Conclusions

The COVID-19 pandemic has raised a fundamental challenge to the global socioeconomic system, forcing countries to reexamine social practices and production systems and generating a severe global economic recession. This study has researched the extent to which fixed broadband networks mitigated the negative economic impact generated by the pandemic in the United States.

The results support the position that US states, such as Delaware and New Jersey, with higher broadband adoption were able to counteract a larger portion of the economic losses caused by the 2020 COVID-19 pandemic than states with lower broadband adoption. The connectivity levels allowed for important parts of the economy to continue functioning during lockdowns. At the national level, if the United States broadband penetration figures were those of the more connected states, the GDP would have contracted only 1% in 2020 because of the virus, a much softer recession than the actual 2.2%.

In conclusion, the pandemic highlighted the critical need to close the digital divide and to ensure universal adoption of high-quality internet connections in the United States.

Today, wide penetration rate disparities exist between states, such as Delaware's rate of 91.4% compared with Arkansas's rate of 39.7%. Because of this, public authorities should focus on creating policy frameworks that allow operators to spur infrastructure deployment and to find the optimal technological mixes to deliver the highest performance to users.

**Author Contributions:** Data curation, J.J.; Formal analysis, J.J.; Project administration, R.K.; Supervision, R.K.; Writing—original draft, R.K. and J.J. All authors have read and agreed to the published version of the manuscript.

**Funding:** This research was funded by Network On, a consortium of companies involved in promoting the development of broadband in the United States.

**Institutional Review Board Statement:** Not applicable.

**Informed Consent Statement:** Not applicable.

**Data Availability Statement:** Not applicable.

**Acknowledgments:** The authors would like to thank Rob Rubinovitz, Jay Schwarz, and three anonymous referees for valuable comments and suggestions.

**Conflicts of Interest:** The authors declare no conflict of interest.

## References

1. Leach, M.; MacGregor, H.; Scoones, I.; Wilkinson, A. Post-pandemic transformations: How and why COVID-19 requires us to rethink development. *World Dev.* **2021**, *138*, 105233. [CrossRef]
2. Hardy, A. The role of the telephone in economic development. *Telecommun. Policy* **1980**, *4*, 278–286. [CrossRef]
3. Karner, J.; Onyeji, R. *Telecom Private Investment and Economic Growth: The Case of African and Central & East European Countries*; Jonkoping International Business School: Jönköping, Sweden, 2007.
4. Jensen, R. The Digital Provide: Information (Technology), Market Performance, and Welfare in the South Indian Fisheries Sector. *Q. J. Econ.* **2007**, *122*, 879–924. [CrossRef]
5. Katz, R.L.; Zenhäusern, P.; Suter, S. *An Evaluation of Socio-Economic Impact of a Fiber Network in Switzerland*; Polynomics and Telecom Advisory Services, LLC: Olten, Switzerland, 2008.
6. Fornefeld, M.; Delaunay, G.; Elixmann, D. *The Impact of Broadband on Growth and Productivity*; European Commission (DG Information Society and Media), MICUS: Düsseldorf, Germany, 2008.
7. Koutroumpis, P. The Economic Impact of Broadband on Growth: A Simultaneous Approach. *Telecommun. Policy* **2009**, *33*, 471–485. [CrossRef]
8. Katz, R.; Vaterlaus, S.; Zenhäusern, P.; Suter, S. The Impact of Broadband on Jobs and the German Economy. *Intereconomics* **2012**, *45*, 26–34. [CrossRef]
9. Rohman, I.K.; Bohlin, E. *Socio-Economic Effects of Broadband Speed*; Ericsson: Stockholm, Sweden, 2012.
10. Mack, E.; Faggian, A. Productivity and broadband: The human factor. *Int. Reg. Sci. Rev.* **2013**, *36*, 392–423. [CrossRef]
11. Arvin, M.; Pradhan, R. Broadband penetration and economic growth nexus: Evidence from cross-country panel data. *J. Appl. Econ.* **2014**, *46*, 4360–4369. [CrossRef]
12. Fernandes, A.M.; Mattoo, A.; Nguyen, H.; Schiffbauer, M. The internet and Chinese exports in the pre-ali baba era. *J. Dev. Econ.* **2019**, *138*, 57–76. [CrossRef]
13. Katz, R.; Jung, J.; Callorda, F. The Economic Contribution of Broadband, Digitization and ICT Regulation and Regional Econometric Modelling. International Telecommunications Union 2020a. Available online: https://www.itu.int/en/publications/ITU-D/pages/publications.aspx?lang=en&media=electronic&parent=D-PREF-EF.BDR-2020 (accessed on 15 August 2022).
14. Lefophane, M.H.; Kalaba, M. Estimating effects of ICT intensity on productivity, employment and output in South Africa: An industry-level analysis. *Inf. Technol. Dev.* **2021**, *28*, 346–371. [CrossRef]
15. Teodorescu, H.N.L. Survey of IC&T in Disaster Mitigation and Disaster Situation Management. In *Improving Disaster Resilience and Mitigation—IT Means and Tools*; NATO Science for Peace and Security Series C: Environmental Security; Teodorescu, H.N., Kirschenbaum, A., Cojocaru, S., Bruderlein, C., Eds.; Springer: Dordrecht, The Netherlands, 2014.
16. O'Reilly, G.; Jrad, A.; Nagarajan, R.; Brown, T.; Conrad, S. Critical Infrastructure Analysis of Telecom for Natural Disasters. Networks. In Proceedings of the 12th International Telecommunications Network Strategy and Planning Symposium, New Delhi, India, 6–9 November 2006; pp. 1–6.
17. Chamola, V.; Hassija, V.; Gupta, V.; Guizani, M. A Comprehensive Review of the COVID-19 Pandemic and the Role of IoT, Drones, AI, Blockchain, and 5G in Managing its Impact. *IEEE Access* **2020**, *8*, 90225–90265. [CrossRef]
18. Biancone, P.; Secinaro, S.; Marseglia, R.; Calandra, D. E-health for the future. Managerial perspectives using a multiple case study approach. *Technovation* **2021**, 102406. [CrossRef]

19. Tortorella, G.L.; Fogliatto, F.S.; Saurin, T.A.; Tonetto, L.M.; McFarlane, D. Contributions of Healthcare 4.0 digital applications to the resilience of healthcare organizations during the COVID-19 outbreak. *Technovation* **2021**, *111*, 102379. [CrossRef]
20. Massaro, M. Digital transformation in the healthcare sector through blockchain technology. Insights from academic research and business developments. *Technovation* **2021**, 102386. [CrossRef]
21. Chi, N.T.K. Innovation capability: The impact of e-CRM and COVID-19 risk perception. *Technol. Soc.* **2021**, *67*, 101725. [CrossRef]
22. Cao, J.; Liu, F.; Shang, M.; Zhou, X. Toward street vending in post COVID-19 China: Social networking services information overload and switching intention. *Technol. Soc.* **2021**, *66*, 101669. [CrossRef]
23. Katz, R.; Jung, J.; Callorda, F. Can digitization mitigate the economic damage of a pandemic? Evidence from SARS. *Telecommun. Policy* **2020**, *44*, 102044. [CrossRef]
24. Katz, R.; Jung, J. *The Economic Impact of Broadband and Digitization through the COVID-19 Pandemic: Econometric Modelling*; International Telecommunication Union: Geneva, Switzerland, 2021.
25. Zhang, X. Broadband and economic growth in China: An empirical study during the COVID-19 pandemic period. *Telemat. Inf.* **2021**, *58*, 101533. [CrossRef]
26. Isley, C.; Low, S. Broadband adoption and availability: Impacts on rural employment during COVID-19. *Telecommun. Policy* **2022**. [CrossRef]
27. Raj, M.; Sundararajan, A.; You, C. *COVID-19 and Digital Resilience: Evidence from Uber Eats 2021*; NYU Stern School of Business: New York, NY, USA, 2021.
28. Carvalho, M.; Hagerman, A.D.; Whitacre, B. Telework and COVID-19 Resiliency in the Southeastern United States. *J. Reg. Anal. Policy* **2022**, *52*, 19–34.
29. ITU. *Economic Impact of COVID-19 on Digital Infrastructure*; Report of an Economic Experts Roundtable Organized by ITU; International Telecommunications Union: Geneva, Switzerland, 2020.
30. Solow, R. A contribution to the theory of economic growth. *Q. J. Econ.* **1956**, *70*, 65–94. [CrossRef]
31. Jung, J.; López-Bazo, E. On the regional impact of broadband on productivity: The case of Brazil. *Telecommun. Policy* **2020**, *44*, 101826. [CrossRef]
32. Hall, R.E.; Jones, C.I. Why Do Some Countries Produce so much more Output per Worker than Others. *Q. J. Econ.* **1999**, *114*, 83–116. [CrossRef]
33. Rohman, I.K.; Bohlin, E. Does Broadband speed really matter as a driver of economic growth? Investigating OECD countries. *Int. J. Manag. Netw. Econ.* **2012**, *2*, 336–356. [CrossRef]
34. Roeller, L.E.; Waverman, L. Telecommunications Infrastructure and Economic Development: A Simultaneous Approach. *Am. Econ. Rev.* **2001**, *91*, 909–923. [CrossRef]
35. Katz, R.; Callorda, F. *The Economic Contribution of Broadband, Digitalization and ICT Regulation*; International Telecommunications Union: Geneva, Switzerland, 2018.
36. Batrancea, L.; Rathnaswamy, M.K.; Batrancea, I. A panel data analysis on determinants of economic growth in seven non-BCBS Countries. *J. Knowl. Econ.* **2022**, *13*, 1651–1665. [CrossRef]
37. Batrancea, L.; Rus, M.I.; Masca, E.S.; Morar, I.D. Fiscal Pressure as a Trigger of Financial Performance for the Energy Industry: An Empirical Investigation across a 16-Year Period. *Energies* **2021**, *14*, 3769. [CrossRef]

Article

# COVID-19 Pandemic and Its Impact on Challenges in the Construction Sector: A Case Study of Slovak Enterprises

Dominika Gajdosikova [1,*], Katarina Valaskova [1,*], Tomas Kliestik [1,2] and Veronika Machova [2]

1. Faculty of Operation and Economics of Transport and Communications, University of Zilina, Univerzitna 1, 010 26 Zilina, Slovakia
2. The Institute of Technology and Business in Ceske Budejovice, School of Expertness and Valuation, Okruzni 517/10, 3701 Ceske Budejovice, Czech Republic
* Correspondence: dominika.gajdosikova@stud.uniza.sk (D.G.); katarina.valaskova@fpedas.uniza.sk (K.V.)

**Abstract:** The corona crisis has affected not only the economic sphere, but also the sphere of health, health care, employment, safety, and health protection in the workplace, shopping habits, and future expectations, to which people adapt their decisions in various areas of daily life. The COVID-19 pandemic, called a global health crisis, was an unpredictable risk of global proportions that paralyzed the entire world. The main aim of this paper is to quantify the impacts of the COVID-19 pandemic on the construction sector, which is considered a crucial sector of the Slovak economy, to evaluate changes in the development of key indicators using adequate quantitative methods. First, a sample of 2000 businesses were analyzed using the 12 financial indicators that were chosen. Second, using the non-parametric Friedman test, a more thorough study was carried out with a focus on analyzing the existence of statistically significant variations in the values of computed indicators as a result of changes in the development of key financial ratios. The Bonferroni adjustments were employed to pinpoint the areas of stochastic dominance at the conclusion of the study. A detailed analysis of the calculated financial indicators showed that the arrival of the pandemic had a negative impact on many aspects of business in the construction sector and affected the financial and economic situation of companies in the construction sector of the Slovak Republic. However, due to the fact that this sector is characterized by slower reactions to changes in the economy, the most significant impacts will be even more noticeable in the future.

**Keywords:** business performance; financial analysis; COVID-19 pandemic; construction sector; Slovak enterprises

**MSC:** 62P20

Citation: Gajdosikova, D.; Valaskova, K.; Kliestik, T.; Machova, V. COVID-19 Pandemic and Its Impact on Challenges in the Construction Sector: A Case Study of Slovak Enterprises. *Mathematics* 2022, 10, 3130. https://doi.org/10.3390/math10173130

Academic Editors: Lina Novickytė, Jolanta Drozdz, Radosław Pastusiak and Michał Soliwoda

Received: 22 July 2022
Accepted: 27 August 2022
Published: 1 September 2022

**Publisher's Note:** MDPI stays neutral with regard to jurisdictional claims in published maps and institutional affiliations.

**Copyright:** © 2022 by the authors. Licensee MDPI, Basel, Switzerland. This article is an open access article distributed under the terms and conditions of the Creative Commons Attribution (CC BY) license (https://creativecommons.org/licenses/by/4.0/).

## 1. Introduction

The global COVID-19 pandemic hit the whole world and stopped all activities and enterprises in their businesses [1]. The COVID-19 pandemic first appeared in Slovakia in the first quarter of 2020, when the first case of the disease was confirmed. Gradually, with increasing cases of coronavirus infection, the epidemiological situation worsened until it gradually resulted in the first wave of the pandemic in Slovakia, which forced enterprises to partially or completely limit their business activities [2]. The uncertainty that accompanied the first wave of the pandemic, the unfavorable epidemiological situation, and the measures associated with it caused many businesses to be unable to respond to the situation flexibly and in a timely manner. The limitation of production naturally had an impact on the added value and the result of management of almost the entire spectrum of business entities [3]. Businesses were forced to optimize costs and often had to reduce the number of employees due to a lack of financial resources. To help entrepreneurs, the Slovak government has taken measures to eliminate the adverse effects of the pandemic on the business economy. However, before the enterprises recovered from the first wave of the pandemic, after the end of the measures, the second wave of the pandemic came, the impact of which on individual sectors of the business economy was different [4]. The construction sector is considered one of the decisive sectors of the Slovak economy. The construction sector as a whole creates works of long-term consumption and durability. At the same time, this sector is considered a contribution to the field of culture, aesthetics, and architecture because it reflects a significant part of the intellectual property of the workers. However, from an ecological point of view, construction creates large amounts of construction waste and emissions [5]. The construction sector is closely related to the economy. It is an important indicator of its development because it directly reacts to every change in the economy and thus other sectors of the national economy. The effects of the pandemic are observed from different perspectives, and it is interesting to monitor and quantify the changes that the COVID-19 pandemic has brought and how it has affected the lives of people in all its aspects [6].

The main aim of this paper is the description and quantification of the impacts of the COVID-19 pandemic on the construction sector (SK NACE 41, 42, and 43), which is considered a crucial sector of the Slovak economy, to evaluate changes in the development of significant indicators and at the same time identifying new trends.

The paper is divided into the following sections. The first part of the paper is focused on literary research, which familiarizes the reader with the principal theoretical background of the issue. The second part describes the methods for meeting the objective of this paper, which is the realization of a financial analysis together with a focus on the existence of statistically significant differences in the values of calculated indicators due to changes in the development of crucial financial ratios. The third part describes the results obtained by the previous calculation of selected indicators and their subsequent statistical verification with a description of the obtained results, which are compared in the context of other relevant studies published worldwide. At the end of this paper, the most important outputs of this research are summarized together with the mentioned limitations and future research of this issue.

## 2. Literature Review

Despite the efforts of economists all over the world to predict the development of economies, crises usually occur very unexpectedly. More if their cause is other than an economic event, as is the case here. The COVID-19 pandemic paralyzed the world, and even the developed economies of the world stopped for a time [7]. According to Durana et al. [8], the COVID-19 pandemic hit the world unexpectedly, and scientists and analysts around the world are trying to measure and quantify its effects on various areas from employment [9] and GDP [10], through analyses of the business environment [11] or enterprises in various sectors [12,13], to the examination of changes in purchasing behavior [14] and others.

Rodrigues-Caballero and Vera-Valdes [15], in a study focusing on the long-term economic effects of a pandemic, examined changes in employment during periods of past pandemics along with the period of the current COVID-19 pandemic. The authors pointed to the fact that, in general, these pandemic shocks have a favorable effect on the development of unemployment not only by increasing the level of employment shortly after the pandemic, but also by increasing its duration. Based on their findings, the authors support the fact that the introduction of timely interventions in the economy can mitigate the pandemic shock itself. In their study, Lahiri and Sinha [16] focused on concerns about the possible emergence of the worst economic crisis in history, which could follow the COVID-19 pandemic. The authors pointed to various changes in consumption or work habits of people brought about by the pandemic, which affect not only individuals, but also all businesses. Valaskova et al. [7] dealt with a similar topic, where the authors, based on a sample of 425 respondents from Slovakia, found out which are the most important factors affecting their financial situation and purchasing behavior even during the ongoing pandemic. As a result, the study showed that the income, profession, and age of the respondents played a significant role in the context of the analyzed questions, and the authors also confirmed the impact of the pandemic on the purchasing behavior of the respondents, which was in line with other global studies on similar topics.

Bonam and Smadu [17] pointed out in their publication that all past pandemics led to an increase in trend inflation in Europe, which lasted for more than a decade. Using a data model, Kocisova and Pastyrikova [18] tracked several microeconomic and macroeconomic aspects of non-performing loans granted in the European Union from 2005 to 2018. The results of their study indicate that the large number of high-value non-performing loans recorded after the financial crisis around 2008 could also adversely affect the economic recovery of economies after the current crisis caused by the COVID-19 pandemic. Orlowski [19] analyzed the financial and economic consequences of the current pandemic, and argues that this pandemic has brought labor problems, which, however, can be solved by structural adjustments in the labor market. At the same time, according to the author, the pandemic has increased all financial risks in enterprises, especially credit, market, or payment risks. Svabova et al. [2] focused on the impact of anti-pandemic measures on the employment rate in Slovakia using the method of comparison before and after the outbreak of the pandemic using various statistical methods based on officially available data on the unemployment rate from 2013 to 2020. Their findings indicate a worsening of the unemployment rate in Slovakia in 2020 by roughly 2% to 3% compared to the previous trend. The results can be used in proposals and measures to mitigate the long-term effects of the pandemic on employment in the Slovak Republic. Subsequently, Svabova and Gabrikova [20] addressed the issue of unemployment during the COVID-19 pandemic focusing on the structure of the unemployed workforce by age, focusing primarily on the young unemployed between 2020 and 2021, compared to the situation if the pandemic had not occurred. Their results pointed out that career opportunities for young people have significantly worsened since the beginning of the pandemic, although this level depends primarily on the sector.

The business environment is a crucial determinant of the economy and enterprises of every country, especially in the field of competition. Hajduova et al. [21] focused on the evaluation of the level of the business environment based on the multi-criteria TOPSIS method, which the authors used to point out the ranking of countries with different levels of business environments from the best to the worst. In the study, the authors came to the conclusion that the business environment levels in Slovakia, the Czech Republic, Poland, Hungary, Lithuania, Latvia, Slovenia, Estonia, and Cyprus are well below the EU average. In a comparative study, Valaskova et al. [22] focused on the topic of the business environment of selected European countries between 2013 and 2018, namely on the comparison of selected macroeconomic factors of Slovakia, the Czech Republic, Poland, Hungary, Croatia, Latvia, Lithuania, Estonia, France, and Germany. These macroeconomic factors were evaluated by the multi-criteria TOPSIS method, and mutual testing of dependence was carried out using analysis of variance and post hoc tests. The results point to a group of countries with a similar business environment, which can be helpful in monitoring the competitiveness of enterprises operating in the market. However, the results showed that Slovakia, Croatia, and Hungary have a similar business environment. Achim et al. [23] analyzed various changes in the activities of Romanian enterprises belonging to different sectors, evaluating the level of business performance in response to the COVID-19 pandemic. The results show that the overall profit of enterprises fell by more than 37% in the period under review, even though better results occurred in sectors such as construction, agriculture, trade, IT, transport, or storage. Furthermore, the authors point to the fact that liquidity management and capital financing improve the performance of enterprises in the area of return on assets and equity, which is crucial information, especially for company managers and investors. Rakha et al. [24] predicted the impacts of the COVID-19 pandemic on three selected sectors in the United Kingdom using artificial intelligence, including the construction sector, and their predictions indicated that although GDP was expected to increase slightly in 2021, it was on average 8.5% lower compared to the pre-pandemic period. Hu and Zhang [25] monitored the mutual relationship between the performance of enterprises and the pandemic was confirmed. At the same time, however, the authors pointed out that countries with better financial or health care systems achieved better results than countries with worse systems.

Zajmi [26] examined not only profitability, but also the level of liquidity of enterprises from 2018 to 2020. In the results, he found that liquidity is generally at half the level of recommendations, and the growth of long-term loans and equity is not sufficient from the point of view of the solvency of enterprises. These solvency problems affect productivity, efficiency, and profitability. However, the fact remains that the COVID-19 pandemic affects small and medium-sized enterprises the most in sectors such as transport, accommodation and tourism, recreation, arts, and construction. The main aim of the study by Lassoued and Khanchel [27] was to determine the impact of the arrival of the pandemic on the use of earnings management in listed companies. Their results point to a tendency of increased use of earnings management during the pandemic period, mainly in the area of revenue management increasing the level of income in 2020 compared to the period before the pandemic, which therefore refers to the acceleration or deferral of expenses or revenue to generate a steady rise in earnings. Salami et al. [28] investigated measures to mitigate the risks associated with non-compliance with commercial contracts of construction enterprises due to COVID-19 pandemic. The most frequently adopted measures include an increased effort to maintain good relations with business partners, analysis of contractual conditions regarding the notice period by both parties, and quick and prompt reporting of potential disputes. At the same time, the authors provided an opportunity to learn from the impact of these measures, which helped to minimize the risks associated with the pandemic and also reduce the expenses related with it. Khalef et al. [29] investigated the long-term consequences of the COVID-19 pandemic on construction projects in various sectors. According to authors, the current pandemic had a significant impact on production, material supplies, availability of human resources, and many other factors that negatively affected construction processes not only in the construction sector, but also in various sectors. The authors focused primarily on contractual consequences and corrective measures in response to the pandemic as support for effective project management practices under pandemic conditions.

In general, the COVID-19 pandemic has visibly affected not only enterprises in various areas of development across all sectors of different countries, but also entrepreneurs, employees, and consumers. However, the construction sector of the Slovak Republic remains specific, on which the effects of the current COVID-19 pandemic will be described in the presented paper.

## 3. Materials and Methods

The main aim of this paper is to perform a financial analysis of enterprises operating in the construction sector, classified as one of the principal manufacturing sectors of the national economy, operating in the territory of the Slovak Republic using adequate quantitative methods. The construction sector is defined as one of the decisive sectors related to the Slovak economy. Therefore, it is considered an important indicator of its development, which directly reacts to every change in the economy and thus brings impacts on other sectors of the national economy as well [30]. The overall position of the construction industry can be easily monitored not only by the industry's share of GDP, but also by the share of total employment of the sector. The share of the construction sector in the creation of GDP had a downward trend after 2010, where it was at the level of 8.1% in 2011, at the level of 7.4% of the total GDP in 2017, and in 2018 only at the level of 7%. Likewise, when monitoring the share of the construction sector in total employment, a downward trend can be seen, where this ratio was at the level of 7.9% in 2011 and only at the level of 6.9% in 2017 [31].

Individual financial data from the ORBIS database, which contains data on 400 million global commercial and public enterprises, served as the basis for the financial study. In total, 3605 businesses were found in Slovakia after searching for ones engaged in the construction industry. The dataset comprised private and public businesses with total assets exceeding

200,000 EUR, as well as limited liability corporations, joint stock companies, limited partnerships, public limited companies, and other legal entities. It was required to adjust the acquired database of financial data before computing the most crucial financial indicators. Businesses who failed to supply all of the essential data for financial analysis throughout the monitored period of 2018–2020 were excluded from the produced dataset (data for the year 2021 are not included as they are not available). Additionally, all outliers that would have diminished the usefulness of the conclusions drawn from the actual financial study were eliminated. After this adjustment, the database contains 2000 enterprises whose elementary identification data are shown in Table 1.

Table 1. The elementary data of the enterprises operating in the construction sector in the period under the review.

| Indicator | | Absolute Frequency | Relative Frequency |
|---|---|---|---|
| Firm size | Small enterprise | 749 | 37.45 |
| | Medium-sized enterprise | 1141 | 57.05 |
| | Large enterprise | 108 | 5.40 |
| | Very large enterprise | 2 | 0.10 |
| Legal form | Limited liability enterprise | 1844 | 92.20 |
| | Joint stock enterprise | 148 | 7.40 |
| | Other legal form | 8 | 0.40 |
| Firm age | <5 | 8 | 0.40 |
| | 5–9 | 311 | 15.55 |
| | 10–19 | 947 | 47.35 |
| | 20–29 | 606 | 30.30 |
| | >30 | 128 | 6.40 |
| Total | | 2000 | 100.00 |

Source: own elaboration.

The basis for the calculation of individual financial indicators was financial data (in thousands of euros), whose basic descriptive statistics, such as mean, median, standard deviation, minimum, maximum, and coefficient of variation (CV), are summarized in Table 2.

Table 2. Descriptive statistics of individual financial indicators (values are given in thousands of euros).

| | Mean | Med. | Std. Dev. | Min. | Max. | CV |
|---|---|---|---|---|---|---|
| CUAS | 1650.578 | 575.200 | 5859.591 | 6.966 | 135,656.852 | 3.550 |
| STOK | 253.372 | 21.781 | 2490.983 | −63.721 | 103,006.656 | 9.831 |
| DEBT | 699.873 | 227.339 | 2009.062 | −3626 | 30,923.053 | 2.871 |
| OCAS | 701.517 | 213.393 | 3310.951 | −182.100 | 101,280.725 | 4.719 |
| CASH | 339.467 | 115.486 | 2108.753 | −244.970 | 88,841.782 | 6.212 |
| TOAS | 2331.388 | 863.141 | 7186.946 | 210.997 | 136,778.224 | 3.083 |
| SHFD | 779.199 | 286.691 | 2362.285 | −5118.237 | 69,851.308 | 3.032 |
| NCLI | 377.573 | 35.582 | 2442.938 | −245.389 | 72,491.123 | 6.470 |
| CULI | 1174.616 | 430.643 | 4313.549 | −46.426 | 129,009.509 | 3.672 |
| CRED | 590.778 | 180.901 | 2037.352 | −34.786 | 46,869.346 | 3.449 |
| OPRE | 3042.036 | 1289.487 | 8396.336 | 0.029 | 226,668.934 | 2.760 |
| TURN | 2890.494 | 1226.787 | 8176.421 | 0.029 | 226,330.071 | 2.829 |
| PLAT | 100.199 | 33.169 | 440.009 | −8260.572 | 9920.586 | 4.391 |

Note: CUAS: Current Assets, STOK: Stocks, DEBT: Debtors, OCAS: Other Current Assets, CASH: Cash and Cash Equivalent, TOAS: Total Assets, SHFD: Shareholders Funds, NCLI: Non-Current Liabilities, CULI: Current Liabilities, CRED: Creditors, OPRE: Operating revenue (Turnover), TURN: Sales, PLAT P/L: after Tax. Source: own elaboration.

The financial analysis of enterprises operating in the construction sector in the Slovak Republic in the monitored period was carried out using 12 crucial indicators, whose formulas necessary for calculation are summarized in Table 3.

Table 3. Summarized formulas of financial indicators.

| Ratio | Algorithm |
|---|---|
| Cash liquidity ratio | Cash and cash equivalent to current liabilities |
| Quick liquidity ratio | Current assets minus inventory to current liabilities |
| Current liquidity ratio | Current assets to current liabilities |
| Inventory turnover ratio | Stocks to operating revenue and sales |
| Collection period ratio | Debtors to operating revenue and sales |
| Credit period ratio | Creditors to operating revenue and sales |
| Return on assets ratio | Profit after tax to total assets |
| Return on equity ratio | Profit after tax to shareholders funds |
| Return on sales ratio | Profit after tax to operating revenue and sales |
| Total indebtedness ratio | Current and non-current liabilities to total assets |
| Equity leverage ratio | Total assets to shareholders funds |
| Insolvency ratio | Current and non-current liabilities to receivables |

Source: [32–34].

The overall financial analysis was carried out in the following methodological steps.

Firstly, significant financial ratios were calculated for individual enterprises in the construction sector operating in Slovakia in the monitored time horizon, set for the period from 2018 to 2020. Individually calculated financial parameters affecting business performance were subsequently analyzed using the methods of analysis, exploration, and explanation.

In the next step, the normality tests (Kolmogorov–Smirnov and Shapiro–Wilk tests) were used to determine if a dataset is well modelled by a normal distribution. The normality tests are supplementary to the graphical assessment of normality, and its ability is to detect whether a sample follows a non-normal distribution.

The $p$-value is interpreted against a significance level of 5% and finds that the test dataset does significantly deviate from normal distribution.

The Friedman test, a nonparametric substitute for one-way ANOVA with repeated measures analysis of variance by levels, was then applied to identify treatment differences over numerous test sessions. The $K$ algorithms under consideration are ranked using the Friedman test on each dataset individually [35]. The information can be set up in a table with $n$ rows and $K$ columns. Typically, the columns indicate the different circumstances, while the rows represent the blocks. The data of the test are ranks ($R_{ik}$, $i = 1, \ldots, n; k = 1, \ldots, K$) of the conditions by blocks; therefore, $1 \leq R_{ik} \leq K$, $i = 1, \ldots, n$ [36]. The data must adhere to two presumptions. The variables must be independent of one another so that the outcomes of one block cannot affect those of another block. The observations in each row may also be prioritized differently based on a variety of factors [37]. Friedman's test examines if the rank totals for each condition deviate noticeably from the predicted values [36]. Friedman's developed the following test statistic:

$$F_r = \frac{12}{nK(k+1)} \sum_{k=1}^{K} R_{.k}^2 - 3n(K+1), \quad (1)$$

where $R_{.k} = \sum_{i=1}^{n} R_{ik}$ is the sum of the ranks for each condition $k$ over the $n$ blocks. As $n$ tends to infinity, under the null hypothesis, this statistic $F_r$ has an asymptotic Chi-square distribution with $K - 1$ degrees of freedom. If $F_r \geq \chi^2_{K-1;1-\alpha}$, where $\chi^2_{K-1;1-\alpha}$ is the $(1-\alpha)$ quantile of the Chi-square distribution with $K - 1$ degrees of freedom, the null hypothesis is rejected at the $\alpha$ level of significance [35].

Friedman's test results indicate a substantial difference across groups, but they do not specify which groups are different in which combinations. Therefore, it is typically required to use a post hoc method for pairwise comparison once the null hypothesis is rejected by these multiple comparison tests [38]. In the literature, there are numerous methods for multiple comparison that may be used to look at differences between median pairs. The Bonferroni adjustment was applied in this study to reduce the likelihood of obtaining a statistically significant result and to address the multiple comparisons issue.

The Bonferroni–Dunn test is adaptable and may be used to determine if there are differences across all conditions as well as between any two conditions [36]. A Bonferroni adjustment, which may change the rejection level for any test by dividing by the total number of tests and necessitates a significantly lower $p$-value to reject any test, was previously outlined by Dunn [39] as a way to deal with this problem. The Bonferroni–Dunn test, as described by Siegel and Castellan [35], makes an adjustment to the critical value used to reject the null hypothesis in order to lower the familywise Type I error rate, i.e., $1 - (1 - \alpha)^c$, where $c = K(K - 1)/2$ is the number of comparisons and $\alpha$ is the per comparison Type I error rate. This correction makes sure that the total likelihood of making at least one Type I error in the collection of comparisons stays below a predefined $\alpha$ value [40]. Pereira et al. [36] state, that the conditions $k$ and $j$ are significantly different if

$$|R_{.k} - R_{.j}| \geq z_{1 - \frac{\alpha}{K(K-1)}} \sqrt{\frac{nK(K+1)}{6}}, \qquad (2)$$

where $z_{1 - \frac{\alpha}{K(K-1)}}$ is the $\left(1 - \frac{\alpha}{K(K-1)}\right)$ quantiles of the standard normal distribution.

## 4. Results and Discussion

It is difficult for enterprises to ensure the long-term success in the current global environment. In general, the enterprise must constantly look for ways to improve its performance. Traditional approaches used to evaluate business performance focus on various financial indicators based on values obtained from financial accounting. Parallel systems of indicators are frequent analytical procedures used to evaluate business performance. Individual ratios are equivalent and are classified into groups according to the area of business management to which they relate. In order to fulfil the main aim of the paper, 12 essential financial indicators were selected (see Table 3).

In the analysis of liquidity, three basic levels are distinguished. Each of them points to the enterprise liquidity from a different point of view, but in general it is true that all types of liquidity should not be negative [41]. Rafaqat and Rafaqat [42] state that it is favorable for enterprises if the value of liquidity ratios gradually increases from year to year. The calculated liquidity indicators for individual enterprises are included in the intervals, summarized in Table 4.

**Table 4.** Liquidity ratios of the enterprises operating in the construction sector during 2018–2020.

| Cash liquidity ratio (EUR) | 2018 | 2019 | 2020 |
| --- | --- | --- | --- |
| mean | 1.18 | 1.11 | 1.82 |
| <0.2 | 940 | 935 | 870 |
| 0.2–0.5 | 456 | 409 | 399 |
| >0.5 | 604 | 656 | 731 |
| **Quick liquidity ratio (EUR)** | **2018** | **2019** | **2020** |
| mean | 3.35 | 2.99 | 3.56 |
| <1 | 808 | 765 | 736 |
| 1–1.5 | 532 | 511 | 484 |
| >1.5 | 660 | 724 | 780 |
| **Current liquidity ratio (EUR)** | **2018** | **2019** | **2020** |
| mean | 3.89 | 3.37 | 3.74 |
| <1.5 | 1198 | 1146 | 1089 |
| 1.5–2.5 | 423 | 446 | 417 |
| >2.5 | 379 | 408 | 494 |

Source: own elaboration.

The *cash liquidity ratio* is given by the relationship of cash and cash equivalent to current liabilities, and according to Canton et al. [43], a value in the range of 0.2 to 0.5 is considered the optimal value of the monitored indicator. This level of liquidity means that from 0.2 EUR to 0.5 EUR of cash accounts for 1 EUR of current liabilities in the enterprise. Between 2018 and 2020, the number of these enterprises decreased from year to year, so the liquidity of the monitored enterprises gradually improved. The average value of this indicator was 1.11 EUR in 2018, and 1.82 EUR in 2020. During the analysis of the cash liquidity ratio, it can be noted that approximately 45% of the monitored enterprises achieved a relatively low value of the given indicator in the monitored period, with an average value of the ratio lower than 0.2. However, the results gradually improved, and the number of such enterprises gradually decreased. The arrival of the COVID-19 pandemic in 2020 did not have a significant impact on this positive decline, and the level of cash liquidity ratio in the industry continued to grow. A similar positive trend was also observed in the analysis of the quick liquidity ratio and current liquidity ratio. Batrancea [44] states that the *quick liquidity ratio* refers to the ability of the enterprise to cover short-term liabilities through current assets, which are reduced by the level of inventories. The indicator thus expresses how many times the enterprise would be able to pay its creditors in the event of monetization of all its current assets, except for the sale of inventory. According to Balina [45], the interval between 1 and 1.5 is considered to be the recommended value of the indicator. The same downward trend can be observed within the enterprises, which means an increase in quick liquidity across enterprises. In 2018, there were 532 enterprises in this interval, while in 2020, the number of these enterprises was only 484. The quick liquidity ratio also showed that even before the pandemic, more than a third of construction enterprises were unable to cover their short-term liabilities through current assets, which means they would have to sell inventory to cover their liabilities. Despite the not the best results of the industry, an improving trend was observed, which was not negatively affected by the pandemic. The *current liquidity ratio* evaluates the development of the solvency of the enterprise in the long term. Da Rocha et al. [46] point to what extent an enterprise covers current assets with its short-term liabilities, i.e., the future solvency of enterprises. In general, the value should not be less than 1, because, in this case, the enterprise becomes illiquid in the long run and faces the risk of bankruptcy. In 2018, 423 enterprises were included in the interval of recommended values from 1.5 to 2.5. However, after the outbreak of the pandemic in 2020, the number of enterprises slightly decreased to 417, which is also related to the increase of enterprises exceeding the optimal values of total liquidity. If the value of the indicator is high, the enterprise becomes excessively liquid, which threatens its efficiency in the long term. In the monitored period, approximately 55% of enterprises faced imminent bankruptcy, but their number decreased. The value of the current liquidity of the sector thus grew again, which is positive in the long term.

The efficiency ratios in financial analysis determine whether individual assets are adequately spent in the enterprise in relation to the specific investigated areas in the present or in the future [47]. The average values of the calculated activity indicators with intervals are summarized in Table 5.

The *inventory turnover ratio* refers to the relationship of stocks to operating revenue and sales [48]. In selected enterprises of the construction sector in Slovakia, the average turnaround time in 2018 was approximately 50 days. In 2019, this period was already 78 days, and in 2020 it was extended to 111 days. According to Boisjoly et al. [49], this is an indicator of turnaround time that needs to be minimized. Between 2018 and 2020, a decrease in the number of enterprises whose inventory turnover ratio is less than 30 days can be observed. In 2018, up to 87.8% of enterprises were in the given interval, compared to 2020, when it was only 84.9%. The value of the ratio indicates a worsening trend, which could be mostly related to the arrival of the COVID-19 pandemic, since the time when inventory was converted to cash significantly increased compared to 2018. However, this ratio development was understandable because the lockdown, which affected the business activities, was implemented across the country at the beginning of the pandemic [50].

The implemented lockdown was manifested primarily by the suspension of construction production [51], while the period during which stocks were tied up in the enterprise was extended. Another indicator is the *collection period ratio* determined by the share of debtors to operating revenue and sales multiplied by the number of days in a year, when the result is the average time from sales to collection of funds [52]. According to Farhan et al. [53], the ratio points to the days when payment collections are withheld in receivables. The indicator needs to be minimized because the lower the indicator, the fewer resources the enterprise needs to finance its receivables [54]. In the monitored period, the collection period gradually lengthened from 2018, with most enterprises having a collection period ranging from 30 to 90 days. The trend of higher collection period can also be observed in the average values for the individual monitored years when the average collection period after the arrival of the COVID-19 pandemic increased from 50 days to 94 days in 2020. According to Mahato and Mahato [55], the *credit period ratio*, another activity ratio, points to the average duration from the origination of the obligation to its repayment, i.e., average length of trade credit from suppliers. Similar to the previous indicator, the credit period ratio needs to be minimized [56]. The enterprise has problems with its liquidity if it has a long maturity period of liabilities [57]. In the monitored period, the most represented enterprises had a maturity period of up to 30 days. In 2018, 1177 enterprises were included in the given interval, and after the arrival of the pandemic a slight increase can be observed. The improving trend of repayment of obligations indicates good liquidity of enterprises, which was not significantly affected even by the arrival of the pandemic. However, the average values of the credit period of liabilities for individual years point to a slightly worsening trend that began before the pandemic and continued even after its outbreak, when it worsened significantly. In 2018, the average credit period ratio of the monitored enterprises was 57 days, while it was extended to 112 days after the arrival of the COVID-19 pandemic. Wang et al. [58] state in their publication that when analyzing the collection period and credit period ratio, it is appropriate to compare these two indicators in the enterprise with each other and to monitor any differences in the observed values. For both indicators, there was a worsening trend in the period before the pandemic (in 2018 and 2019), while the collection period and credit period ratio were made even worse by the arrival of the pandemic in 2020.

**Table 5.** Efficiency ratios of the enterprises operating in the construction sector during 2018–2020.

| Inventory turnover ratio (Days) | 2018 | 2019 | 2020 |
|---|---|---|---|
| mean | 49.8 | 77.7 | 111.2 |
| <30 days | 1755 | 1730 | 1697 |
| 30–120 days | 172 | 190 | 207 |
| > 120 days | 73 | 80 | 96 |
| Collection period ratio (days) | 2018 | 2019 | 2020 |
| mean | 50 | 56.2 | 93.6 |
| <30 days | 882 | 892 | 871 |
| 30–90 days | 959 | 930 | 896 |
| >90 days | 159 | 178 | 233 |
| Credit period ratio (days) | 2018 | 2019 | 2020 |
| mean | 57.1 | 69.0 | 111.7 |
| <30 days | 1177 | 1195 | 1216 |
| 30–90 days | 677 | 646 | 590 |
| >90 days | 146 | 159 | 194 |

Source: own elaboration.

When analyzing the profitability of enterprises in the construction sector, the value of the net profit enters the numerator of all indicators, and the relevant investigated unit based on the ratio enters the denominator. Trang et al. [59] state that profitability indicators express the profitability of business efforts and point to the efficiency of business activity and indicate the intensity of use, reproduction, and appreciation of the capital invested in the business. Average values of individual profitability indicators are summarized in Table 6.

Table 6. Profitability ratios of the enterprises operating in the construction sector during 2018–2020.

| Return on assets ratio (%) | 2018 | 2019 | 2020 |
| --- | --- | --- | --- |
| mean | 6.72 | 5.86 | 3.26 |
| <5% | 1058 | 1149 | 1286 |
| 5%10% | 380 | 321 | 309 |
| >10% | 562 | 530 | 405 |
| **Return on equity ratio (%)** | **2018** | **2019** | **2020** |
| mean | 168.10 | 22.82 | −272.92 |
| <15% | 964 | 1035 | 1226 |
| 15%–20% | 140 | 183 | 176 |
| >20% | 896 | 782 | 598 |
| **Return on sales ratio (%)** | **2018** | **2019** | **2020** |
| mean | −18.04 | −20.17 | −15.11 |
| <5% | 1672 | 1670 | 1707 |
| 5%–10% | 301 | 219 | 197 |
| >10% | 27 | 111 | 96 |

Source: own elaboration.

The first monitored profitability indicator is the *return on assets ratio*, which according to Eldridge et al. [60] indicates the production force and relates the profit to the total assets invested in the business, regardless of the method of financing. The higher the ratio, the more efficient the enterprise is at generating profit [61], while the optimal interval of the monitored indicator is considered to be between 5 and 10% [62], and when interpreted it can be claimed that every 1 EUR of invested assets produced between 0.05 EUR and 0.10 EUR of net profit. A slight decline can be observed in the group of enterprises with asset profitability at an optimal level, even if the changes from year to year are significant. In the period before the pandemic, approximately 53% of enterprises did not reach the optimal level of the monitored indicator. However, in 2020, most businesses in the construction sector already faced the pandemic crisis, as their number increased to 64%. When monitoring the average values of the monitored indicator, a significant trend of decreasing profitability of assets can be observed. According to Xu and Liu [63], return on assets needs to be evaluated with return on equity because these two indicators are interconnected. The *return on equity ratio* is an indicator showing the profitability of invested capital, which, according to Soewarno and Tjahjadi [64], makes it possible to point out whether the invested capital of the enterprise is sufficiently profitable. Bolton et al. [65] state that every investor also faces increased risk related to different business activities. These risks can be divided into risks associated not only with the production itself, market development, legislation, inflation, and technological progress [66], but also risks associated with unpredictable events, such as the current pandemic [67]. Again, the higher the return on equity, the better the enterprise at generating profit from its existing assets [68], and the range from 15% to 20% is considered the optimal value. The level of return on equity in the monitored enterprises decreased, and less than 20% were in the optimal interval. Before the pandemic, approximately 964 enterprises operating in the construction sector had a return on equity of less than 15%, but in 2020, the number of these enterprises increased to 1226. According to Balatsky [69], a low return on equity ratio means the enterprise earns less compared to its shareholder's equity. When monitoring the average values of the return on equity indicator for individual years, a sharp drop can be observed, when enterprises were able to produce less than 1 EUR of equity capital in the monitored years. Another indicator that points to the size of the achieved profit concerning sales is the *return on sales ratio*, the results of which are very individual across industries. Zimon and Tarighi [70] state that an indicator between 5% and 10% is excellent, while it is generally true that if the return on sales is above 0%, the enterprise is turning a profit. From the results, most enterprises have revenue profitability of up to 5%, i.e., business units with less than 0.05 EUR of net profit per 1 EUR of revenue. However, after the arrival of the pandemic in 2020, the number of enterprises in this interval slightly increased. On the contrary, a downward trend can be observed in the following two intervals. The sales profitability development trend described so far is easy to see because it is clear from the analysis that 2020, together with the pandemic it brought, was a shock for the construction sector that significantly affected the internal conditions of the enterprises.

A debt analysis is focused on the structure of the financial resources of the enterprise, which affects its financial stability. In general, an enterprise with a high share of equity is stable and independent, and vice versa, an enterprise with a low share of them is financially unstable [34]. Within the debt analysis, it was possible to monitor the combination of equity and debt through debt indicators, which decline due to debt repayment from sold assets [71], as well as the ability of enterprises to bear the indebtedness between 2018 and 2020, i.e., in the period before and after the COVID-19 pandemic. Average values of individual indebtedness ratios are summarized in Table 7.

**Table 7.** Indebtedness ratios of the enterprises operating in the construction sector during 2018–2020.

| Total indebtedness ratio (%) | 2018 | 2019 | 2020 |
|---|---|---|---|
| mean | 0.648 | 0.633 | 0.623 |
| <50% | 598 | 652 | 705 |
| 50%–75% | 621 | 628 | 600 |
| >75% | 781 | 720 | 695 |
| **Equity leverage ratio (coef.)** | **2018** | **2019** | **2020** |
| mean | 9.47 | 6.53 | 12.76 |
| <2 | 701 | 753 | 827 |
| 2–3 | 397 | 389 | 366 |
| >3 | 902 | 858 | 807 |
| **Insolvency ratio (coef.)** | **2018** | **2019** | **2020** |
| mean | 2.89 | 3.22 | 2.60 |
| <1 | 971 | 1019 | 1031 |
| >1 | 1029 | 981 | 969 |

Source: own elaboration.

The *total indebtedness ratio* is an indicator of indebtedness that compares current and non-current liabilities to total assets, and its complementary indicator is the self-financing ratio. It is clear that the debt level of the monitored enterprises was slowly decreasing from year to year, and not only in the period before the pandemic, but also after it started, this trend continued. According to Stefko et al. [72], the range from 50% to 75% is considered to be the optimal level of indebtedness of enterprises operating in the construction sector.

At the same time, from a pure risk perspective, lower debt ratios are considered better, while a higher debt ratio makes the enterprise more difficult to borrow money [73]. In general, there is a risk associated with an enterprise carrying too much debt, while a low value of the total indebtedness ratio suggests greater creditworthiness [74]. In the monitored period, most enterprises are in the debt group at the level of 75% and above. More than 75% of the financial resources of the enterprise are in debt, and they may face an increased risk of instability. After the arrival of the COVID-19 pandemic in 2020, the number of enterprises with optimal indebtedness decreased to 600. The rest of the enterprises reached a debt level of less than 50%, which represents their increasing autonomy and independence of them in the field of finance but, on the contrary, according to Mouandat [75], equity financing is generally considered more expensive compared to debt financing. The average value of the total indebtedness ratio was at the level of 64.8% in 2018, and a gradual decrease in corporate indebtedness can be observed until the outbreak of the pandemic. Another monitored indicator is the *equity leverage ratio*, the inverse value of the degree of self-financing, is calculated as the ratio of total assets to shareholders' funds. Rahmati et al. [76] state that if the indicator value is 1, the enterprise uses only equity to finance its business activity. In the case of an increase in the value, it can be pointed to an increasing use of debt in the enterprise, while an interval from 2 to 3 is considered the optimal ratio. In the monitored period, there was an increase in the number of enterprises whose value of the equity leverage ratio was 2, i.e., business units in which debt was located in the proportion of up to 50%. On the contrary, the largest group of enterprises with a financial leverage higher than the value of 3 gradually decreased. The last indicator is the *insolvency ratio*, which gives the relationship of current and non-current liabilities to receivables of the enterprise. According to de Rezende [77], it is generally considered together with liquidity indicators in financial analysis because these indicators give a better picture of the enterprise. The ratio examines whether the enterprise insolvency is caused by its own business activities [78]. If the value of the insolvency ratio is higher than 1, primary insolvency can be pointed out. On the contrary, in the case of a value lower than 1, it is possible to mention secondary insolvency caused as a consequence of primary insolvency of the enterprise [79]. In 2018, in the monitored enterprises in the construction sector, there were more enterprises whose insolvency was caused by their own business activities, i.e., the insolvency ratio value was greater than 1. This number of enterprises decreased over time, and from 2019 there were more enterprises whose value of the indicator was less than 1. Therefore, the insolvency ratio is often assessed with liquidity indicators, where, based on the results of the analysis, it was shown that the arrival of the pandemic in 2020 did not significantly affect the financial situation of the examined enterprises in the area of liquidity, nor in the area of solvency, since the changes were not significant, and more or less only they continued the trend from previous years, i.e., from the period before the pandemic.

The detailed financial analysis, focused on the enterprises operating in the construction sector in Slovakia, was aimed at monitoring the existence of statistically significant differences between the individual indicators because of the period in which the enterprises achieved these values. The main aim of this more detailed analysis was to examine whether the average values of the financial indicators are the same in all years of the period under review (2018, 2019, and 2020) or whether the individual values of the indicators differ significantly from each other.

Firstly, it was necessary to verify the normality of the dataset using the Kolmogorov–Smirnov and Shapiro–Wilk tests. The results of these tests rejected the null hypothesis that the data came from a normal distribution. Subsequently, the Friedman test, the non-parametric alternative to the one-way ANOVA with repeated measures, was used to determine a statistically significant difference between the calculated indicators concerning the year. The Friedman test tests the existence of differences between groups when the measured dependent variable is ordinal. Table 8 summarizes the result of the Friedman test, which points to the fact that the $p$-value of the test is less than the chosen level of significance for some financial ratios, which means that the null hypothesis of equal median values of indicators is rejected. Based on the result, it can be claimed that there are statistically significant differences in the individual indicators concerning the monitored year, except the two activity indicators. There are no statistically significant differences in the collection period and credit period ratio.

Because there are statistically significant differences between the 10 financial indicators, in the next step, a post hoc analysis was performed, the result of which was the determination between which monitored periods the differences in the individual indicators are the most significant. The result of pairwise comparison of the monitored years is included in Table 9.

The results of the pairwise comparison (see column Adj. Sig.) indicate that those periods, where the test value is below the significance level 0.05 (marked in bold), are the periods with significant differences in the values of the analyzed indicators. It is evident that in 2020 there were significant changes in the development of the financial indicators compared to the previous periods.

The construction sector is closely related to the national economy, which means that it responds to every change in the development of the economy [80]. At the same time, these reactions affect other sectors, even though the position of the construction industry in the national economy from the point of view of the share in GDP formation is not significant in percentage terms and is gradually decreasing year-by-year [81]. Before the arrival of the COVID-19 pandemic in 2019, the construction industry was predicted to grow slightly, and on the contrary, a slight decline or stagnation was subsequently expected in 2020. However,

Narayanamurthy and Tortorella [82] pointed out that the construction sector was primarily characterized by a high rate of insolvencies and generally worse payment morale before the pandemic. The authors pointed out that the payment terms of the construction sector are set for more than 90 days, and their repayment occurs even after the due date. This sector produces lots of bad debts, which in the long term has a negative impact on its future development.

Table 8. The output of the Friedman test.

|  |  | CashR | QR | CurrR | IT | CollP | CredP |
|---|---|---|---|---|---|---|---|
| Mean Rank | 2018 | 1.91 | 1.86 | 1.84 | 1.94 | 1.99 | 2.00 |
|  | 2019 | 1.94 | 1.98 | 1.98 | 1.95 | 1.98 | 2.00 |
|  | 2020 | 2.15 | 2.15 | 2.19 | 2.12 | 2.03 | 1.99 |
| N |  | 2000 | 2000 | 2000 | 2000 | 2000 | 2000 |
| Chi-Square |  | 69.303 | 86.131 | 122.557 | 49.717 | 3.333 | 0.158 |
| Df |  | 2 | 2 | 2 | 2 | 2 | 2 |
| Asymp. Sig. |  | 0.000 | 0.000 | 0.000 | 0.000 | 0.189 | 0.924 |
|  |  | ROA | ROE | ROS | TI | EL | Ins |
| Mean Rank | 2018 | 2.14 | 2.22 | 2.09 | 2.18 | 2.19 | 2.13 |
|  | 2019 | 2.03 | 2.03 | 2.01 | 2.00 | 2.01 | 2.01 |
|  | 2020 | 1.82 | 1.75 | 1.89 | 1.82 | 1.80 | 1.86 |
| N |  | 2000 | 2000 | 2000 | 2000 | 2000 | 2000 |
| Chi-Square |  | 106.255 | 226.688 | 41.128 | 133.170 | 153.830 | 75.230 |
| Df |  | 2 | 2 | 2 | 2 | 2 | 2 |
| Asymp. Sig. |  | 0.000 | 0.000 | 0.000 | 0.000 | 0.000 | 0.000 |

Note: CashR: Cash liquidity ratio, QR: Quick liquidity ratio, CurrR: Current liquidity, IT: Inventory turnover ratio, CollP: Collection period ratio, CredP: Credit period ratio, ROA: Return on assets ratio, ROE: Return on equity ratio, ROS: Return on sales ratio, TI: Total indebtedness ratio, EL: Equity leverage ratio, Ins: Insolvency ratio. Source: own elaboration.

In 2020, many researchers began to focus on the issue of the coronavirus pandemic and its impact on the economy, employment, enterprises, individuals, and society as a whole.

Orlowski [19] identified labor force problems with the arrival of the COVID-19 pandemic that could be solved by structural changes in the labor market. Similarly, Svabova et al. [2] examined the impact of anti-pandemic measures on the development of employment in the Slovak Republic and found that in 2020 unemployment worsened by approximately 2% to 3% in contrast to its development before the pandemic. This situation also affected self-employed people in the construction sector, who were significantly more affected by the pandemic than employees. According to Davidescu et al. [83], the wages of self-employed people were already at a lower level than the wages of employees before the pandemic. The arrival of the pandemic at the turn of March and April in 2020 worsened this development, while many self-employed people suspended their work activities. However, Jha [84] pointed to the fact that the direct cash benefits provided during the pandemic to construction sector employees were of significant help as they helped them to overcome financial hardship more easily. Unfortunately, this support was primarily associated not only with the dysfunctionality of the institutions in the handling process but with several financial problems [85]. Such aid was introduced in Slovakia in the form of First Aid I and First Aid II, which offered a large number of self-employed people in the construction sector to draw benefits calculated on the basis of the decrease in their cash income during the pandemic compared to the amount of their income in the period before the pandemic.

Table 9. The output of the pairwise comparison of the monitored years.

| Cash Liquidity Ratio | Test Statistics | Std. Error | Str. Test Statistics | Sig. | Adj. Sig. |
|---|---|---|---|---|---|
| 2018–2019 | 0.030 | 0.032 | 0.949 | 0.343 | 1.000 |
| 2018–2020 | 0.241 | 0.032 | 7.637 | 0.000 | 0.000 |
| 2019–2020 | 0.211 | 0.032 | 6.688 | 0.000 | 0.000 |
| **Quick liquidity ratio** | **Test Statistics** | **Std. Error** | **Std. Test Statistics** | **Sig.** | **Adj. Sig.** |
| 2018–2019 | 0.120 | 0.032 | 3.811 | 0.000 | 0.000 |
| 2018–2020 | 0.292 | 0.032 | 9.234 | 0.000 | 0.000 |
| 2019–2020 | 0.172 | 0.032 | 5.423 | 0.000 | 0.000 |
| **Current liquidity ratio** | **Test Statistics** | **Std. Error** | **Std. Test Statistics** | **Sig.** | **Adj. Sig.** |
| 2018–2019 | 0.137 | 0.032 | 4.332 | 0.000 | 0.000 |
| 2018–2020 | 0.347 | 0.032 | 10.989 | 0.000 | 0.000 |
| 2019–2020 | 0.210 | 0.032 | 6.657 | 0.000 | 0.000 |
| **Inventory turnover ratio** | **Test Statistics** | **Std. Error** | **Std. Test Statistics** | **Sig.** | **Adj. Sig.** |
| 2018–2019 | 0.007 | 0.032 | 0.221 | 0.825 | 1.000 |
| 2018–2020 | 0.176 | 0.032 | 5.566 | 0.000 | 0.000 |
| 2019–2020 | 0.169 | 0.032 | 5.344 | 0.000 | 0.000 |
| **Return on assets ratio** | **Test Statistics** | **Std. Error** | **Std. Test Statistics** | **Sig.** | **Adj. Sig.** |
| 2020–2019 | −0.210 | 0.032 | −6.639 | 0.000 | 0.000 |
| 2020–2018 | −0.321 | 0.032 | −10.148 | 0.000 | 0.000 |
| 2019–2018 | −0.111 | 0.032 | −3.509 | 0.000 | 0.001 |
| **Return on equity ratio** | **Test Statistics** | **Std. Error** | **Std. Test Statistics** | **Sig.** | **Adj. Sig.** |
| 2020–2019 | −0.284 | 0.032 | −8.994 | 0.000 | 0.000 |
| 2020–2018 | −0.473 | 0.032 | −14.954 | 0.000 | 0.000 |
| 2019–2018 | −0.188 | 0.032 | −5.959 | 0.000 | 0.000 |
| **Return on sales ratio** | **Test Statistics** | **Std. Error** | **Std. Test Statistics** | **Sig.** | **Adj. Sig.** |
| 2020–2019 | −0.121 | 0.032 | −3.825 | 0.000 | 0.000 |
| 2020–2018 | −0.201 | 0.032 | −6.370 | 0.000 | 0.000 |
| 2019–2018 | −0.080 | 0.032 | −2.545 | 0.011 | 0.033 |
| **Total indebtedness ratio** | **Test Statistics** | **Std. Error** | **Std. Test Statistics** | **Sig.** | **Adj. Sig.** |
| 2020–2019 | −0.179 | 0.032 | −5.675 | 0.000 | 0.000 |
| 2020–2018 | −0.365 | 0.032 | −11.539 | 0.000 | 0.000 |
| 2019–2018 | −0.185 | 0.032 | −5.865 | 0.000 | 0.000 |
| **Equity leverage ratio** | **Test Statistics** | **Std. Error** | **Std. Test Statistics** | **Sig.** | **Adj. Sig.** |
| 2020–2019 | −0.209 | 0.032 | −6.623 | 0.000 | 0.000 |
| 2020–2018 | −0.392 | 0.032 | −12.393 | 0.000 | 0.000 |
| 2019–2018 | −0.182 | 0.032 | −5.770 | 0.000 | 0.000 |
| **Insolvency ratio** | **Test Statistics** | **Std. Error** | **Std. Test Statistics** | **Sig.** | **Adj. Sig.** |
| 2020–2019 | −0.149 | 0.032 | −4.711 | 0.000 | 0.000 |
| 2020–2018 | −0.274 | 0.032 | −8.662 | 0.000 | 0.000 |
| 2019–2018 | −0.125 | 0.032 | −3.952 | 0.000 | 0.000 |

Source: own elaboration.

When analyzing the effects of past pandemics on the economy, Bonam and Smadu [17] pointed to the fact that in the past, pandemics primarily brought with them an increase in inflation, which subsequently lasted for more than 10 years. Given the current situation, this essential information indicates potential future developments that could occur even after the outbreak of the coronavirus pandemic. Currently, it is possible to point out that the arrival of the pandemic brought a crisis, which is increasingly beginning to manifest itself mainly in high inflation [86]. According to the National Bank of Slovakia, inflation was at an acceptable level of 1.6% in January 2021, rising slightly over time to 6.4% in November 2021. This growth trend continued in the following year as inflation reached 8.4% in January and an incredible 9% in February [87]. At the same time, the National Bank of Slovakia evaluates the current development of the economy and also provides a prediction of the expected development in the medium term. Not only the ongoing COVID-19 pandemic, but also the current war in Ukraine, will slow down the recovery of the world economy in the near future, and increasing global inflationary pressures will lead to further price increases across all sectors. In one of the predictions for 2022, Karmazin [88] expects a continued trend of inflation growth throughout the year due to the ongoing pandemic, crisis, and situation in Ukraine. The author also stated that, in the long term, he expects an increase in interest rates from the National Bank of Slovakia as a reaction to high inflation in an effort to reduce it, which will also have a direct impact on investments in the construction sector and thus a worsening of the conditions for providing mortgages and loans. Since the beginning of the pandemic, a significant increase in the prices not only of materials consumed in the construction sector [89], but also of construction works, which have grown at a dizzying pace since April 2021 [90], can be observed. Given the increased inflation, this trend was expected, although the real growth in the prices of materials and real estate dramatically exceeded expectations. The prices of construction materials as of the third quarter of 2021 increased by an average of 23% compared to October 2020. The cause of this growth is not only the growth of inflation, but also high energy prices and the ongoing demand for real estate [91]. Khalef et al. [29] emphasized that the current pandemic had an impact on construction projects in all sectors, specifically in material supply and human resources. In Slovakia, however, one can currently observe the problem of a lack of construction material, which is not only pointed out by many construction enterprises and individuals, but also faced by state contracts, where prices can increase by 15% to 20% [92].

When investigating the effects of the corona crisis on the business performance, Hu and Zhang [25] found a statistically significant relationship between the arrival of the pandemic and the deteriorated performance of the monitored enterprises. Achim et al. [23] found that the total profit of the monitored enterprises was up to 37% lower after the pandemic than before the pandemic, while according to Lam et al. [93], the construction sector performed significantly better than other sectors. Lassoued and Khanchel [27], on the contrary, pointed to the fact that in enterprises operating in the construction sector, the use of earnings management increased during the pandemic, especially in 2020, which brings with it a reduced reliability of financial statements during the pandemic. However, since the arrival of the COVID-19 pandemic, the construction sector has not been significantly affected compared to other sectors. Although there has been a sharp decline in construction production since the beginning of the pandemic, caused by the measures of the government in the form of a lockdown and its persistence even after the short-term restart of production during the last months of 2020, this development did not reach the values from the period before the pandemic.

Based on the findings, it can be argued that the COVID-19 pandemic brought about a sharp decline in construction output, which affected enterprises across the industry, but has recovered over time [94]. Increased consumption only supported the already started increase in inflation, which led to price increases not only in the entire economy but in the construction sector [95]. According to Iqbal et al. [96], the increased prices in the construction sector are caused not only by inflation but prices of input raw materials, such as oil or metals, while this increase is reflected in the growth of prices of new buildings and existing apartments [97]. However, a slight correction in the prices of apartments and houses can be expected in the future, which could slow down the possible future growth of this industry.

## 5. Conclusions

Even before the arrival of the COVID-19 pandemic, the world economy felt a decline in global demand, which began to manifest itself, especially towards the end of 2019. However, measures introduced in developed countries associated with the new coronavirus pandemic, which affected overall global consumption, had a considerable impact. In general, there is a decrease in the production of industrial production with a sharp decline in demand and consumption.

Based on the results of the liquidity analysis, it can be said that the enterprises operating in the construction sector in Slovakia during the period under review are improving the financial situation, reducing their indebtedness, guarding the financing of non-current assets, ensuring a sufficient level of liquidity against possible bankruptcy. At the same time, it turned out that at the beginning of the pandemic, the enterprises in the construction sector reacted very quickly because they decided to create higher reserves, thereby improving the results of the monitored indicators. Enterprises thus prepared for the new situation that the pandemic brought. These conclusions are supported by the results from the realized debt analysis, which pointed to a trend of decreasing corporate indebtedness, which started before the pandemic and continued after the arrival of the coronavirus crisis. Based on the results of the total indebtedness ratio, the average indebtedness of enterprises between 2018 and 2020 was at a level of up to 65% and gradually decreased. Similarly, the financial leverage indicator, the inverse of the self-financing coefficient, confirmed these results. On the contrary, when analyzing other ratios, it is possible to claim that the arrival of the COVID-19 pandemic had a negative impact on many aspects of business in this sector. The efficiency ratios are the most affected by the pandemic, as the average inventory turnover time is more than 111 days in 2020, compared to 2018, when it was only 50 days. In the case of the average collection period and the average credit period ratio, a disparity between these two indicators was revealed, which became more and more profound from year to year in the examined companies and worsened even more significantly with the arrival of the pandemic. The average collection period was 50 days in 2018, and in 2020, i.e., after the pandemic, it was almost 94 days. The average credit period was similar at the level of 57 days in 2018, and in 2020 the number of days until maturity doubled. In the analysis of profitability, a worsening trend across all selected indicators was also recorded, which confirmed their interconnectedness, i.e., if the enterprise does not have a favorable ROA indicator, then it cannot create positive results even in the ROE and ROS ratios. These indicators faced a worsening trend even before the pandemic, and the arrival of the pandemic only helped it in the form of a significant, even jumpy deterioration. Overall, based on the findings of the detailed analysis, the arrival of the pandemic had a clear impact on the financial and economic situation of the examined enterprises from the Slovak construction sector. However, the most significant impacts will be even more noticeable in the future due to the fact that this sector is characterized by slower reactions to changes in the economy.

Construction sector enterprises operating in Slovakia are trying to make the right decisions in the long term, thus facing the pandemic sensibly, primarily by maintaining good liquidity or reducing indebtedness. On the contrary, enterprises are trying to increase the use of earnings management techniques and reduce the reliability of annual reports during the pandemic. This situation could improve after the end of the entire pandemic period. In the long term, high inflation at approximately 10% to 15% is expected in the coming years, followed by its gradual reduction. At the same time, an increase in interest rates is expected not only for mortgages but for loans, which can significantly slow down the sector growth and, therefore, reduce investment in this area.

Despite the contribution of this paper to the extant literature, the following limitation needs to be highlighted. The scope of the paper (i.e., the focus only on one national economy of Slovakia) limits the generalization of the findings. Future research should examine this phenomenon in more national economies or in a longer time horizon than what was set for this research to determine whether there will be differences in the findings and allow for greater generalization and applicability.

**Author Contributions:** Conceptualization, D.G. and K.V.; methodology, D.G. and K.V.; software, T.K.; validation, D.G., K.V. and V.M.; formal analysis, T.K. and D.G.; investigation, V.M.; resources, K.V. and T.K.; data curation, D.G. and T.K.; writing—original draft preparation, D.G. and K.V.; writing—review and editing, D.G., K.V. and T.K.; visualization, V.M.; supervision, T.K.; project administration, K.V. All authors have read and agreed to the published version of the manuscript.

**Funding:** This research was financially supported by the Slovak Research and Development Agency–Grant Vega 1/0121/20: Research of transfer pricing system as a tool to measure the performance of national and multinational companies in the context of earnings management in conditions of the Slovak Republic and V4 countries and faculty institutional research 1/KE/2021: The use of quantitative methods to assess corporate indebtedness.

**Institutional Review Board Statement:** Not applicable.

**Informed Consent Statement:** Not applicable.

**Data Availability Statement:** The data presented in this research paper are available on request from the corresponding authors.

**Acknowledgments:** The paper is an output of the project NFP313010BWN6 "The implementation framework and business model of the Internet of Things, Industry 4.0 and smart transport".

**Conflicts of Interest:** The authors declare no conflict of interest.

# References

1. Kovacova, M.; Krajcik, V.; Michalkova, L.; Blazek, R. Valuing the Interest Tax Shield in the Central European Economies: Panel Data Approach. *J. Compet.* **2022**, *14*, 41–59. [CrossRef]
2. Svabova, L.; Tesarova, E.N.; Durica, M.; Strakova, L. Evaluation of the impacts of the COVID-19 pandemic on the development of the unemployment rate in Slovakia: Counterfactual before-after comparison. *Equilib. Q. J. Econ. Econ. Policy* **2021**, *16*, 261–284. [CrossRef]
3. Belas, J.; Gavurova, B.; Dvorsky, J.; Cepel, M.; Durana, P. The impact of the COVID-19 pandemic on selected areas of a management system in SMEs. *Econ. Res. Ekon. Istraz.* **2021**, *35*, 3754–3777. [CrossRef]
4. Penakova, Z. Tax policy in the Slovak and Czech economies. *Polit Ekon.* **2021**, *69*, 689–707. [CrossRef]
5. Strukova, Z.; Liska, M. Application of automation and robotics in construction work execution. *Ad Alta J. Interd. Res.* **2012**, *2*, 121–125.
6. Deep, S.; Joshi, R.; Patil, S. Identifying the Contractor's core competencies in post-COVID-19 scenario: Developing a survey instrument. *Eng. Constr. Archit. Manag.* **2022**. [CrossRef]
7. Valaskova, K.; Durana, P.; Adamko, P. Changes in consumers' purchase patterns as a consequence of the COVID-19 pandemic. *Mathematics* **2021**, *9*, 1788. [CrossRef]
8. Durana, P.; Valaskova, K.; Blazek, R.; Palo, J. Metamorphoses of Earnings in the Transport Sector of the V4 Region. *Mathematics* **2022**, *10*, 1204. [CrossRef]
9. Svabova, L.; Kramarova, K.; Gabrikova, B. Counterfactual Assessment of the Allowance for School-leaver Practice Performance as a Measure of Active Labour Market Policy in Slovakia. *Ekon. Cas.* **2022**, *70*, 99–123. [CrossRef]
10. Binh, L.H.; Ha, L.T. Vietnam Economy Under the Impact of COVID-19. *Rus. J. Vietn. Stud.* **2022**, *5*, 45–70.
11. Wang, Q.; Zhang, C. Can COVID-19 and environmental research in developing countries support these countries to meet the environmental challenges induced by the pandemic? *Environ. Sci. Pollut. Res.* **2021**, *28*, 41296–41316. [CrossRef] [PubMed]
12. Adnan, A.T.M.; Hasan, M.M. The emergence of COVID-19 and capital market reaction: An emerging market scenario analysis. *Asian Acad. Manag. J. Account.* **2021**, *17*, 35–62. [CrossRef]
13. Valaskova, K.; Nagy, M.; Zabojnik, S.; Lazaroiu, G. Industry 4.0 Wireless Networks and Cyber-Physical Smart Manufacturing Systems as Accelerators of Value-Added Growth in Slovak Exports. *Mathematics* **2022**, *10*, 2452. [CrossRef]
14. Tesarova, E.N.; Krizanova, A. The Impact of COVID-19 on Sustainability and Changing Consumer Behavior in the Textile Industry. Is it Significant? *Manag. Dyn. Knowl. Econ.* **2022**, *10*, 95–105.
15. Rodríguez-Caballero, C.V.; Vera-Valdes, J.E. Long-lasting economic effects of pandemics: Evidence on growth and unemployment. *Econ. J.* **2020**, *8*, 16.
16. Lahiri, S.; Sinha, M. A study of the socio-economic implications of the COVID-19 pandemic. *Australas. Account. Bus. Financ. J.* **2021**, *15*, 51–69. [CrossRef]
17. Bonam, D.; Smadu, A. The long-run effects of pandemics on inflation: Will this time be different? *Econ. Lett.* **2021**, *208*, 110065. [CrossRef]
18. Kocisova, K.; Pastyrikova, M. Determinants of non-performing loans in European Union countries. *Proc. Econ. Financ. Conf.* **2020**, 64–71. [CrossRef]
19. Orlowski, L.T. The 2020 Pandemic: Economic repercussions and policy responses. *Rev. Financ. Econ.* **2021**, *39*, 20–26. [CrossRef]
20. Svabova, L.; Gabrikova, B. The rise in youth employment? Impact evaluation of COVID-19 consequences. *J. East. Eur. Cent. Asian Res.* **2021**, *8*, 511–526. [CrossRef]
21. Hajduova, Z.; Hurajova, J.C.; Smorada, M.; Srenkel, L. Competitiveness of the Selected Countries of the EU with a Focus on the Quality of the Business Environment. *J. Compet.* **2021**, *13*, 43–59. [CrossRef]

22. Valaskova, K.; Gajdosikova, D.; Pavic Kramaric, T. How Important Is the Business Environment for The Performance of Enterprises? Case Study of Selected European Countries. *Cent. Eur. Bus. Rev.* **2022**. [CrossRef]
23. Achim, M.V.; Safta, I.L.; Vaidean, V.L.; Mureșan, G.M.; Borlea, N.S. The impact of COVID-19 on financial management: Evidence from Romania. *Econ. Res.-Ekon. Istraz.* **2021**, *35*, 1807–1832. [CrossRef]
24. Rakha, A.; Hettiarachchi, H.; Rady, D.; Gaber, M.M.; Rakha, E.; Abdelsamea, M.M. Predicting the economic impact of the COVID-19 pandemic in the United Kingdom using time-series mining. *Economies* **2021**, *9*, 137. [CrossRef]
25. Hu, S.; Zhang, Y. COVID-19 pandemic and firm performance: Cross-country evidence. *Int. Rev. Econ.* **2021**, *74*, 365–372. [CrossRef]
26. Zajmi, S. Liquidity and solvency analysis of the real sector of the economy of serbia for 2018–2019. *Cas. ekon. trz. komun.* **2021**, *11*, 294–306. [CrossRef]
27. Lassoued, N.; Khanchel, I. Impact of COVID-19 pandemic on earnings management: An evidence from financial reporting in European firms. *Glob. Bus. Rev.* **2021**. [CrossRef]
28. Salami, B.A.; Ajayi, S.O.; Oyegoke, A.S. Tackling the impacts of COVID-19 on construction projects: An exploration of contractual dispute avoidance measures adopted by construction firms. *Int. J. Constr. Manag.* **2021**. [CrossRef]
29. Khalef, R.; Ali, G.G.; El-adaway, I.H.; Gad, G.M. Managing construction projects impacted by the COVID-19 pandemic: A contractual perspective. *Constr. Manag. Econ.* **2022**, *40*, 313–330. [CrossRef]
30. Vetrakova, M.; Potkany, M.; Hitka, M. Outsourcing of facility management. *E. M. Ekon. Manag.* **2013**, *16*, 80–92.
31. Hanak, T.; Chadima, T.; Selih, J. Implementation of online reverse auctions: Comparison of Czech and Slovak construction industry. *Eng. Econ.* **2017**, *28*, 271–279. [CrossRef]
32. Lalithchandra, B.N.; Rajendhiran, N. Liquidity Ratio: An Important Financial Metrics. *Turk. J. Comp. Math. Educ.* **2021**, *12*, 1113–1114.
33. Santosuosso, P. Do efficiency ratios help investors to explore firm performances? Evidence from Italian listed firms. *Int. Bus. Rev.* **2014**, *7*, 111. [CrossRef]
34. Valaskova, K.; Kliestik, T.; Gajdosikova, D. Distinctive determinants of financial indebtedness: Evidence from Slovak and Czech enterprises. *Equilib. Q. J. Econ. Econ. Policy* **2021**, *16*, 639–659. [CrossRef]
35. Siegel, S.; Castellan, N.J., Jr. *Nonparametric Statistics for the Behavioral Sciences*, 2nd ed.; McGraw-Hill: New York, NY, USA, 1988.
36. Pereira, D.G.; Afonso, A.; Medeiros, F.M. Overview of Friedman's test and post-hoc analysis. *Commun. Stat. Simul. Comput.* **2015**, *44*, 2636–2653. [CrossRef]
37. Conover, W.J. *Practical Nonparametric Statistics*; Wiley: New York, NY, USA, 1999.
38. Liu, J.; Xu, Y. T-Friedman Test: A New Statistical Test for Multiple Comparison with an Adjustable Conservativeness Measure. *Int. J. Comput. Intell.* **2022**, *15*, 1–19. [CrossRef]
39. Dunn, O.J. Multiple comparisons among means. *J. Am. Stat. Assoc.* **1961**, *56*, 52–64. [CrossRef]
40. Dinno, A. Nonparametric pairwise multiple comparisons in independent groups using Dunn's test. *Stata J.* **2015**, *15*, 292–300. [CrossRef]
41. Musa, H.; Musova, Z.; Natorin, V.; Lazaroiu, G.; Boda, M. Comparison of factors influencing liquidity of European Islamic and conventional banks. *Oeconomia Copernicana.* **2021**, *12*, 375–398. [CrossRef]
42. Rafaqat, S.; Rafaqat, S. The Impact of Merger and Acquisition on the Financial Performance of the Nasdaq Listed Small Size Technology Companies. *Econ. Financ. Let.* **2020**, *7*, 200–217. [CrossRef]
43. Canton, C.; Muller, M.; da Silva, T.P.; Rodrigues, M.M. Accounting conservatism effect on speed of adjustment of the cash. *Rev. Ges. Organiz.* **2019**, *12*, 3–17.
44. Batrancea, L. The Influence of Liquidity and Solvency on Performance within the Healthcare Industry: Evidence from Publicly Listed Companies. *Mathematics* **2021**, *9*, 2231. [CrossRef]
45. Balina, R. Forecasting bankruptcy risk in the contexts of credit risk management—A case study on wholesale food industry in Poland. *J. Int. Econ. Sci.* **2018**, *7*, 1–15. [CrossRef]
46. da Rocha, E.M.; de Oliveira, F.I.S.; Valdevino, R.Q.S. PROFUT: An analysis of the capital of Brazilian times. *Rev. Ambient. Cont.* **2021**, *13*, 145–164.
47. Jelavic, S.R.; Brkic, I.; Kozul, A. Financial Indicators of the Cement Industry in Croatia. *Econ. Thought Pract.* **2016**, *25*, 565–586.
48. Almomani, T.M.; Almomani, M.A.; Obeidat, M.I. The relationship between working capital management and financial performance: Evidence from Jordan. *J. As. Finance Econ. Bus.* **2021**, *8*, 713–720.
49. Boisjoly, R.P.; Conine, T.E., Jr.; McDonald, M.B., IV. Working capital management: Financial and valuation impacts. *J. Bus. Res.* **2020**, *108*, 1–8. [CrossRef]
50. Goolsbee, A.; Syverson, C. Fear, lockdown, and diversion: Comparing drivers of pandemic economic decline 2020. *J. Public Econ.* **2021**, *193*, 104311. [CrossRef]
51. Bera, B.; Bhattacharjee, S.; Shit, P.K.; Sengupta, N.; Saha, S. Significant impacts of COVID-19 lockdown on urban air pollution in Kolkata (India) and amelioration of environmental health. *Environ. Dev. Sustain.* **2021**, *23*, 6913–6940. [CrossRef]
52. Aregbeyen, O. The effects of working capital management on the profitability of Nigerian manufacturing firms. *J. Bus. Econ.* **2013**, *14*, 520–534. [CrossRef]
53. Farhan, N.H.; Belhaj, F.A.; Al-ahdal, W.M.; Almaqtari, F.A. An analysis of working capital management in India: An urgent need to refocus. *Cogent Bus. Manag.* **2021**, *8*, 1924930. [CrossRef]

54. Kumaraswamy, S. Goods and services tax shock on small and medium enterprises working capital in India. *Entrepreneurship Sustain. Issues* **2020**, *7*, 3464–3476. [CrossRef]
55. Mahato, C.; Mahata, G.C. Decaying items inventory models with partial linked-to-order upstream trade credit and downstream full trade credit. *J. Manag. Anal.* **2022**, *9*, 137–168. [CrossRef]
56. Ghoul, S.E.; Guedhami, O.; Kim, Y. Country-level institutions, firm value, and the role of corporate social responsibility initiatives. *J. Int. Bus.* **2017**, *48*, 360–385. [CrossRef]
57. Barbuta-Misu, N. Analysis of factors influencing managerial decision to use trade credit in construction sector. *Econ. Res.-Ekon. Istraz.* **2018**, *31*, 1903–1922.
58. Wang, X.; Han, L.; Huang, X.; Mi, B. The financial and operational impacts of European SMEs' use of trade credit as a substitute for bank credit. *Eur. J. Finance* **2021**, *27*, 796–825. [CrossRef]
59. Trang, L.N.T.; Nhan, D.T.T.; Phuong, D.N.T.; Wong, W.K. The Effects of Selected Financial Ratios on Profitability: An Empirical Analysis of Real Estate Firms in Vietnam. *Ann. Econ. Financ.* **2022**, *17*, 2250006. [CrossRef]
60. Eldridge, D.; Nisar, T.M.; Torchia, M. What impact does equity crowdfunding have on SME innovation and growth? An empirical study. *Small Bus. Econ.* **2021**, *56*, 105–120. [CrossRef]
61. Lee, W.M. The determinants and effects of board committees. *J. Corp. Financ.* **2020**, *65*, 101747. [CrossRef]
62. Nguyen, T.N.L.; Nguyen, V.C. The determinants of profitability in listed enterprises: A study from Vietnamese stock exchange. *J. As. Financ. Econ. Bus.* **2020**, *7*, 47–58. [CrossRef]
63. Xu, J.; Liu, F. Nexus between intellectual capital and financial performance: An investigation of Chinese manufacturing industry. *J. Bus. Econ.* **2021**, *22*, 217–235. [CrossRef]
64. Soewarno, N.; Tjahjadi, B. Measures that matter: An empirical investigation of intellectual capital and financial performance of banking firms in Indonesia. *J. Intellect. Cap.* **2020**, *21*, 1085–1106. [CrossRef]
65. Bolton, P.; Kacperczyk, M. Do investors care about carbon risk? *J. Financ. Econ.* **2021**, *142*, 517–549.
66. Gangi, F.; Daniele, L.M.; Varrone, N. How do corporate environmental policy and corporate reputation affect risk-adjusted financial performance? *Bus. Strategy Environ.* **2020**, *29*, 1975–1991. [CrossRef]
67. Korzeb, Z.; Niedziolka, P. Resistance of commercial banks to the crisis caused by the COVID-19 pandemic: The case of Poland. *Equilib. Q. J. Econ. Econ. Policy* **2020**, *15*, 205–234. [CrossRef]
68. Kumar, S.; Zbib, L. Firm performance during the COVID-19 crisis: Does managerial ability matter? *Financ. Res. Lett.* **2022**, *47*, 102720. [CrossRef]
69. Balatsky, E.V. Return on equity as an economic growth driver. *Econ. Soc. Chang. Fac. Tr. For.* **2021**, *14*, 26–40. [CrossRef]
70. Zimon, G.; Tarighi, H. Effects of the COVID-19 global crisis on the working capital management policy: Evidence from Poland. *J. Risk Financ. Manag.* **2021**, *14*, 169. [CrossRef]
71. Durana, P.; Michalkova, L.; Privara, A.; Marousek, J.; Tumpach, M. Does the life cycle affect earnings management and bankruptcy? *Oeconomia Copernican.* **2021**, *12*, 425–461. [CrossRef]
72. Stefko, R.; Vasanicova, P.; Jencova, S.; Pachura, A. Management and economic sustainability of the Slovak industrial companies with medium energy intensity. *Energies* **2021**, *14*, 267. [CrossRef]
73. Cerkovskis, E.; Gajdosikova, D.; Ciurlau, C.F. Capital structure theories: Review of literature. *Ekon.-Manaz. Spektrum* **2022**, *16*, 12–24.
74. Jencova, S.; Petruska, I.; Lukacova, M. Relationship between roa and total indebtedness by threshold regression model. *Montenegrin J. Econ.* **2021**, *17*, 37–46. [CrossRef]
75. Mouandat, S.R. Is Foreign Debt Management in Gabon Efficient? *Manag. Dyn. Knowl. Economy* **2022**, *10*, 82–94.
76. Rahmati, Z.; Noshadi, A.; Bozorgmehrian, S. Studying the Variations in Ratio of Capital Resources toward the Equity Returnin Tehran Stock Exchange. *J. Life Sci.* **2012**, *9*, 664–669.
77. de Rezende, F.A.C.; de Albuquerque, A.A.; de Souza, G.H.S. Solvency index at differentiated levels of corporate governance according to the models from Elizabetsky (1976), Kanitz (1978), Matias (1978) and Altman (1979): The case of the Brazilian electricity sector. *Ind. J. Man. Prod.* **2014**, *5*, 921–946. [CrossRef]
78. Cai, J.; Landriault, D.; Shi, T.; Wei, W. Joint insolvency analysis of a shared map risk process: A capital allocation application. *N. Am. Actuar. J.* **2017**, *21*, 178–192. [CrossRef]
79. Centes, J.; Krajcovic, M. Consideration of the effectiveness of flat-rate compensation for damage in insolvency proceedings. *Entrep. Sustain. Issues* **2019**, *7*, 1435–1449.
80. Krulicky, T.; Horak, J. Business performance and financial health assessment through artificial intelligence. *Ekon. Manaz. Spektrum* **2021**, *15*, 38–51.
81. Mai, X.; Chan, R.C.; Zhan, C. Which sectors really matter for a resilient Chinese economy? A structural decomposition analysis. *Sustainability* **2019**, *11*, 6333. [CrossRef]
82. Narayanamurthy, G.; Tortorella, G. Impact of COVID-19 outbreak on employee performance–moderating role of industry 4.0 base technologies. *Int. J. Prod. Econ.* **2021**, *234*, 108075. [CrossRef]
83. Davidescu, A.A.; Apostu, S.A.; Stoica, L.A. Socioeconomic Effects of COVID-19 Pandemic: Exploring Uncertainty in the Forecast of the Romanian Unemployment Rate for the Period 2020–2023. *Sustainability* **2021**, *13*, 7078. [CrossRef]
84. Jha, A. Vulnerability of construction workers during COVID-19: Tracking welfare responses and challenges. *Indian J. Labour Econ.* **2021**, *64*, 1043–1067. [CrossRef]

85. Ortensi, L.E.; di Belgiojoso, E.B. Welfare and social protection: What is the link with secondary migration? Evidence from the 2014-crisis hit Italian region of Lombardy. *Popul. Space Place* **2022**, *28*, e2469. [CrossRef]
86. Fetzer, T.; Hensel, L.; Hermle, J.; Roth, C. Coronavirus perceptions and economic anxiety. *Rev. Econ. Stat.* **2021**, *103*, 968–978. [CrossRef]
87. Karmazin, B. Rychle komentare: Ceny vstupov posunuli inflaciu na 9%. Narodna banka Slovenska. 2022. Available online: https://nbs.sk/dokument/4de47406-2779-4b8e-8d76-a4e0d2a79b96/stiahnut?force=false/ (accessed on 24 May 2022).
88. Karmazin, B. Rychle komentare: Regulované ceny potiahli infláciu nad 8%. Narodna banka Slovenska. 2022. Available online: https://nbs.sk/komentare/regulovane-ceny-potiahli-inflaciu-nad-8/ (accessed on 28 May 2022).
89. Assaad, R.; El-adaway, I.H. Guidelines for responding to COVID-19 pandemic: Best practices, impacts, and future research directions. *J. Manag. Eng.* **2021**, *37*, 06021001. [CrossRef]
90. Araya, F. Modeling the spread of COVID-19 on construction workers: An agent-based approach. *Saf. Sci.* **2021**, *133*, 105022. [CrossRef] [PubMed]
91. Vandana; Singh, R.; Yaday, D.; Sarkar, B.; Sarkar, M. Impact of Energy and Carbon Emission of a Supply Chain Management with Two-Level Trade-Credit Policy. *Energies* **2021**, *14*, 1569. [CrossRef]
92. Vrbovsky, R. Rychle komentare: Rast cien nehnutelnosti pokracuje aj na zaciatku roku 2022. Narodna banka Slovenska. 2022. Available online: https://nbs.sk/komentare/rast-cien-nehnutelnosti-pokracuje-aj-na-zaciatku-roku-2022/ (accessed on 18 March 2022).
93. Lam, W.S.; Lam, W.H.; Jaaman, S.H.; Liew, K.F. Performance evaluation of construction companies using integrated entropy–fuzzy VIKOR model. *Entropy* **2021**, *23*, 320. [CrossRef]
94. Ayat, M.; Malikah; Kang, C.W. Effects of the COVID-19 pandemic on the construction sector: A systemized review. *Eng. Constr. Archit. Manag.* **2021**. [CrossRef]
95. Gillman, M. Macroeconomic trends among Visegrad countries, EU Balkans, and the US, 1991–2021. *Cent. Eur. Bus. Rev.* **2021**, *10*, 1–20. [CrossRef]
96. Iqbal, M.; Ahmad, N.; Waqas, M.; Abrar, M. COVID-19 pandemic and construction industry: Impacts, emerging construction safety practices, and proposed crisis management. *Braz. J. Oper. Prod. Manag.* **2021**, *18*, 1–17. [CrossRef]
97. Alsamhi, M.H.; Al-Ofairi, F.A.; Farhan, N.H.; Al-ahdal, W.M.; Siddiqui, A. Impact of COVID-19 on firms' performance: Empirical evidence from India. *Cogent Bus. Manag.* **2022**, *9*, 2044593. [CrossRef]

*Article*

# Post-COVID-19 Family Micro-Business Resources and Agritourism Performance: A Two-Mediated Moderated Quantitative-Based Model with a PLS-SEM Data Analysis Method

Ibrahim A. Elshaer [1,2], Ahmad M. AboAlkhair [3,4], Sameh Fayyad [2] and Alaa M. S. Azazz [5,6,*]

1. Department of Management, College of Business Administration, King Faisal University, Al-Ahsaa 380, Saudi Arabia
2. Hotel Studies Department, Faculty of Tourism and Hotels, Suez Canal University, Ismailia 41522, Egypt
3. Quantitative Methods Department, College of Business Administration, King Faisal University, Al-Ahsaa 380, Saudi Arabia
4. Department of Applied Statistics and Insurance, Mansoura University, Mansoura 35516, Egypt
5. Department of Tourism and Hospitality, Arts College, King Faisal University, Al-Ahsaa 380, Saudi Arabia
6. Tourism Studies Department, Faculty of Tourism and Hotels, Suez Canal University, Ismailia 41522, Egypt
* Correspondence: aazazz@kfu.edu.sa

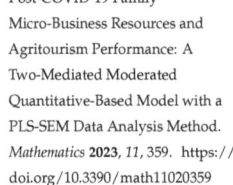

Citation: Elshaer, I.A.; AboAlkhair, A.M.; Fayyad, S.; Azazz, A.M.S. Post-COVID-19 Family Micro-Business Resources and Agritourism Performance: A Two-Mediated Moderated Quantitative-Based Model with a PLS-SEM Data Analysis Method. *Mathematics* 2023, 11, 359. https://doi.org/10.3390/math11020359

Academic Editor: Manuel Alberto M. Ferreira

Received: 24 November 2022
Revised: 28 December 2022
Accepted: 6 January 2023
Published: 10 January 2023

**Copyright:** © 2023 by the authors. Licensee MDPI, Basel, Switzerland. This article is an open access article distributed under the terms and conditions of the Creative Commons Attribution (CC BY) license (https://creativecommons.org/licenses/by/4.0/).

**Abstract:** The global spread of coronavirus (COVID-19) has had a devastating impact on thousands of small businesses. Many businesspeople, especially those who own and run micro-businesses, have been hampered by the unprecedented scale of the lockdown of social activities and the restrictions placed on their freedom of movement. The reciprocity process between small rural businesses and residents is ultimately in the interest of improving agrotourism performance. Integrating the non-zero-sum games theory and the social exchange theory, this study aims to achieve the following: (1) testing the relationship between family micro-businesses resources and agritourism performance; (2) examining the impact of two mediating variables (resident–micro-business interaction and support for agritourism development); and (3) testing the intervention of one moderating variable (personal resident benefit) on the tested relationships. Dyads data was collected from 293 residents/family small businesses operators. Partial least squares-based structural equation modelling (PLS-SEM) with the SmartPLS program was employed to analyze the collected data. Family micro-business resources were found to have a positive and significant impact on agritourism performance, moreover, resident–micro-business interaction and support for agritourism development were found to partially mediate the relationship between family micro-business resources and agritourism performance, and the personal resident benefit significantly moderated the relationship between family micro-business resources and resident–micro-business interaction. Several implications for academics and policymakers were elaborated. The limitations and further study opportunities were also discussed.

**Keywords:** rural hospitality and tourism; agritourism; micro-businesses; agritourism performance; support for agritourism development; personal resident benefit; resident–micro-business interaction

**MSC:** 91C99

## 1. Introduction

The perspectives of rural residents toward agritourism enterprises directly influence their behavior in engaging with agritourism enhancement and, thus, are a crucial factor that can determine the resilience ability and the success or failure of the organization [1]. Research has indicated that rural residents might participate in resistance actions that can significantly prevent rural tourism development if they believe that they are responsible for the majority of the rural core tourism attractions while having the least access to those that are useful to tourists [2,3]. They believe tourism developments that do not use local businesses will not provide clear economic benefits such as jobs and higher family incomes [2]; as agritourism's main players, they will defend their rights and interests.

In developing countries, agritourism micro-businesses are frequently associated with family-related enterprises, such as farming or tourist-related activities on farms [4]. Family-owned agritourism small businesses often do not aim to become large entities and the owners often see themselves as emotionally attached to their communities and businesses [5]. However, micro-business success is predicated not just on the individual ventures' success but also on the overall contributions each makes to its local community [6]. In the same vein, drawing on the social exchange theory, [7] it can be argued that "local residents are prepared to participate in an exchange with tourists if they believe that it is likely they will obtain benefits without incurring unacceptable costs". The reciprocity process between family micro-businesses and local residents is ultimately in the interest of improving agrotourism performance.

According to the social exchange theory (SET), economic and socio-emotional resources are exchanged. Economic resources include everything of monetary value that might meet financial needs. Socio-emotional resources include supportiveness, helpfulness, and friendliness [8]. On examination, micro-businesses are frequently perceived as non-'mainstream', boosted by the owners' interests rather than by commercial motivations, offering little opportunity for growth and greater value in promoting social inclusion. Hence, the economic activities of the micro-business are embedded within the broader social and economic relationships of the household [9]. Local residents' ownership of family micro-businesses is expected to increase resident–micro-business interaction (or client interaction) due to high-quality social exchanges (i.e., economic and socio-emotional relationships) [8]. Furthermore, personal benefits play a significant role in the exchange process for residents' favorable attitudes toward tourism [10]. Thus, maximizing the residents' personal benefits will reflect positively on resident–micro-business interaction [11]. Overall, local residents' involvement in tourism development strengthens their perceptions of tourism's benefits, increasing their willingness to support agritourism development in their community [12,13].

Based on the arguments mentioned earlier, the current study uses game theory (GT) as a theoretical background to explain the intercorrelations in our study. According to Friedenberg and Keisler [14], the application of the game theory to economic behavior and alliances is extensive. The theory is instrumental in gaining insights into how market players behave and interact in certain situations [15] and provides a way of analyzing both competitor and partner behavior, as well as what is likely to happen if the rules are changed. Game theorists have suggested the notion of a non-zero-sum game (see Figure 1). This is one of the considerable critical assumptions of game theory. The idea proposes that players—i.e., in our study are (player 1) family micro-businesses and (player 2) local residents—may profit from collaboration by revealing their approach beforehand and making an "irrevocable commitment" to it [16].

|  | | Residents | |
|---|---|---|---|
|  |  | Win | lose |
| Micro-businesses | Win | 1,1 | 0,0 |
|  | Lose | 0,0 | 4,4 |

- Microbusinesses will win when able to gain revenue and will lose when unable to generate revenue.
- Residents will win when being able to gain benefits (i.e., job creation, and other community services) and will lose when be unable to gain benefits.

**Figure 1.** Non-zero game theory.

Zhang et al. described this notion as "the realization of maximizing the interests of both sides, which is a harmonious development with mutual benefits" [17]. Accordingly, this study, depending on the game theory along with the social exchange theory (SET), aims to (1) test the associations between family micro-business resources (FM) and agritourism performance (AP), (2) explore the mediating role of resident–micro-business interaction (RMI) and support for agritourism development (SAD), and finally, (3) test the moderating role of personal resident benefit (PRB) on the proposed relationships.

Previous studies on agritourism were found to have focused on the social, ecological, cultural, authenticity variables [18], and agritourism marketing endeavors [19]. Still, they have not addressed the micro-business as a tool for the success of agritourism enterprises in local rural communities [20]. Furthermore, most agritourism research has been conducted in Western nations, resulting in a need for more awareness of the sector's condition in less developed countries [21]. Consequently, this study attempts to fill this gap by (1) exploring the role of establishing family micro-businesses in improving agritourism performance and (2) conducting a field study in one of the developing countries (i.e., KSA). To the authors' best knowledge, this study is one of the first that explores all these direct, moderating, and mediating relationships in one model and in one context using partial least squares-based structural equation modelling (PLS-SEM) as the main data analysis technique.

## 2. Literature Review and Development of Hypotheses

*2.1. The Mediating Role of Resident–Micro-Business Interaction (RMI) and Support for Agritourism Development (SAD)*

Traditional agricultural production methods are becoming less feasible, especially in developing countries, and farming residents have faced economic and social problems due to lower farming revenues. Hence, farmers have resorted to agritourism activities [22]. Agritourism promotes local economic development by revitalizing traditional industries, farming-related tourist activities, and older styles of life that react to the post-modern customers' pursuit of authenticity [23]. Thus, it generates services and employment chances and provides additional foreign sources of income. Therefore, agritourism is increasingly regarded as a tool for enhancing the economic and social circumstances for local residents [24,25].

Agritourism operators (agritourism practices include on-farm direct sales, accommodation/lodging, leisure/special events, open-air recreation, and educational activities) are often smaller, family-owned businesses originating in the host community and frequently showcase host agricultural goods and cultural practices [26]. These micro-businesses employ 10 or fewer employees and have progressively more significant roles in local economic growth [27] by creating entrepreneurship chances for women [28], and family groups [29]. Employing the resource-based view (RBV) approach [30], family micro-business resources (FM) can be categorized as business-based resources and structural resources, where "business resources are those created and possessed by individual business owners". While structural resources are considered externally based in nature "...that owners may benefit from or contribute to but do not possess individually". Business-based resources—that include small business orientation, social capital, and social networking links—for family micro-businesses are critical strategic resources for competitive advantage. These resources are valuable, rare, hard to imitate, and hard to substitute [31] as they are based on culture, community environment, and family-entrepreneurship processes [32].

Family micro-businesses that operate a small business orientation are "any business that is independently owned and operated, not dominant in its field, and does not engage in any new marketing or innovative practices" [33]. The limited size of agritourism markets may be unattractive to large businesses. Thus, small family agritourism firms may be more stable and prosperous in niches with less competition [34]. Social capital as a business resource is a core resource or group of social assets that performers utilize to track their interests through the membership of social networks/structures [35], which can facilitate mutual collaboration between individuals [36]. Based on the social capital theory, family micro-businesses can benefit from social capital in sharing information, working toward joint goals with the community, and creating trust among group members [20]. On the other hand, as the third business resource, social network ties may be a precursor to forming possible social capital, yet "they are not equivalent or interchangeable terms" [37]. These social network ties are more significant to micro-businesses and those in the difficult conditions seen in rural areas [38]. Based on SET, we argue that the business-based resources of family micro-businesses (social network ties, small business orientation, and social capital) involve many economic and socio-emotional resource exchanges between micro-businesses and the community. Therefore, they are vital to boosting these micro-businesses' success in particular, and the agritourism performance in general [39]. Thus, we can propose the below hypothesis:

**Hypothesis 1 (H1).** *Family micro-business resources have a relationship with agritourism performance.*

Contact in tourism occurs between tourists and hosts, other guests, service providers, and fellow tourists [40]. Positive communication between service providers and their guests or residents is the most important of these contacts and can boost friendly attitudes and good behaviors, which are essential for the success of any tourism business [41,42]. In the agritourism sector, farm owners themselves are the owners of agritourism businesses in many cases [43]. Thus, the residents feel psychological ownership of these businesses. According to the affective events theory (AET), when locals experience psychological ownership of the family micro-businesses, they support them and express their loyalty. This is because of their psychological connection with the businesses [44,45]. Given the nature of the resources on which family micro-businesses depend and which require a lot of exchanges of interests between these businesses and the residents, resident–micro-business interaction has become significant [40]. Therefore, we introduce the below hypothesis:

**Hypothesis 2 (H2).** *Family micro-business resources have a relationship with resident–micro-business interaction.*

The positive social contact and interactions inherent in agritourism between agritourism operators and local residents associate strongly and positively with profitability and successful agritourism endeavors [46]. In the same vein, such interactions can succeed in the mutual objectives of exchanging economic and socio-emotional resources among agritourism entrepreneurs and local communities and reinforce collaborative dual partnerships between agritourism companies [47]. Aiming to assess the contribution of resident–micro-business interaction to enhancing agritourism performance, we hypothesize that:

**Hypothesis 3 (H3).** *Resident–micro-business interactions have a relationship with agritourism performance.*

Local communities' perceptions of tourism benefits affect their support for tourism development [48]. Furthermore, locals dependent on the tourist business or perceiving a more significant economic benefit have a more favorable impression of tourism's economic influence than other residents [49]. Although economic benefits were a crucial indicator, social and emotional factors better predicted local residents' support for tourism development [50]. Hence, we argue that resident–micro-business interaction, besides the participation of the residents in tourism development, demonstrates the economic, social, and emotional benefits of agritourism development, thus increasing societal support for agritourism and improving its performance. On this basis, the following two hypotheses were derived (as seen in Figure 2).

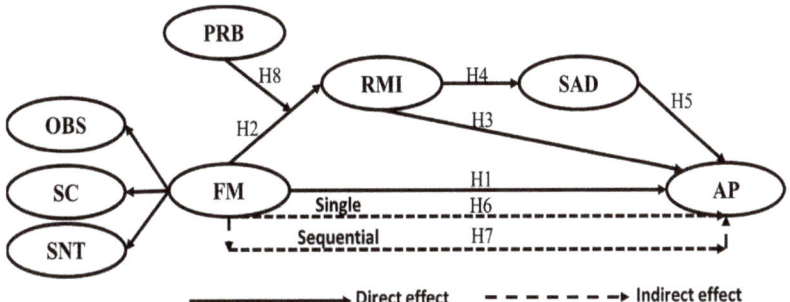

**Figure 2.** The proposed conceptual framework and hypotheses. FM: family micro-business resources, AP: agritourism performance, RMI: resident–micro-business interaction, SAD: support for agritourism development, PRB: personal resident benefit, SBO: small business orientation, SC: social capital, SNY: social network ties.

**Hypothesis 4 (H4).** *Resident–micro-business interactions have a relationship with residents' support for agritourism development.*

**Hypothesis 5 (H5).** *Residents' support for agritourism development has a relationship with agritourism performance.*

Based on the non-zero-sum games theory and combining prior pieces of evidence, and drawing on the previous justifications of the proposed five hypotheses, we suggested the following hypotheses for mediation relationships:

**Hypothesis 6 (H6).** *Resident–micro-business interaction mediates the association between family micro-business resources and agritourism performance.*

**Hypothesis 7 (H7).** *Resident–micro-business interaction and residents' support for agritourism development mediate the relationship between family micro-business resources and agritourism performance.*

*2.2. The Moderating Role of Personal Resident Benefit (PRB)*

The level of residents' perception of tourism benefits shifts from a macro to a micro perspective, when treating it as a personal benefit [51]. According to the rationality theory, people's motivation to join in some economic actions is defined by their surface appearance and formal rationality. Formal rationality focuses on financial incentives, while substantive (surface appearance) rationality concentrates on non-financial stimuli, such as morals, philosophy, and psychological dimensions [52]. As a consequence of this, when locals base their decisions regarding whether or not to support tourism on their perceptions of justice (substantive rationality), they take into consideration the personal and material rewards that might be gained from tourism (formal rationality) [53]. Thus, the host's perception of the unique personal benefits from tourism is also essential in the context of residents' interaction with agritourism operators [7]. Therefore, personal resident benefits significantly affect the link between family micro-business resources and resident–micro-business interaction. Thus, we developed the hypothesis:

**Hypothesis 8 (H8).** *Personal resident benefit moderates the impact of family micro-business resources on resident–micro-business interaction (the association will be more robust when the personal resident benefit is high).*

## 3. Methods

This paper aims to give answers that explain and test the impact of building family micro-businesses and the performance of agritourism through two mediating variables: resident–micro-business interaction and support for agritourism development. Moreover, the paper tested the moderating role of personal resident benefit in the tested relationships. A quantitative-based research methodology was considered to attain and accomplish the assumed aims by employing a self- structured survey to gather the dyadic data (from residents and micro-businesses). PLS-SEM was utilized as the main data analysis procedure. PLS-SEM is a proper approach for investigating and approving the early levels of theory development [54]. PLS-SEM was conducted to calculate the measurement and structural models' validity due to its multivariate nature and predictive power with a small sample size. Furthermore, 5000 bootstraps repeats of 293 dyadic data (total of 686) samples were run to assess the significance ($p$) level of all path coefficients.

### 3.1. Scale and Measure Development

An extensive review of the related previous studies was conducted to develop the study scale and create the questionnaire items. This process yielded five significant measures that could be employed as the study scale. The FM (family microbusinesses' business-based resources variable)—as we explained previously, business-based resources were selected for their importance in agritourism—was tested by 13 items derived from Campbell and Kubickova [20], three variables to measure small business orientation (SMO), six items for social capital (SC), and four variables for social networking ties (SNT). At the same time, agritourism performance (AP) was operationalized by the eight-item scale suggested by Domi and Belletti [55]. Five items from Reimer et al. [56] were employed to measure resident–micro-business interaction (RMI). The SAD (support for agritourism development) was measured by three items created by Wang et al. [53]. Finally, the PRB (personal resident benefit) was measured using the eight-item scale proposed by Vukovic et al. [7]. A Likert scale of 1 (strongly disagree) to 5 (strongly agree) was employed. Eight academics and eight professionals in the field area tested the instrument. The text was transcribed and clarified. The scale content was retained and employed with no changes.

### 3.2. Participants and Collection of the Study Data

Family micro-businesses in rural destinations in Saudi Arabia's eastern province (Al Ahsa governance) were selected to participate in the field study. Data collection was achieved via the drop-and-collect method. The survey was split into two sequential phases. Residents were asked to answer and provide the information necessary for the PRB and SAD variables in the first phase. One month after, family micro-businesses operators and employees within the same rural area were asked to complete the FM, AP, and RMI questionnaire items. In the two phases, 400 questionnaires were disseminated. After removing all the unqualified and irrelevant questionnaires, we were left with 293 residents/family micro-businesses operators and employees whose dyads data were tested, with an effective recovery rate of 73.25%. The data was collected in September and October 2022, post COVID-19 pandemic, when the small businesses in these rural places had returned back to their normal operation. The final residents sample included 224 males (76.5%) and 69 females (23.5%). Most of them were between the ages of 26 and 45. For family micro-business operators and employees, the final family micro-business operators and employees sample comprised 246 males, accounting for 84% of the total, and 43 women (16%). Most of them were between the ages of 28 and 53, and the vast majority held university degrees (91.5%).

## 4. Findings of the Data Analysis

The SmartPLS-4.0 program was used to test the previously justified research hypotheses using SEM (structural equation modeling) via "Partial least squares PLS 4". The proposed theoretical model was tested in two sequential stages [57].

## 4.1. Evaluation of the Outer Model (Validity Assessment)

Following the suggestions of [57–59], the scale validity (discriminant and convergent) and reliability were assessed through several criteria. First, for reliability, Cronbach's alpha (α) and composite reliability (C_R) were used, as shown in Table 1. All values exceeded the threshold of 0.7, which gives a signal of a proper level of reliability.

**Table 1.** Assessment of the outer model validity.

| Abbreviation | Items | Loading | α | C_R | AVE | VIF |
|---|---|---|---|---|---|---|
| FM | | | 0.948 | 0.954 | 0.617 | |
| SBO | | | 0.900 | 0.938 | 0.834 | |
| SBO_1 | I established this business/farm because it fit my personal life better than working for others. | 0.931 | | | | 4.659 |
| SBO_2 | I love my business/farm. | 0.907 | | | | 2.543 |
| SBO_3 | I have plans to expand this business/farm in size/sales revenue. | 0.901 | | | | 3.116 |
| SC | | | 0.897 | 0.921 | 0.661 | |
| SC_1 | Others would say I am trustworthy. | 0.766 | | | | 3.940 |
| SC_2 | I can be trusted by others not to take advantage of them. | 0.820 | | | | 3.472 |
| SC_3 | Others are generally fair in dealing with me. | 0.839 | | | | 4.185 |
| SC_4 | Others visit my business because I support the community. | 0.826 | | | | 2.927 |
| SC_5 | Others share the same ambitions and visions for our community. | 0.785 | | | | 2.542 |
| SC_6 | Others like to work toward achieving community goals. | 0.841 | | | | 3.012 |
| SNT | | | 0.863 | 0.908 | 0.713 | |
| SNT_1 | We in the community know each other by name. | 0.894 | | | | 3.380 |
| SNT_2 | We in the community talk to each other regularly about business/farming issues. | 0.874 | | | | 3.064 |
| SNT_3 | I am similar to these people in terms of my business/community/farm philosophy. | 0.884 | | | | 2.506 |
| SNT_4 | I am similar to these people in terms of my values and beliefs. | 0.712 | | | | 3.360 |
| AP | | | 0.939 | 0.949 | 0.701 | |
| AP_1 | Through agritourism we have achieved revenue targets. | 0.827 | | | | 3.058 |
| AP_2 | Through the farm we have achieved profit goals. | 0.796 | | | | 2.504 |
| AP_3 | Through the farm we have achieved a good stabilisation of income. | 0.847 | | | | 3.302 |
| AP_4 | Through the farm we have generated out-of-season income. | 0.859 | | | | 3.641 |
| AP_5 | Through the farm we have made better use of the company's human resources. | 0.867 | | | | 3.934 |
| AP_6 | We have improved the way in which products are sold. | 0.815 | | | | 3.472 |
| AP_7 | We have improved the loyalty of existing customers. | 0.843 | | | | 4.055 |
| AP_8 | We have attracted a significant number of new customers. | 0.843 | | | | 3.448 |
| RMI | | | 0.926 | 0.944 | 0.773 | |
| RMI_1 | How often did you experience being supported in contact with local residents? | 0.858 | | | | 1.421 |
| RMI_2 | How often did you experience being helped in contact with local residents? | 0.865 | | | | 2.811 |
| RMI_3 | How often did you experience being complimented in contact with local residents? | 0.892 | | | | 3.642 |
| RMI_4 | How often did you experience being befriended in contact with local residents? | 0.907 | | | | 3.986 |
| RMI_5 | How often did you experience being welcomed in contact with local residents? | 0.873 | | | | 3.164 |
| SAD | | | 0.900 | 0.938 | 0.834 | |
| SAD_1 | I welcome tourists to visit our village. | 0.917 | | | | 3.166 |
| SAD_2 | I intend to support rural tourism development. | 0.941 | | | | 4.005 |
| SAD_3 | I intend to support the local government's tourism decisions. | 0.880 | | | | 2.362 |

Table 1. Cont.

| Abbreviation | Items | Loading | α | C_R | AVE | VIF |
|---|---|---|---|---|---|---|
| PRB | | | 0.960 | 0.965 | 0.777 | |
| PRB_1 | My understanding of other cultures has increased. | 0.826 | | | | 2.945 |
| PRB_2 | The quality of my personal life has improved. | 0.859 | | | | 3.397 |
| PRB_3 | My property value has increased. | 0.884 | | | | 3.910 |
| PRB_4 | I got in touch with others and expanded my business. | 0.889 | | | | 3.920 |
| PRB_5 | My children will stay in the countryside to work. | 0.915 | | | | 4.080 |
| PRB_6 | I care more about my community's cultural resources. | 0.897 | | | | 4.172 |
| PRB_7 | I care more about my community's natural resources. | 0.899 | | | | 3.765 |
| PRB_8 | I feel my community is better place to live. | 0.880 | | | | 3.711 |

SBO (small business orientation), SC (social capital), and SNT (social networking) are the components of family micro-business resources.

Second, the standardized factor loading for all reflective items was higher than 0.7, further supporting the scale's convergent validity. Furthermore, the average variance extracted (AVE) values exceeded the value of 0.50, which approves convergent validity [54]. Finally, three main indices were checked to test discriminant validity: (1) cross-loading, (2) the Fronell-Larcker index, and (3) the heterotrait-monotrait value (HTMT). As revealed in Table 2, the outer loading for the latent variables (bolded) exceeded the cross-loading with other items.

Table 2. Cross-loading output.

| | SBO | SC | SNT | RMI | SAD | AP | PRB |
|---|---|---|---|---|---|---|---|
| SBO_1 | 0.931 | 0.745 | 0.726 | 0.659 | 0.579 | 0.700 | −0.337 |
| SBO_2 | 0.907 | 0.695 | 0.629 | 0.539 | 0.509 | 0.701 | −0.346 |
| SBO_3 | 0.901 | 0.771 | 0.656 | 0.595 | 0.500 | 0.545 | −0.265 |
| SC_1 | 0.675 | 0.766 | 0.568 | 0.563 | 0.414 | 0.480 | −0.252 |
| SC_2 | 0.750 | 0.820 | 0.642 | 0.587 | 0.456 | 0.559 | −0.266 |
| SC_3 | 0.629 | 0.839 | 0.598 | 0.477 | 0.524 | 0.536 | −0.223 |
| SC_4 | 0.641 | 0.826 | 0.695 | 0.552 | 0.586 | 0.585 | −0.264 |
| SC_5 | 0.551 | 0.785 | 0.627 | 0.477 | 0.515 | 0.532 | −0.305 |
| SC_6 | 0.688 | 0.841 | 0.763 | 0.598 | 0.654 | 0.666 | −0.341 |
| SNT_1 | 0.650 | 0.714 | 0.894 | 0.679 | 0.528 | 0.572 | −0.245 |
| SNT_2 | 0.667 | 0.673 | 0.874 | 0.610 | 0.575 | 0.544 | −0.257 |
| SNT_3 | 0.602 | 0.699 | 0.884 | 0.728 | 0.675 | 0.707 | −0.302 |
| SNT_4 | 0.559 | 0.613 | 0.712 | 0.460 | 0.570 | 0.646 | −0.237 |
| RMI_1 | 0.679 | 0.673 | 0.703 | 0.858 | 0.577 | 0.644 | −0.222 |
| RMI_2 | 0.583 | 0.582 | 0.623 | 0.865 | 0.576 | 0.634 | −0.234 |
| RMI_3 | 0.499 | 0.566 | 0.658 | 0.892 | 0.591 | 0.636 | −0.174 |
| RMI_4 | 0.548 | 0.560 | 0.647 | 0.907 | 0.567 | 0.581 | −0.177 |
| RMI_5 | 0.564 | 0.546 | 0.607 | 0.873 | 0.486 | 0.555 | −0.048 |
| SAD_1 | 0.558 | 0.626 | 0.657 | 0.627 | 0.917 | 0.776 | −0.270 |
| SAD_2 | 0.550 | 0.581 | 0.624 | 0.545 | 0.941 | 0.749 | −0.406 |
| SAD_3 | 0.478 | 0.565 | 0.617 | 0.573 | 0.880 | 0.696 | −0.356 |

**Table 2.** Cont.

|       | SBO    | SC     | SNT    | RMI    | SAD    | AP     | PRB    |
|-------|--------|--------|--------|--------|--------|--------|--------|
| AP_1  | 0.666  | 0.677  | 0.634  | 0.557  | 0.714  | 0.827  | −0.306 |
| AP_2  | 0.620  | 0.528  | 0.627  | 0.517  | 0.606  | 0.796  | −0.271 |
| AP_3  | 0.569  | 0.589  | 0.668  | 0.722  | 0.699  | 0.847  | −0.259 |
| AP_4  | 0.611  | 0.596  | 0.690  | 0.670  | 0.732  | 0.859  | −0.354 |
| AP_5  | 0.601  | 0.556  | 0.567  | 0.657  | 0.700  | 0.867  | −0.354 |
| AP_6  | 0.534  | 0.467  | 0.512  | 0.519  | 0.636  | 0.815  | −0.323 |
| AP_7  | 0.536  | 0.546  | 0.537  | 0.453  | 0.643  | 0.843  | −0.288 |
| AP_8  | 0.607  | 0.646  | 0.620  | 0.536  | 0.692  | 0.843  | −0.266 |
| PRB_1 | −0.270 | −0.219 | −0.207 | −0.098 | −0.232 | −0.300 | 0.826  |
| PRB_2 | −0.263 | −0.245 | −0.189 | −0.121 | −0.292 | −0.241 | 0.859  |
| PRB_3 | −0.325 | −0.300 | −0.236 | −0.160 | −0.293 | −0.297 | 0.884  |
| PRB_4 | −0.262 | −0.242 | −0.234 | −0.143 | −0.317 | −0.295 | 0.889  |
| PRB_5 | −0.354 | −0.409 | −0.399 | −0.243 | −0.413 | −0.398 | 0.915  |
| PRB_6 | −0.301 | −0.278 | −0.273 | −0.155 | −0.334 | −0.325 | 0.897  |
| PRB_7 | −0.327 | −0.332 | −0.308 | −0.236 | −0.369 | −0.348 | 0.899  |
| PRB_8 | −0.285 | −0.248 | −0.194 | −0.128 | −0.290 | −0.269 | 0.880  |

Table 3 shows bolded AVEs which are higher than the correlation coefficient between variables. Hair Jr et al. [54] suggested that the readings on the HTMT should be less than 0.90, as the rule stated. In the study, the levels of HTMT were significantly lower than this. Based on the findings, it is clear that the model structure possesses the necessary discriminant validity. As a direct consequence of this, the outputs of the outer measurement model were considered adequate to move forward with the evaluation of the structural model.

**Table 3.** AVE values and HTMT results.

|     | AVE Values |        |        |        |       | HTMT  |       |       |       |
|-----|--------|--------|--------|--------|-------|-------|-------|-------|-------|
|     | FM     | AP     | RMI    | PRB    | SAD   | FM    | AP    | RMI   | PRB   | SAD   |
| FM  | 0.786  |        |        |        |       |       |       |       |       |       |
| AP  | 0.763  | 0.837  |        |        |       | 0.805 |       |       |       |       |
| RMI | 0.741  | 0.696  | 0.879  |        |       | 0.785 | 0.738 |       |       |       |
| PRB | −0.358 | −0.362 | −0.198 | 0.881  |       | 0.357 | 0.369 | 0.194 |       |       |
| SAD | 0.695  | 0.812  | 0.639  | −0.375 | 0.913 | 0.751 | 0.879 | 0.696 | 0.390 |       |

## 4.2. Structural Model Evaluation (Hypotheses Testing)

The model should possess adequate predictive and explanatory power before testing the path coefficient [58]. Furthermore, the multicollinearity test should show adequate results based on the VIF values not exceeding 5. The VIF values in our model ranged between 1.421 and 4.659 (<5.0), which supports the nonexistence of multicollinearity in the model. Furthermore, the lower level of $R^2$ values is 0.10 for a good model fit [58]. Consequently, the $R^2$ values for the study variables—AP ($R^2 = 0.745$), RMI ($R^2 = 0.591$), and SAD ($R^2 = 0.408$)—are appropriate (Table 4). Likewise, the Stone–Geisser ($Q^2$) index revealed the AP, RMI, and SAD values to be higher than zero (Table 4), suggesting the sufficient predictive validity of our model [59]. As a direct result of this, an adequate level of predictive validity was also demonstrated for the structural model.

**Table 4.** Model goodness-of-fit $R^2$ and $Q^2$ values.

| Endogenous Variables | ($R^2$) | ($Q^2$) |
|---|---|---|
| AP | 0.745 | 0.485 |
| RMI | 0.591 | 0.420 |
| SAD | 0.408 | 0.320 |

A bootstrapping method was used to conduct the final analysis, which consisted of a path coefficient and t-value analysis of the hypothesized paths. The results of the hypothesis test are displayed below in Table 5, along with Figure 3, which includes the path coefficient values and their relevant significance. FM was found to be in positive and significant correlation with AP ($\beta$ = 0.632) and RMI ($\beta$ = 0.299), hence, we can accept hypothesis one (H1) and hypothesis two (H2). The results also demonstrated that RMI has a significant ($p < 0.001$) and positive association with AP ($\beta$ = 0.150) and SAD ($\beta$ = 0.639), which led us to support hypothesis three (H3) and hypothesis four (H4). Hypothesis five (H5) was supported as well due to the correlation between SAD and AP being positive and significant ($\beta$ = 0.508). The mediation impact of RMI in the link between FM-AP was supported with a significant effect size of $\beta$ = 0.095. Thus hypothesis six (H6) was accepted. Similarly, the sequential mediation effect of RMI and SAD in the link between FM and AP showed a significant effect size of $\beta$ = 0.205, which leads us to support hypothesis (H7). Lastly, the findings supported the positive moderation impact of PRB on the link between FM and RMI at a significant path coefficient value of $\beta$ = 0.287, which confirms hypothesis (H8).

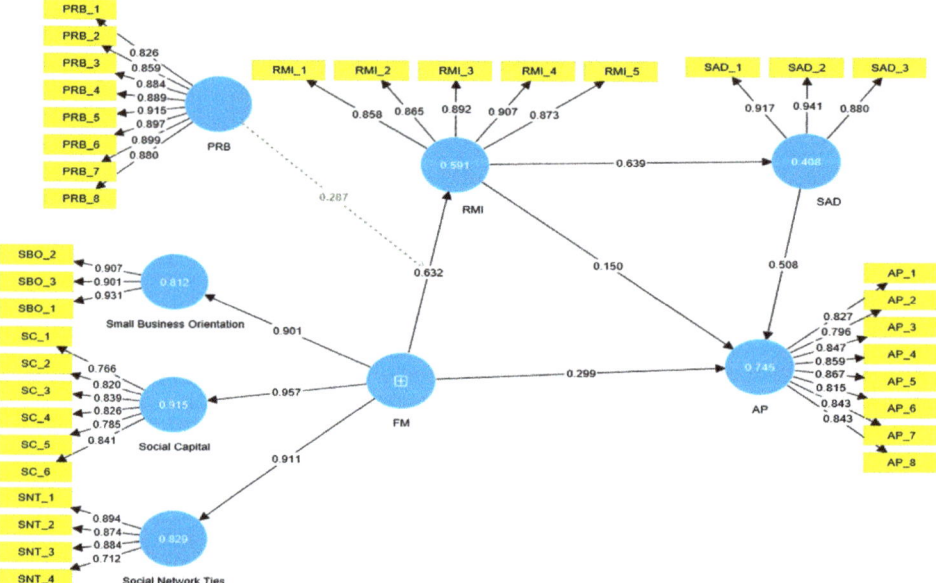

**Figure 3.** The tested structural and measurement model. FM: family micro-business resources, AP: agritourism performance, RMI: resident–micro-business interaction, SAD: support for agritourism development, PRB: personal resident benefit, SBO: small business orientation, SC: social capital, SNT: social network ties.

Table 5. The structural inner model findings.

| | Hypotheses | Beta (β) | (T-Value) | p Values | Results of Hypotheses |
|---|---|---|---|---|---|
| H1 | FM → AP | 0.299 | 3.518 | 0.000 | Supported |
| H2 | FM → RMI | 0.632 | 11.568 | 0.000 | Supported |
| H3 | RMI → AP | 0.150 | 2.536 | 0.012 | Supported |
| H4 | RMI → SAD | 0.639 | 15.075 | 0.000 | Supported |
| H5 | SAD → AP | 0.508 | 6.906 | 0.000 | Supported |
| H6 | FM → RMI → AP | 0.095 | 2.285 | 0.023 | Supported |
| H7 | FM → RMI → SAD → AP | 0.205 | 5.625 | 0.000 | Supported |
| H8 | Moderating imapct 1(FM × PRB) → RMI | 0.287 | 3.290 | 0.001 | Supported |

## 5. Discussion and Implications

*5.1. Family Microbusiness Resources, Agritourism Performance, Resident–Micro-Business Interaction and Support for Agritourism Development (Direct Relationship)*

This study revealed a direct, significant, and positive association between FM and AP (H1). This result is consistent with the studies of Kangasharju [27] and Tamilmani [29]. Given the features of the limited agritourism market and the nature of the resources on which micro-businesses depend in rural destinations, especially business-based resources (small business orientation, social capital, and social networking links), we find that it is a favorable environment for improving agritourism performance in general and achieving profitability for agritourism operators [34,39]. This study confirms that FM is an antecedent facet in RMI practice implementation (H2). In most rural destinations, the owners of agritourism businesses themselves are farm owners in many cases [43]. Thus, the contact between rural micro-business operators and their guests or residents is rational and practical and boosts friendly attitudes and good behaviors [42].

Furthermore, our findings assist in verifying the positive effect of RMI on AP (H3). In line with this result, Li and Barbieri [46] pointed out that the positive interaction inherent in the agritourism field between agritourism operators and their guests, residents, and agritourism operators themselves correlates strongly and positively with profitability and successful agritourism efforts. It follows from the results obtained that RMI positively influences the SAD achieved (H4). In explanation of this result, the residents' perceptions of tourism's benefits increase due to positive resident–micro-business interactions. Thus, the greater the positive resident–micro-business interaction, the more the residents understand and perceive the benefits of tourism. Therefore, the residents' support for tourism development in their rural destinations is increasing [49]. The final direct relationship in our study is the positive influence of SAD on AP (H5). In an agritourism business environment, business owners need the support of the local community as it is a crucial determinant of the success or failure of such businesses and ensures that they avoid any resistance from them to tourism development [1].

*5.2. Results of the Moderating Effect*

The empirical results supported the moderation effects of the PRB on the link between FM and RMI (H6). In other words, according to the interaction plot in Figure 4, PRB made the connection between FM and RMI strengthen. This result can be justified based on the SET and the non-zero-sum games theory. When an individual in the community realizes the personal benefit generated by the agritourism development business, he will enhance his positive interaction with them to improve personal benefit and respect for the principle of reciprocity.

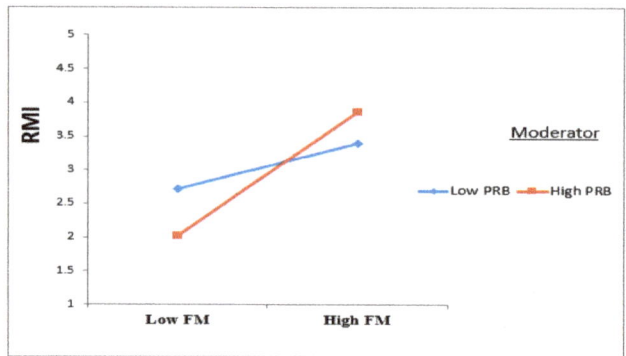

**Figure 4.** Interaction plot for the PRB moderation effect on FM towards RMI.

*5.3. The Mediating Effect of RMI and SAD in the Tested Model*

One of the paper's basic purposes was to evaluate the mediating effects of RMI and SAD on the link between FM and AP. Concerning H7, the results prove that the impact of RMI as a single mediating variable in the link between FM and AP is significant and positive. Finally, the empirical evidence obtained allows us to confirm that the sequential mediation exerted by the RMI and SAD variables indirectly influences the relationship between FM and AP (H8). Based on the SET and the non-zero-sum games theory, the significance of mediation can be justified, whether single or sequential. Given the residents' sense of psychological ownership of family micro-businesses in rural destinations, we assert that the resident–micro-business interaction is effective and supports the development and performance of agritourism (single mediation) [45]. Regarding sequential mediation, with the positive interaction and mutual interaction between residents and family micro-businesses, the individual's perception of the personal and societal benefits resulting from the development of tourism in rural destinations increases, and thus their support for agritourism increases, reflected in improving the agritourism performance [7,50].

By comparing the single and sequential mediations, we find that the indirect impact of the sequential mediation of RMI and SAD variables between FM and AP ($\beta = 0.205$, $p < 0.000$) was more significant than the single mediation effect of RMI ($\beta = 0.095$, $p < 0.023$) in the same relationship. In both cases, the mediation was partial. Hence, the resident–micro-business interaction must generate outcomes (economic and socio-emotional) that motivate the residents and communities to support tourism development to boost agritourism performance. This literature review offers direct theoretical and practical implications. Concerning the theoretical implications, this examination promotes the comprehension of the micro-businesses economy and adds a unique role to this economy in rural destinations by exploiting family micro-businesses' features and benefits to support local rural communities via developing agritourism. Regarding the practical implications, this article provides a valuable synthesis of micro-businesses' economic role and family micro-businesses' local community exchange connections that should be beneficial to both. Supporting this type of micro-business makes it feasible to build local economies to protect farmers from economic and social problems caused by lower farming revenues from unfeasible traditional agricultural production methods, especially in developing countries.

## 6. Conclusions and Avenues for Further Research

Rural local hosts may resist rural tourism development if they believe they are responsible for most of the key attractions but have the least access to those helpful to tourists. Dyadic data were gathered targeting 400 residents—owners and employees in family micro-businesses. A total of 293 valid responses were prepared for further analysis with PLS-SEM. After ensuring that the study scale possesses adequate convergent and discriminant validity, the proposed hypotheses were tested. The results supported the direct association between family micro-business resources (small business orientation, social capital, and social network ties) and agritourism performance. Additionally, the results highlighted the critical mediating roles of resident–micro-business interaction and support for agritourism development in improving the tested direct relationships. Furthermore, the PLS-SEM result supported the moderating role of personal resident benefit in strengthening the tested interrelationships. These results are consistent with different previous study results, but the main contribution of our study is that it tested all of these relationships (direct, mediating, and moderating), for the first time, in one model employing a sophisticated data analysis technique (PLS-SEM), in one context (family micro-businesses in KSA), post COVID-19 pandemic. Future studies could employ a qualitative research design to improve and extend our understanding of how to enhance agritourism performance. Moreover, in future studies, other mediating dimensions (i.e., tourist satisfaction, resident satisfaction) can be explored to decide whether they can act as mediators in the relationship between FM and AP. In conclusion, it should be noted that this research was only conducted using a cross-sectional research strategy, and the results do not allow for the inference of a causal relationship. It would be beneficial to undertake longitudinal research in order to support or disprove the outcomes of the study.

**Author Contributions:** Methodology, S.F. and A.M.S.A.; Software, A.M.A.; Writing—original draft, I.A.E.; Writing—review & editing, I.A.E., S.F. and A.M.S.A.; Supervision, I.A.E.; Funding acquisition, I.A.E. and A.M.S.A. All authors have read and agreed to the published version of the manuscript.

**Funding:** This work was supported by the Deanship of Scientific Research, Vice Presidency for Graduate Studies and Scientific Research, King Faisal University, Saudi Arabia (Grant No. 2012).

**Institutional Review Board Statement:** The study was conducted according to the guidelines of the Declaration of Helsinki and approved by the deanship of the scientific research ethical committee, King Faisal University (project number: GRANT2012, date of approval: 1 August 2022).

**Informed Consent Statement:** Informed consent was obtained from all subjects involved in the study.

**Data Availability Statement:** Data is available upon request from researchers who meet the eligibility criteria. Kindly contact the first author privately by e-mail.

**Acknowledgments:** We thank for the support by the Deanship of Scientific Research, Vice Presidency for Graduate Studies and Scientific Research, King Faisal University, Saudi Arabia (Grant No. 2012).

**Conflicts of Interest:** The authors declare no conflict of interest.

# References

1. Ma, X.L.; Wang, R.; Dai, M.L.; Ou, Y.H. The Action Logic and Interpretation Framework of Residents' Resistance in Rural Tourism Development. *J. Hosp. Tour. Manag.* **2022**, *51*, 79–87. [CrossRef]
2. Loperena, C.A. Honduras Is Open for Business: Extractivist Tourism as Sustainable Development in the Wake of Disaster? *J. Sustain. Tour.* **2017**, *25*, 618–633. [CrossRef]
3. Yang, J.; Ryan, C.; Zhang, L. Sustaining Culture and Seeking a Just Destination: Governments, Power and Tension—A Life-Cycle Approach to Analysing Tourism Development in an Ethnic-Inhabited Scenic Area in Xinjiang, China. *J. Sustain. Tour.* **2014**, *22*, 1151–1174. [CrossRef]
4. Tew, C.; Barbieri, C. The Perceived Benefits of Agritourism: The Provider's Perspective. *Tour. Manag.* **2012**, *33*, 215–224. [CrossRef]
5. Stewart Jr, W.H.; Roth, P.L. Risk Propensity Differences between Entrepreneurs and Managers: A Meta-Analytic Review. *J. Appl. Psychol.* **2001**, *86*, 145. [CrossRef]
6. Campbell, J.M.; Line, N.; Runyan, R.C.; Swinney, J.L. The Moderating Effect of Family-Ownership on Firm Performance: An Examination of Entrepreneurial Orientation and Social Capital. *J. Small Bus. Strategy* **2010**, *21*, 27–46.
7. Vukovic, D.B.; Maiti, M.; Vujko, A.; Shams, R. Residents' Perceptions of Wine Tourism on the Rural Destinations Development. *Br. Food J.* **2020**, *122*, 2739–2753. [CrossRef]
8. Mitchell, M.S.; Cropanzano, R.S.; Quisenberry, D.M. Social Exchange Theory, Exchange Resources, and Interpersonal Relationships: A Modest Resolution of Theoretical Difficulties. In *Handbook of Social Resource Theory*; Springer: Berlin/Heidelberg, Germany, 2012; pp. 99–118.
9. Oughton, E.; Wheelock, J.; Baines, S. Micro-Businesses and Social Inclusion in Rural Households: A Comparative Analysis. *Sociol. Rural.* **2003**, *43*, 331–348. [CrossRef]

10. Wang, Y.; Pfister, R.E. Residents' Attitudes toward Tourism and Perceived Personal Benefits in a Rural Community. *J. Travel Res.* **2008**, *47*, 84–93. [CrossRef]
11. Petrović, M.D.; Blešić, I.; Vujko, A.; Gajić, T. The Role of Agritourism's Impact on the Local Community in a Transitional Society: A Report from Serbia. *Transylv. Rev. Adm. Sci.* **2017**, *13*, 146–163. [CrossRef]
12. Lepp, A. Attitudes towards Initial Tourism Development in a Community with No Prior Tourism Experience: The Case of Bigodi, Uganda. *J. Sustain. Tour.* **2008**, *16*, 5–22. [CrossRef]
13. Jaafar, M.; Noor, S.M.; Rasoolimanesh, S.M. Perception of Young Local Residents toward Sustainable Conservation Programmes: A Case Study of the Lenggong World Cultural Heritage Site. *Tour. Manag.* **2015**, *48*, 154–163. [CrossRef]
14. Friedenberg, A.; Keisler, H.J. Iterated Dominance Revisited. *Econ. Theory* **2021**, *72*, 377–421. [CrossRef]
15. Dixit, A.K.; Nalebuff, B.J. *Thinking Strategically: The Competitive Edge in Business, Politics, and Everyday Life*; WW Norton & Company: New York, NY, USA, 1991.
16. Tlemsani, I.; Mohamed Hashim, M.A.; Matthews, R. Games Theory and Strategic Alliances: Applications to British Russian Partnership. *High. Educ. Ski. Work-Based Learn.* **2022**, *12*, 689–704. [CrossRef]
17. Zhang, S.; Zang, X.; Zhang, F. Development and Validation of the Win-Win Scale. *Front Psychol.* **2021**, *12*, 657015. [CrossRef]
18. Flanigan, S.; Blackstock, K.; Hunter, C. Agritourism from the Perspective of Providers and Visitors: A Typology-Based Study. *Tour. Manag.* **2014**, *40*, 394–405. [CrossRef]
19. Joyner, L.; Kline, C.; Oliver, J.; Kariko, D. Exploring Emotional Response to Images Used in Agritourism Destination Marketing. *J. Destin. Mark. Manag.* **2018**, *9*, 44–55. [CrossRef]
20. Campbell, J.M.; Kubickova, M. Agritourism Microbusinesses within a Developing Country Economy: A Resource-Based View. *J. Destin. Mark. Manag.* **2020**, *17*, 100460. [CrossRef]
21. Grillini, G.; Sacchi, G.; Chase, L.; Taylor, J.; Van Zyl, C.C.; Van Der Merwe, P.; Streifeneder, T.; Fischer, C. Qualitative Assessment of Agritourism Development Support Schemes in Italy, the USA and South Africa. *Sustainability* **2022**, *14*, 7903. [CrossRef]
22. Busby, G.; Rendle, S. The Transition from Tourism on Farms to Farm Tourism. *Tour. Manag.* **2000**, *21*, 635–642. [CrossRef]
23. Iorio, M.; Corsale, A. Rural Tourism and Livelihood Strategies in Romania. *J. Rural. Stud.* **2010**, *26*, 152–162. [CrossRef]
24. Sharpley, R. Tourism and Sustainable Development: Exploring the Theoretical Divide. *J. Sustain. Tour.* **2000**, *8*, 1–19. [CrossRef]
25. Rasoolimanesh, S.M.; Ringle, C.M.; Jaafar, M.; Ramayah, T. Urban vs. Rural Destinations: Residents' Perceptions, Community Participation and Support for Tourism Development. *Tour. Manag.* **2017**, *60*, 147–158. [CrossRef]
26. Dimitrovski, D.D.; Todorović, A.T.; Valjarević, A.D. Rural Tourism and Regional Development: Case Study of Development of Rural Tourism in the Region of Gruţa, Serbia. *Procedia Environ. Sci.* **2012**, *14*, 288–297. [CrossRef]
27. Kangasharju, A. Growth of the Smallest: Determinants of Small Firm Growth during Strong Macroeconomic Fluctuations. *Int. Small Bus. J.* **2000**, *19*, 28–43. [CrossRef]
28. Tamilmani, B. Rural Women Microentrepreneurs: An Empirical Study on Their Social Profile, Business Aspects and Economic Impact. *IUP J. Entrep. Dev.* **2009**, *6*, 7–20.
29. Chell, E.; Baines, S. Networking, Entrepreneurship and Microbusiness Behaviour. *Entrep. Reg. Dev.* **2000**, *12*, 195–215. [CrossRef]
30. Runyan, R.C. *Predicting Downtown and Small Business Success: A Resource-Based View*; Michigan State University: East Lansing, MI, USA, 2005.
31. Barney, J. Firm Resources and Sustained Competitive Advantage. *J. Manag.* **1991**, *17*, 99–120. [CrossRef]
32. Adiguna, R. Organisational Culture and the Family Business. In *Theoretical Perspectives on Family Businesses*; Edward Elgar Publishing: Cheltenham, UK, 2015; pp. 156–174.
33. Carland, J.W.; Hoy, F.; Boulton, W.R.; Carland, J.A.C. Differentiating Entrepreneurs from Small Business Owners: A Conceptualization. *Acad. Manag. Rev.* **1984**, *9*, 354–359. [CrossRef]
34. Phillipson, J.; Tiwasing, P.; Gorton, M.; Maioli, S.; Newbery, R.; Turner, R. Shining a Spotlight on Small Rural Businesses: How Does Their Performance Compare with Urban? *J. Rural. Stud.* **2019**, *68*, 230–239. [CrossRef]
35. Dai, M.; Fan, D.X.; Wang, R.; Ou, Y.; Ma, X. Residents' Social Capital in Rural Tourism Development: Guanxi in Housing Demolition. *J. Destin. Mark. Manag.* **2021**, *22*, 100663. [CrossRef]
36. Grafton, R.Q. Social Capital and Fisheries Governance. *Ocean. Coast. Manag.* **2005**, *48*, 753–766. [CrossRef]
37. Lin, N. A Network Theory of Social Capital. *Handb. Soc. Cap.* **2008**, *50*, 69.
38. Tuitjer, G.; Küpper, P. Local and Vertical Networking as Drivers of Innovativeness and Growth in Rural Businesses. *J. Rural. Stud.* **2022**, *95*, 412–422. [CrossRef]
39. Paige, R.C.; Littrell, M.A. Craft Retailers' Criteria for Success and Associated Business Strategies. *J. Small Bus. Manag.* **2002**, *40*, 314–331. [CrossRef]
40. Choo, H.; Petrick, J.F. Social Interactions and Intentions to Revisit for Agritourism Service Encounters. *Tour. Manag.* **2014**, *40*, 372–381. [CrossRef]
41. Luo, X.; Brown, G.; Huang, S. (Sam) Host Perceptions of Backpackers: Examining the Influence of Intergroup Contact. *Tour. Manag.* **2015**, *50*, 292–305. [CrossRef]
42. Tu, H.; Ma, J. Does Positive Contact Between Residents and Tourists Stimulate Tourists' Environmentally Responsible Behavior? The Role of Gratitude and Boundary Conditions. *J. Travel. Res.* **2022**, *61*, 1774–1790. [CrossRef]
43. Wilson, L. The Family Farm Business? Insights into Family, Business and Ownership Dimensions of Open-Farms. *Leis. Stud.* **2007**, *26*, 357–374. [CrossRef]

44. Elshaer, I.A.; Azazz, A.M.S.; Ameen, F.A.; Fayyad, S. Agritourism and Peer-to-Peer Accommodation: A Moderated Mediation Model. *Agriculture* **2022**, *12*, 1586. [CrossRef]
45. Pierce, J.L.; Kostova, T.; Dirks, K.T. The State of Psychological Ownership: Integrating and Extending a Century of Research. *Rev. Gen. Psychol.* **2003**, *7*, 84–107. [CrossRef]
46. Li, J.; Barbieri, C. Demystifying Members' Social Capital and Networks within an Agritourism Association: A Social Network Analysis. *Tour. Hosp.* **2020**, *1*, 41–58. [CrossRef]
47. Hollas, C.R.; Chase, L.; Conner, D.; Dickes, L.; Lamie, R.D.; Schmidt, C.; Singh-Knights, D.; Quella, L. Factors Related to Profitability of Agritourism in the United States: Results from a National Survey of Operators. *Sustainability* **2021**, *13*, 13334. [CrossRef]
48. Wang, S.; Berbekova, A.; Uysal, M. Pursuing Justice and Quality of Life: Supporting Tourism. *Tour. Manag.* **2022**, *89*, 104446. [CrossRef]
49. McGehee, N.G.; Andereck, K.L. Factors Predicting Rural Residents' Support of Tourism. *J. Travel Res.* **2004**, *43*, 131–140. [CrossRef]
50. Demirović Bajrami, D.; Radosavac, A.; Cimbaljević, M.; Tretiakova, T.N.; Syromiatnikova, Y.A. Determinants of Residents' Support for Sustainable Tourism Development: Implications for Rural Communities. *Sustainability* **2020**, *12*, 9438. [CrossRef]
51. Xu, S.; Barbieri, C.; Anderson, D.; Leung, Y.-F.; Rozier-Rich, S. Residents' Perceptions of Wine Tourism Development. *Tour. Manag.* **2016**, *55*, 276–286. [CrossRef]
52. Kalberg, S. Max Weber's Types of Rationality: Cornerstones for the Analysis of Rationalization Processes in History. *Am. J. Sociol.* **1980**, *85*, 1145–1179. [CrossRef]
53. Wang, R.; Dai, M.; Ou, Y.; Ma, X. Residents' Happiness of Life in Rural Tourism Development. *J. Destin. Mark. Manag.* **2021**, *20*, 100612. [CrossRef]
54. Hair, J., Jr.; Hult, G.T.M.; Ringle, C.M.; Sarstedt, M.; Danks, N.P.; Ray, S. *Partial Least Squares Structural Equation Modeling (PLS-SEM) Using R: A Workbook*; Springer Nature: New York, NY, USA, 2021; ISBN 978-3-030-80519-7.
55. Domi, S.; Belletti, G. The Role of Origin Products and Networking on Agritourism Performance: The Case of Tuscany. *J. Rural. Stud.* **2022**, *90*, 113–123. [CrossRef]
56. Reimer, N.K.; Becker, J.C.; Benz, A.; Christ, O.; Dhont, K.; Klocke, U.; Neji, S.; Rychlowska, M.; Schmid, K.; Hewstone, M. Intergroup Contact and Social Change: Implications of Negative and Positive Contact for Collective Action in Advantaged and Disadvantaged Groups. *Pers. Soc. Psychol. Bull.* **2017**, *43*, 121–136. [CrossRef] [PubMed]
57. Leguina, A. A Primer on Partial Least Squares Structural Equation Modeling (PLS-SEM). *Int. J. Res. Method Educ.* **2015**, *38*, 220–221. [CrossRef]
58. Chin, W.W. The Partial Least Squares Approach for Structural Equation Modeling. In *Modern Methods for Business Research*; Methodology for business and management; Lawrence Erlbaum Associates Publishers: Mahwah, NJ, USA, 1998; pp. 295–336. ISBN 978-0-8058-2677-7.
59. Henseler, J.; Ringle, C.M.; Sinkovics, R.R. The Use of Partial Least Squares Path Modeling in International Marketing. In *New Challenges to International Marketing*; Sinkovics, R.R., Ghauri, P.N., Eds.; Advances in International Marketing; Emerald Group Publishing Limited: Bingley, UK, 2009; Volume 20, pp. 277–319. ISBN 978-1-84855-469-6.

**Disclaimer/Publisher's Note:** The statements, opinions and data contained in all publications are solely those of the individual author(s) and contributor(s) and not of MDPI and/or the editor(s). MDPI and/or the editor(s) disclaim responsibility for any injury to people or property resulting from any ideas, methods, instructions or products referred to in the content.

*Article*

# Time-Varying Granger Causality of COVID-19 News on Emerging Financial Markets: The Latin American Case

**Semei Coronado [1], Jose N. Martinez [2], Victor Gualajara [3], Rafael Romero-Meza [4] and Omar Rojas [5,6,*]**

1. Palomar College, San Marcos, CA 92069, USA
2. Accounting, Finance and Economics Department, California State University, Dominguez Hills, Carson, CA 90747, USA
3. Departamento de Métodos Cuantitativos, Centro Universitario de Ciencias Económico Administrativas, Universidad de Guadalajara, Guadalajara 44100, Jalisco, Mexico
4. Departamento de Gestión y Negocios, Facultad de Economía y Negocios, Universidad Alberto Hurtado, Santiago 6500620, Chile
5. Facultad de Ciencias Económicas y Empresariales, Universidad Panamericana, Zapopan 45010, Jalisco, Mexico
6. Faculty of Economics and Business, Universitas Airlangga, Surabaya 60286, East Java, Indonesia
* Correspondence: orojas@up.mx; Tel.: +52-331-368-2200

**Abstract:** This study uses daily COVID-19 news series to determine their impact on financial market volatility. This paper assesses whether U.S. financial markets react differently to COVID-19 news than emerging markets and if such markets are impacted differently by country-specific and global news. To detect the spillover effects from news on market volatility, a time-varying DCC-GARCH model was applied. The results suggest that the U.S. and emerging markets are affected differently by pandemic news, global series have a stronger impact on emerging markets than country-specific ones, and misleading information plays a significant role in financial market volatility, especially for the U.S.

**Keywords:** COVID-19 news; volatility; granger causality; time-varying; time series; financial markets

**MSC:** 37M10; 62P05; 91B28

## 1. Introduction

The pandemic, declared by the World Health Organization (WHO) on 11 March, 25 2020 [1], caused by the coronavirus (COVID-19), represents an unprecedented shock to the world economy. Starting in Wuhan, China, in December 2019, the shock rapidly spread throughout the world due to its simultaneous impacts on the world's demand and supply sectors. However, its economic impacts have been particularly hard for Latin American countries [2]. This pandemic has been followed by a climate of panic, misinformation, and uncertainty that has shocked global financial markets. For some, this uncertainty has forced economic agents to leave the stock market altogether, which created additional volatility and uncertainty due to COVID-19 [3–5].

In the U.S., the Standard and Poor's 500 index (S&P), which measures the performance of 500 major companies in the U.S. stock market, lost almost 30% of its value at the beginning of the pandemic (1 January–18 March 2020). Between 6 March and 18 March 2020, the index fell by almost 15% [6]. Government interventions, such as the implementation of the Coronavirus Aid, Relief, and Economic Security (CARES) Act in the U.S., helped stabilize financial markets and the economy [7,8]. In Latin America, countries usually tend to lack the financial resources that might help lessen the impacts of the pandemic on financial markets and their economies, which can lead to further reductions in capital investments and economic growth [9,10]. Moreover, it has been found that government response time and the size of the stimulus package are important to offset the impact of COVID-19 on emerging stock markets [11]. In general terms, financial markets have reacted to the heightened level of uncertainty and volatility brought about by the pandemic. This increase in uncertainty and volatility has led researchers to understand the direct implications for financial markets, specifically in terms of volatility for different commodities and markets, which can be used as a diversification and hedging strategy [12].

Several studies have examined the link between the COVID-19 pandemic and financial markets. Several studies relate financial market volatility to economic, financial, and other types of variables during the pandemic [13–15]. Financial volatility can also be clustered throughout time—volatility today tends to be followed by high volatility tomorrow [16]—and these changes in market volatility might be related to COVID-19 news. Specifically, there are studies that link financial markets' volatility to infectious disease news, such as the Infectious Disease Equity Market Volatility Tracker (EMV-ID) series from [17], which considers COVID-19 news and the impact on different economic and financial variables [18–21]. There are also other real-time news indexes, such as the Coronavirus Media Monitor [22], that have been linked to different financial and economic variables [23–25]. These news series have been analyzed to assess the asymmetry between the stock market returns and COVID-19 news [26,27]. Others have measured the lead–lag correlation between the news and volatility of central commercial banks traded in the Chinese stock market [24], while others [28] have evaluated how the stock markets have integrated public information about COVID-19 and used it to forecast the volatility of China's crude oil [29].

In terms of specific COVID-19 news series that might impact investor psychology (sentiment), studies analyze the impact of sentiment variables on stock market volatility [30,31], and others have shown that investor sentiment in one of the leading causes of stock return asymmetry [32]. Furthermore, the authors of [33] propose a new approach to estimating investor sentiment and its implications for global financial markets. The authors of [34] emphasize that the COVID-19 pandemic has resulted in unprecedented news coverage and an outpouring of opinion in this age of rapid information, and this has created uncertainty in financial markets that leads to greater volatility in prices. There is also the possibility that investors, overwhelmed by the volume of sometimes conflicting news, prefer to do nothing and make no changes to their portfolios. This behavior is known as the ostrich effect [35,36].

Regarding the specific nature of the news–financial market relation, there seems to be evidence of time-varying predictability of several predictors from the literature on stock markets' returns [37]. It is suggested that predictability might exist only over some phases of time and not necessarily over the entire sample period. This paper considers a similar dynamic relationship between COVID-19 news indexes and stock market volatilities in the U.S. and emerging markets. Given the unprecedented nature of the COVID-19 pandemic, it is not clear if this dynamic relationship holds in the case of Latin American markets. This paper considers global, U.S.-based, and country-specific COVID-19 news indexes, in order to analyze such a relationship in detail. In that regard, the impact of COVID-19 pandemic news on emerging market economies might differ for the news source. The differential impact of these news indexes on distinct stock markets may be due to each country's financial and cultural differences, which condition investors' decision-making processes. In that sense, a group of heterogeneous investors analyzes and interprets local and global pandemic information, and that can have an impact on fundamental valuations and market conditions for each country [38,39].

Considering the predominant role of the U.S. in the global economy, particularly in the case of Mexico and other Latin American countries, and the relative close fitting of country-specific news indexes, we might observe a different impact from global news indexes than from country-specific ones. However, the unprecedented nature of the COVID-19 pandemic shock makes it particularly hard to predict. Furthermore, emerging markets, given their financial constraints and cultural idiosyncrasies, might react significantly differently than developed countries in regard to similar COVID-19 pandemic news.

In summary, the main goals of this study are to analyze country-specific COVID-19 news indexes through time and determine how they might affect the volatility of financial markets in the U.S. and several emerging markets and to analyze how global news indexes might impact the volatility of financial markets of emerging economies.

This study also contributes to the literature on how COVID-19 news might cause panic and uncertainty in financial markets [34]. In this regard, the news' impacts might not be realized immediately in financial markets, so the effects might be asynchronous—the news one day might be reflected on a later day—and this, in turn, might affect the market volatility. Accordingly, a cross-correlation approach will be used to capture the Granger causality using a time-varying model such as DCC-GARCH [40]. This model can capture the spillover effects from instantaneous information on financial markets, as the news keeps flowing.

The result shows that global news indexes impacted the stock market's volatility more than local news indexes. One to three local news indexes caused stock volatility in Latin American markets. In contrast, the global news indexes demonstrated greater causality in Latin America.

The remainder of this work is organized as follows: Section 2 presents the data and methods; Section 3 the result and discussion; Section 4 presents the conclusions.

## 2. Data and Methods

The daily COVID-19 news series range from 22 January to 12 November 2020, for a total of 204 observations per series (data obtained from Bloomberg.com, accessed on 20 November 2022). Six stock market indexes were considered in this study: S&P from the U.S., MEXBOL from Mexico, COLCAP from Colombia, BOVESPA from Brazil, IPSA from Chile, MERVAL from Argentina, and IGBVL from Peru. The local series contain news specific to each country and include the Panic Index (PI), the level of news conversations related to panic about COVID-19; the Media Hype Index (MHI), the percentage of news about COVID-19 relative to the total news; the Fake News Index (FNI), the percentage of false news about COVID-19; the Sentiment Index (SI), the difference between positive and negative COVID-19 news; the Coronavirus Infodemic Index (CII), the percentage of COVID-19 information to which the user is exposed from unreliable sources; the Media Coverage Index (MCI), the proportion of all news sources covering the coronavirus (data obtained from https://www.ravenpack.com, accessed on 20 November 2022). All of these series use a scale between 0 and 100, except for the SI, which goes from −100 to 100. A value of 0 is considered neutral. These series contain information gathered from news outlets such as the Dow Jones Newswire, Wall Street Journal, and Stocktwits, among others [26,41]. This analysis also considers the EMV-ID index, which contains information about several infectious diseases news from almost 3000 newspapers in the U.S., from January of 1985 until today (data obtained from https://www.policyuncertainty.com/infectious_EMV.html, accessed on 20 November 2022). From the perspective of emerging markets, this index is considered a global index. In terms of other global news indexes, this paper considers the Global Fear Index (GFI), the fear and panic about the transmission and severity of COVID-19 [42]. This index is composed of two separate indexes, the COVID-19 Case Reporting Index (CRI) and the Death Reporting Index (DRI) (GFI provided by [42]). All three indexes are on a scale of 0 to 100, where a value of 50 represents moderate fear. Another set of global news indexes includes the COVID-19-Induced Uncertainty Stock Tracker composite index (ciustk.cmp, accessed on 20 November 2022), which combines an index of global news related to COVID-19 (ciustk.news, accessed on 20 November 2020) and the index of uncertainty due to global economic indicators (ciustk.mac, accessed on 20 November 2022), which contains information for the price of oil, gold, and raw materials, exchange rates, and stock prices [43] (indexes provided by [43]). Like the GFI, the scale of the indexes is from 0 to 100; the larger the value, the greater the perceived vulnerability of the stock market due to the effects of COVID-19. The last set of global news indexes includes the Aggregate Index of COVID-19 (A_COVID _I), Medical Index (MI), Travel

Index (TI), Uncertainty Index (UI), Vaccine Index (VI), and COVID Index (COVID_I) [44] (data obtained from: https://ael.scholasticahq.com/article/23491-new-measures-of-the-covid-19-pandemic-a-new-time-series-dataset, accessed on 20 November 2022). These indexes consider the number of reported COVID-19 deaths and cases but also the results from the 45 most popular worldwide newspapers' keyword searches to capture important events in the pandemic, such as vaccine development, medical advances, travel restrictions, and overall uncertainty.

To start with, the country-specific news series were standardized, given that growth rates or logarithmic transformations cannot be used due to having several zero values in the EMV-ID and SI series (the series' names for each country: add "_M" for Mexico; "_B" for Brazil; "_C" for Colombia; "_P" for Peru; "_CHI" for Chile; "_A" for Argentina; "_US" for the U.S.). Once standardized, the series show asymmetry and excess kurtosis. Accordingly, the Jarque–Bera test [45] was applied. The hypothesis of normality was rejected for all series, except for the SI for Mexico, Colombia, Chile, Brazil, and Argentina (the descriptive statistics and Jarque-Bera test results are available upon request). According to the Residual Augmented Least Squares-Lagrange Multiplier test results (RALS-LM) [46], the series were stationary and each one of them presents two breaks. Therefore, transformations of the series were not applied (results are available upon request.). Then, the ARCH-LM tests [47] were applied, and the results were not statistically significant for the PI and FNI of Mexico, Colombia, Brazil, and Peru. For the rest of the series, the hypothesis of not having ARCH effects was rejected (ARCH-LM test results are available upon request.). These results suggest that volatility in the series is implied, which might be due to having a kurtosis greater than zero. Accordingly, the Pruned Exact Linear Time test (PELT) [48] was applied to determine the changes in the variance of each series.

Table 1 presents the dates for changes in the variance for the series. The FNI series for Latin American countries tend to have more breaks in the variance than the other indexes. On the other hand, the SI series has breaks close to FNI's dates with lags of a day or two. The rest of the series have dates for the changes in variance that are close to each other. The EMV-ID, for its part, has only one break in its variance.

The results obtained are significant because investors and governments can use the information to apply or adapt investment decisions such as portfolio diversification or market politics such as lockdowns during the pandemic. These structural breaks in the volatility are due to skewness, leptokurtosis, and non-normality according to their descriptive statistics. For this reason, the DCC-GARCH model is suitable for this analysis.

The next step was to apply the Dechert and Scheinkman test (BDS) [49]. The results for the PI and FNI series for Mexico, Colombia, Brazil, and Peru were not statistically significant. For the rest of the series, the null hypothesis that the residuals are independent and identically distributed (iid) was rejected (BDS test results are available upon request.). This exact same process was applied to global news indexes, and the results indicate the appropriateness of applying causality tests on all the global news series. Table 2 presents breaks in the variance for the ten global indexes. This indicates that applying a DCC-GARCH Hong test is appropriate in order to determine the instantaneous causality of the COVID-19 news series' volatility on the specific country's stock market volatility (series that were not statistically significant in different tests were not considered for TV-DCC-GARH modeling).

The DCC-GARCH Hong test is widely used to analyze time-varying causality between pairs of economic and financial time series [20,50–52], and it offers several advantages when applied to test for instantaneous Granger causality [40,53]: (1) it allows identifying any immediate impact of news information on the stock market at any point in time, which occurs asynchronously due to how the information flows [52,54]; (2) it uses dynamic cross-correlation to assess causality according to the width of the time window [40]; (3) it allows determining the causal relationship in a unidirectional and bidirectional manner; (4) it allows determining the causality both in the mean and in the variance in a dynamic way; (5) it allows determining the volatility cluster where the causality occurs [55].

Table 1. Breaks in the variance for all countries and country-specific indexes.

| Mexico | | Brazil | | | | Colombia | | |
|---|---|---|---|---|---|---|---|---|
| **MEXBOL** | **CII_M** | **BOVESPA** | **MHI_B** | **CII_B** | **MCI_B** | **COLCAP** | **MHI_C** | **CII_C** |
| 02/25/20 | 03/10/20 | 06/02/20 | 03/12/20 | 03/09/20 | 03/06/20 | 08/21/20 | 09/01/20 | 06/08/20 |
| 04/28/20 | 07/31/20 | 07/03/20 | 05/15/20 | 06/12/20 | | 08/21/20 | 09/01/20 | 06/08/20 |
| 06/11/20 | | 09/17/20 | 09/08/20 | | | 09/14/20 | 10/19/20 | |
| 07/08/20 | | 10/12/20 | 10/19/20 | | | | | |
| 07/21/20 | | | 10/26/20 | | | | | |
| 08/28/20 | | | | | | | | |
| 10/07/20 | | | | | | | | |
| 10/27/20 | | | | | | | | |

| Chile | | | | Peru | | | Argentina | | |
|---|---|---|---|---|---|---|---|---|---|
| **IPSA** | **PI_CH** | **MCI_CH** | **IGBVL** | **SI_P** | **CII_P** | **MARVEL** | **MCI_A** | **FNI_A** | |
| 04/02/20 | 05/27/20 | 03/04/20 | 06/03/20 | 07/08/20 | 04/13/20 | 02/12/20 | 02/26/20 | 03/23/20 | |
| 07/16/20 | 06/03/20 | 07/07/20 | 08/04/20 | 08/13/20 | 08/13/20 | 03/06/20 | 06/02/20 | 03/26/20 | |
| 09/08/20 | 07/16/20 | | | 08/25/20 | | 05/08/20 | | 04/24/20 | |
| | 07/29/20 | | | | | 06/02/20 | | | |
| | 09/21/20 | | | | | 06/10/20 | | | |
| | 09/23/20 | | | | | 07/13/20 | | | |
| | | | | | | 09/15/20 | | | |
| | | | | | | 09/30/20 | | | |

| U.S.A | | | | |
|---|---|---|---|---|
| **S&P** | **PI_US** | **FNI_US** | **CII_US** | **EMV-ID** |
| 03/06/20 | 05/11/20 | 05/04/20 | 03/09/20 | 04/07/20 |
| 04/07/20 | | 05/21/20 | 05/29/20 | |
| 05/26/20 | | | 08/14/20 | |
| 07/31/20 | | | | |

Table 2. Breaks in the variance for global indexes.

| Indexes | | | | | | | | | |
|---|---|---|---|---|---|---|---|---|---|
| **GFI** | **A_COVID_I** | **MI** | **TI** | **UI** | **VI** | **COVID_I** | **Ciustk.news** | **Ciustk.mac** | **Ciustk.cmp** |
| 04/03/20 | 05/22/20 | 05/22/20 | 03/05/20 | 06/01/20 | 04/03/20 | 05/15/20 | 04/13/20 | 04/01/20 | 04/13/20 |
| 10/23/20 | 06/05/20 | 10/20/20 | 03/27/20 | 10/22/20 | 11/06/20 | 06/05/20 | 05/29/20 | 07/07/20 | 05/28/20 |
| | 08/13/20 | | 05/21/20 | | | 08/14/20 | 07/30/20 | 10/06/20 | 07/08/20 |
| | | | 05/29/20 | | | | | | 08/26/20 |
| | | | 09/23/20 | | | | | | |

To apply the test, we start by analyzing the standardized residuals for each stationary series $\{y_{i,t}\}$, for $i = 1, 2$ and $t = 1, \ldots T$ is the sample size from a univariate GARCH(1,1) model, in order to remove any autocorrelation effects. To analyze the dynamic correlation, we introduce a DCC-GARCH model $y_t(j) = \begin{pmatrix} y_{1,t} \\ y_{2,t-j} \end{pmatrix}$, where $j$ = lag order. Following the procedure from [40,51,52], the DCC-GARCH model is defined by:

$$y_t(j)I_{t-1} \sim N(0, D_{t,j}R_{t,j}D_{t,j})$$
$$D_{t,j}^2 = diag\{\omega_{i,j}\} + diag\{\kappa_{i,j}\} \circ y_t(j)y_t'(j) + diag\{\lambda_{i,j}\} \circ D_{t-1,j}^2$$
$$u_{t,j} = D_{t-1,j}^{-1}y_t(j) \quad (1)$$
$$Q_{t,j} = S \circ (u' - A - B) + Au_{t-1,j}u_{t-1,j}' + BQ_{t-1,j}$$
$$R_{t,j} = diag\{Q_{t,j}\}^{-1}Q_{t,j}diag\{Q_{t,j}\}^{-1}.$$

The dynamic correlation $\rho_{pq,t(j)}$ in the DCC-GARCH(1,1) is defined by:

$$\rho_{pq,t}(j) = \overline{\rho_{pq}}(j) + \alpha_j \left( u_{p,t-1} u_{q,t-1-j} - \overline{\rho_{pq}}(j) \right)$$
$$+ \beta_j \left( \rho_{pq,t-1}(j) - \overline{\rho_{pq}}(j) \right) r_{pq}(j) \frac{\rho_{pq,t}(j)}{\sqrt{\rho_{11,t} \rho_{22,t}(j)}} \quad (2)$$

where $p, q = 1, 2$.

The univariant Granger causality time varying is defined as $H_{3,t}(k)$:

$$H_{3,t}(k) = \frac{T \sum_{j=0}^{T-2} k^2 \left( \frac{j+1}{M} \right) r_{12,t}^2(j) - C_{1T}(k)}{\sqrt{2 D_{1T}(k)}} \quad (3)$$

where $M$ is a positive integer and has a small impact on the size of the DCC-GARCH Hong test (we also used $M = 2$, $M = 5$, and $M = 10$, but results remain relatively constant.) $k(x)$ is the Bartlett kernel function; $C_{1T} = \sum_{j=1}^{T-1} \left(1 - \frac{j}{M}\right) k^2 \left(\frac{j}{M}\right)$, $D_{1,T}(k) = \sum_{j=1}^{T-1} \left(1 - \frac{j}{T}\right) \left(1 - \frac{j+1}{T}\right) k^4 \left(\frac{j}{M}\right)$; $H_{3,t}(k) \sim N(0,1)$. If $H_{3,t}(k)$ is larger than the critical value of the normal distribution, the null hypothesis of no causality is rejected.

Given that the majority of the news and stock market series have ARCH effects, a GARCH (1,1) model is applied to each of these series to obtain the residuals, removing any autocorrelation effects. Then, a DCC-GARCH model is applied in order to determine the instantaneous, one-way Granger causality between the COVID-19 news series and the stock market series for the U.S. and emerging markets.

## 3. Results and Discussion

Table 3 and Figures 1–7 present the results of the instantaneous, one-way Granger-causality tests for different news series for each country. For the sake of space, only statistically significant results are presented. The line graph represents the causality estimates through time, and the vertical blue lines at the bottom of the figures represent the statistically significant causality at the 5% level. The "→" symbol represents the direction of causality.

For statistically significant results, MEXBOL and COLCAP each have eight news series; BOVESPA has nine series; IPSA and IGBVL each have twelve series; MERVAL has seven series; S&P has eight news series. Overall, global news tends to have more impact on Latin American stock markets than country-specific news. Brazil and Mexico, the largest Latin American stock markets by far, represent evidence of this.

Among country-specific news series, the CII series is statistically significant for five of the seven countries considered here. As mentioned before, the Coronavirus Infodemic Index represents the percentage of Coronavirus news considered false rumors and unreliable information. This particular news index shows how susceptible countries, including the U.S., can be to the circulation and spreading of false and misleading information. Interestingly, only the most southern economies (Chile and Argentina) are not affected by this news index. This could mean that these countries have different or better ways to "filter out" misleading information or simply that investors in these countries receive significantly different information than most Latin American countries and the U.S. In addition to the CII, the MCI also affects three of the six Latin American markets considered.

Table 3. One-way Granger-causality tests.

| New Index | Stock Market Index | | | | | | |
|---|---|---|---|---|---|---|---|
| | MEXBOL | BOVESPA | COLCAP | IPSA | IGBVL | MARVEL | S&P |
| CII_M | x | | | | | | |
| MHI_B | | x | | | | | |
| CII_B | | x | | | | | |
| MCI_B | | x | | | | | |
| MHI_C | | | x | | | | |
| CII_C | | | x | | | | |
| PI_CH | | | | x | | | |
| MCI_CH | | | | x | | | |
| SI_P | | | | | x | | |
| CII_P | | | | | x | | |
| FNI_A | | | | | | x | |
| MCI_A | | | | | | x | |
| PI_US | | | | | | | x |
| FNI_US | | | | | | | x |
| CII_US | | | | | | | x |
| GFI | x | x | x | x | x | x | x |
| A_COVID_I | x | | | x | x | | |
| MI | | | | x | x | | |
| TI | | x | x | x | | x | |
| UI | | | x | x | x | | |
| VI | x | x | | x | x | | |
| COVID_I | | x | x | x | x | | |
| Ciustk.news | x | x | x | x | x | x | x |
| Ciustk.mac | x | | | x | x | x | x |
| Ciustk.cmp | x | x | x | x | x | x | x |
| EMV-ID | x | | | x | x | | x |

Note: x represents where one-way Granger-causality tests for different news series for each country.

Considering only the largest stock markets—the U.S., Brazil, and Mexico—one thing to note is that the Panic Index and the Fake News Index are statistically significant only for the U.S. This could mean that the U.S. market might be exposed to significantly more misleading information and this generates more panic and uncertainty than in other countries, but it could also mean that investors in the U.S. are simply more susceptible to this type of news. On the other hand, this feeling of fear on the part of investors may cause the direction of the stock price to change, leading to stocks being oversold or overbought, which could create bubbles in the market, and volatility. Investors' decisions depend on governments' actions regarding COVID-19 so they can make effective decisions to reduce their risk. Considering the CII, this suggests the latter is more likely for the U.S. Investors in the U.S. might be too quick to react to new COVID-19 information, but this could also mean they have little time to discern whether the information is accurate [56].

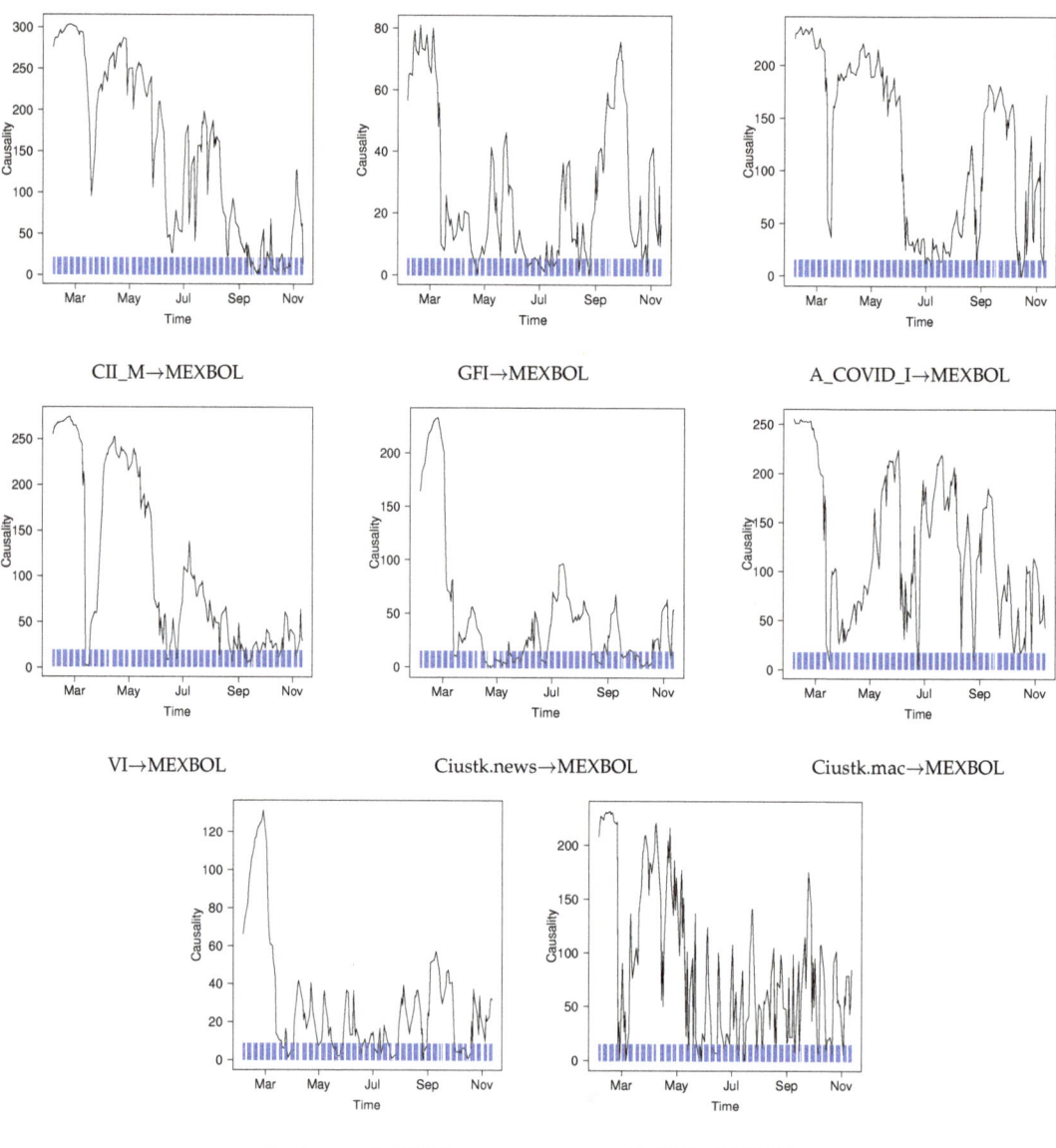

**Figure 1.** Instantaneous, one-way Granger-causality from news series to MEXBOL (DCC-GARCH model).

For Brazil, only the CII, MHI, and MCI are statistically significant, but the last two indexes capture only the proportion of COVID-19 news relative to all the news. For Mexico, the CII is the only local series that is statistically significant. Overall, these countries represent evidence that global news series tend to have a more significant impact than local news series.

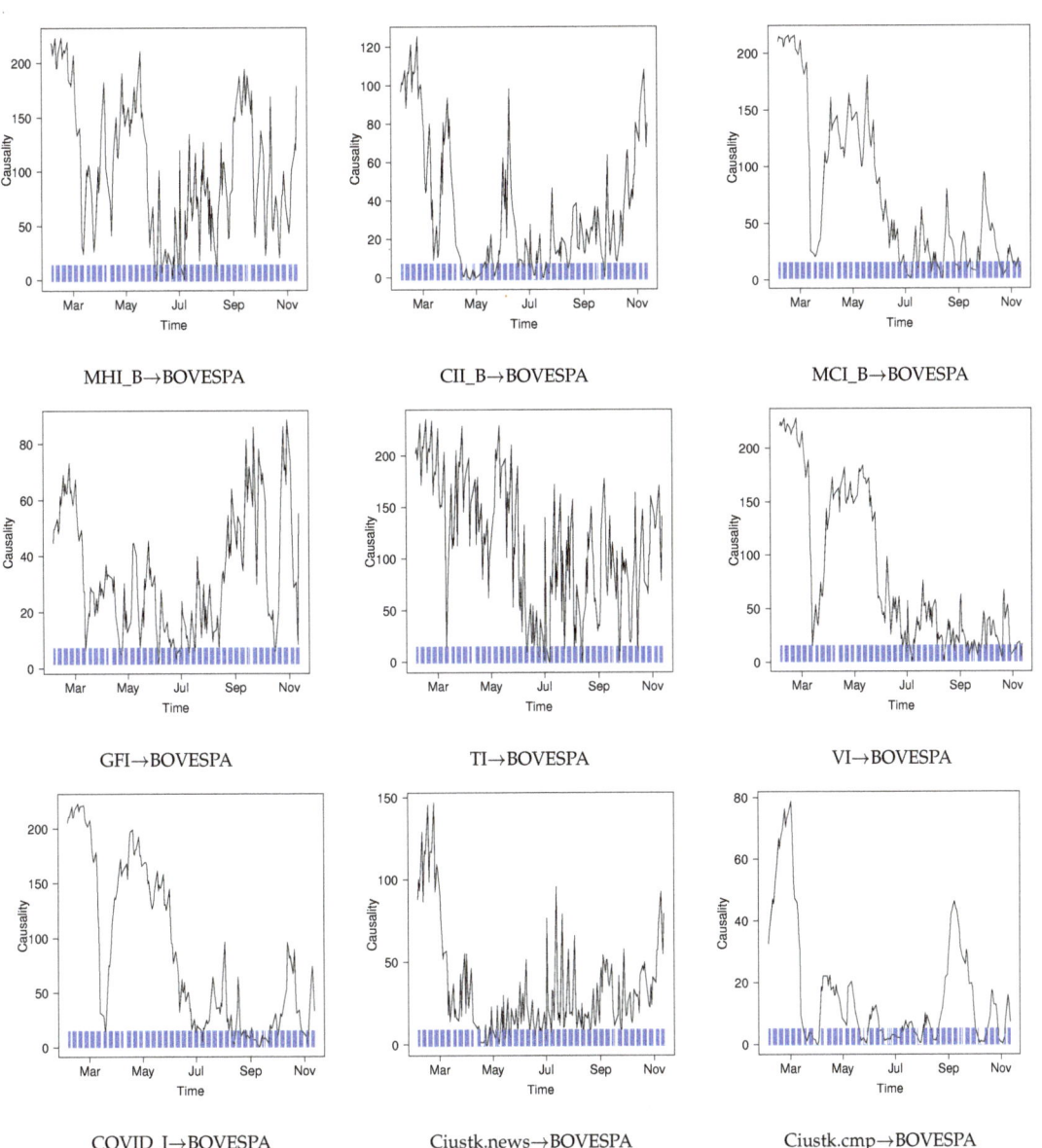

**Figure 2.** Instantaneous, one-way Granger-causality from news series to BOVESPA (DCC-GARCH model).

In terms of global news indexes, the ciustk.cmp and ciustk.news series are statistically significant for all countries, including the U.S. Considering how these indexes are constructed, it is not a surprise to observe statistically significant results. These results are consistent with the findings in [57,58], who found there is a relation between some macro-level news and price volatility. Given the inherently uncertain nature of the COVID-19 pandemic, it is reasonable to see an overall reduction in the flow of capital, which could lead to increased volatility and stock markets' decmidrule [59,60]. With the exception of Chile, the GFI is also statistically significant for all countries, which could be due to economic agents' concerns about how the volatility is impacting financial markets [61].

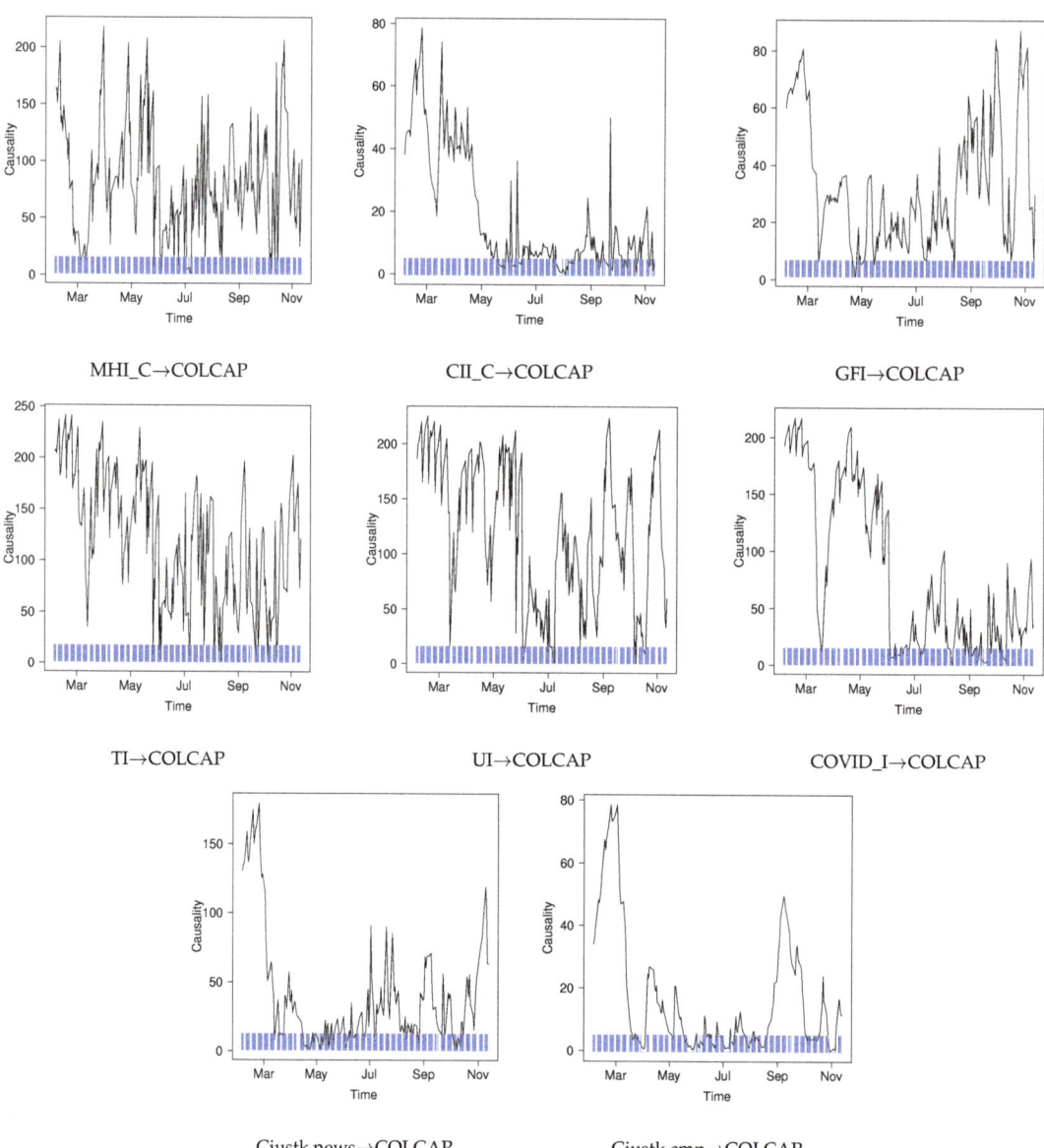

**Figure 3.** Instantaneous, one-way Granger-causality from news series to COLCAP (DCC-GARCH model).

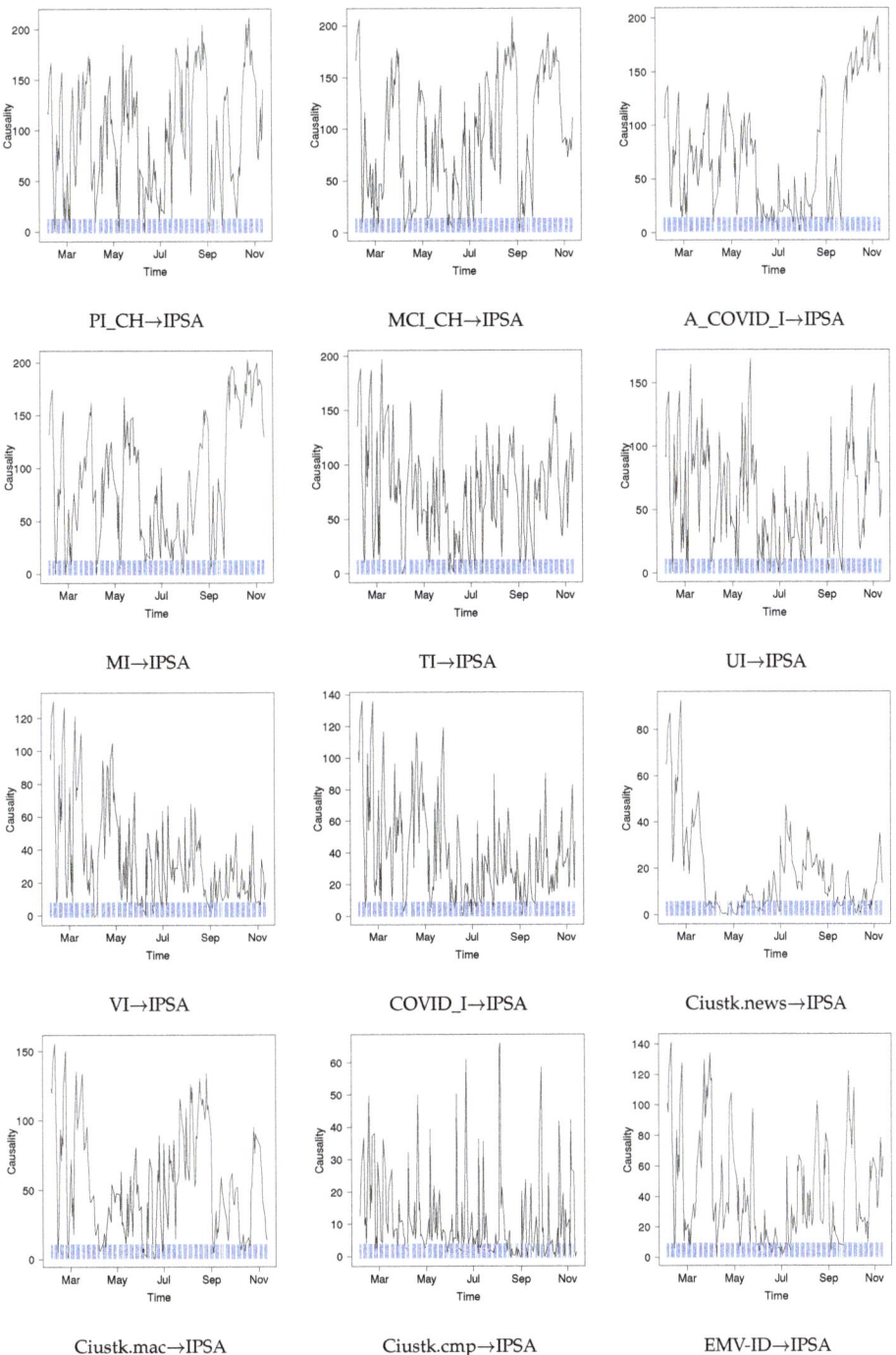

**Figure 4.** Instantaneous, one-way Granger-causality from news series to IPSA (DCC-GARCH model).

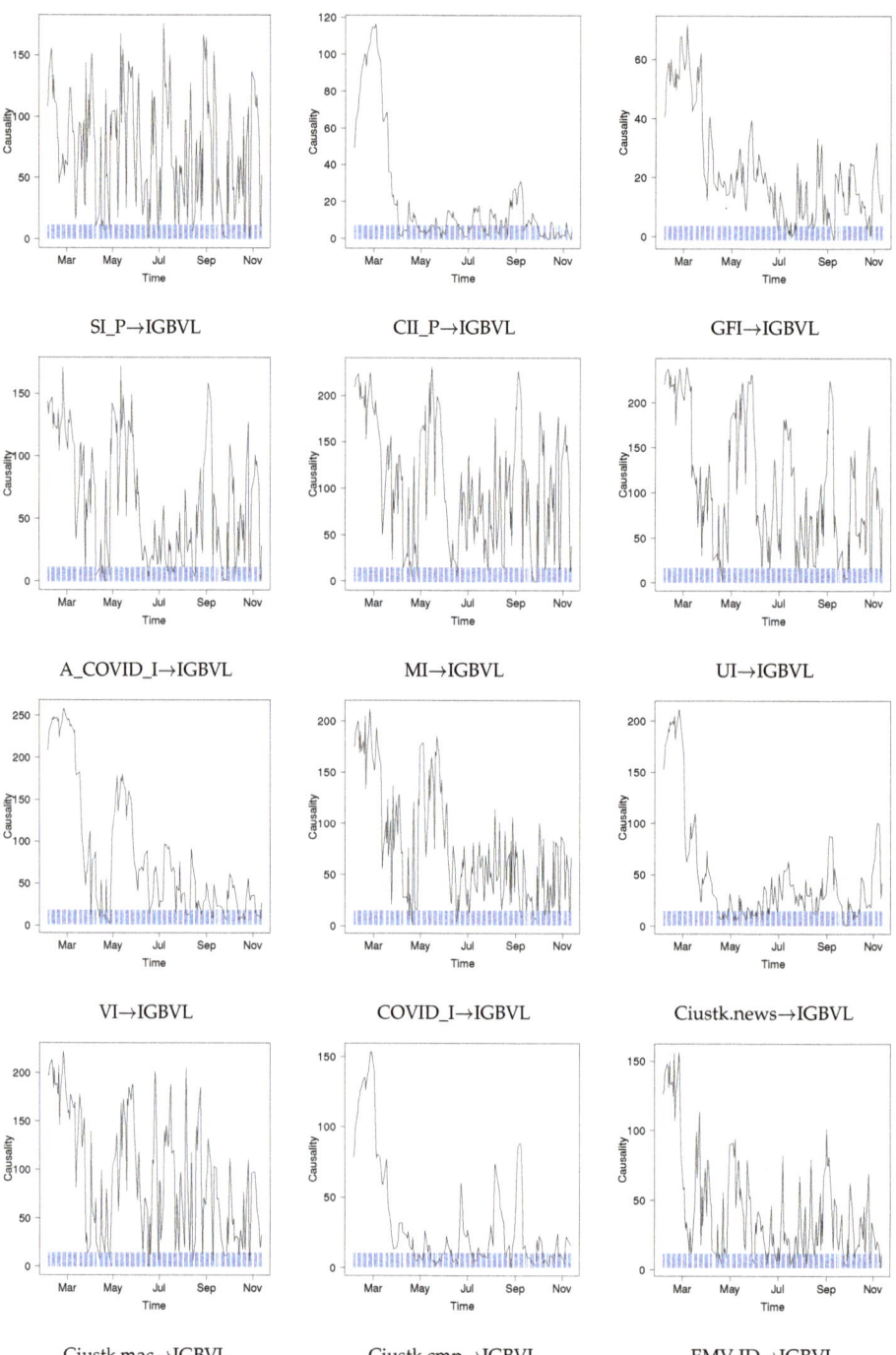

**Figure 5.** Instantaneous, one-way Granger-causality from news series to IGBVL (DCC-GARCH model).

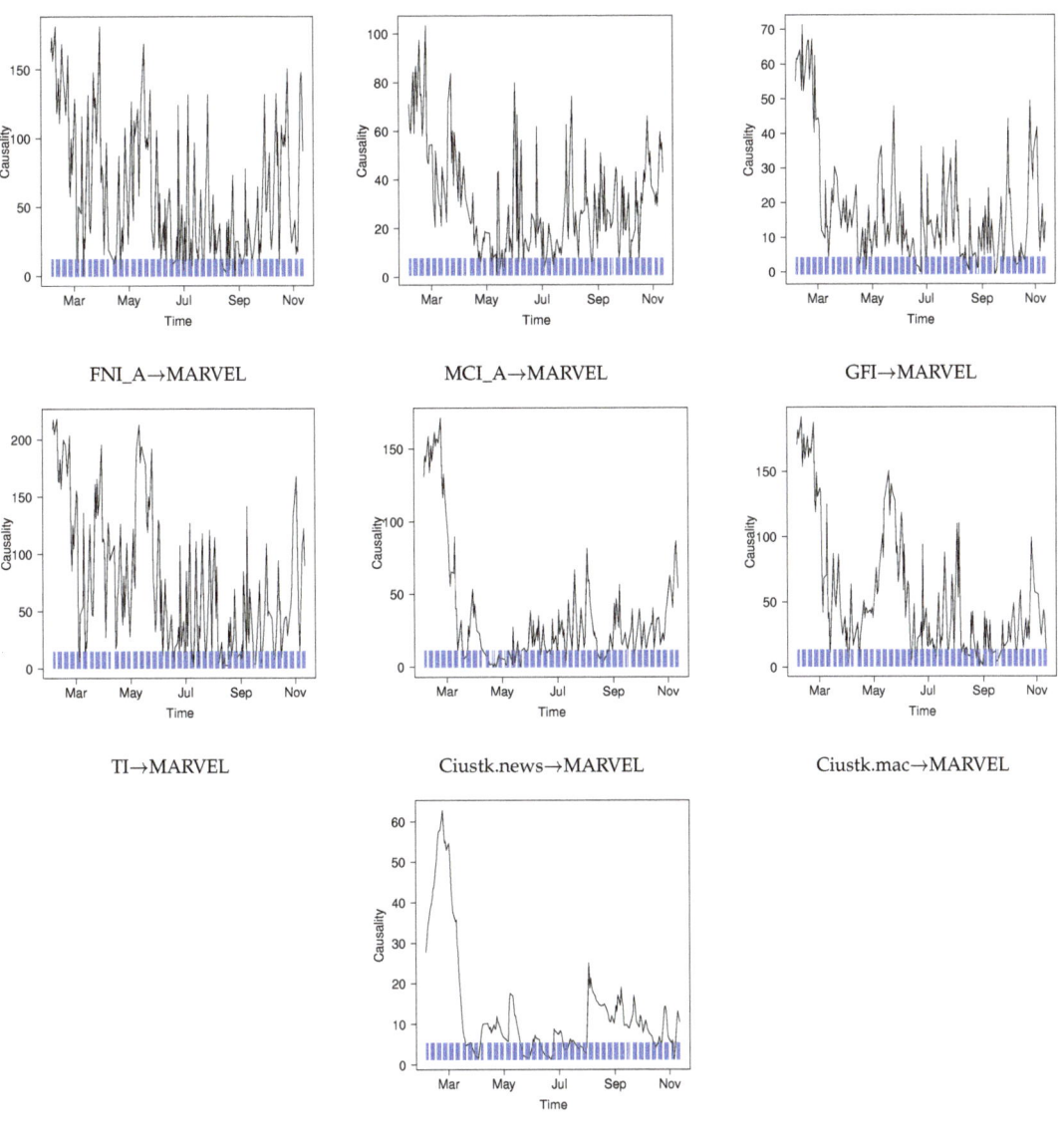

**Figure 6.** Instantaneous, one-way Granger-causality from news series to MARVEL (DCC-GARCH model).

The EMV-ID series is statistically significant for the U.S., Mexico, Chile, and Peru. These results are consistent with the findings in [62,63], which analyzed the correlation of the EMV-ID in several Latin American markets.

The Travel Index, Vaccine Index, and the COVID news series are statistically significant for the majority of Latin American markets but not for the U.S. This represents further evidence that Latin American markets respond differently to global news series than the U.S. The Travel Index is statistically significant for Brazil, Colombia, Chile, and Argentina, countries that imposed travel restrictions. Interestingly, Mexico did not impose travel restrictions during the pandemic, and its results are statistically insignificant. On the other hand, the U.S. imposed severe travel restrictions, but the result for the TI is statistically insignificant. The Vaccine Index, which captures information on vaccine development, is also statistically significant for most Latin American countries, including Mexico and Brazil, but not for the U.S. Once again, this might be due to the significant impact of false rumors and unreliable information on financial markets during the pandemic.

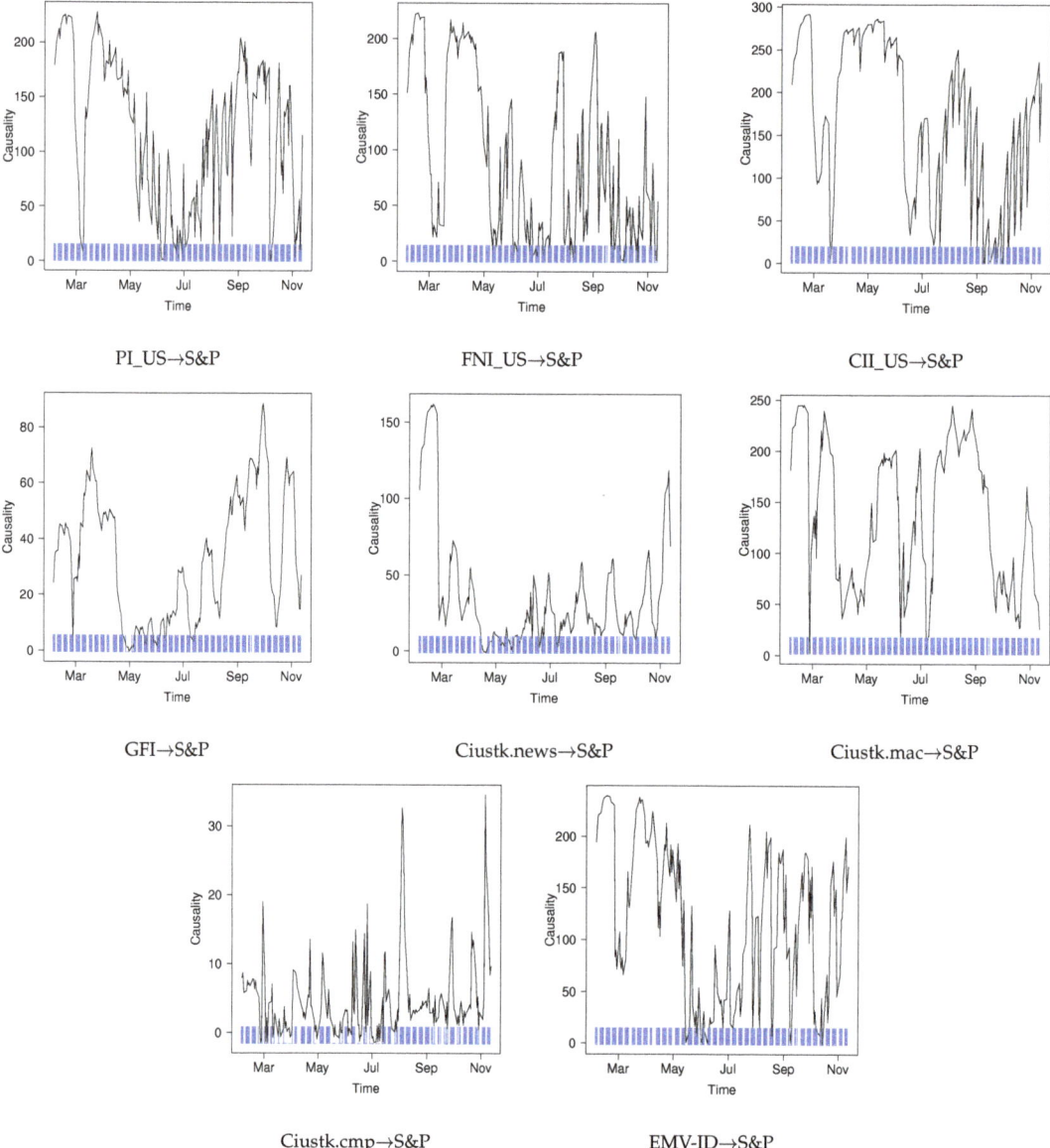

**Figure 7.** Instantaneous, one-way Granger-causality from news series to S&P (DCC-GARCH model).

## 4. Conclusions

This study analyzed different types of COVID-19 news series over time to determine how they might affect the volatility of stock markets in the U.S. and several Latin American countries. Given the unprecedented nature of the COVID-19 pandemic, this paper investigates whether or not U.S. financial markets reacted differently to pandemic news than emerging financial markets. This paper also investigates whether or not country-specific news series tend to have a more significant impact than global news series on financial markets. Furthermore, the current analysis allows us to ascertain the relative impact of unreliable information.

Stock market indexes were considered, along with local and global daily COVID-19 news series. Using both types of series, a DCC-GARCH model was applied to each pair of series to determine the instantaneous, one-way Granger causality between the news series and the stock market series in the U.S. and emerging markets.

The beliefs of economic agents about the news triggers their irrational decision-making since they do not have all the information available. The results may also be related to the fact that economic agents are not homogeneous since they depend on the financial culture of the country. Therefore, their emotions and feelings can affect the market, which varies over time with the degree of market maturity.

Overall, COVID-19 news impacted U.S. financial markets differently than emerging markets. Additionally, global indexes tend to have a more statistically significant impact on Latin American stock markets than local news. The results for Brazil and Mexico, the largest Latin American stock markets by far, support this.

In terms of country-specific news series, the CII is statistically significant for five of the seven countries analyzed, including the U.S., Brazil, and Mexico. This particular news index shows how susceptible countries, including the U.S., can be to the circulation and spreading of false and misleading information. In addition, the Panic Index and the Fake News Index are statistically significant only for the U.S. This could mean that the U.S. financial market might be exposed to significantly more misleading information and, therefore, it generates more panic and market volatility than in other countries, but it could also mean that investors in the U.S. are simply more susceptible to this type of news. Considering that the CII series is also statistically significant for the U.S., this suggests the latter is more likely.

In terms of policy implications, the main results suggest that investors in Latin American markets tend to pay more attention to global and U.S.-based news series than to local ones. Whether this is good for the stability of financial markets in emerging markets remains to be determined, and it could be part of an extension of this work. To the extent that global and U.S.-based news series might be more complete and up-to-date, this could represent a desired feature of Latin American financial markets. In terms of false rumors and unreliable information, the results suggest that investors across the world should do a better job at filtering out this type of information and try not to be so quick to react. This hastened reaction might produce even more volatility and uncertainty in financial markets worldwide. The results suggest this might be particularly true for the U.S.

Some of the limitations of this work are the fact that comparisons should be included with these same variables with other countries from other regions, both developed and undeveloped, to determine their causality. At the same time, these same markets could be analyzed with other variables related to COVID-19, such as those provided in the coronanet database, which includes more than 1,300 data points related to the pandemic in 195 countries. Finally, the results could be compared with time-varying models that do not require the series to be stationary or through entropy. This study only focused on the univariate Granger causality of different series of local and global news towards that of the volatility of Latin American stock markets.

**Author Contributions:** Conceptualization, methodology, software, validation, writing—original draft preparation, writing—review, and editing, J.N.M., S.C., V.G., R.R.-M. and O.R. All the authors commented on the final version before the submission. All authors have read and agreed to the published version of the manuscript.

**Funding:** This research received no external funding.

**Institutional Review Board Statement:** Not applicable.

**Data Availability Statement:** Not applicable.

**Conflicts of Interest:** The authors declare no conflict of interest.

## References

1. World Health Organization. Rolling Updates on Coronavirus Disease (COVID-19). Available online: https://www.who.int/emergencies/diseases/novel-coronavirus-2019/events-as-they-happen (accessed on 20 November 2022 ).
2. Economic Commission for Latin America and the Caribbean. *Informe Sobre El Impacto Económico En América Latina y El Caribe De La Enfermedad Por Coronavirus (COVID-19)*; UNECLAC: Santiago, Chile, 2020; ISBN 9789210054140.
3. Hasan, Md.B.; Mahi, M.; Hassan, M.K.; Bhuiyan, A.B. Impact of COVID-19 Pandemic on Stock Markets: Conventional vs. Islamic Indices Using Wavelet-Based Multi-Timescales Analysis. *N. Am. J. Econ. Financ.* **2021**, *58*, 101504. [CrossRef]
4. Yarovaya, L.; Elsayed, A.H.; Hammoudeh, S. Determinants of Spillovers between Islamic and Conventional Financial Markets: Exploring the Safe Haven Assets during the COVID-19 Pandemic. *Financ. Res. Lett.* **2021**, *43*, 101979. [CrossRef]
5. Albulescu, C.T. COVID-19 and the United States Financial Markets' Volatility. *Financ. Res. Lett.* **2021**, *38*, 101699. [CrossRef] [PubMed]
6. Shehzad, K.; Xiaoxing, L.; Bilgili, F.; Koçak, E. COVID-19 and Spillover Effect of Global Economic Crisis on the United States' Financial Stability. *Front. Psychol.* **2021**, *12*, 632175. [CrossRef] [PubMed]
7. Nicola, M.; Alsafi, Z.; Sohrabi, C.; Kerwan, A.; Al-Jabir, A.; Iosifidis, C.; Agha, M.; Agha, R. The Socio-Economic Implications of the Coronavirus Pandemic (COVID-19): A Review. *Int. J. Surg.* **2020**, *78*, 185–193. [CrossRef]
8. Wei, S.-J. Ten Keys to Beating Back COVID-19 and the Associated Economic Pandemic. In *Mitigating the COVID Economic Crisis: Act Fast and Do Whatever It Takes*; Baldwin, R., Weder di Mauro, B., Eds.; CEPR Press: London, UK, 2020; pp. 71–76, ISBN 978-1-912179-29-9.
9. Sharma, S.S. A Note on the Asian Market Volatility During the COVID-19 Pandemic. *Asian Econ. Lett.* **2020**, *1*, 17661. [CrossRef]
10. Hong, H.; Bian, Z.; Lee, C.C. COVID-19 and Instability of Stock Market Performance: Evidence from the U.S. *Financ. Innov.* **2021**, *7*, 12. [CrossRef]
11. Topcu, M.; Gulal, O.S. The Impact of COVID-19 on Emerging Stock Markets. *Financ. Res. Lett.* **2020**, *36*, 101691. [CrossRef]
12. Umar, Z.; Gubareva, M.; Teplova, T. The Impact of COVID-19 on Commodity Markets Volatility: Analyzing Time Frequency Relations between Commodity Prices and Coronavirus Panic Levels. *Resour. Policy* **2021**, *73*, 102164. [CrossRef]
13. Corbet, S.; Hou, Y.; Hu, Y.; Lucey, B.; Oxley, L. Aye Corona! The Contagion Effects of Being Named Corona during the COVID-19 Pandemic. *Financ. Res. Lett.* **2021**, *38*, 101591. [CrossRef]
14. Shaikh, I. On the Relation between the Crude Oil Market and Pandemic COVID-19. *Eur. J. Manag. Bus. Econ.* **2021**, *30*, 331-356. [CrossRef]
15. Phan, D.H.B.; Narayan, P.K. Country Responses and the Reaction of the Stock Market to COVID-19 a Preliminary Exposition. *Emerg. Mark. Financ. Trade* **2021**, *56*, 2138–2150. [CrossRef]
16. Javed, F.; Mantalos, P. Sensitivity of the Causality in Variance Test to the GARCH (1,1) Parameters. *Chil. J. Stat.* **2015**, *6*, 49–65. [CrossRef]
17. Baker, S.R.; Bloom, N.; Kost, K.; Sammon, M.; Viratyosin, T. *The Unprecedented Stock Market Impact of COVID-19*; National Bureau of Economic Research, Cambridge, MA, USA, 2020.
18. Bai, L.; Wei, Y.; Wei, G.; Li, X.; Zhang, S. Infectious Disease Pandemic and Permanent Volatility of International Stock Markets: A Long-Term Perspective. *Financ. Res. Lett.* **2020**, *40*, 101709. [CrossRef] [PubMed]
19. Bouri, E.; Gkillas, K.; Gupta, R.; Pierdzioch, C. Forecasting Power of Infectious Diseases-Related Uncertainty for Gold Realized Variance. *Financ. Res. Lett.* **2021**, *42*, 101936. [CrossRef]
20. Gupta, R.; Subramaniam, S.; Bouri, E.; Ji, Q. Infectious Disease-Related Uncertainty and the Safe-Haven Characteristic of US Treasury Securities. *Int. Rev. Econ. Financ.* **2021**, *71*, 289–298. [CrossRef]
21. Li, Y.; Liang, C.; Ma, F.; Wang, J. The Role of the IDEMV in Predicting European Stock Market Volatility during the COVID-19 Pandemic. *Financ. Res. Lett.* **2020**, *36*, 101749. [CrossRef]
22. RavenPack Coronavirus. Available online: https://coronavirus.ravenpack.com (accessed on 20 November 2022).
23. Baig, A.S.; Butt, H.A.; Haroon, O.; Rizvi, S.A.R. Deaths, Panic, Lockdowns and US Equity Markets: The Case of COVID-19 Pandemic. *Financ. Res. Lett.* **2021**, *38*, 101701. [CrossRef]
24. Ho, K.-Y.; Shi, Y.; Zhang, Z. News and Return Volatility of Chinese Bank Stocks. *Int. Rev. Econ. Financ.* **2020**, *69*, 1095–1105. [CrossRef]

25. Akhtaruzzaman, M.; Boubaker, S.; Umar, Z. COVID-19 Media Coverage and ESG Leader Indices. *Financ. Res. Lett.* **2021**, *45*, 102170. [CrossRef]
26. Cepoi, C.O. Asymmetric Dependence between Stock Market Returns and News during COVID-19 Financial Turmoil. *Financ. Res. Lett.* **2020**, *36*, 101658. [CrossRef]
27. Tan, Ö. The Effect of Pandemic News on Stock Market Returns During the Covid-19 Crash: Evidence from International Markets. *Connect. Istanb. Univ. J. Commun. Sci* **2021**, *60*, 217–240. [CrossRef]
28. Capelle-Blancard, G.; Desroziers, A. The Stock Market Is Not the Economy? Insights from the COVID-19 Crisis. *SSRN Electron. J.* **2020**, 1–40. [CrossRef]
29. Niu, Z.; Liu, Y.; Gao, W.; Zhang, H. The Role of Coronavirus News in the Volatility Forecasting of Crude Oil Futures Markets: Evidence from China. *Resour. Policy* **2021**, *73*, 102173. [CrossRef]
30. Naseem, S.; Mohsin, M.; Hui, W.; Liyan, G.; Penglai, K. The Investor Psychology and Stock Market Behavior During the Initial Era of COVID-19: A Study of China, Japan, and the United States. *Front. Psychol.* **2021**, *12*, 626934. [CrossRef]
31. Xiang, Y.-T.; Yang, Y.; Li, W.; Zhang, L.; Zhang, Q.; Cheung, T.; Ng, C.H. Timely Mental Health Care for the 2019 Novel Coronavirus Outbreak Is Urgently Needed. *Lancet Psychiatry* **2020**, *7*, 228–229. [CrossRef] [PubMed]
32. Jawadi, F.; Namouri, H.; Ftiti, Z. An Analysis of the Effect of Investor Sentiment in a Heterogeneous Switching Transition Model for G7 Stock Markets. *J. Econ. Dyn. Control* **2018**, *91*, 469–484. [CrossRef]
33. Huynh, T.L.D.; Foglia, M.; Nasir, M.A.; Angelini, E. Feverish Sentiment and Global Equity Markets during the COVID-19 Pandemic. *J. Econ. Behav. Organ.* **2021**, *188*, 1088–1108. [CrossRef] [PubMed]
34. Haroon, O.; Rizvi, S.A.R. COVID-19: Media Coverage and Financial Markets Behavior—A Sectoral Inquiry. *J. Behav. Exp. Financ.* **2020**, *27*, 100343. [CrossRef] [PubMed]
35. Dong, H.; Gil-Bazo, J.; Ratiu, R.V. Information Demand during the COVID-19 Pandemic. *J. Account. Public Policy* **2021**, *40*, 106917. [CrossRef]
36. Galai, D.; Sade, O. The "Ostrich Effect" and the Relationship between the Liquidity and the Yields of Financial Assets. *J. Bus.* **2006**, *79*, 2741–2759. [CrossRef]
37. Devpura, N.; Narayan, P.K.; Sharma, S.S. Is Stock Return Predictability Time-Varying? *J. Int. Financ. Mark. Institutions Money* **2018**, *52*, 152–172. [CrossRef]
38. Fernandez-Perez, A.; Gilbert, A.; Indriawan, I.; Nguyen, N.H. COVID-19 Pandemic and Stock Market Response: A Culture Effect. *J. Behav. Exp. Financ.* **2021**, *29*, 100454. [CrossRef] [PubMed]
39. Namouri, H.; Jawadi, F.; Ftiti, Z.; Hachicha, N. Threshold Effect in the Relationship between Investor Sentiment and Stock Market Returns: A PSTR Specification. *Appl. Econ.* **2018**, *50*, 559–573. [CrossRef]
40. Lu, F.; Hong, Y.; Wang, S.; Lai, K.; Liu, J. Time-Varying Granger Causality Tests for Applications in Global Crude Oil Markets. *Energy Econ.* **2014**, *42*, 289–298. [CrossRef]
41. Blitz, D.; Huisman, R.; Swinkels, L.; van Vliet, P. Media Attention and the Volatility Effect. *Financ. Res. Lett.* **2020**, *36*, 101317. [CrossRef]
42. Salisu, A.A.; Akanni, L.O. Constructing a Global Fear Index for the COVID-19 Pandemic. *Emerg. Mark. Financ. Trade* **2020**, *56*, 2310–2331. [CrossRef]
43. Salisu, A.A.; Ogbonna, A.E.; Oloko, T.F.; Adediran, I.A. A New Index for Measuring Uncertainty Due to the COVID-19 Pandemic. *Sustainability* **2021**, *13*, 3212. [CrossRef]
44. Narayan, P.K.; Iyke, B.N.; Sharma, S.S. New Measures of the COVID-19 Pandemic: A New Time-Series Dataset. *Asian Econ. Lett.* **2021**, *2*, 1–14. [CrossRef]
45. Bera, A.K.; Jarque, C.M. Efficient Tests for Normality, Homoscedasticity and Serial Independence of Regression Residuals. *Econ. Lett.* **1981**, *7*, 313–318. [CrossRef]
46. Meng, M.; Lee, J.; Payne, J.E. RALS-LM Unit Root Test with Trend Breaks and Non-Normal Errors: Application to the Prebisch-Singer Hypothesis. *Stud. Nonlinear Dyn. Econom.* **2017**, *21*, 31–45. [CrossRef]
47. Engle, R. Autoregressive Conditional Heteroscedasticity with Estimates of the Variance of United Kingdom Inflation. *Econometrica* **1982**, *50*, 987–1007. [CrossRef]
48. Killick, R.; Fearnhead, P.; Eckley, I.A. Optimal Detection of Changepoints with a Linear Computational Cost. *J. Am. Stat. Assoc.* **2012**, *107*, 1590–1598. [CrossRef]
49. Broock, W.A.; Scheinkman, J.A.; Dechert, W.D.; LeBaron, B. A Test for Independence Based on the Correlation Dimension. *Econom. Rev.* **1996**, *15*, 197–235. [CrossRef]
50. Cevik, E.I.; Atukeren, E.; Korkmaz, T. Oil Prices and Global Stock Markets: A Time-Varying Causality-in-Mean and Causality-in-Variance Analysis. *Energies* **2018**, *11*, 2848. [CrossRef]
51. Gupta, R.; Kanda, P.; Wohar, M.E. Predicting Stock Market Movements in the United States: The Role of Presidential Approval Ratings. *Int. Rev. Financ.* **2021**, *21*, 324–335. [CrossRef]
52. Coronado, S.; Gupta, R.; Hkiri, B.; Rojas, O. Time-Varying Spillovers between Currency and Stock Markets in the USA: Historical Evidence from More than Two Centuries. *Adv. Decis. Sci.* **2020**, *24*, 1–32. [CrossRef]
53. Engle, R. Dynamic Conditional Correlation. *J. Bus. Econ. Stat.* **2002**, *20*, 339–350. [CrossRef]
54. Kanda, P.; Burke, M.; Gupta, R. Time-Varying Causality between Equity and Currency Returns in the United Kingdom: Evidence from over Two Centuries of Data. *Phys. A Stat. Mech. Appl.* **2018**, *506*, 1060–1080. [CrossRef]

55. Jammazi, R.; Ferrer, R.; Jareño, F.; Shahzad, S.J.H. Time-Varying Causality between Crude Oil and Stock Markets: What Can We Learn from a Multiscale Perspective? *Int. Rev. Econ. Financ.* **2017**, *49*, 453–483. [CrossRef]
56. Gallotti, R.; Valle, F.; Castaldo, N.; Sacco, P.; De Domenico, M. Assessing the Risks of 'Infodemics' in Response to COVID-19 Epidemics. *Nat. Hum. Behav.* **2020**, *4*, 1285–1293. [CrossRef] [PubMed]
57. Evans, K.P. Intraday Jumps and US Macroeconomic News Announcements. *J. Bank Financ.* **2011**, *35*, 2511–2527. [CrossRef]
58. Jawadi, F.; Louhichi, W.; ben Ameur, H.; Ftiti, Z. Do Jumps and Co-Jumps Improve Volatility Forecasting of Oil and Currency Markets? *Energy J.* **2019**, *40*, 131–150 . [CrossRef]
59. Youssef, M.; Mokni, K.; Ajmi, A.N. Dynamic Connectedness between Stock Markets in the Presence of the COVID-19 Pandemic: Does Economic Policy Uncertainty Matter? *Financ. Innov.* **2021**, *7*, 13. [CrossRef] [PubMed]
60. Azimli, A. The Impact of COVID-19 on the Degree of Dependence and Structure of Risk-Return Relationship: A Quantile Regression Approach. *Financ. Res. Lett.* **2020**, *36*, 101648. [CrossRef] [PubMed]
61. Engelhardt, N.; Krause, M.; Neukirchen, D.; Posch, P.N. Trust and Stock Market Volatility during the COVID-19 Crisis. *Financ. Res. Lett.* **2021**, *38*, 101873. [CrossRef]
62. Coronado, S.; Martinez, J.N.; Romero-Meza, R. Time-Varying Multivariate Causality among Infectious Disease Pandemic and Emerging Financial Markets: The Case of the Latin American Stock and Exchange Markets. *Appl. Econ.* **2021**, *54*, 3924–3932. [CrossRef]
63. Romero-Meza, R.; Coronado, S.; Ibañez-Veizaga, F. COVID-19 y Causalidad En La Volatilidad Del Mercado Accionario Chileno. *Estud. Gerenciales* **2021**, *37*, 242–250. [CrossRef]

**Disclaimer/Publisher's Note:** The statements, opinions and data contained in all publications are solely those of the individual author(s) and contributor(s) and not of MDPI and/or the editor(s). MDPI and/or the editor(s) disclaim responsibility for any injury to people or property resulting from any ideas, methods, instructions or products referred to in the content.

Article

# The Bitcoin Halving Cycle Volatility Dynamics and Safe Haven-Hedge Properties: A MSGARCH Approach

Jireh Yi-Le Chan [1], Seuk Wai Phoong [2,*], Seuk Yen Phoong [3], Wai Khuen Cheng [4] and Yen-Lin Chen [5,*]

[1] Institute for Advanced Studies, Universiti Malaya, Kuala Lumpur 50603, Malaysia
[2] Department of Management, Faculty of Business and Economics, Universiti Malaya, Kuala Lumpur 50603, Malaysia
[3] Department of Mathematics, Faculty of Science and Mathematics, Universiti Pendidikan Sultan Idris, Tanjong Malim 35900, Malaysia
[4] Faculty of Information and Communication Technology, Universiti Tunku Abdul Rahman, Kampar 31900, Malaysia
[5] Department of Computer Science and Information Engineering, National Taipei University of Technology, Taipei 106344, Taiwan
* Correspondence: phoongsw@um.edu.my (S.W.P.); ylchen@mail.ntut.edu.tw (Y.-L.C.)

**Abstract:** This paper introduces a unique perspective towards Bitcoin safe haven and hedge properties through the Bitcoin halving cycle. The Bitcoin halving cycle suggests that Bitcoin price movement follows specific sequences, and Bitcoin price movement is independent of other assets. This has significant implications for Bitcoin properties, encompassing its risk profile, volatility dynamics, safe haven properties, and hedge properties. Bitcoin's institutional and industrial adoption gained traction in 2021, while recent studies suggest that gold lost its safe haven properties against the S&P500 in 2021 amid signs of funds flowing out of gold into Bitcoin. Amid multiple forces at play (COVID-19, halving cycle, institutional adoption), the potential existence of regime changes should be considered when examining volatility dynamics. Therefore, the objective of this study is twofold. The first objective is to examine gold and Bitcoin safe haven and hedge properties against three US stock indices before and after the stock market selloff in March 2020. The second objective is to examine the potential regime changes and the symmetric properties of the Bitcoin volatility profile during the halving cycle. The Markov Switching GARCH model was used in this study to elucidate regime changes in the GARCH volatility dynamics of Bitcoin and its halving cycle. Results show that gold did not exhibit safe haven and hedge properties against three US stock indices after the COVID-19 outbreak, while Bitcoin did not exhibit safe haven or hedge properties against the US stock market indices before or after the COVID-19 pandemic market crash. Furthermore, this study also found that the regime changes are associated with low and high volatility periods rather than specific stages of a Bitcoin halving cycle and are asymmetric. Bitcoin may yet exhibit safe haven and hedge properties as, at the time of writing, these properties may manifest through sustained adoption growth.

**Keywords:** MSGARCH; symmetry; regime changes; safe haven; hedge properties; Bitcoin; gold

**MSC:** 62M45

## 1. Introduction

A Bitcoin halving event is defined as an event that decreases a Bitcoin miner's reward by half, which occurs roughly every four years [1]. Bitcoin price chart and past studies showed that the halving event impacted Bitcoin price in specific manners that formed the Bitcoin halving cycle.

In Figure 1, each cycle is segregated by vertical dash lines. Each of the three boxes within a cycle represents the Bitcoin bull market, bear market, and stagnation, respectively. By examining the Bitcoin price chart illustrated in Figure 1, it can be seen that a Bitcoin halving cycle typically consists of three stages: a one-year bull market, followed by a one-year bear market, followed by a two-year stagnation. During the one-year bull market, Bitcoin surpasses its previous high to achieve a new all-time high, per Meynkhard's [1] findings and has stood the test of time as of the time of this writing. It can also be seen in Figure 1 that Bitcoin is in its third halving cycle and has completed its one-year bull market. Therefore, Bitcoin is expected to be in the one-year bear market stage as of the time of this writing.

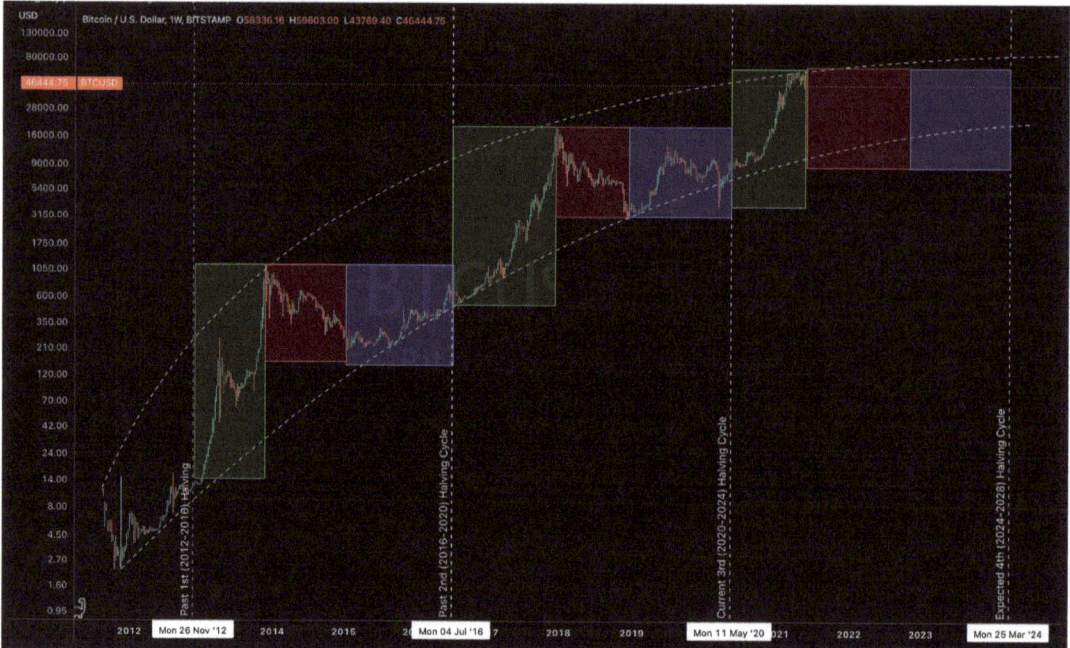

**Figure 1.** The Bitcoin Halving Cycle. Figure 1 represents a log-scale weekly candlestick chart of the Bitcoin price and illustrates the consistent occurrence of the 3 distinct phases (bull market, bear market, recovery phase) during each cycle. The green box represents the bull market, the red box represents the bear market, and the blue box represents the recovery phase. The first halving cycle occurred on 28 November 2012. The second halving cycle occurred on 9 July 2016. The third halving cycle occurred on 11 May 2020. The start of each halving cycle is indicated by a vertical line marking the date of the beginning of the respective weeks, as Figure 1 is a weekly chart.

1. There are specific sequences of events during each of the three stages of a Bitcoin halving cycle. Figures 2–5 illustrate the five sequences of events consistently taking place during a bear market in Bitcoin's past two halving cycles. Below are the five sequences of events:
2. Occurrence of reversal pattern at an all-time high;
3. Followed by a 50% crash from the all-time high;
4. Followed by a recovery back to 20% away from the all-time high;
5. Followed by a 70% crash from the all-time high;
6. Eventually bottoming out at 85% from the all-time high.

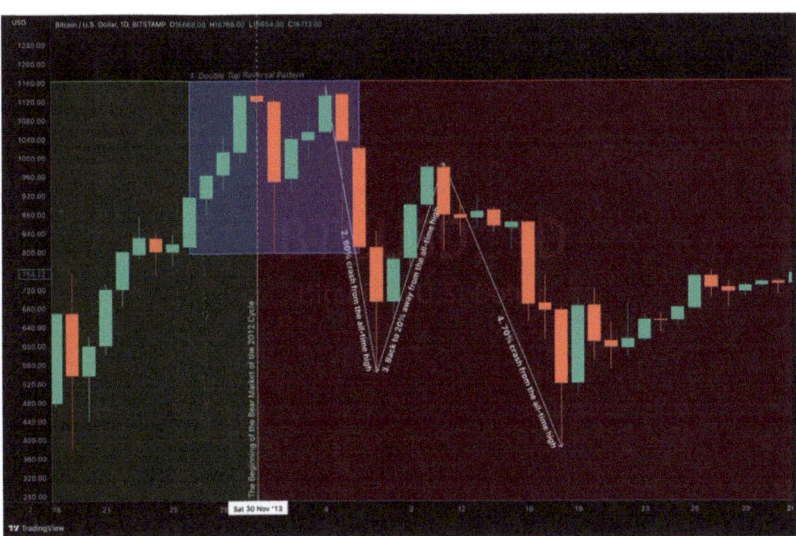

**Figure 2.** The first 4 sequences of the 2014 bear market during the Bitcoin 2012–2016 halving cycle. The Bitcoin price reached a historical all-time high of $1160. A double top reversal pattern first occurred and indicated a potential reversal, followed by a 50% crash to $550. The Bitcoin price recovered back to 20% away from the historical all-time high ($1000) before making a 70% crash away from the historical all-time high ($340).

**Figure 3.** The 5th sequence of the 2014 bear market during the Bitcoin 2012–2016 halving cycle. The Bitcoin price finally bottomed at $200 (85% away from the historical all-time high) before entering the recovery phase.

**Figure 4.** The first 4 sequences of the 2017 bear market during the Bitcoin 2016–2020 halving cycle. During this cycle, the Bitcoin price reached a new all-time high of $20,000 before entering the bear market. Figure 4 highlights 4 out of 5 primary sequences of events that are similar to Figure 2. A reversal pattern was first indicated at the new all-time high of $20,000. Then, Bitcoin suffered an approximately 50% crash to $11,000. The Bitcoin price recovered back to approximately 20% away from the historical all-time high ($17,000) before making a 70% crash away from the historical all-time high down to $6000.

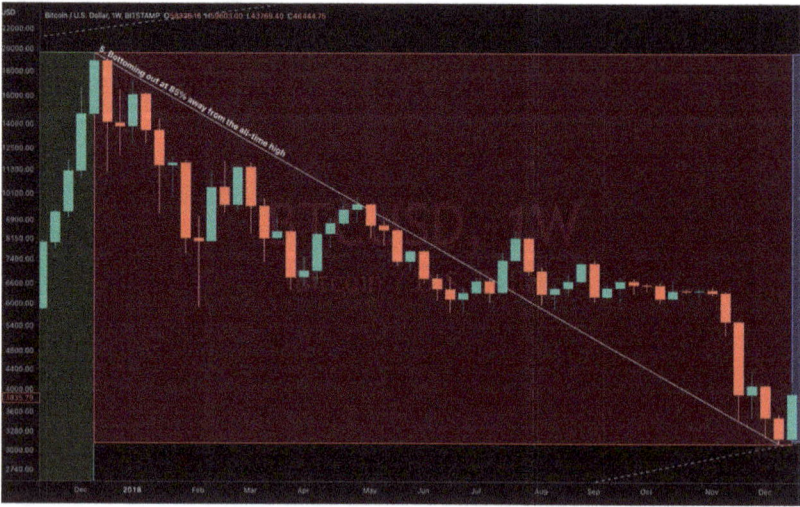

**Figure 5.** The 5th sequence of the 2017 bear market during the Bitcoin 2016–2020 halving cycle. Similar to Figure 3, the Bitcoin price ended the bear market by bottoming at $3100 (approximately 85% away from the historical all-time high) before entering the recovery phase again.

The Bitcoin halving cycle suggests that Bitcoin price movement follows specific sequences, and is independent of other assets. This has significant implications for Bitcoin properties, encompassing its risk profile, volatility dynamics, safe haven properties, and hedge properties. For instance, Bitcoin should be negatively correlated to the stock market to exhibit safe haven and hedge properties according to the framework proposed by Baur and McDermott [2]. However, Bitcoin halving cycle implies independence (no correlation) of stock market movements. Given the predictability of the Bitcoin price movement, Bitcoin could exhibit time-varying properties that might not be inherent. Furthermore, given the distinctiveness of the three stages within a cycle, there could be certain volatility dynamics that are specific to each stage. While the Bitcoin halving cycle may impact Bitcoin safe haven, hedge properties, and volatility dynamics, these findings may not hold significance without significant industrial and institutional exposures and interests.

Bitcoin is rapidly gaining recognition as an investment vehicle at the retail, institutional, and federal levels. The deputy governor of the People's Bank of China (PBOC), Li Bo, acknowledged Bitcoin as an investment alternative [3]. The first two Bitcoin Exchange Traded Funds (ETF), were approved in Canada and launched in February 2021. In an interview with CNBC in 2021, Rick Rieder, BlackRock's chief investment officer of global income, revealed that BlackRock, one of the world's largest asset managers, has entered the Bitcoin space [4].

Many significant events also occurred in early 2021, suggesting the beginning of the increasing industrial adoption of Bitcoin. These events include big corporations accepting or facilitating payments via Bitcoin, S&P500 companies buying billions of dollars worth in Bitcoin, approval of the first-ever Bitcoin Exchange Traded Funds (ETF), and the world's largest asset management company entering the Bitcoin space [4]. Additionally, Apple Pay officially announced support of payments via Bitcoin in February 2021, while Google Pay and Samsung Pay have plans to support payments via Bitcoin in Q1 2021. According to SEC Filings, in January 2021, Tesla Inc., an S&P500 company, purchased USD 1.5 billion worth of Bitcoin for diversification and returned maximization of cash not required to maintain operating liquidity. Tesla Inc. also added that it expects to accept Bitcoin for payments soon.

An aspect of industrial adoption is reflected by the rapid expansion in the Bitcoin supply chain. One component of the supply chain is the Bitcoin mining operation. Several well-known Bitcoin mining companies are Bitfarms, Riot Blockchain, and Marathon Digital Holdings. In May 2020, Bitfarms announced the acquisition of 6600 miners, costing an estimated ~USD 43 million. A company's Bitcoin mining capacity is measured in hast rate per second (H/s), and Bitfarm's acquisition of 6600 miners will increase its mining capacity to 2.5 EH/s. Bitfarms stated that the company aims to achieve 8 EH/s by the end of 2022, implying that the company would be required to invest an estimated ~USD 80 mil before 2022 to achieve that milestone. Riot Blockchain, Marathon Digital Holdings, and other mining companies are also aggressively expanding their operations.

Another aspect of industrial adoption is the emergence of crypto-asset exchanges and institutional trading volume. For example, Coinbase went public on 14 April 2021, at a valuation of ~USD 65 billion. It is the second world's largest crypto exchange after Binance. In addition, Coinbase reported that institutional trading volume was double that of retail trading volume in Q1 2021, citing that institutional interest has surpassed retail traders' [5]. With other major crypto exchanges, such as Gemini, also planning to go public, more capital will be invested into Bitcoin and its supply chain.

*1.1. Implications of Bitcoin Rapid Adoption and the Halving Cycle*

Firstly, the extensive industrial and institutional adoption suggests that the importance of Bitcoin risk assessment is becoming apparent as more capital is being risked into Bitcoin and its supply chain. According to Ark Invest [6], Bitcoin would be lifted to ~USD 400,000 per coin if institutions allocate 5% of their funds to Bitcoin. Bitcoin's drastic increase in adoption suggests that its role may go beyond that of the medium of payment or store of value to a hedge against the stock market.

Bitcoin is referred to as digital gold [7], and this comparison is apt as gold can be used as a hedge against many stock markets [8]. The notion of Bitcoin as digital gold is echoed by prolific portfolio manager Cathie Wood of ARK Invest. Two common properties of gold are being a safe haven and a hedge against the stock market and economic turmoil [2,9,10]. However, Bitcoin's role in this context is highly disputed. Some previous studies regarded Bitcoin as a speculative asset based on transaction data [11,12], while others believe that Bitcoin exhibits safe haven properties and diversification benefits [13,14], implying that the safe haven property of both Bitcoin and gold is dependent on markets, market conditions, time horizon, and other factors such as government intervention and market participant reactions to market events [15–18]. Moreover, the properties of Bitcoin and gold could begin to interrelate. There may be signs that funds are flowing out of gold to the Bitcoin [19]. A recent contrasting finding suggests that gold did not exhibit safe haven properties against one of the US stock indices (S&P500) during the COVID-19 pandemic [17]. As a result, there might be a possibility that Bitcoin is displacing gold as a safe haven asset amidst the rising momentum of its adoption.

Secondly, the stages and sequences of events in the Bitcoin halving cycle suggest that there may be the existence of regimes in Bitcoin volatility dynamics during each stage or sequence of events. A deeper open problem suggested by past studies [20] is the lack of a fundamental approach to assessing the value and risk of Bitcoin. The potential existence of regimes that are associated with different stages in the Bitcoin halving cycle will only add to the challenges of Bitcoin risk assessment. For instance, Value-at-risk (VaR) is one of the statistical measurements that assess Bitcoin volatility over a specific time frame by determining Bitcoin probability and severity of losses. Since VaR is sensitive toward volatility, regime changes can cause the VaR computed throughout low volatility to understate the actual risk level. Aside from the potential existence of regimes associated with the Bitcoin cycle, black-swan events, such as the COVID-19 pandemic, can also result in the same effect.

The lack of a fundamental approach to Bitcoin risk assessment also has another set of significant implications for Altcoins such as Ethereum (ETH). Agosto and Cafferata [20] examined the co-explosivity in the crypto market and the interdependencies of crypto prices. The authors found high interdependence in the crypto market and that the Bitcoin explosive periods also coincide with the Altcoins'. This finding also aligns with other recent notable studies [21–23]. For instance, Bitcoin is found to be negatively related to Ripple (XRP), and this negative relationship is amplified during bubble periods. The interdependence between cryptocurrency prices, such as the Bitcoin–Ripple relationship, is found to be related to the function of the cryptocurrencies.

In short, due to the extent of Bitcoin's impact on the wider crypto market, it is even more essential to access the Bitcoin risk assessment (VaR) under specific contexts (or regimes). Limited past studies considered the Bitcoin risk assessment (VaR) in the context of the recent COVID-19 pandemic, a spike in the USA's money supply, and a drastic increase in industrial and institutional participation in Bitcoin and Bitcoin supply chain. Furthermore, Bitcoin completed its second halving cycle in May 2020 and entered its third cycle.

Ardia, Bluteau, and Rüede [24] found that regime changes existed in the Bitcoin GARCH volatility dynamics between 19 August 2011, and 2 March 2018. The authors accounted for regime changes in Bitcoin volatility using regime-switching GARCH models, such as the Markov Switching GARCH (MSGARCH) model. The authors found that regime-switching GARCH models suited Bitcoin volatility better than a single-regime GARCH based on Deviance Information Criterion (DIC) and VaR forecasting. Maciel [25] also reported similar findings during this period and showed that regime-switching GARCH forecasted VaR more accurately than its single-regime counterparts. There is also a similar recent study that analyzed how prices transit between different regimes ("bull", "stable, and "bear"), but this study examines the Bitcoin price dynamics at a more granular level based on the unique and well-defined decade-old four-year cycle consisting of three phases with distinctive sequences of events illustrated in Figures 1–3.

*1.2. Objective*

Therefore, the goal of this study is twofold: (1) to examine the safe haven and hedge properties of gold and Bitcoin specifically against the US stock indices before and after the market crash in March 2020; (2) to examine Bitcoin volatility dynamics via Markov-Switching (MS) GARCH models under the above-mentioned context. This work primarily extends the two past studies where one study, [26], examined the safe haven and hedge properties of Bitcoin and gold against the G7 stock market indices between 2010–2018, while the other, [24], studied the regime changes existed in Bitcoin GARCH volatility dynamics between 2011–2018. This study extends these two past studies by investigating periods after 2018 (from 2017 to 2021) where the COVID-19 black-swan event and major developments in Bitcoin adoption occurred that could displace gold.

## 2. The Literature Review

*2.1. Is Gold the Undisputed Hedge against Stock Market Risk*

Gold is a popular commodity for hedging the market and economic turmoil [2,9]. However, contrary to popular belief, the safe haven and hedge properties of gold are not uniform across markets, market conditions, time horizon, and other factors, such as market participant reaction and government intervention [15–18].

Chkili [16] studied the safe haven effect of gold against BRICS (Brazil, Russia, India, China, and South Africa) stock market risk during three major geopolitical and economic crises: the 911 terrorist attacks, the global financial crisis in 2008, and the European debt crisis in 2009. Chkili [16] suggested that gold has a safe haven effect during crises, but the effect varies across the three crises and is also dependent on the magnitude of the shock of the stock market participants toward events. Iqbal [15] reported similar findings, where the hedge effectiveness of gold is not uniformly strong across the gold market conditions in the USA, India, and Pakistan. For example, Iqbal [15] reported that gold could only hedge against the US stock market risk during the gold bull market of 1991–2013. However, a more recent study reported that gold failed to exhibit safe haven properties uniformly across four global stock market indices in the US, Europe, Japan, and China after 16 March 2020 [17]. Akhtaruzzaman et al. [17] attributed this to government intervention via relaxed fiscal and monetary policies.

If gold loses its safe haven properties, investors would be expected to search for alternate assets, such as Bitcoin, for a safe haven. According to Blomberg [27], JPMorgan is predicting a significant shift from gold to Bitcoin. JPMorgan reported that gold has been suffering net money outflows, while more money has been pouring into Bitcoin as it observed a net inflow of $2 billion into Grayscale Bitcoin Trust from October to December and a net outflow of $7 billion for ETF backed by gold [19]. Since Bitcoin is referred to as a digital gold [7], this observation suggests that investors consider Bitcoin a gold replacement as a safe haven during stock market distress. However, there are also studies arguing that Bitcoin is unable to replace gold due to regulatory restrictions (such as anti-money laundering and counterterrorism regulations) and asset security issues (such as the risk of hacking and theft) [28–30].

*2.2. The Safe Haven and Hedge Properties of Gold and Bitcoin against the Stock Market*

There is no consensus on the safe haven properties and hedge ability of Bitcoin toward the stock market, as these properties of an asset are not uniform across markets, market conditions, time horizon, and other factors, such as market participant reaction and government intervention [15–18,31]. Although these studies were conducted before Bitcoin bottomed out in November 2018, these findings can be used to manage stakeholders' expectations when using Bitcoin to hedge against stock market risks.

Thampanya, Nasir, and Huynh [18] examined Bitcoin and gold asymmetric correlation and hedging effectiveness against the Thai stock market and found that neither is a good hedge against the stock market because the correlation between the two commodities and the Thai stock market were found to be positive in most cases for 2000–2019.

Shahzad et al. [26] also studied the safe haven and hedge properties of both gold and Bitcoin against the G7 stock market indices for 2010–2018 and found that Bitcoin was more effective in hedging against the Canadian stock market index relative to gold. This could be because the safe haven property of gold is undermined by the higher concentration of natural resource companies in the Canadian stock index [32]. In terms of safe haven properties, Shahzad et al. [26] found that gold exhibited safe haven and hedge properties against six out of the seven G7 stock market indices, including the US stock market index. On the other hand, Bitcoin only exhibited safe haven properties for two out of seven of the G7 stock market indices and hedge properties against four out of seven of the G7 stock market indices. These findings agree with previous studies during Bitcoin's infancy stage [12,33].

Previous studies also suggested that Bitcoin can hedge against the US stock market. For example, Dyhrbeg [34] argued that Bitcoin shares many similarities with gold based on their similar reactions to variables, such as Federal Funds Rates, the USDEUR exchange rate, and the FTSE index. However, Bitcoin reacts faster to market sentiment relative to gold due to the former's smaller market capitalization.

In summary, disputes related to the safe haven and hedge properties of assets, such as gold and Bitcoin, arise because an asset's safe haven and hedge properties are not uniform across markets, market conditions, time horizon, and other factors, such as market participant reaction and government intervention. For example, one of the most notable and recent findings suggests that gold did not exhibit safe haven properties after the COVID-19 pandemic [17]. Therefore, this study extends Shahzad et al.'s [26] work by examining the safe haven and hedge properties of Bitcoin and gold against three US Stock indices before the COVID-19 pandemic and after the V-shaped recovery from the bottoming out event caused by the COVID-19 pandemic in March 2020.

*2.3. Presence of Regime Changes in Bitcoin GARCH Volatility Dynamics*

Researchers and practitioners extensively use the single-regime GARCH-type models to forecast volatility [24]. One popular application of forecasting volatility using GARCH-type models is to measure the hedge effectiveness of an asset [35]. More recent innovative and novel methods address the non-linear and time-varying characteristics of volatility forecasting. One of the approaches uses non-linear machine learning models to compensate for the linearity of the GARCH models [36]. Hu et al. [36] combined the Long Short Term Memory (LSTM) neural networks, Artificial Neural Networks (ANN), and GARCH to address the non-linear and time-varying characteristics of the factors affecting volatility in copper prices, where GARCH was used to model copper price time-varying volatility while the neural networks were used to engineer more presentative non-linear features from the GARCH model's volatility forecasts along with the other market factors to better forecast copper price volatility. The results showed that GARCH volatility forecasts are meaningful and can significantly improve volatility forecasting when used in conjunction with other market variables and non-linear models.

Recent developments in the field of artificial intelligence also presented new ways to expand Hu et al.'s [36] work. Chan et al. [37,38] developed a novel correlation-embedded attention model that allows the model to learn and associate input variables (also known as 'features') by correlation. This method is useful to mitigate an inherent statistical problem known as multicollinearity. Multicollinearity is a problem where models' features are highly correlated to one another, and the resulting impact is the reduction in generalization ability. Mathematical models, including machine learning models, are prone to the multicollinearity problem [38]. Chan et al. [37,38] found that by introducing a correlation-embedded module, a variation of the attention module, in between the features and the main model, the main model's predictive ability can improve.

Progress in GARCH volatility modeling has advanced its application in financial risk management. The Value-at-Risk (VaR) is widely accepted as an approach to the risk management [39]. VaR measures the quantile distribution of log returns over a specified time horizon [40]. The distribution can then be used to assess asset allocation strategies and the performance of the risk models via the backtesting [41]. Additionally, GARCH is often used to estimate the volatility component of VaR [42], and VaR is also used to benchmark volatility models, such as GARCH models [25].

However, Krause [43] reported that VaR is prone to significant estimation errors and downside bias via manipulation under certain circumstances. For instance, VaR-modeled low volatility can understate the risk of a black-swan event, such as the COVID-19 pandemic. The occurrence of black swan events and time-varying characteristics of market factors suggest a potential presence in an asset's volatility dynamic. Although there are innovative and novel applications related to GARCH volatility forecasting, there are limited studies considering the existence of regimes in GARCH's conditional variance process. Ignoring the potential existence of regimes in GARCH's conditional variance process can lead to inaccurate and biased volatility forecasts [44].

Ardia, Bluteau, and Rüede [24] found that regime changes existed in Bitcoin's GARCH volatility dynamics between 19 August 2011 and 2 March 2018. The authors accounted for regime changes in Bitcoin volatility using regime-switching GARCH models such as the Markov Switching GARCH (MSGARCH) model. The authors found that regime-switching GARCH models Bitcoin volatility better than single-regime GARCH based on Deviance Information Criterion (DIC) and VaR forecasting. Maciel [25] also reported similar findings during this period and showed that regime-switching GARCH forecasted VaR more accurately than its single-regime counterparts. However, due to the events occurring beyond 2018 (the COVID-19 black-swan event and major development in Bitcoin adoption), it is crucial to investigate whether these findings could be extrapolated beyond 2018.

## 3. Methodology

The model used in this study to test the safe haven property of a hedge asset is proposed by Baur and McDermott [2]. The presence of regime changes in Bitcoin volatility dynamics is assessed via regime-switching models.

*3.1. The Dataset*

The three US stock indices examined in this study are the Dow Jones Industrial Average, Nasdaq 100, and the S&P500. US stock indices were specifically selected out of the G7 countries because only the US (fifth) was ranked among the top 10 in the 2022 Global Crypto Adoption Index [45]. The daily price data was extracted directly from the respective stock exchanges. The daily price data of Bitcoin was extracted from CoinDesk, while the daily price data of spot gold was extracted from Investing.com. Similar to Shahzad et al. [26], the empirical analysis was conducted with the percentage change of the daily data (daily return) from October 2017 to February 2021. The sample period covered a brief period before and after the COVID-19 pandemic to examine the timely properties of gold and Bitcoin right before the pandemic and during the pandemic.

The dataset is split into two subsets. The first subset covers the period before the COVID-19 market crash, from 1 October 2017 to 28 February 2020, while the second subset is identical to the original dataset, covering the period between October 2017 to February 2021.

*3.2. Safe Haven and Hedge Properties Testing*

According to Baur and McDermott [2], the safe haven and hedge properties are estimated via the following equations:

$$r_{hedgeasset,t} = a + b_t r_{stock,t} + e_t \qquad (1)$$

$$b_t = c_0 + c_1 D(r_{stock}, q_{10}) + c_2 D(r_{stock}, q_5) + c_3 D(r_{stock}, q_1), \qquad (2)$$

where:

1. $r_t$ denotes the return of an asset at time $t$;

2. $D(.)$ denotes dummy variables;
3. $Q_i$ denotes the $i$-th quantile of an asset's return;
4. $e_t$ is the error term at time $t$.

The parameters to estimate in Equations (1) and (2) are $a$, $c_0$, $c_1$, $c_2$, and $c_3$. The dummy variable $D(.)$ is used to capture extreme stock movements. The respective dummy variables $D(.)$ equals 1 when a stock index return exceeds 10%, 5%, and 1% quantile of the return's distribution. The haven benchmark for a hedge asset (Bitcoin or gold) is shown in Table 1.

**Table 1.** Safe Haven and Hedge Properties Benchmark.

| Condition | Conclusion |
| --- | --- |
| If $c_1$, $c_2$ or $c_3$ is significantly different from 0 | There is a non-linear relationship between the hedged asset and the stock index. |
| If $c_0$, $c_1$, $c_2$ and $c_3$ are less than or equal to 0 | The hedge asset is a weak safe haven |
| If $c_1$, $c_2$ and $c_3$ are less than 0 and is statistically significant | The hedge asset is a strong safe haven |
| If $c_0$ is zero, and the sum of $c_1$, $c_2$, and $c_3$ is less than 0 and $c_0$ | The hedge asset is a weak hedge |
| If $c_0$ is less than zero, and the sum of $c_1$, $c_2$, and $c_3$ is less than 0 and $c_0$ | The hedge asset is a strong hedge |

Adekoya, Oliyide, and Oduyemi [46] argued that time-variation and regime changes should also be considered in the estimation process. By taking into account regime changes, the general theoretical exposition can be defined as:

$$r_{hedgeasset,t} = (\beta_1 + \alpha_1 r_{stock\ market,t})\ I[q_t \leq \gamma] + (\beta_2 + \alpha_2 r_{stock\ market,t})\ I[q_t > \gamma] + error_t, \quad (3)$$

where $qt$ is the threshold variable and y is the threshold value.

The threshold value, y, divides the observations (extracted daily prices of the seven market indices, spot gold, and Bitcoin) into distinct regimes (assuming two regimes). $I(.)$ is the indicator operator, where $I(.)$ equals one if the observation falls into the specified regime [46]. The switching regression model assumes a total of two distinct regression models, one for each regime. Referring to Equation (1), the conditional mean in each regime, n, is assumed to adhere to the following specifications:

$$\phi t(n) = \alpha_n + Z'_t \delta_m, \quad (4)$$

where $\alpha_n$ and $\delta_m$ are regime-specific coefficients, while $Z'_t$ denotes the vector of regressor (the logarithmic first difference of a stock market index price).

This study adopts Baur and McDermott's [2] framework to examine the safe haven and hedge properties of gold and Bitcoin due to arbitrariness of the threshold variable, $qt$, from Adekoya, Oliyide, and Oduyemi's [46] proposed framework. Therefore, regime changes were examined following the framework proposed by Ardia, Bluteau, and Rüede [24].

### 3.3. Testing Presence of Regime Changes

The MSGARCH model is defined as follows:

$$y_t\ |\ (s_t = k, I_{t-1}) \sim D(0, h_{k,t}, \xi_k), \quad (5)$$

where:
1. $y_t$ denotes the Bitcoin daily log-return at time t;
2. $s_t$ denotes the state variable;
3. k denotes the number of states;
4. $I_{t-1}$ denotes the information set available up to $t-1$;
5. $\xi_k$ is a vector of additional shape parameters;
6. $h_{k,t}$ is a time-varying conditional variance in regime k;

7. $D(0, h_{k,t}, \xi_k)$ is a continuous distribution with zero mean.

The asymmetric properties of the Bitcoin cycle can be identified by computing the expected duration for each state/regime [31]. The expected duration can be estimated by using the following formula:

$$E(D) = 1/(1 - p_{ii}),  \quad (6)$$

where $p_{ii}$ is the transition probability from state/regime i to state/regime i.

Symmetric GARCH(1,1) and asymmetric GJR(1,1) specifications for the conditional variance are considered and defined as Equation. Furthermore, (7) and (8), respectively, are as follows:

$$h_{k,t} \equiv w_k + \alpha_k y^2_{t-1} + \beta_k h_{k,t-1} \quad (7)$$

$$h_{k,t} \equiv w_k + (\alpha_k + \gamma_k I y_{t-1} < 0\}) y^2_{t-1} + \beta_k h_{k,t-1}),  \quad (8)$$

where $I$ denotes an indicator function.

Normal distribution was used, and up to two regimes were considered, leading to four models overall. This methodology aligns with Ardia, Bluteau, and Rüede's [24] findings that the two-regime is preferable because it offers better fitting quality and model complexity than the single-regime counterpart while gains from the three-regime counterpart are attributed to normal distribution variability. The models were optimized using the maximum likelihood estimation (MLE), and the performances of the models were evaluated with Akaike's Information Criteria (AIC) and Bayesian Information Criteria (BIC).

The prediction performance of MSGARCH and traditional single-regime models were also evaluated against the out-sample one-step-ahead VaR prediction. A total of 2490 daily observations from 18 September 2014 to 19 July 2021 were used, where a rolling window of 1500 log returns was backtested over 990 out-of-sample daily observations from October 27th, 2018, to July 19th, 2021. Bitcoin's past two halving cycles suggest that each cycle would span four years (or 1460 days). Hence, a rolling window size of 1500 was used. The model parameters were updated every hundredth observation. The accuracy of the 5% VaR prediction was evaluated using conditional coverage (CC) test statistics and the Dynamic Quantile (DQ) test [24,47,48].

## 4. Results and Discussions

This section reports the findings using the methodology discussed in the previous section. The discussion is divided into two main subsections, Section 4.1 presents the results and discussion for Bitcoin and gold, while Section 4.2 report the findings of MSGARCH, and in-sample and out-of-sample analysis for the changes in Bitcoin price.

### 4.1. Bitcoin Safe Haven and Hedging Properties

The results and discussions are discussed in the following section. Section 4.1.1 discuss the descriptive statistics and the findings of the stationarity test, and Section 4.1.2 presents the hedge properties results for gold and Bitcoin.

4.1.1. Results for Descriptive Statistics and Stationarity Test

Daily prices for Bitcoin (BTC), gold (XAU), S&P500 (SPY), Nasdaq (NAS), and Dow Jones Index (DJI) from October 2017 to July 2021 were obtained. According to Table 2, all five assets have positive average returns during the designated period. Bitcoin has the highest return and the highest volatility, implying that its high risk (volatility) is met with high returns, consistent with [26]. Sharpe Ratio represents the trade-off between return and risk. Although Bitcoin's high volatility is compensated with high returns, Bitcoin Sharpe Ratio showed that it does not provide the optimal risk-return trade-off during the designated period. All five assets are negatively skewed, indicating that Bitcoin, gold, and the US stock market are skewed towards positive returns during the period. ADF test shows that all datasets are stationary.

Table 2. Descriptive Statistics and stationarity test for gold, Bitcoin, and 3 US stock indices. *** represents 99% confidence level.

| Assets | Number of Observations | Mean | Std Dev | ADF Statistics | Skewness | Kurtosis | Sharpe Ratio |
|---|---|---|---|---|---|---|---|
| BTC | 955 | 0.2 | 5.064 | −16.15 *** | −0.981 | 10.568 | 0.039 |
| XAU | 955 | 0.037 | 0.877 | −16.13 *** | −0.669 | 4.724 | 0.042 |
| SPY | 955 | 0.056 | 1.357 | −9.07 *** | −1.074 | 18.245 | 0.041 |
| NAS | 955 | 0.094 | 1.577 | −9.88 *** | −0.754 | 9.78 | 0.06 |
| DJI | 955 | 0.045 | 1.427 | −9.39 *** | −1.098 | 20.609 | 0.032 |

4.1.2. Safe Haven and Hedge Properties Test Findings and Results

The safe haven and hedge properties test results of Bitcoin and gold before and after the COVID-19 market crash are discussed here. By referring to Table 3, before the pandemic (October 2017 to February 2020), gold was a safe haven for the S&P500 and the Nasdaq and a strong hedge against all three stock indices. The estimates also indicated that gold is not a safe haven against the Dow Jones Index because the relationship between the two respective assets is positive during extreme market movements and c1 and c3, though the relationship is generally negative (c0). For a portfolio comprising all three US stock indices equally weighted, gold would be both a safe haven and a hedge toward the portfolio.

Table 3. Estimated Parameters for Safe Haven and Hedge Testing for gold and Bitcoin from October 2017 to February 2020. ** represents 95% confidence level.

| | Gold | | | | Bitcoin | | | |
|---|---|---|---|---|---|---|---|---|
| | Hedge ($c_0$) | 0.1 ($c_1$) | 0.05 ($c_2$) | 0.01 ($c_3$) | Hedge ($c_0$) | 0.1 ($c_1$) | 0.05 ($c_2$) | 0.01 ($c_3$) |
| S&P500 | −0.322 | −0.154 | −0.185 ** | −0.078 | −0.024 | −0.676 | −0.0073 | 0.7462 |
| NASDAQ | −0.0435 | −0.082 | −0.0823 | −0.0471 | 0.0478 | −0.444 | −0.133 | 0.4 |
| Dow Jones Index | −0.0693 | 0.064 | −0.195 ** | 0.02516 | 0.01 | −0.24 | −0.28 | 0.87 |
| US Market Portfolio | −0.0501 | −0.13 | −0.113 | −0.051 | 0.121 | −1.01 | −0.27 | 0.65 |

However, by referring to Table 4, this study found that gold did not exhibit safe haven and hedge properties against all three stock indices for the period after the COVID-19 market crash in March 2020. This result aligns with Akhtaruzzaman et al. [17] and can be explained by the change in the correlation between gold and the three US stock market indices before and after the COVID-19 market crash in March 2020.

Table 4. Estimated Parameters for Safe Haven and Hedge Testing for gold and Bitcoin from October 2017 to February 2021. * Represents 90% confidence level; ** represents 95% confidence level; *** represents 99% confidence level.

| | Gold | | | | Bitcoin | | | |
|---|---|---|---|---|---|---|---|---|
| | Hedge ($c_0$) | 0.1 ($c_1$) | 0.05 ($c_2$) | 0.01 ($c_3$) | Hedge ($c_0$) | 0.1 ($c_1$) | 0.05 ($c_2$) | 0.01 ($c_3$) |
| S&P500 | 0.069 ** | 0.113 | 0.201 *** | 0.037 | 0.563 *** | 0.652 | 0.297 | 1.162 *** |
| NASDAQ | 0.052 ** | 0.013 | 0.096 * | 0.059 | 0.473 *** | 0.497 | 0.117 | 1.244 *** |
| Dow Jones Index | 0.027 | 0.053 | 0.192 *** | 0.078 | 0.418 ** | 0.124 | 0.315 | 1.152 *** |
| US Market Portfolio | 0.074 ** | 0.25 *** | 0.143 ** | 0.031 | 0.581 *** | 1.056 ** | 0.21 | 1.112 *** |

Correlation can be a simple precursor toward a hedge asset's safe haven and hedge properties (gold or Bitcoin). As per Baur and McDermott's [2] model, safe haven and hedge properties are determined by the coefficients (relationship) between the asset and the hedged asset during normal and extreme downside market movements, as captured by the parameters c0, c1, c2, and c3. The discrepancy between the correlation and Baur and McDermott's model [2] is due to measuring the relationship between the asset and hedge asset during extreme market movements. Correlation aggregates all market movements, while Baur and McDermott [2] separate the measurements for regular market movements (c0) and extreme downside market movements (c1,c2, and c3), which means that the relationship between the asset and hedge asset must also be zero or negative even during extreme negative market movements to be regarded as a safe haven and a hedge using Baur and McDermott's [2] framework, where parameters c0, c1, c2, and c3 would be zero or negative if the hedge assets (gold and Bitcoin) have no or negative correlation to the assets (the three US stock indices) during normal and extreme market movements.

According to Table 5, gold is negatively correlated to the three US stock indices relative to Bitcoin, implying that gold could generally be an excellent safe haven and hedge. When the safe haven properties and hedge properties are scrutinized further using Baur and McDermott's [2] model, gold is indeed a strong hedge against all three US stock indices and a safe haven against the S&P500 and NASDAQ. Although gold was negatively correlated to the Dow Jones index, gold was not a safe haven for the Dow Jones Index because the relationship between gold and the Dow Jones Index was not zero or negative during extreme movements (c1 and c3), even though it was generally negative (c0).

**Table 5.** Correlation Table for the period October 2017 to February 2020.

|  | SPY | NAS | DJI |
| --- | --- | --- | --- |
| BTC | 0.009589 | 0.008211 | 0.016471 |
| XAU | −0.14366 | −0.13702 | −0.14673 |

According to Table 6, gold's negative correlation to the three US stock indices turned positive, implying that gold was unlikely to retain its safe haven and hedge properties. This implication was confirmed by Baur and McDermott's [2] model's test results. Tables 5 and 6 indicate that Bitcoin was positively correlated to all three stock indices before and after the COVID-19 market crash, suggesting that Bitcoin is unlikely to exhibit safe haven or hedge properties against the US stock indices. This implication can also be confirmed by Baur and McDermott's [2] model test results, where Bitcoin is neither a safe haven nor a hedge against the US stock market.

**Table 6.** Correlation Table for the Period from October 2017 to July 2021.

|  | SPY | NAS | DJI |
| --- | --- | --- | --- |
| BTC | 0.214 | 0.207 | 0.204 |
| XAU | 0.058 | 0.085 | 0.039 |

It is not surprising that Bitcoin failed to exhibit safe haven and hedge properties. This is because Baur and McDermott's [2] model suggests that the relationship between the hedge asset (Bitcoin) price and an asset (stock index) should be negative to exhibit safe haven and hedge properties. However, the Bitcoin halving cycle suggests that Bitcoin price movement strictly follows specific sequences of events and not the stock market. Hence, there are instances when Bitcoin is positively or negatively correlated to the stock market as Bitcoin follows through its halving cycles. This explains Bitcoin's time-varying safe haven and hedge properties reported by previous studies [15–18].

*4.2. Presence of Regime Changes in Bitcoin Volatility*

4.2.1. Descriptive Statistics and Stationarity Test for Bitcoin Price

The dataset used to test the regime changes in Bitcoin volatility extends from 18 September 2014 to 19 July 2021, because more data is required to conduct the rolling window one step ahead of VaR forecasting. Table 7 represents the descriptive statistics and stationarity tests for the daily log return of Bitcoin for the period from 18 September 2014 to 19 July 2021. The mean and median values are 0.167% and 0.19742%, respectively. The standard deviation is 3.96% or 75.65%, annually. Thus, similar to the values in Table 1, Bitcoin is moderately skewed towards positive returns during the designated period.

**Table 7.** Descriptive Statistics and stationarity test for Bitcoin.

| Statistics | Value |
| --- | --- |
| Observations | 2490 |
| Mean (%) | 0.167 |
| Median (%) | 0.19742 |
| Standard Deviation (%) | 3.96 |
| ADF $p$-value | 0.01 |
| Skewness | −0.824 |
| Kurtosis | 11.624 |
| Sharpe Ratio | 0.042 |
| VaR (5%) (%) | 11.35 |
| JB $p$-value | <0.01 |

4.2.2. In-Sample and Out-of-Sample Analysis

Based on the Bitcoin halving cycle, this study expects the two-regime Markov-switching models to outperform their single-regime counterparts because each cycle consists of distinct stages, and each stage consists of a specific sequence of events. The distinctiveness between each stage suggests the presence of regime changes.

The in-sample analysis is considered by fitting the four models to Bitcoin's complete historical data from 18 September 2014 to 19 July 2021. The goodness-of-fit of the models is evaluated using AIC and BIC. Table 8 shows the AIC and BIC of the four models. It can be seen that both the two-regime models offer better fitting quality and model complexity trade-offs than their single-regime counterparts for all specifications. Table 9 shows the parameter estimates of the best in-sample model, which is the two-regime Markov-switching GJR model. For comparison, the parameter estimates for the single-regime GJR model are also reported. The results showed that the positive leverage effect of the single-regime GJR and both regimes of the two-regime Markov-Switching GJR are positive, implying a negative correlation between volatility and Bitcoin returns [49,50].

**Table 8.** Goodness-of-fit.

|  | AIC | BIC |
| --- | --- | --- |
| Single-regime |  |  |
| GARCH | −9453 | −9436 |
| GJR | −9461 | −9437 |
| Two-regime |  |  |
| GARCH | −10,172 | −10,126 |
| GJR | −10,184 | −10,126 |

The results in Table 9 showed the unconditional volatilities of the two-regime Markov-Switching GJR as 8.1% and 250%, suggesting that the regimes are associated with low and high unconditional volatilities, respectively.

However, the high volatility regime is not as persistent as the low volatility regime, with transition probabilities p11 and p22 at 0.8142 and 0.3526, respectively. The resulting expected duration for state/regime one and state/regime two is 5.382 days and 1.545 days, respectively. This implies that the relationship between the Bitcoin high volatility regime and the low volatility regime is asymmetric.

Table 9. Parameter Estimate.

|  | Single Regime | 2-Regime |
|---|---|---|
| Regime k = 1 |  |  |
| w1 | 0.0001 | 0 |
| a1 | 0.1143 | 0.459 |
| y1 | 0.0605 | 0.0001 |
| b1 | 0.8243 | 0.594 |
| UV1 | 93.74% | 8.10% |
| Regime k = 2 |  |  |
| w2 |  | 0.008 |
| a2 |  | 0.08 |
| y2 |  | 0.2704 |
| b2 |  | 0.7388 |
| UV2 |  | 250% |

The persistence of the low volatility regime one is illustrated in Figure 6, where the smoothed probabilities P[st = k | It] for the low volatility and high volatility regimes are plotted.

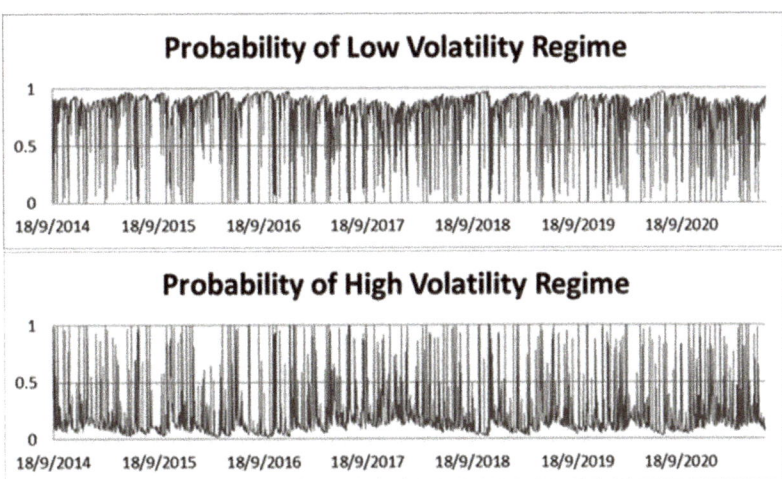

Figure 6. Smoothed Probabilities for two-regime GJR model.

The out-of-sample analysis is considered via the performance of the four models to forecast the one-day VaR. Table 10 reports the one-day ahead VaR results at 5% risk levels.

The results show that the single regime GJR failed the CC test at a 10% confidence level, while the null hypothesis of correct VaR forecasting for the two-regime cannot be rejected.

Overall, the Markov-switching GARCH models have the best in-sample performance and out-of-sample VaR forecasting performance. Furthermore, since the Markov-switching model can account for the structural breaks in GARCH, the Markov-switching GARCH model's superior in-sample and out-of-sample performance suggest regime changes in Bitcoin volatility [24,25].

Table 10. *p*-values for the CC test and DQ test for the one-day ahead 5% VaR.

|  | CC-Test | DQ-Test |
|---|---|---|
| **Single-Regime** | | |
| GJR | 0.115 | 0.552 |
| GARCH | 0.0576 | 0.42 |
| **2-Regime** | | |
| GJR | 0.43 | 0.94 |
| GARCH | 0.313 | 0.913 |

Although the results align with the expectations based on the Bitcoin halving cycle, the whole expectation was not realized. Due to the non-persistence of regime two illustrated in Figure 4, this study found that the regime changes are associated with low and high volatility rather than the distinct stages during the Bitcoin halving cycle.

## 5. Conclusions

This study introduces a unique perspective on the Bitcoin safe haven and hedge properties through Bitcoin's decade-old halving cycle. This study showed that Bitcoin halving cycle might be able to explain the time-varying safe haven and hedge properties reported by previous studies [15–18], where time periods with safe haven and hedge properties might coincide with periods of negative correlation (as required by Baur and McDermott's framework [2]). This might also be the reason Bitcoin failed to exhibit safe haven and hedge properties despite major industrial and institutional Bitcoin adoption and the fund outflow from gold into Bitcoin. Practically, this finding suggests that investors should not invest in Bitcoin for Bitcoin safe haven and hedge properties because time periods with safe haven and hedge properties might coincide with periods of negative correlation. On the other hand, this study provided additional evidence showing that gold also failed to exhibit safe haven and hedge properties after the pandemic; this aligns with the findings of past studies. One possible explanation for gold's loss of safe haven and hedge properties is the funds' outflow from gold-related ETFs during the pandemic. Since Bitcoin also failed to exhibit safe haven and hedge properties, Bitcoin has yet to displace gold as the new safe haven commodity.

As shown in this study, Bitcoin halving cycle is well-defined in terms of price volatility and timing and is also independent (not correlated) to the stock market. This violates one of the conditions required, proposed by Baur and McDermott [2], to exhibit safe haven and hedge properties, which are a negative correlation to the stock market. Therefore, in this respect, findings related to the safe haven and hedge properties of Bitcoin and gold may not extrapolate beyond the COVID-19 black-swan event and should be reinvestigated in the future.

Findings related to regime changes in Bitcoin's GARCH volatility dynamics could be extrapolated well beyond the COVID-19 black-swan event, as this study is consistent with the findings from past studies before the COVID-19 pandemic. This study found that regimes do exist in Bitcoin's GARCH volatility dynamics through the pandemic. Therefore, the Markov-switching model remains recommended over its single-regime counterparts with low and high volatility periods rather than the distinct stages of a Bitcoin halving cycle. Moreover, the relationship between low and high volatility regimes are asymmetric. Future studies could consider using more recent techniques to improve the robustness of the safe haven and hedge properties framework [2] and regime change models [24] to better address Bitcoin's time-varying properties. We also recommend future studies revisit Bitcoin safe haven and hedge properties in the future as continued industrial and institutional adoption may break Bitcoin's decade-old halving cycle.

**Author Contributions:** J.Y.-L.C. investigated the ideas, and reviewed the systems and methods; J.Y.-L.C. provided the survey studies and methods; J.Y.-L.C. conceived of the presented ideas and wrote the manuscript with support from S.W.P., S.Y.P., W.K.C. and Y.-L.C.; S.W.P., S.Y.P., W.K.C. and Y.-L.C. provided the suggestions on the experimental setup and the analytical results; J.Y.-L.C. and S.W.P. provided the suggestions on the research ideas, analytical results, and wrote the manuscript; S.W.P. and Y.-L.C. provided funding supports and wrote the manuscript. All authors have read and agreed to the published version of the manuscript.

**Funding:** The author(s) disclosed receipt of the following financial support for this research, authorship, and/or publication of this article: this research was funded by the Fundamental Research Grant Scheme (FRGS) provided by the Ministry of Higher Education, Malaysia, Grant number FRGS/1/2019/STG06/UM/02/9. This work was also funded by the National Science and Technology Council in Taiwan, under grant numbers MOST-109-2628-E-027-004–MY3, MOST-111-2218-E-027-003, and MOST-110-2622-8-027-006, and also supported by the Ministry of Education of Taiwan under Official Document No. 1112303249 entitled "The study of artificial intelligence and advanced semiconductor manufacturing for female STEM talent education and industry–university value-added cooperation pro-motion".

**Institutional Review Board Statement:** Not applicable.

**Informed Consent Statement:** Not applicable.

**Data Availability Statement:** There are no data applicable to this study.

**Conflicts of Interest:** The authors declare no conflict of interest.

## References

1. Meynkhard, A. Fair market value of bitcoin: Halving effect. *Invest. Manag. Financ. Innov.* **2019**, *16*, 72–85. [CrossRef]
2. Baur, D.G.; McDermott, T.K. Is gold a safe haven? International evidence. *J. Bank. Financ.* **2010**, *34*, 1886–1898. [CrossRef]
3. Kharpal, A. After a Bitcoin Crackdown, China Now Calls It an 'Investment Alternative' in a Significant Shift in Tone. Available online: https://www.cnbc.com/2021/04/19/china-calls-bitcoin-an-investment-alternative-marking-shift-in-tone.html (accessed on 30 September 2022).
4. Stankiewicz, K. BlackRock's Rick Rieder Says the World's Largest Asset Manager Has 'Started to Dabble' in Bitcoin. Available online: https://www.cnbc.com/2021/02/17/blackrock-has-started-to-dabble-in-bitcoin-says-rick-rieder.html (accessed on 30 September 2022).
5. CoinBase. Shareholder Letter. Available online: https://www.sec.gov/Archives/edgar/data/1679788/000167978821000005/q121shareholderletter.htm (accessed on 30 September 2022).
6. Figueras, V. Bitcoin Price Prediction: $400,000 Possible If This Happens, Ark CEO Reveals. Available online: https://www.ibtimes.com/bitcoin-price-prediction-400000-possible-if-happens-ark-ceo-reveals-3143300 (accessed on 2 November 2021).
7. Su, C.-W.; Qin, M.; Tao, R.; Zhang, X. Is the status of gold threatened by Bitcoin? *Econ. Res.-Ekon. Istraživanja* **2020**, *33*, 420–437. [CrossRef]
8. Chang, B.H.; Rajput, S.K.O.; Ahmed, P.; Hayat, Z. Does gold act as a hedge or a safe haven? Evidence from Pakistan. *Pak. Dev. Rev.* **2020**, *59*, 69–80. [CrossRef]
9. Lin, F.-L.; Yang, S.-Y.; Marsh, T.; Chen, Y.-F. Stock and bond return relations and stock market uncertainty: Evidence from wavelet analysis. *Int. Rev. Econ. Financ.* **2018**, *55*, 285–294. [CrossRef]
10. Phoong, S.W.; Sek, S.K. A Markov switching vector error correction model on oil price and gold price effect on stock market returns. *Inf. Manag. Bus. Rev.* **2013**, *5*, 331–336. [CrossRef]
11. Baur, D.G.; Hong, K.; Lee, A.D. Bitcoin: Medium of exchange or speculative assets? *J. Int. Financ. Mark. Inst. Money* **2018**, *54*, 177–189. [CrossRef]
12. Klein, T.; Thu, H.P.; Walther, T. Bitcoin is not the New Gold–A comparison of volatility, correlation, and portfolio performance. *Int. Rev. Financ. Anal.* **2018**, *59*, 105–116. [CrossRef]
13. Gkillas, K.; Longin, F. Is Bitcoin the new digital gold? Evidence from extreme price movements in financial markets. In *Evidence From Extreme Price Movements in Financial Markets*; 2018. Available online: https://papers.ssrn.com/sol3/papers.cfm?abstract_id=3245571 (accessed on 30 September 2022).
14. EBouri, E.; Molnár, P.; Azzi, G.; Roubaud, D.; Hagfors, L.I. On the hedge and safe haven properties of Bitcoin: Is it really more than a diversifier? *Financ. Res. Lett.* **2017**, *20*, 192–198.
15. Iqbal, J. Does gold hedge stock market, inflation and exchange rate risks? An econometric investigation. *Int. Rev. Econ. Financ.* **2017**, *48*, 1–17. [CrossRef]

16. Chkili, W. Dynamic correlations and hedging effectiveness between gold and stock markets: Evidence for BRICS countries. *Res. Int. Bus. Financ.* **2016**, *38*, 22–34. [CrossRef]
17. Akhtaruzzaman, M.; Boubaker, S.; Lucey, B.M.; Sensoy, A. Is gold a hedge or safe haven asset during COVID–19 crisis? *Econ. Model.* **2020**, *102*, 105588. [CrossRef]
18. Thampanya, N.; Nasir, M.A.; Huynh, T.L.D. Asymmetric correlation and hedging effectiveness of gold & cryptocurrencies: From pre-industrial to the 4th industrial revolution☆. *Technol. Forecast. Soc. Chang.* **2020**, *159*, 120195. [PubMed]
19. Spence, E. JPMorgan Says Gold Will Suffer for Years Because of Bitcoin. Available online: https://www.bloomberg.com/news/articles/2020-12-09/jpmorgan-says-gold-will-suffer-for-years-because-of-bitcoin (accessed on 30 September 2022).
20. Agosto, A.; Cafferata, A. Financial Bubbles: A Study of Co-Explosivity in the Cryptocurrency Market. *Risks* **2020**, *8*, 34. [CrossRef]
21. Corbet, S.; Meegan, A.; Larkin, C.; Lucey, B.; Yarovaya, L. Exploring the dynamic relationships between cryptocurrencies and other financial assets. *Econ. Lett.* **2018**, *165*, 28–34. [CrossRef]
22. Yi, S.; Xu, Z.; Wang, G.-J. Volatility connectedness in the cryptocurrency market: Is Bitcoin a dominant cryptocurrency? *Int. Rev. Financ. Anal.* **2018**, *60*, 98–114. [CrossRef]
23. Giudici, P.; Abu-Hashish, I. What determines bitcoin exchange prices? A network VAR approach. *Financ. Res. Lett.* **2019**, *28*, 309–318. [CrossRef]
24. Ardia, D.; Bluteau, K.; Rüede, M. Regime changes in Bitcoin GARCH volatility dynamics. *Financ. Res. Lett.* **2019**, *29*, 266–271. [CrossRef]
25. Maciel, L. Cryptocurrencies value-at-risk and expected shortfall: Do regime-switching volatility models improve forecasting? *Int. J. Financ. Econ.* **2020**, *26*, 4840–4855. [CrossRef]
26. Shahzad, S.J.H.; Bouri, E.; Roubaud, D.; Kristoufek, L. Safe haven, hedge and diversification for G7 stock markets: Gold versus bitcoin. *Econ. Model.* **2020**, *87*, 212–224. [CrossRef]
27. Spence, E. JPMorgan Says Gold Will Suffer for Years Because of Bitcoin. Available online: https://www.bnnbloomberg.ca/jpmorgan-says-gold-will-suffer-for-years-because-of-bitcoin-1.1533933 (accessed on 30 September 2022).
28. Bradbury, D. The problem with Bitcoin. *Comput. Fraud. Secur.* **2013**, *2013*, 5–8. [CrossRef]
29. Conti, M.; Kumar, E.S.; Lal, C.; Ruj, S. A survey on security and privacy issues of bitcoin. *IEEE Commun. Surv. Tutor.* **2018**, *20*, 3416–3452. [CrossRef]
30. Zaghloul, E.; Li, T.; Mutka, M.W.; Ren, J. Bitcoin and blockchain: Security and privacy. *IEEE Internet Things J.* **2020**, *7*, 10288–10313. [CrossRef]
31. Phoong, S.W.; Phoong, S.Y.; Phoong, K.H. Analysis of structural changes in financial datasets using the breakpoint test and the Markov switching model. *Symmetry* **2020**, *12*, 401. [CrossRef]
32. Beckmann, J.; Berger, T.; Czudaj, R. Does gold act as a hedge or a safe haven for stocks? A smooth transition approach. *Econ. Model.* **2015**, *48*, 16–24. [CrossRef]
33. Chowdhury, A. Is Bitcoin the "Paris Hilton" of the currency world? Or are the early investors onto something that will make them rich? *J. Invest.* **2016**, *25*, 64–72. [CrossRef]
34. Dyhrberg, A.H. Bitcoin, gold and the dollar—A GARCH volatility analysis. *Financ. Res. Lett.* **2016**, *16*, 85–92. [CrossRef]
35. Dai, Z.; Zhu, H.; Zhang, X. Dynamic spillover effects and portfolio strategies between crude oil, gold and Chinese stock markets related to new energy vehicle. *Energy Econ.* **2022**, *109*, 105959. [CrossRef]
36. Hu, Y.; Ni, J.; Wen, L. A hybrid deep learning approach by integrating LSTM-ANN networks with GARCH model for copper price volatility prediction. *Phys. A Stat. Mech. Its Appl.* **2020**, *557*, 124907. [CrossRef]
37. Chan, J.Y.-L.; Leow, S.M.H.; Bea, K.T.; Cheng, W.K.; Phoong, S.W.; Hong, Z.-W.; Lin, J.-M.; Chen, Y.-L. A Correlation-Embedded Attention Module to Mitigate Multicollinearity: An Algorithmic Trading Application. *Mathematics* **2022**, *10*, 1231. [CrossRef]
38. Chan, J.Y.-L.; Leow, S.M.H.; Bea, K.T.; Cheng, W.K.; Phoong, S.W.; Hong, Z.-W.; Chen, Y.-L. Mitigating the Multicollinearity Problem and Its Machine Learning Approach: A Review. *Mathematics* **2022**, *10*, 1283. [CrossRef]
39. Liu, W.; Semeyutin, A.; Lau, C.K.M.; Gozgor, G. Forecasting Value-at-Risk of Cryptocurrencies with RiskMetrics type models. *Res. Int. Bus. Financ.* **2020**, *54*, 101259. [CrossRef]
40. Philippe, J. *Value at Risk: The New Benchmark for Managing Financial Risk*; McGraw-Hill: New York, NY, USA, 2001.
41. Ardia, D.; Bluteau, K.; Boudt, K.; Catania, L. Forecasting risk with Markov-switching GARCH models: A large-scale performance study. *Int. J. Forecast.* **2018**, *34*, 733–747. [CrossRef]
42. Emenogu, N.G.; Adenomon, M.O.; Nweze, N.O. On the volatility of daily stock returns of Total Nigeria Plc: Evidence from GARCH models, value-at-risk and backtesting. *Financ. Innov.* **2020**, *6*, 18. [CrossRef]
43. Krause, A. Exploring the limitations of value at risk: How good is it in practice? *J. Risk Financ.* **2003**, *4*, 19–28. [CrossRef]
44. Lamoureux, C.G.; Lastrapes, W.D. Persistence in variance, structural change, and the GARCH model. *J. Bus. Econ. Stat.* **1990**, *8*, 225–234.
45. The 2022 Global Crypto Adoption Index: Emerging Markets Lead in Grassroots Adoption, China Remains Active Despite Ban, and Crypto Fundamentals Appear Healthy. Available online: https://blog.chainalysis.com/reports/2022-global-crypto-adoption-index/ (accessed on 30 September 2022).
46. Adekoya, O.B.; Oliyide, J.A.; Oduyemi, G.O. How COVID-19 upturns the hedging potentials of gold against oil and stock markets risks: Nonlinear evidences through threshold regression and markov-regime switching models. *Resour. Policy* **2020**, *70*, 101926. [CrossRef]

47. Christoffersen, P.F. Evaluating interval forecasts. *Int. Econ. Rev.* **1998**, *39*, 841–862. [CrossRef]
48. Engle, R.F.; Manganelli, S. CAViaR: Conditional autoregressive value at risk by regression quantiles. *J. Bus. Econ. Stat.* **2004**, *22*, 367–381. [CrossRef]
49. Ait-Sahalia, Y.; Fan, J.; Li, Y. The leverage effect puzzle: Disentangling sources of bias at high frequency. *J. Financ. Econ.* **2013**, *109*, 224–249. [CrossRef]
50. de Sousa Filho, F.; Silva, J.; Bertella, M.; Brigatti, E. The leverage effect and other stylized facts displayed by Bitcoin returns. *Braz. J. Phys.* **2021**, *51*, 576–586. [CrossRef]

**Disclaimer/Publisher's Note:** The statements, opinions and data contained in all publications are solely those of the individual author(s) and contributor(s) and not of MDPI and/or the editor(s). MDPI and/or the editor(s) disclaim responsibility for any injury to people or property resulting from any ideas, methods, instructions or products referred to in the content.

*Article*

# Government Interventions and Sovereign Bond Market Volatility during COVID-19: A Quantile Analysis

Claudiu Tiberiu Albulescu and Eugenia Grecu *

Management Department, Politehnica University of Timisoara, P-ta Victoriei, No. 2, 300006 Timisoara, Romania
* Correspondence: eugenia.grecu@upt.ro

**Abstract:** We test the interaction between governments' COVID-19 interventions, COVID-19-induced uncertainty, and the volatility of sovereign bonds. Different from previous literature, we investigate the asymmetric response of bond market volatility to both governmental interventions and COVID-19-induced uncertainty. With a focus on the first waves of the pandemic and using a panel quantile approach and a comprehensive dataset of 31 countries worldwide, we document that containment and closure policies tend to amplify volatility. Furthermore, the price variability is augmented by the spread of the pandemic itself. On the contrary, economic support policies have a substantial stabilizing effect on bond price fluctuations. Both phenomena are not subsumed by additional control variables and are robust to multiple considerations. Our findings may serve financial market participants in their risk management decisions, as well as policymakers to better shape their preparedness for future pandemics.

**Keywords:** COVID-19; government bond price volatility; government policy responses; international financial markets; containment and closure; economic support; panel quantile regression

**MSC:** 62P25; 62J02; 62F35

**Citation:** Albulescu, C.T.; Grecu, E. Government Interventions and Sovereign Bond Market Volatility during COVID-19: A Quantile Analysis. *Mathematics* **2023**, *11*, 1171. https://doi.org/10.3390/math11051171

Academic Editors: Lina Novickytė, Jolanta Drozdz, Radosław Pastusiak and Michał Soliwoda

Received: 28 December 2022
Revised: 13 February 2023
Accepted: 21 February 2023
Published: 27 February 2023

**Copyright:** © 2023 by the authors. Licensee MDPI, Basel, Switzerland. This article is an open access article distributed under the terms and conditions of the Creative Commons Attribution (CC BY) license (https://creativecommons.org/licenses/by/4.0/).

## 1. Introduction

A careful mapping of the COVID-19 research shows that much of its efforts and attention has, so far, been focused on the possible impact of government interventions on the equity market [1–19]. To be specific, only a handful of studies focus on the impact of the pandemic on bond yields, prices, liquidity, or term spreads [20–27]. Hence, the primary goal of this study is to improve the understanding of the COVID-19–bond market nexus. Specifically, we scrutinize the effect of the government policy responses to the pandemic and of the COVID-19-induced uncertainty on sovereign bond volatility, showing that this effect is asymmetric, being influenced by the volatility level. Ours is the first paper assessing the asymmetric, nonlinear effect of government interventions on sovereign bond market volatility during COVID-19.

During the COVID-19 outbreak, financial markets have experienced extraordinary levels of uncertainty leading to significant price drawdowns, volatility spikes, and liquidity shortages [28–33]. Importantly, besides the pandemic itself, which generated a specific form of uncertainty associated with the increased number of new infection cases and deaths [34] or with news related to COVID-19 [35], global economies have faced unprecedented government policy responses. These interventions may significantly affect financial market volatility; however, the direction of these forces is far from trivial. On the one hand, any government action may induce additional uncertainty [36], which in turn, leads to an increase in the volatility of government bond markets. On the other hand, several other papers consider government interventions as responsible actions that may curb the adverse effects of crises and uncertainty [37–39], which can also be the case for sovereign debt.

Furthermore, the interventions may take different forms. Some of them include containment and closure policies that are targeted at curbing the spread of the pandemic;

others provide economic support to both enterprises and consumers. The impacts of these very different actions do not need to be identical [38]. If we consider for instance the containment and closure policies, we expect an immediate negative impact of these measures on the real economy. However, these policies limit COVID-19 propagation and might restore investor confidence. In this case, containment policies might reduce bond price volatility. This is also the case with economic support measures which in the short run generate a positive market sentiment but in the long run might be associated with fiscal imbalances, increasing thus the market uncertainty. Consequently, we attempt to shed light on this issue and explore the impact of different government policy responses on government bond volatility.

To this end, we examine the behavior of sovereign bonds in 31 countries during the recent pandemic. Contrary to earlier studies [25,38], we employ Canay's panel quantile regression [40] approach with fixed effects to determine whether the relationship is consistent across several parts of the bond volatility distribution. In other words, we investigate if the impact of interventions on sovereign bond market volatility differs depending on the volatility level.

We, therefore, build upon the work of Zaremba et al. [25] and extend their analysis in three ways. First, we posit that the effect of government interventions on bond market volatility is not linear and is influenced by the level of volatility recorded in each market. More precisely, it is well known that countries with more developed financial markets tend to record a reduced volatility level [41]. These mature markets do not react to news and uncertainty in the same way the emerging financial markets do. Therefore, we expect that the governmental interventions will have a stronger impact on bond price volatility at upper quantiles, that is, for more volatile bond markets. Highlighting the asymmetric effect of governmental interventions on bond market volatility represents the main advantage of a panel quantile approach over the classic panel data models. In addition, a quantile approach has other advantages, including its robustness to non-normality, as well as to heteroscedasticity, skewness, and leptokurtosis, all of which are typical financial data features [40]. The estimated conditional quantile functions provide a much more complete image of the covariates' effect on the location, scale, and shape of the distribution of a response variable [42]. The application of this method to study the relationship between COVID-19 and sovereign bond volatility is uncovered by the extant literature. We demonstrate that both the spread of the infections and the policy measures augment the bond market volatility. As a novel finding, we show that the impact of government interventions increases for upper quantiles, that is, for more volatile markets. The effect is driven principally by containment and closure policies, such as lockdowns or school closings. On the other hand, economic support policies tend to stabilize bond price fluctuations.

Second, we cover the first two waves of the pandemic, while Zaremba et al.'s [25] data span only covers the first wave. We investigate the two waves of the pandemic (for a description, please refer to the work of Duttilo et al. [43]) given the high level of uncertainty and volatility recorded in 2020. Starting with 2021, financial market volatility decreased, pointing in favor of shock accommodation and uncertainty downturn. Moreover, the bond purchase measures (see, for example, the Federal Reserve quantitative easing program) diminished the market volatility. Third, we check for the "Monday effect" of new infection cases. The new infections are reported on the date "t" for the tests performed on the date "t-1" [1]. Given that fewer tests are performed during the weekend, the number of new infection cases is smaller Monday compared with the other days of the week.

In summary, previous literature does not investigate the asymmetric response of bond market volatility to both governmental interventions and COVID-19-induced uncertainty. Starting from this limitation, we derive the following hypotheses for our empirical research:

**Hypothesis 1.** *Government interventions and new COVID-19 infection cases have different impacts on bond market volatility, depending on the volatility level.*

**Hypothesis 2.** *The containment measures amplify the volatility by increasing the uncertainty, whereas the economic support policies have a stabilizing effect on bond price fluctuations.*

**Hypothesis 3.** *The "Monday effect" of new infection cases is significant.*

Our findings contribute to the literature on the effect of the COVID-19 outbreak on bond market volatility [20–22,24] in several ways. Our focus is on sovereign bond market volatility. A concurrent strand of the literature [44–48] investigates the pandemic's effect on sovereign bond risk. In particular, our study is most closely related to the study of Zaremba et al. [25], who applied simple panel regressions to delve into the pandemic–bond volatility nexus. Significantly, our conclusions expand the findings of that study, showing that the impact of interventions is influenced by the bond volatility distribution. Whereas Zaremba et al. [25] only found a link between bond volatility and economic support policies, we also document the essential role of containment and closure interventions, which amplify the price variability. Consequently, while Zaremba et al. [19] find the overall stabilizing effect of government interventions, we demonstrate their detrimental impact.

The structure of the paper is as follows: Section 2 describes materials and methods. Section 3 presents the results regarding empirical findings and robustness checks. Section 4 discusses the findings in relation to the research hypotheses, and Section 5 presents conclusions.

## 2. Materials and Methods

### 2.1. Materials

As in the work of Zaremba et al. [25], the data consist of information on different policy responses from 31 countries that are covered by Datastream: Australia, Austria, Belgium, Canada, China, Czech Republic, Denmark, Finland, France, Germany, Greece, Hungary, India, Indonesia, Ireland, Italy, Japan, Korea, Mexico, the Netherlands, New Zealand, Norway, Poland, Portugal, Singapore, South Africa, Spain, Sweden, Switzerland, the United Kingdom, and the United States. This data sample is representative of developed and emerging market economies having adopted complex governmental measures as a response to the COVID-19 public health crisis. All of the bond-related data and variables are derived from the Datastream 10-Year Government Bond Total Returns indices. The 10-year maturities are the primary choice in asset pricing literature due to high liquidity and broad international coverage [49,50]. The sample period encompasses the spread of the pandemic, running from 1 January 2020 through 3 November 2020, covering thus the first two waves of COVID-19. Most of the existing works on this topic focus on the first wave of the pandemic (March–May 2020). In our opinion, the second wave of the public health crisis (September–November 2020) is equally important in studying the impact of COVID-19 on sovereign bond market volatility, given the additional measures imposed by governments to fight against the pandemic. However, the study of the third wave of the pandemic (February–March 2021) should be placed in a totally different context given the start of the vaccination campaign. Following the typical approach in international bond pricing studies [51], we express the market data in U.S. dollars, and the risk-free rate is proxied by the U.S. one-month treasury-bill rate from Kenneth R. French's website [52].

To quantify day-to-day changes in volatility, we build on the work of Antonakakis and Kizys [53], Khalifa et al. [54], and Zaremba et al. [11,25] (all of whom employ absolute measures of daily returns). Furthermore, to extract the country-specific volatility component, free of the impact of systematic risks, we replace the raw returns with residuals from a factor model. To be precise, in order to capture the multidimensionality of bond returns, we utilize the comprehensive seven-factor model originating from Zaremba et al. [25]:

$$R_{i,t} = \alpha_i + \beta_i^{MKT}MKT_t^F + \beta_i^{DUR}DUR_t^F + \beta_i^{CRED}CRED_t^F + \beta_i^{SIZE}SIZE_t^F + \beta_i^{MOM}MOM_t^F + \beta_i^{REV}REV_t^F + \beta_i^{CAR}CAR_t^F + \varepsilon_{i,t}. \quad (1)$$

where $R_{i,t}$ indicates the daily payoff on a country government i on day t, $\alpha_i$ measures the abnormal return, and $\varepsilon_{i,t}$ is the error term. The regression coefficients $\beta_i^{MKT}$, $\beta_i^{DUR}$, $\beta_i^{CRED}$, $\beta_i^{SIZE}$, $\beta_i^{MOM}$, $\beta_i^{REV}$, and $\beta_i^{CAR}$ reflect the exposures to the market risk (MKT$^F$), duration (DUR$^F$), credit risk (CRED$^F$), size (SIZE$^F$), momentum (MOM$^F$), long-term reversal (REV$^F$), and carry (CAR$^F$) risk factors, respectively. A detailed description of factor construction is provided in Table A1 in the Appendix. Indeed, according to Fama and French [55], unexpected changes in the interest rate represent a source of risks and volatility in the bond market. Further, the shift in economic conditions, measured as the difference between the return on a market portfolio and the long-term government bond return, explains the bond price volatility. In addition, the excess return on a value-weighted aggregate market proxy represents another element of risk explaining the financial market volatility [56].

We derive look-ahead bias-free absolute daily residuals by performing the following steps: To begin, for each day t we run the regression (1) using five years of trailing data ending on day t-1. Subsequently, we utilize the coefficient estimates and factor realizations from day t to calculate the expected daily returns. Finally, we compute the residual returns as the difference between the actual return realizations on day t and their expected values implied by the model (1).

Our main explanatory variables are based on the policy response indices from the Oxford COVID-19 Government Response Tracker [57]. The indices aggregate data on different government interventions following the COVID-19 outbreak, such as canceling public gatherings and closing workplaces, social distancing requirements, debt relief, and income support. In our baseline approach, we use three different indices: the Government Response Index (gvt), which incorporates information on all types of policies, as well as the Containment and Health Index (cntm) and the Economic Support Index (eco). The latter two constitute sub-indices of "gvt" and reflect different types of policies. Whereas "cntm" concentrates on containment and closure policies aimed at curbing the pandemic, eco is about economic support to consumers and enterprises during the pandemic.

Besides the primary independent variable, we include a range of additional control variables. These include bond duration (dur), default risk (cred), money market rate (mmr) and convexity (cx), carry (car), momentum (mom), reversal (rev), and "Monday effect" dummy (dummy). The detailed descriptions for all variables are presented in Table A2 in the Appendix A.

Table 1 reports the descriptive statistics for the key variables. Though not reported here, all variables are stationary according to Maddala and Wu's [58], and Pesaran's [59] unit root tests.

**Table 1.** Summary Statistics.

|  | Mean | Std. Dev. | Min | Max |
| --- | --- | --- | --- | --- |
| $R_1$ | 3.392 | 4.283 | 0.001 | 104.7 |
| $R_2$ | 5.607 | 6.966 | 0.000 | 125.0 |
| gvt | 49.32 | 24.61 | 0.000 | 95.54 |
| cntm | 49.28 | 24.70 | 0.000 | 98.96 |
| stg | 47.99 | 26.62 | 0.000 | 100.0 |
| eco | 49.57 | 35.21 | 0.000 | 100.0 |
| inf | 4.578 | 3.097 | 0.000 | 11.49 |
| dur | 8.559 | 1.124 | 5.390 | 10.45 |
| cred | 4.623 | 3.663 | 1.000 | 13.00 |
| mmr | 0.788 | 1.805 | −1.957 | 7.300 |
| car | 0.693 | 1.107 | −1.269 | 7.623 |
| cx | 81.47 | 20.98 | 34.86 | 119.9 |
| size | 16.09 | 0.902 | 14.13 | 18.38 |

Table 1. Cont.

|  | Mean | Std. Dev. | Min | Max |
|---|---|---|---|---|
| mom | −0.496 | 0.589 | −3.138 | 3.220 |
| rev | −0.656 | 1.547 | −16.54 | 3.680 |

Notes: (i) $R_1$—daily absolute residuals from a seven-factor model, $R_2$—daily absolute returns in U.S. dollars, gvt—government response index, cntm—containment and health index, eco—economic support index, stg—original stringency index, inf—new infection cases, dur—duration, cred—credit rating, mmr—money market rate, car—yield-based carry, cx—convexity, size—bond market value, mom—momentum, and rev—reversal; (ii) 6789 observations. The sovereign bond price volatility variables ($R_1$ and $R_2$) are adjusted ($|\ln(1 + R)|$) and multiplied by 1000 before running the regression.

## 2.2. Methods

Quantile regression models are useful to account for unobserved heterogeneity and asymmetry [40]. In addition, when relying on fixed-effect models, researchers can control for unobserved covariates. A combination of these approaches represents the basis of panel quantile fixed-effect models that are proposed in the literature [42,60–62].

Let us consider the following model:

$$Y_{it} = X'_{it}\theta(U_{it}) + \alpha_i \quad (2)$$

where $t = 1,\ldots,T$; $i = 1,\ldots,n$; $Y_{it}$ and $X_{it}$ represent the observable variables; $U_{it}$ is an unobservable component; $X'_{it}$ includes a constant term; and $\theta(\tau)$ is the parameter of interest.

It is assumed that the function $\tau \to X'\theta(\tau)$ is increasing in $\tau \in (0,1)$. In the case $\alpha_i$ is observable, it follows that:

$$P[Y_{it} \leq X'_{it}\theta(U_{it}) + \alpha_i | X_i, \alpha_i] = \tau, \quad (3)$$

where $U_{it} \sim U[0,1]$, conditional on $X_i = (X'_{i1},\ldots,X'_{iT})'$ and $\alpha_i$.

The challenge is the $\theta(\tau)$ identification, which cannot be accomplished by imposing only covariate quantile restrictions [42]. If $Q_Y(\tau|X)$ is the $\tau$-quantile of a random variable Y conditional on X and $e_{it}(\tau) \equiv X'_{it}[\theta(U_{it}) - \theta(\tau)]$, Equation (2) can be written as follows:

$$Y_{it} = X'_{it}\theta(U_{it}) + \alpha_i + e_{it}(\tau), \quad (4)$$

Canay [40] proves that $\theta(\tau)$ is identified for $T \geq 2$ under independence restrictions and the existence of moments. When we move from identification to estimation, we eliminate the fixed effects under the assumption that $\alpha_i$ is a location shift. Practically, Canay [33] assumes that only $\theta(\tau)$ and $e_{it}(\tau)$ depend on $\tau$ and transforms Equation (4) as follows:

$$Y_{it} = X'_{it}\theta\mu + \alpha_i + u_{it}, \quad E(u_{it}|X_i, \alpha_i) = 0. \quad (5)$$

This way $\alpha_i$ is present in the conditional mean of $Y_{it}$, allowing Canay [40] to compute the two-step estimator $\hat\theta\mu$. First, we obtain a consistent estimator of $\alpha_i$ ($\sqrt{T}$) and $\theta\mu$ ($\sqrt{nT}$), with $\hat\alpha_i \equiv E_T[Y_{it} - X'_{it}\hat\theta\mu]$. Second, we define $\hat Y_i \equiv Y_{it} - \hat\alpha_i$, and $\hat\theta\mu$ becomes

$$\hat\theta\mu \equiv \underset{\theta \in \Theta}{\text{argmin}}\mathbb{E}_{nT}[\rho_\tau(\hat Y_{it} - X'_{it}\hat\theta\mu)], \quad (6)$$

where $\mathbb{E}_{nT}(\cdot) \equiv (nT)^{-1}\sum_{t=1}^{T}\sum_{i=1}^{n}(\cdot)$.

Starting from this framework, similar to Li et al. [63], we use the first lag of explanatory variables to avoid any endogeneity bias. Indeed, some governmental responses to the COVID-19 pandemic have an economic nature (i.e., financial aid, fiscal facilities, etc.). Therefore, the governmental decisions in this line are influenced by the state financing costs, that is, by the bond returns. As a result, we test the following general regression:

$$R_{it} = \alpha_0 + \alpha_1 X_{it-1} + \alpha_2 Z_{it-1} + \mu_i + \gamma_t + \varepsilon_{it}, \quad (7)$$

where $R_{it}$ is the daily measure of sovereign bond volatility in the country i on day t, i.e., the absolute residuals from the model (1); $\alpha_0$ represents a constant term; $X_{it-1}$ is the vector of COVID-19 variables, represented by new cases of infection and governmental response to the SARS-CoV-2 pandemic; $Z_{it-1}$ is the vector of control variables defined in Section 2; and $\mu_i$ are the time-invariant country-specific effects, $\gamma_t$ are the time-specific effects, and $\varepsilon_{it}$ are the error terms.

## 3. Results

### 3.1. Empirical Findings

Table 2 reports the results of the quantile regressions that account for the overall role of the policy responses. The positive and highly significant coefficients on "gvt" suggest that government interventions amplify bond market volatility. The effect is robust across the majority of quantiles tested. The impact of policy measures increases when we shift from lower to higher quantiles. In other words, a volatile financial market environment implies a stronger reaction to COVID-19-induced policy measures. The only exception is the most volatile quantile, where the "gvt" does not differ significantly from zero.

**Table 2.** Panel Conditional Quantile Regression—Government Response Index.

|  | Lower Quantiles | | | | Middle Quantiles | | | | Upper Quantiles | |
| --- | --- | --- | --- | --- | --- | --- | --- | --- | --- | --- |
|  | 0.05 | 0.15 | 0.25 | 0.35 | 0.45 | 0.55 | 0.65 | 0.75 | 0.85 | 0.95 |
| gvt | 0.007 *** | 0.006 *** | 0.005 *** | 0.007 *** | 0.010 *** | 0.012 *** | 0.014 *** | 0.013 *** | 0.011 ** | −0.007 |
|  | (0.002) | (0.002) | (0.002) | (0.001) | (0.002) | (0.002) | (0.002) | (0.003) | (0.005) | (0.012) |
| inf | 0.201 *** | 0.188 *** | 0.192 *** | 0.181 *** | 0.163 *** | 0.159 *** | 0.136 *** | 0.135 *** | 0.117 *** | 0.097 |
|  | (0.021) | (0.017) | (0.016) | (0.014) | (0.016) | (0.018) | (0.022) | (0.025) | (0.041) | (0.100) |
| dur | −2.444 *** | −2.857 *** | −2.373 *** | −2.218 *** | −2.088 *** | −2.034 *** | −1.890 *** | −1.529 *** | −1.482 * | −3.128 |
|  | (0.475) | (0.374) | (0.357) | (0.318) | (0.361) | (0.394) | (0.495) | (0.559) | (0.899) | (2.190) |
| cred | −0.379 *** | −0.382 *** | −0.329 *** | −0.327 *** | −0.326 *** | −0.326 *** | −0.321 *** | −0.328 *** | −0.343 *** | −0.443 *** |
|  | (0.020) | (0.015) | (0.015) | (0.013) | (0.015) | (0.016) | (0.020) | (0.023) | (0.038) | (0.092) |
| mmr | 2.361 *** | 2.518 *** | 2.535 *** | 2.558 *** | 2.617 *** | 2.689 *** | 2.753 *** | 2.869 *** | 2.946 *** | 3.495 *** |
|  | (0.045) | (0.036) | (0.034) | (0.030) | (0.034) | (0.038) | (0.047) | (0.053) | (0.086) | (0.211) |
| car | 2.250 *** | 2.422 *** | 2.338 *** | 2.435 *** | 2.484 *** | 2.598 *** | 2.696 *** | 2.879 *** | 3.220 *** | 4.721 *** |
|  | (0.071) | (0.056) | (0.053) | (0.048) | (0.054) | (0.059) | (0.074) | (0.084) | (0.135) | (0.329) |
| cx | 0.121 *** | 0.151 *** | 0.127 *** | 0.120 *** | 0.114 *** | 0.114 *** | 0.105 *** | 0.085 *** | 0.083 | 0.192 |
|  | (0.027) | (0.021) | (0.020) | (0.018) | (0.021) | (0.023) | (0.028) | (0.032) | (0.052) | (0.127) |
| size | −0.445 *** | −0.506 *** | −0.540 *** | −0.621 *** | −0.717 *** | −0.844 *** | −0.936 *** | −1.073 *** | −1.274 *** | −1.568 *** |
|  | (0.054) | (0.042) | (0.040) | (0.036) | (0.041) | (0.044) | (0.056) | (0.063) | (0.102) | (0.248) |
| mom | −0.534 *** | −0.689 *** | −0.616 *** | −0.673 *** | −0.773 *** | −0.859 *** | −0.930 *** | −1.102 *** | −1.562 *** | −2.664 *** |
|  | (0.082) | (0.065) | (0.062) | (0.055) | (0.062) | (0.068) | (0.086) | (0.097) | (0.156) | (0.381) |
| rev | 0.565 *** | 0.482 *** | 0.470 *** | 0.491 *** | 0.494 *** | 0.528 *** | 0.543 *** | 0.519 *** | 0.591 *** | 0.658 *** |
|  | (0.036) | (0.029) | (0.027) | (0.024) | (0.028) | (0.030) | (0.038) | (0.043) | (0.069) | (0.169) |
| dummy | 0.004 | −0.062 | −0.087 | −0.118 | −0.1537 | −0.148 * | −0.156 | −0.062 | 0.0663 | −0.110 |
|  | (0.108) | (0.085) | (0.081) | (0.072) | (0.082) | (0.089) | (0.112) | (0.127) | (0.205) | (0.498) |

Notes: The table reports slope coefficients from panel regressions along with the corresponding standard errors. (i) Standard error in parentheses; (ii) *** $p < 0.01$, ** $p < 0.05$, * $p < 0.1$; (iii) 6788 observations; (iv) gvt—government response index, inf—new infection cases, dur—duration, cred—credit rating, mmr—money market rate, car—yield-based carry, cx—convexity, size—bond market value, mom—momentum, rev—reversal, and dummy—binary variable that takes value 1 if Monday and 0 for the rest of the weekdays.

Besides the impact of policy responses to the pandemic, our baseline regression analysis uncovers the role of the pandemic itself: growth in the number of new infections translates into an increase in the bond market volatility. This observation matches similar earlier findings from equity markets [3,11,34] showing that COVID-19-induced uncertainty contributes to the instability of stock prices. Interestingly, the COVID-19 figures more strongly influence the sovereign bond prices located at the lower and medium volatility quantiles when compared with high-volatility bonds. Consequently, less volatile financial markets—typically found in developed countries—are more sensitive to changes in COVID-19 figures.

The overall government response index, as examined in Table 2, encompasses various interventions that may exhibit differing economic impacts. Therefore, in the subsequent analysis, we distinguish containment and closure measures from economic support policies. These two categories are measured with "cntm" and "eco", respectively.

Table 3 presents the influence of containment and closure measures on bond market volatility.

Table 3. Panel Conditional Quantile Regression—Containment and Health Index.

|  | Lower Quantiles | | | | Middle Quantiles | | | | Upper Quantiles | |
| --- | --- | --- | --- | --- | --- | --- | --- | --- | --- | --- |
|  | 0.05 | 0.15 | 0.25 | 0.35 | 0.45 | 0.55 | 0.65 | 0.75 | 0.85 | 0.95 |
| cntm | 0.010 *** | 0.009 *** | 0.007 *** | 0.009 *** | 0.013 *** | 0.015 *** | 0.017 *** | 0.019 *** | 0.019 *** | 0.007 |
|  | (0.002) | (0.002) | (0.002) | (0.002) | (0.002) | (0.002) | (0.002) | (0.003) | (0.005) | (0.012) |
| inf | 0.182 *** | 0.170 *** | 0.174 *** | 0.166 *** | 0.143 *** | 0.135 *** | 0.116 *** | 0.101 *** | 0.075 * | 0.001 |
|  | (0.021) | (0.017) | (0.016) | (0.014) | (0.016) | (0.017) | (0.022) | (0.025) | (0.041) | (0.101) |
| dur | −2.209 *** | −2.498 *** | −2.067 *** | −1.858 *** | −1.744 *** | −1.697 *** | −1.596 *** | −1.243 ** | −1.115 | −2.561 |
|  | (0.466) | (0.375) | (0.364) | (0.325) | (0.364) | (0.386) | (0.480) | (0.562) | (0.910) | (2.221) |
| cred | −0.374 *** | −0.374 *** | −0.317 *** | −0.324 *** | −0.314 *** | −0.322 *** | −0.315 *** | −0.315 *** | −0.329 *** | −0.424 *** |
|  | (0.019) | (0.015) | (0.015) | (0.013) | (0.015) | (0.016) | (0.020) | (0.023) | (0.038) | (0.093) |
| mmr | 2.293 *** | 2.470 *** | 2.475 *** | 2.492 *** | 2.538 *** | 2.611 *** | 2.676 *** | 2.791 *** | 2.886 *** | 3.419 *** |
|  | (0.044) | (0.036) | (0.035) | (0.031) | (0.035) | (0.037) | (0.046) | (0.054) | (0.087) | (0.213) |
| car | 2.170 *** | 2.314 *** | 2.249 *** | 2.345 *** | 2.389 *** | 2.535 *** | 2.608 *** | 2.782 *** | 3.070 *** | 4.610 *** |
|  | (0.070) | (0.056) | (0.054) | (0.049) | (0.054) | (0.058) | (0.072) | (0.084) | (0.137) | (0.334) |
| cx | 0.110 *** | 0.131 *** | 0.111 *** | 0.099 *** | 0.095 *** | 0.095 *** | 0.089 *** | 0.070 ** | 0.062 | 0.164 |
|  | (0.027) | (0.021) | (0.021) | (0.019) | (0.021) | (0.022) | (0.028) | (0.032) | (0.053) | (0.129) |
| size | −0.453 *** | −0.516 *** | −0.553 *** | −0.625 *** | −0.716 *** | −0.836 *** | −0.936 *** | −1.084 *** | −1.302 *** | −1.535 *** |
|  | (0.052) | (0.042) | (0.041) | (0.036) | (0.041) | (0.043) | (0.054) | (0.063) | (0.103) | (0.251) |
| mom | −0.521 *** | −0.668 *** | −0.583 *** | −0.642 *** | −0.748 *** | −0.821 *** | −0.878 *** | −1.082 *** | −1.518 *** | −2.690 *** |
|  | (0.080) | (0.065) | (0.063) | (0.056) | (0.063) | (0.067) | (0.083) | (0.097) | (0.158) | (0.385) |
| rev | 0.588 *** | 0.493 *** | 0.481 *** | 0.496 *** | 0.508 *** | 0.539 *** | 0.554 *** | 0.531 *** | 0.607 *** | 0.698 *** |
|  | (0.035) | (0.028) | (0.028) | (0.025) | (0.028) | (0.029) | (0.036) | (0.043) | (0.070) | (0.170) |
| dummy | −0.012 | −0.051 | −0.080 | −0.131 * | −0.148 * | −0.162 * | −0.161 | −0.057 | 0.044 | 0.004 |
|  | (0.106) | (0.085) | (0.082) | (0.074) | (0.082) | (0.087) | (0.109) | (0.128) | (0.207) | (0.505) |

Notes: The table reports slope coefficients from panel regressions along with the corresponding standard errors. (i) Standard error in parentheses; (ii) *** $p < 0.01$, ** $p < 0.05$, * $p < 0.1$; (iii) 6788 observations; (iv) cntm—Containment and Health Index, inf—new infection cases, dur—duration, cred—credit rating, mmr—money market rate, car—yield-based carry, cx—convexity, size—bond market value, mom—momentum, rev—reversal, and dummy—binary variable that takes value 1 if Monday and 0 for the rest of the weekdays.

This additional analysis unequivocally reveals the underlying source of the impact of government policy responses on market volatility. Highly significant "cntm" coefficients indicate that these containment and closure interventions constitute a major contributor to bond price variability. In accordance with previous results, the policy measures generate a more substantial impact when we test the higher quantiles of the distribution, whereas the spread of the pandemic as measured by the "inf" variable is more powerful in low quantiles. Finally, similar to the previous case, the effect of policy measures (or the spread of the disease) on bond price volatility is not significant for very volatile markets (i.e., the 0.95 quantile).

Let us now turn to the role of the other category of government interventions: economic support policies (eco). Table 4 demonstrates the results of another set of quantile regressions to capture the role of this category of government actions. Our analysis uncovers a negative impact on bond price volatility for lower and upper quantiles, but not for middle quantiles (Table 4). For sovereign bonds with smaller and higher volatility, economic support interventions stabilize the markets. The effect is more substantial for the upper quantiles, which is in line with the impact generated by other policy interventions (see, for example, the results reported in Table 3).

Table 4. Panel Conditional Quantile Regression—Economic Support Index.

| | Lower Quantiles | | | | Middle Quantiles | | | | Upper Quantiles | |
| --- | --- | --- | --- | --- | --- | --- | --- | --- | --- | --- |
| | 0.05 | 0.15 | 0.25 | 0.35 | 0.45 | 0.55 | 0.65 | 0.75 | 0.85 | 0.95 |
| eco | −0.002 | −0.004 *** | −0.002 * | −0.001 | −0.001 | −0.001 | −0.001 | −0.004 ** | −0.010 *** | −0.025 *** |
| | (0.001) | (0.001) | (0.001) | (0.001) | (0.001) | (0.001) | (0.001) | (0.002) | (0.003) | (0.007) |
| inf | 0.273 *** | 0.255 *** | 0.240 *** | 0.236 *** | 0.239 *** | 0.238 *** | 0.224 *** | 0.243 *** | 0.209 *** | 0.170 ** |
| | (0.016) | (0.014) | (0.012) | (0.011) | (0.013) | (0.014) | (0.019) | (0.023) | (0.033) | (0.085) |
| dur | −3.718 *** | −4.251 *** | −3.546 *** | −3.272 *** | −3.264 *** | −3.125 *** | −3.131 *** | −2.733 *** | −2.920 *** | −3.751 |
| | (0.444) | (0.378) | (0.337) | (0.316) | (0.362) | (0.391) | (0.507) | (0.614) | (0.884) | (2.282) |
| cred | −0.366 *** | −0.370 *** | −0.314 *** | −0.314 *** | −0.325 *** | −0.331 *** | −0.332 *** | −0.348 *** | −0.345 *** | −0.424 *** |
| | (0.018) | (0.015) | (0.014) | (0.013) | (0.015) | (0.016) | (0.021) | (0.025) | (0.037) | (0.095) |
| mmr | 2.343 *** | 2.546 *** | 2.572 *** | 2.594 *** | 2.664 *** | 2.721 *** | 2.814 *** | 2.902 *** | 3.006 *** | 3.394 *** |
| | (0.043) | (0.036) | (0.032) | (0.030) | (0.035) | (0.038) | (0.049) | (0.059) | (0.086) | (0.221) |
| car | 2.348 *** | 2.463 *** | 2.351 *** | 2.437 *** | 2.555 *** | 2.654 *** | 2.777 *** | 3.006 *** | 3.217 *** | 4.479 *** |
| | (0.066) | (0.056) | (0.050) | (0.047) | (0.054) | (0.058) | (0.075) | (0.091) | (0.132) | (0.340) |
| cx | 0.187 *** | 0.226 *** | 0.191 *** | 0.176 *** | 0.178 *** | 0.172 *** | 0.172 *** | 0.148 *** | 0.161 *** | 0.215 |
| | (0.025) | (0.022) | (0.019) | (0.018) | (0.021) | (0.022) | (0.029) | (0.035) | (0.051) | (0.132) |
| size | −0.331 *** | −0.419 *** | −0.468 *** | −0.544 *** | −0.640 *** | −0.757 *** | −0.840 *** | −0.982 *** | −1.175 *** | −1.347 *** |
| | (0.050) | (0.042) | (0.038) | (0.035) | (0.041) | (0.044) | (0.057) | (0.069) | (0.100) | (0.258) |
| mom | −0.542 *** | −0.697 *** | −0.630 *** | −0.660 *** | −0.770 *** | −0.850 *** | −0.928 *** | −1.016 *** | −1.392 *** | −2.258 *** |
| | (0.077) | (0.066) | (0.059) | (0.055) | (0.063) | (0.068) | (0.089) | (0.107) | (0.155) | (0.399) |
| rev | 0.475 *** | 0.388 *** | 0.383 *** | 0.413 *** | 0.416 *** | 0.430 *** | 0.416 *** | 0.377 *** | 0.427 *** | 0.442 ** |
| | (0.034) | (0.029) | (0.026) | (0.024) | (0.028) | (0.030) | (0.039) | (0.047) | (0.069) | (0.177) |
| dummy | 0.001 | −0.068 | −0.085 | −0.107 | −0.196 ** | −0.175 ** | −0.185 | −0.019 | −0.012 | −0.100 |
| | (0.101) | (0.086) | (0.076) | (0.072) | (0.082) | (0.089) | (0.115) | (0.139) | (0.201) | (0.519) |

Notes: The table reports slope coefficients from panel regressions along with the corresponding standard errors. (i) Standard error in parentheses; (ii) *** $p < 0.01$, ** $p < 0.05$, * $p < 0.1$; (iii) 6788 observations; (iv) eco—Economic Support Index, inf—new infection cases, dur—duration, cred—credit rating, mmr—money market rate, car—yield-based carry, cx—convexity, size—bond market value, mom—momentum, rev—reversal, and dummy—binary variable that takes value 1 if Monday and 0 for the rest of the weekdays.

To sum up our considerations, we find that market volatility is affected by containment and closure restrictions as well as economic support policies; however, the directions of the impacts are opposite. Whereas the first category tends to boost market fluctuations, the latter helps to stabilize the market.

### 3.2. Robustness Checks

To assure the validity of our findings, we run a number of additional robustness checks. First, we use a different metric to compute the sovereign bond price volatility, relying on absolute raw returns rather than on risk-adjusted returns (residuals). In an unreported analysis, we also consider different nested models. The major results remain unaffected. These results are reported in Table 5 and are very similar to those reported in Section 3.1.

Table 5. Panel Conditional Quantile Regression—Robustness Analysis Using Daily USD Returns as a Proxy for Bond Price Volatility.

| | Lower Quantiles | | | | Middle Quantiles | | | | Upper Quantiles | |
| --- | --- | --- | --- | --- | --- | --- | --- | --- | --- | --- |
| | 0.05 | 0.15 | 0.25 | 0.35 | 0.45 | 0.55 | 0.65 | 0.75 | 0.85 | 0.95 |
| gvt | 0.002 | 0.019 *** | 0.020 *** | 0.023 *** | 0.030 *** | 0.033 *** | 0.032 *** | 0.034 *** | 0.029 *** | −0.036 * |
| | (0.004) | (0.003) | (0.003) | (0.003) | (0.003) | (0.003) | (0.004) | (0.006) | (0.009) | (0.020) |
| inf | 0.310 *** | 0.264 *** | 0.246 *** | 0.238 *** | 0.203 *** | 0.195 *** | 0.217 *** | 0.217 *** | 0.249 *** | 0.349 ** |
| | (0.033) | (0.026) | (0.025) | (0.024) | (0.027) | (0.031) | (0.037) | (0.049) | (0.076) | (0.165) |
| dur | −5.950 *** | −4.269 *** | −4.197 *** | −4.576 *** | −5.363 *** | −6.754 *** | −8.351 *** | −9.593 *** | −12.41 *** | −16.18 *** |
| | (0.734) | (0.576) | (0.545) | (0.529) | (0.589) | (0.674) | (0.805) | (1.066) | (1.655) | (3.604) |
| cred | −0.330 *** | −0.340 *** | −0.363 *** | −0.360 *** | −0.357 *** | −0.342 *** | −0.320 *** | −0.313 *** | −0.235 *** | −0.257 * |
| | (0.031) | (0.024) | (0.023) | (0.022) | (0.024) | (0.028) | (0.034) | (0.045) | (0.069) | (0.152) |
| mmr | 3.716 *** | 3.965 *** | 4.187 *** | 4.258 *** | 4.309 *** | 4.432 *** | 4.540 *** | 4.782 *** | 5.056 *** | 6.006 *** |
| | (0.070) | (0.055) | (0.052) | (0.051) | (0.056) | (0.065) | (0.077) | (0.102) | (0.159) | (0.347) |
| car | 3.341 *** | 3.305 *** | 3.543 *** | 3.693 *** | 3.887 *** | 4.119 *** | 4.290 *** | 4.455 *** | 4.791 *** | 6.643 *** |
| | (0.110) | (0.086) | (0.082) | (0.079) | (0.088) | (0.101) | (0.121) | (0.160) | (0.249) | (0.542) |

Table 5. Cont.

|  | Lower Quantiles | | | | Middle Quantiles | | | | Upper Quantiles | |
|---|---|---|---|---|---|---|---|---|---|---|
|  | 0.05 | 0.15 | 0.25 | 0.35 | 0.45 | 0.55 | 0.65 | 0.75 | 0.85 | 0.95 |
| cx | 0.323 *** | 0.233 *** | 0.231 *** | 0.254 *** | 0.300 *** | 0.388 *** | 0.479 *** | 0.556 *** | 0.726 *** | 0.972 *** |
|  | (0.042) | (0.033) | (0.031) | (0.030) | (0.034) | (0.039) | (0.046) | (0.062) | (0.096) | (0.210) |
| size | −0.560 *** | −0.689 *** | −0.734 *** | −0.867 *** | −0.946 *** | −1.107 *** | −1.278 *** | −1.531 *** | −1.995 *** | −2.608 *** |
|  | (0.083) | (0.065) | (0.061) | (0.060) | (0.066) | (0.076) | (0.091) | (0.121) | (0.187) | (0.408) |
| mom | −0.371 *** | −0.609 *** | −0.791 *** | −0.904 *** | −0.947 *** | −1.046 *** | −1.117 *** | −1.175 *** | −1.770 *** | −3.300 *** |
|  | (0.127) | (0.100) | (0.095) | (0.092) | (0.102) | (0.117) | (0.140) | (0.185) | (0.288) | (0.627) |
| rev | 0.846 *** | 0.812 *** | 0.721 *** | 0.799 *** | 0.878 *** | 0.939 *** | 1.006 *** | 1.121 *** | 1.322 *** | 1.588 *** |
|  | (0.057) | (0.044) | (0.042) | (0.041) | (0.045) | (0.052) | (0.062) | (0.082) | (0.128) | (0.279) |
| dummy | −0.101 | −0.188 | −0.312 ** | −0.319 *** | −0.375 *** | −0.330 ** | −0.423 ** | −0.413 * | −0.134 | −0.458 |
|  | (0.167) | (0.131) | (0.124) | (0.120) | (0.134) | (0.153) | (0.183) | (0.243) | (0.377) | (0.821) |

Notes: The table reports slope coefficients from panel regressions along with the corresponding standard errors. (i) Standard error in parentheses; (ii) *** $p < 0.01$, ** $p < 0.05$, * $p < 0.1$; (iii) 6788 observations; (iv) gvt—government response index, inf—new infection cases, dur—duration, cred—credit rating, mmr—money market rate, car—yield-based carry, cx—convexity, size—bond market value, mom—momentum, rev—reversal, and dummy—binary variable that takes value 1 if Monday and 0 for the rest of the weekdays.

Second, we work with alternative sets of control variables, and we show a similar effect of governmental interventions and COVID-19-related uncertainty (Table 6).

Table 6. Panel Conditional Quantile Regression—Robustness Analysis Using a Different Set of Control Variables.

|  | Lower Quantiles | | | | Middle Quantiles | | | | Upper Quantiles | |
|---|---|---|---|---|---|---|---|---|---|---|
|  | 0.05 | 0.15 | 0.25 | 0.35 | 0.45 | 0.55 | 0.65 | 0.75 | 0.85 | 0.95 |
| gvt | 0.009 *** | 0.015 *** | 0.014 *** | 0.012 *** | 0.012 *** | 0.016 *** | 0.018 *** | 0.018 *** | 0.011 ** | −0.002 |
|  | (0.003) | (0.002) | (0.002) | (0.002) | (0.002) | (0.002) | (0.003) | (0.004) | (0.005) | (0.012) |
| inf | 0.095 *** | 0.060 *** | 0.042 *** | 0.046 *** | 0.043 *** | 0.031 * | 0.018 | 0.017 | 0.026 | −0.133 |
|  | (0.025) | (0.017) | (0.016) | (0.014) | (0.016) | (0.017) | (0.022) | (0.028) | (0.044) | (0.102) |
| dur | −0.126 ** | −0.223 *** | −0.200 *** | −0.168 *** | −0.182 *** | −0.158 *** | −0.166 *** | −0.188 *** | −0.188 * | −0.084 |
|  | (0.055) | (0.039) | (0.035) | (0.031) | (0.036) | (0.038) | (0.050) | (0.063) | (0.097) | (0.227) |
| cred | 0.153 *** | 0.205 *** | 0.225 *** | 0.252 *** | 0.258 *** | 0.262 *** | 0.273 *** | 0.261 *** | 0.284 *** | 0.218 ** |
|  | (0.022) | (0.015) | (0.014) | (0.012) | (0.014) | (0.015) | (0.020) | (0.025) | (0.039) | (0.090) |
| car | 0.036 | −0.067 | −0.052 | 0.006 | 0.138 *** | 0.232 *** | 0.396 *** | 0.702 *** | 1.044 *** | 2.473 *** |
|  | (0.071) | (0.050) | (0.045) | (0.040) | (0.046) | (0.048) | (0.064) | (0.081) | (0.125) | (0.290) |
| size | −0.801 *** | −0.876 *** | −0.881 *** | −0.929 *** | −1.008 *** | −1.139 *** | −1.232 *** | −1.352 *** | −1.615 *** | −1.762 *** |
|  | (0.061) | (0.043) | (0.039) | (0.034) | (0.040) | (0.042) | (0.056) | (0.070) | (0.108) | (0.252) |
| mom | 0.967 *** | 0.924 *** | 0.935 *** | 0.851 *** | 0.734 *** | 0.599 *** | 0.470 *** | 0.260 ** | −0.348 ** | −1.264 *** |
|  | (0.091) | (0.064) | (0.058) | (0.051) | (0.059) | (0.062) | (0.083) | (0.104) | (0.160) | (0.371) |
| rev | 1.242 *** | 1.138 *** | 1.140 *** | 1.102 *** | 1.125 *** | 1.190 *** | 1.211 *** | 1.249 *** | 1.364 *** | 1.473 *** |
|  | (0.037) | (0.026) | (0.023) | (0.020) | (0.024) | (0.025) | (0.033) | (0.042) | (0.065) | (0.151) |
| dummy | 0.007 | −0.036 | −0.092 | −0.091 | −0.126 | −0.141 * | −0.116 | −0.061 | 0.112 | 0.080 |
|  | (0.124) | (0.087) | (0.080) | (0.070) | (0.080) | (0.085) | (0.113) | (0.142) | (0.218) | (0.507) |

Notes: The table reports slope coefficients from panel regressions along with the corresponding standard errors. (i) Standard error in parentheses; (ii) *** $p < 0.01$, ** $p < 0.05$, * $p < 0.1$; (iii) 6788 observations; (iv) gvt—government response index, inf—new infection cases, dur—duration, cred—credit rating, car—yield-based carry, size—bond market value, mom—momentum, rev—reversal, and dummy—binary variable that takes value 1 if Monday and 0 for the rest of the weekdays.

Third, in an unreported analysis, we employ a modified measure of the strictness of government policies, namely the Stringency Index, which is also sourced from the Oxford COVID-19 Government Response Tracker. None of these extra robustness checks materially affect our findings. Our overall conclusions remain unaffected.

## 4. Discussion

The novelty of our analysis consists in investigating the asymmetric, nonlinear effect of government interventions and COVID-19-induced uncertainty on bond price volatility. Our first hypothesis points in favor of a nonlinear impact of government interventions and new COVID-19 infection cases on bond market volatility. The empirical findings confirm this hypothesis. More specifically, we have shown that government interventions and new COVID-19 infection cases have different impacts on bond market volatility, depending on the volatility level. Indeed, the governmental interventions' effect is less strong at lower quantiles, that is, for less volatile markets. Consequently, the intervention impact is influenced by the bond volatility distribution. This result thus validates the first hypothesis of our empirical exercise and can be explained by the fact that the government interventions during the pandemic were stronger in the developed countries, generating a higher uncertainty and thus amplifying the bond price volatility. On contrary, the financial markets had a stronger reaction to new infection cases in more developed countries. This is an original result, never reported by the previous literature.

Making the differentiation between containment and economic measures, our second research hypothesis posits that containment measures amplify volatility, whereas economic measures have the opposite effect. This is because the travel restrictions generate additional uncertainty which amplifies the volatility, while the economic measures are designed to restore investor confidence. Indeed, we have shown that the containment measure amplified the volatility whereas the economic measures reduced the bond price volatility level. However, the positive impact the containment and closure measures have on the volatility level cannot be compensated by the stabilizing effect of economic measures. Similar to the main results, the containment measures' impact is stronger at upper quantiles, whereas the impact of economic measures is significant only at lower and upper quantiles, but not at middle quantiles. This finding brings some clarification to the previous results reported in the empirical literature, showing a mixed effect of government interventions on financial market volatility. Our findings contrast those reported by Zaremba et al. [25], who reported an overall stabilizing effect of government interventions. We, therefore, validate our second research hypothesis.

Lastly, we partially validate the third hypothesis of our research. Indeed, the "Monday effect", associated with fewer reported infection cases, is significant at middle quantiles only.

## 5. Conclusions

We examine the impact of government interventions and COVID-19 numbers on the volatility of sovereign bonds. We apply quantile regressions to a sample of 31 countries to scrutinize the importance of different types of policy responses during the first two waves of the pandemic. We show that the impact of COVID-19 on sovereign bonds is influenced by the level of market volatility, which represents an original result of our analysis.

Our findings demonstrate that the direction of the effect on government bond return volatility depends strongly on the type of interventions. Confinement and closure restrictions increase market uncertainty and, in consequence, drive the return volatility up. In contrast, economic support measures tend to calm the volatility level in trading and enhance market stability. Further, we show that the impact of COVID-19-induced policy measures and related uncertainty is higher in the case of less volatile markets (i.e., at lower quantiles).

The conclusions from this study yield clear, practical implications. Since confinement and closure restrictions amplify volatility, our results imply that governments should be transparent and clear with their plans about this type of intervention in the short and longer terms. The COVID-19 period is characterized by increased uncertainty, and government interventions may amplify this uncertainty. Hence, providing information publicly as soon as possible may calm the adverse effect of closures. In addition, even though economic interventions seem to be associated with positive responses, this does not mean that transparency about economic steps is not needed, especially if such supportive actions are expected to increase the fiscal deficit.

The findings also imply that investors can exploit this information to better shape their investment decisions. They should be aware that non-economic interventions, which are not directly related to financial markets, may spill over to capital markets and are not limited to the equity markets. Therefore, investors, particularly those operating in the fixed-income markets, should monitor the changes in government policy and make the required adjustments to their portfolios. More precisely, to anticipate the volatility dynamics, they need to analyze the type of interventions and the sovereign bond markets' characteristics.

Our research has several limitations and can be extended in the following ways: First, our analysis covers only the first two waves of the pandemic. Although governmental interventions and COVID-19-induced uncertainty were vitally important in 2020, a different set of measures was adopted in 2021 during the third and fourth waves of the pandemic. Second, in the context of the high volatility recorded by the bond markets in the post-pandemic period, it is recommended to investigate the sources of this volatility. On the one hand, COVID-19 might change investor behavior for a long period. On the other hand, other elements of uncertainty, represented by the energy crisis or the Russo-Ukrainian War, can explain the volatility level. Third, additional robustness analyses can be performed using alternative approaches to derive the day-to-day changes in volatility, relying on Fama and French's [55] three-factor model or on Carhart's [56] four-factor model.

**Author Contributions:** Conceptualization, C.T.A.; Methodology, C.T.A.; Software, C.T.A.; Validation, C.T.A. and E.G.; Formal Analysis, C.T.A.; Investigation, C.T.A.; Resources, C.T.A. and E.G.; Data Curation, C.T.A.; Writing—Original Draft Preparation, C.T.A.; Writing—Review and Editing, C.T.A. and E.G.; Visualization, C.T.A. and E.G.; Supervision, C.T.A. and E.G.; Project Administration, C.T.A. and E.G.; Funding Acquisition, C.T.A. and E.G. All authors have read and agreed to the published version of the manuscript.

**Funding:** This research was funded by a Grant from the Romanian National Authority for Scientific Research and Innovation, CNCS–UEFISCDI, Project Number PN-III-P1–1.1-TE-2019-0436.

**Data Availability Statement:** Data available on http://mba.tuck.dartmouth.edu/pages/faculty/ken.french/data_library.html and https://www.bsg.ox.ac.uk/research/research-projects/coronavirus-government-response-tracker.

**Acknowledgments:** We are grateful to David Y. Aharon and Adam Zaremba for their input on the earlier versions of this paper.

**Conflicts of Interest:** The authors declare no conflict of interest.

## Appendix A

Table A1. Construction of the Cross-Sectional Asset Pricing Factors.

| Symbol | Factor | Description |
| --- | --- | --- |
| $MKT^F$ | Market risk factor | $MKT^F$ is the excess return on the market, i.e., the value-weighted return of all the bond indices in the sample at the end of month $t$ minus the risk-free rate, i.e., the one-month T-Bill return. |
| $DUR^F$ | Duration factor | The factor is represented by a long–short zero-investment portfolio that buys (sells) the value-weighted portfolio comprising 30% of bond indices with the highest (lowest) adjusted duration. |
| $CRED^F$ | Credit risk factor | The factor is represented by a long–short zero-investment portfolio that buys (sells) the value-weighted portfolio comprising 30% of bond indices with the highest (lowest) adjusted credit risk score. The credit risk score for each market is calculated as the average numerical rating from three major rating agencies: Moody's, S&P, and Fitch. To obtain the numerical ratings, we convert all the ratings linearly so that the top rating (AAA/Aaa) is associated with 1 and the bottom rating (C) is associated with 21. |
| $SIZE^F$ | Size factor | The factor is represented by a long–short zero-investment portfolio that buys (sells) the value-weighted portfolio comprising 30% of bond indices with the highest (lowest) market value of the relevant bond basket. |
| $MOM^F$ | Momentum factor | The factor is represented by a long–short zero-investment portfolio that buys (sells) the value-weighted portfolio comprising 30% of bond indices with the lowest (highest) change in yield-to-maturity from t-12 to t-1. This corresponds with going long (short) bonds with the highest (lowest) return induced by the change in YTMs. |

**Table A1.** *Cont.*

| Symbol | Factor | Description |
|---|---|---|
| $REV^F$ | Reversal factor | The factor is represented by a long–short zero-investment portfolio that buys (sells) the value-weighted portfolio comprising 30% of bond indices with the highest (lowest) change in the yield-to-maturity (YTM) from t-60 to t-13. This corresponds with going long (short) bonds with the lowest (highest) return induced by the change in YTMs. |
| $CAR^F$ | Carry factor | The factor is represented by a long–short zero-investment portfolio that buys (sells) the value-weighted portfolio comprising 30% of bond indices with the highest (lowest) lowest carry. The carry variable is measured as the difference between the yield-to-maturity on 10-year government bonds and the 3-month interbank interest rate. |

Notes: The table displays the procedures used to calculate the returns on asset pricing factors used in this study.

**Table A2.** Major Variables Used in the Study.

| Symbol | Variable | Description |
|---|---|---|
| | | Panel A: Dependent variables |
| $R_1$ | Daily absolute residuals from a seven-factor model | $R_1$ represents the residuals from the seven-factor model (1), computed as $|\ln(1+R)|$. |
| $R_2$ | Daily absolute returns in U.S. dollars | $R_2$ represents the daily returns computed as $|\ln(1+R)|$. |
| | | Panel B: Explanatory variables of interest |
| gvt | Government Response Index | COVID-19 government policy response index aggregating all types of policies and rescaling them to create a score between 0 and 100 on day $t$ |
| cntm | Containment and Health Index | COVID-19 containment and health index aggregating only containment, closure, and health policies and rescaling them rescaled to create a score between 0 and 100 on day t. |
| stg | Stringency Index | COVID-19 containment and health index aggregating only containment and closure policies and rescaling them rescaled to create a score between 0 and 100 on day t. |
| eco | Economic Support Index | COVID-19 economic support index aggregating only the goverment policy responses targeting and providing economic support and rescaling them to create a score between 0 and 100 on day t. |
| inf | New infections | The new cases of infection are computed as $\ln(1 + \Delta INF')$, where INF' is the number of infected cases. |
| | | Panel C: Control variables |
| dur | Duration | Average adjusted duration of the bond market index on day t-1. |
| cred | Quantified credit rating | Numerical sovereign rating of the government bonds in the index on day t-1. The credit risk score for each market is calculated as the average numerical rating from three major rating agencies: Moody's, S&P, and Fitch. To obtain the numerical ratings, we convert all the ratings linearly, so that the top rating (AAA/Aaa) is associated with 1 and the bottom rating (C) is associated with 21. |
| mmr | Money market rate | Three-month interbank rate that is available in a given country at t-1. |
| car | Carry | The difference between the yield-to-maturity on 10-year government bonds and the 3-month interbank interest rate. |
| cx | Convexity | Average adjusted convexity of the bond market index on day t-1. |
| size | Market value | Natural logarithm of the market value of the bond index portfolio expressed in U.S. dollars on day t-1. |
| mom | Momentum | Change in the yield-to-maturity level on the government bond index in months t-12 to t-1. |
| rev | Reversal | Change in the yield-to-maturity level on the government bond index in months t-60 to t-13. |
| dummy | "Monday effect" dummy | The variable takes the value 1 if the day of the week is Monday and 0 otherwise. |

Notes: The table presents the variables that are used in the study.

## References

1. Albulescu, C.T. COVID-19 and the United States financial markets' volatility. *Financ. Res. Lett.* **2021**, *38*, 101699. [CrossRef] [PubMed]
2. Alexakis, C.; Eleftheriou, K.; Patsoulis, P. COVID-19 containment measures and stock market returns: An international spatial econometrics investigation. *J. Behav. Exp. Financ.* **2021**, *29*, 100428. [CrossRef] [PubMed]
3. Baig, A.S.; Butt, H.A.; Haroon, O.; Rizvi, S.A.R. Deaths, panic, lockdowns and U.S. equity markets: The case of COVID-19 pandemic. *Financ. Res. Lett.* **2021**, *38*, 101701. [CrossRef] [PubMed]
4. Duan, Y.; Liu, L.; Wang, Z. COVID-19 Sentiment and the Chinese Stock Market: Evidence from the Official News Media and Sina Weibo. *Res. Int. Bus. Financ.* **2021**, *58*, 101432. [CrossRef]
5. Gao, X.; Ren, Y.; Umar, M. To what extent does COVID-19 drive stock market volatility? A comparison between the U.S. and China. *Econ. Res.-Ekon. Istraživanja* **2021**, *35*, 1686–1706. [CrossRef]
6. Goodell, J.W.; Huynh, T.L.D. Did Congress trade ahead? Considering the reaction of U.S. industries to COVID-19. *Financ. Res. Lett.* **2020**, *36*, 101578. [CrossRef]
7. James, N.; Menzies, M. Association between COVID-19 cases and international equity indices. *Phys. D Nonlinear Phenom.* **2021**, *417*, 132809. [CrossRef]
8. Ozkan, O. Impact of COVID-19 on stock market efficiency: Evidence from developed countries. *Res. Int. Bus. Financ.* **2021**, *58*, 101445. [CrossRef]
9. Seven, Ü.; Yılmaz, F. World equity markets and COVID-19: Immediate response and recovery prospects. *Res. Int. Bus. Financ.* **2021**, *56*, 101349. [CrossRef]
10. Szczygielski, J.J.; Bwanya, P.R.; Charteris, A.; Brzeszczyński, J. The only certainty is uncertainty: An analysis of the impact of COVID-19 uncertainty on regional stock markets. *Financ. Res. Lett.* **2021**, *43*, 101945. [CrossRef]
11. Zaremba, A.; Kizys, R.; Aharon, D.Y.; Demir, E. Infected markets: Novel coronavirus, government interventions, and stock return volatility around the globe. *Financ. Res. Lett.* **2020**, *35*, 101597. [CrossRef] [PubMed]
12. Zaremba, A.; Aharon, D.Y.; Demir, E.; Kizys, R.; Zawadka, D. COVID-19, government policy responses, and stock market liquidity around the world: A note. *Res. Int. Bus. Financ.* **2021**, *56*, 101359. [CrossRef] [PubMed]
13. Zhang, D.; Hu, M.; Ji, Q. Financial markets under the global pandemic of COVID-19. *Financ. Res. Lett.* **2020**, *36*, 101528. [CrossRef]
14. Škrinjarić, T. Profiting on the Stock Market in Pandemic Times: Study of COVID-19 Effects on CESEE Stock Markets. *Mathematics* **2021**, *9*, 2077. [CrossRef]
15. Aziz, M.I.A.; Ahmad, N.; Zichu, J.; Nor, S.M. The Impact of COVID-19 on the Connectedness of Stock Index in ASEAN+3 Economies. *Mathematics* **2022**, *10*, 1417. [CrossRef]
16. Bouri, E.; Demirer, R.; Gupta, R.; Nel, J. COVID-19 Pandemic and Investor Herding in International Stock Markets. *Risks* **2021**, *9*, 168. [CrossRef]
17. Hui, E.C.M.; Chan, K.K.K. How does Covid-19 affect global equity markets? *Financ. Innov.* **2021**, *8*, 25. [CrossRef] [PubMed]
18. Navratil, R.; Taylor, S.; Vecer, J. On equity market inefficiency during the COVID-19 pandemic. *Int. Rev. Financ. Anal.* **2021**, *77*, 101820. [CrossRef] [PubMed]
19. Nguyen, D.T.; Phan, D.H.B.; Ming, T.C.; Nguyen, V.L. An assessment of how COVID-19 changed the global equity market. *Econ. Anal. Policy* **2021**, *69*, 480–491. [CrossRef]
20. Arellano, C.; Bai, Y.; Mihalache, G.P. *Deadly Debt Crises: COVID-19 in Emerging Markets*; National Bureau of Economic Research: Cambridge, MA, USA, 2020; No. w27275.
21. Gubareva, M. The impact of Covid-19 on liquidity of emerging market bonds. *Financ. Res. Lett.* **2020**, *41*, 101826. [CrossRef]
22. He, Z.; Nagel, S.; Song, Z. *Treasury Inconvenience Yields during the COVID-19 Crisis*; National Bureau of Economic Research: Cambridge, MA, USA, 2020; No. w27416.
23. O'Hara, M.; Zhou, X.A. Anatomy of a liquidity crisis: Corporate bonds in the COVID-19 crisis. *J. Financ. Econ.* **2021**, *142*, 46–68. [CrossRef] [PubMed]
24. Sène, B.; Mbengue, M.L.; Allaya, M.M. Overshooting of sovereign emerging Eurobond yields in the context of COVID-19. *Financ. Res. Lett.* **2021**, *38*, 101746. [CrossRef] [PubMed]
25. Zaremba, A.; Kizys, R.; Aharon, D.Y. Volatility in international sovereign bond markets: The role of government policy responses to the COVID-19 pandemic. *Financ. Res. Lett.* **2021**, *43*, 102011. [CrossRef] [PubMed]
26. Zaremba, A.; Kizys, R.; Aharon, D.Y.; Umar, Z. Term spreads and the COVID-19 pandemic: Evidence from international sovereign bond markets. *Financ. Res. Lett.* **2022**, *44*, 102042. [CrossRef] [PubMed]
27. Gubareva, M.; Umar, Z.; Sokolov, T.; Vinh Vo, X. Astonishing insights: Emerging market debt spreads throughout the pandemic. *Appl. Econ.* **2022**, *18*, 2067–2076. [CrossRef]
28. Baker, S.R.; Bloom, N.; Davis, S.J.; Kost, K.; Sammon, M.; Viratyosin, T. The unprecedented stock market reaction to COVID-19. *Rev. Asset Pricing Stud.* **2020**, *10*, 742–758. [CrossRef]
29. Belaid, F.; Amar, A.B.; Goutte, S.; Guesmi, K. Emerging and advanced economies markets behaviour during the COVID-19 crisis era. *Int. J. Financ. Econ.* **2021**. [CrossRef]
30. Fakhfekh, M.; Jeribi, A.; Salem, M.B. Volatility dynamics of the Tunisian stock market before and during the COVID-19 outbreak: Evidence from the GARCH family models. *Int. J. Financ. Econ.* **2021**. [CrossRef]

31. Fetzer, T.R.; Witte, M.; Hensel, L.; Jachimowicz, J.; Haushofer, J.; Ivchencko, A.; Caris, S.; Reutskaja, E. *Global Behaviors and Perceptions at the Onset of the COVID-19 Pandemic*; National Bureau of Economic Research: Cambridge, MA, USA, 2020; WORKING PAPER 27082. Available online: https://www.nber.org/papers/w27082 (accessed on 29 November 2020).
32. Lee, C.-C.; Lee, C.-C.; Wu, Y. The impact of COVID-19 pandemic on hospitality stock returns in China. *Int. J. Financ. Econ.* **2021**. [CrossRef]
33. Lyócsa, Š.; Baumöhl, E.; Výrost, T.; Molnár, P. Fear of the coronavirus and the stock markets. *Financ. Res. Lett.* **2020**, *36*, 101735. [CrossRef]
34. Albulescu, C.T.; Mina, M.; Oros, C. Oil-US Stock Market Nexus: Some insights about the New Coronavirus Crisis. *Econ. Bull.* **2021**, *41*, 588–593. [CrossRef]
35. Ftiti, Z.; Ameur, H.B.; Louhichi, W. Does non-fundamental news related to COVID-19 matter for stock returns? Evidence from Shanghai stock market. *Econ. Model.* **2021**, *99*, 105484. [CrossRef] [PubMed]
36. Pastor, L.; Veronesi, P. Uncertainty about government policy and stock prices. *J. Financ.* **2012**, *67*, 1219–1264. [CrossRef]
37. Amengual, D.; Xiu, D. Resolution of policy uncertainty and sudden declines in volatility. *J. Econom.* **2018**, *203*, 297–315. [CrossRef]
38. Kizys, R.; Tzouvanas, P.; Donadelli, M. From COVID-19 herd immunity to investor herding in international stock markets: The role of government and regulatory restrictions. *Int. Rev. Financ. Anal.* **2020**, *74*, 101663. [CrossRef]
39. Albulescu, C.T.; Tiwari, A.K.; Kyophilavong, P. Nonlinearities and Chaos: A New Analysis of CEE Stock Markets. *Mathematics* **2021**, *9*, 707. [CrossRef]
40. Canay, I.A. A simple approach to quantile regression for panel data. *Econom. J.* **2011**, *14*, 368–386. [CrossRef]
41. Wang, P.; Wen, Y.; Xu, Z. Financial development and long-run volatility trends. *Rev. Econ. Dyn.* **2018**, *28*, 221–251. [CrossRef]
42. Rosen, A.M. Set identification via quantile restrictions in short panels. *J. Econom.* **2012**, *166*, 127–137. [CrossRef]
43. Duttilo, P.; Gattone, S.A.; Di Battista, T. Volatility Modeling: An Overview of Equity Markets in the Euro Area during COVID-19 Pandemic. *Mathematics* **2021**, *9*, 1212. [CrossRef]
44. Andrieș, A.M.; Ongena, S.; Sprincean, N. The COVID-19 pandemic and sovereign bond risk. *N. Am. J. Econ. Finance* **2021**, *58*, 101527. [CrossRef]
45. Augustin, P.; Sokolovski, V.; Subrahmanyam, M.G.; Tamio, D. In sickness and in debt: The COVID-19 impact on sovereign credit risk. *J. Financ. Econ.* **2021**, *143*, 1251–1274. [CrossRef] [PubMed]
46. Cevik, S.; Öztürkkal, B. Contagion of fear: Is the impact of COVID-19 on sovereign risk really indiscriminate? *Int. Financ.* **2021**, *24*, 134–154. [CrossRef]
47. Daehler, T.; Aizenman, J.; Jinjarak, Y. Emerging markets sovereign CDS spreads during COVID-19: Economics versus epidemiology news. *Econ. Model.* **2020**, *100*, 105504. [CrossRef] [PubMed]
48. Pan, W.F.; Wang, X.; Wu, G.; Xu, W. The COVID-19 pandemic and sovereign credit risk. *China Financ. Rev. Int.* **2021**, *11*, 287–301. [CrossRef]
49. Andres, C.; Betzer, A.; Doumet, M. Measuring Abnormal Credit Default Swap Spreads. 2016. Available online: https://ssrn.com/abstract=2194320 (accessed on 8 May 2021).
50. Baltussen, G.; Swinkels, L.; van Vliet, P. Global factor premiums. Journal of Financial Economics (JFE), Forthcoming. 2020. Available online: https://ssrn.com/abstract=3325720 (accessed on 8 May 2021).
51. Asness, C.S.; Moskowitz, T.J.; Pedersen, L.H. Value and momentum everywhere. *J. Financ.* **2013**, *68*, 929–985. [CrossRef]
52. Available online: http://mba.tuck.dartmouth.edu/pages/faculty/ken.french/data_library.html (accessed on 3 November 2020).
53. Antonakakis, N.; Kizys, R. Dynamic spillovers between commodity and currency markets. *Int. Rev. Financ. Anal.* **2015**, *41*, 303–319. [CrossRef]
54. Khalifa, A.A.A.; Miao, H.; Ramchander, S. Return distributions and volatility forecasting in metal futures markets: Evidence from gold, silver, and copper. *J. Futur. Mark.* **2011**, *31*, 55–80. [CrossRef]
55. Fama, E.F.; French, K.R. Common risk factors in the returns on stocks and bonds. *J. Financ. Econ.* **1993**, *33*, 3–56. [CrossRef]
56. Carhart, M.M. On Persistence in Mutual Fund Performance. *J. Financ.* **1997**, *52*, 57–82. [CrossRef]
57. Available online: https://www.bsg.ox.ac.uk/research/research-projects/coronavirus-government-response-tracker (accessed on 3 November 2020).
58. Maddala, G.S.; Wu, S. A comparative study of unit root tests with panel data and a new simple test. *Oxf. Bull. Econ. Stat.* **1999**, *61* (Suppl. 1), 631–652. [CrossRef]
59. Pesaran, M.H. A simple panel unit root test in the presence of cross-section dependence. *J. Appl. Econom.* **2007**, *22*, 265–312. [CrossRef]
60. Koenker, R. Quantile regression for longitudinal data. *J. Multivar. Anal.* **2004**, *91*, 74–89. [CrossRef]
61. Lamarche, C. Robust penalized quantile regression estimation for panel data. *J. Econom.* **2010**, *157*, 396–408. [CrossRef]
62. Galvao, A.F., Jr. Quantile regression for dynamic panel data with fixed effects. *J. Econom.* **2011**, *164*, 142–157. [CrossRef]
63. Li, J.; Ding, H.; Hu, Y.; Wan, G. Dealing with dynamic endogeneity in international business research. *J. Int. Bus. Stud.* **2021**, *52*, 339–362. [CrossRef]

**Disclaimer/Publisher's Note:** The statements, opinions and data contained in all publications are solely those of the individual author(s) and contributor(s) and not of MDPI and/or the editor(s). MDPI and/or the editor(s) disclaim responsibility for any injury to people or property resulting from any ideas, methods, instructions or products referred to in the content.

MDPI
St. Alban-Anlage 66
4052 Basel
Switzerland
www.mdpi.com

*Mathematics* Editorial Office
E-mail: mathematics@mdpi.com
www.mdpi.com/journal/mathematics

Disclaimer/Publisher's Note: The statements, opinions and data contained in all publications are solely those of the individual author(s) and contributor(s) and not of MDPI and/or the editor(s). MDPI and/or the editor(s) disclaim responsibility for any injury to people or property resulting from any ideas, methods, instructions or products referred to in the content.

www.ingramcontent.com/pod-product-compliance
Lightning Source LLC
LaVergne TN
LVHW070420100526
838202LV00014B/1497